T0330950

Henry A. Abbati: Keynes' Forgotten Precursor

Henry A. Abbati was not an economist by profession. After retiring from business, in 1924 he published his first book, *The Unclaimed Wealth: How Money Stops Production* in which he expounded his theory of 'effective demand' (terminology of his own) and its differences with respect to current theories on economic fluctuations. He was advocating public intervention in the economy in the crisis. His second book, *The Final Buyer* marshalled his criticisms of current theories and further clarified salient aspects of his theory, such as 'saving' and its various definitions, the working of the banking system, the interest rate and the role of public works as a means of reducing unemployment. Later work in the 30s and 40s looked at full employment, through reflections on the economic crisis and further analysis of the concept of unclaimed wealth.

In many ways Abbati's work in the twenties was an important precursor to Keynes' *Treatise on Money* and was admired by Robertson and indeed Keynes. Nevertheless his work is today largely unknown and entirely ignored by the numerous authors who have examined the debate of the twenties and thirties on the crises and business cycles and by academic opinion in general. In this book, Di Gaspare restores Abbati's position as a pioneer in macroeconomic theory with a selection of his writings and a far reaching introduction to his contribution to the history of economic thought.

An important contribution to the literature on both this period and the history of economic thought more generally, this will appeal both to scholars and researchers alike.

Serena Di Gaspare is Assistant Professor of Economic Policy at the University of Turin, Italy.

Routledge Studies in the History of Economics

Henry A. Abbati: Keynes' Forgotten Precursor

Selected writings

Edited by Serena Di Gaspare

Routledge
Taylor & Francis Group

LONDON AND NEW YORK

First published 2011
by Routledge
2 Park Square, Milton Park, Abingdon, Oxon, OX14 4RN

Simultaneously published in the USA and Canada
by Routledge
270 Madison Avenue, New York, NY 10016

*Routledge is an imprint of the Taylor & Francis Group, an informa
business*

© 2011 Serena Di Gaspare

The right of Serena Di Gaspare to be identified as editor of this work has
been asserted by her in accordance with sections 77 and 78 of the
Copyright, Designs and Patents Act 1988.

Typeset in Times New Roman by RefineCatch Limited, Bungay, Suffolk

British Library Cataloguing in Publication Data
A catalogue record for this book is available
from the British Library

Library of Congress Cataloging in Publication Data
A catalog record for this book has been requested

ISBN: 978–0–415–57345–0 (hbk)
ISBN: 978–0–203–83379–7 (ebk)

Contents

Acknowledgements

I wish first to thank Mrs Joy Abbati Yeoman for having placed her trust in me, for having willingly provided me with valuable material and information concerning her father, and for having given me permission to use his writings in this book.

My especial thanks go to Augusto Graziani, with whom I drew up the initial project for this book.

I am very grateful to Terenzio Cozzi and Roberto Marchionatti for their patient discussion with me of various aspects of my research and for their useful suggestions.

For discussions of specific problems and various forms of support I am indebted to Daniele Besomi, Maria Laura Di Tommaso, Hirotaka Kojima, Ferruccio Maggiora, Don Moggridge, Fiorenzo Mornati and John Presley.

I finally wish to thank my daughter Claudia, without whose helpfulness and computer skills it would have been much more difficult for me to give a body to the name of Abbati.

I would like to thank Mrs Judith Brown for permission to quote from the unpublished and published writings of D.H. Robertson. I also wish to thank Peter Jones and the Provost and Scholars of King's College, Cambridge, for permission to quote from the unpublished writings of J.M. Keynes. I also thank the following institutions and their staff: Jonathan Smith, Wren Library, Trinity College, Cambridge; Marshall Library of Economics, Cambridge; British Library of Political and Economic Science, London School of Economics; Dolph Briscoe Center for American History, University of Texas at Austin.

Financial support from University of Turin is gratefully acknowledged.

All reasonable effort has been made to seek permission from the original publishers. Any interested parties should contact us.

Biography of Henry A. Abbati[1]

1889 Henry A. Abbati was born on 6 April at 10 Kemplay Road, Hampstead, London. His father Camille, of French origin,[2] had been born in 1846 on Syra, one of the islands of the Greek archipelago, and obtained British naturalization in 1893. Camille developed a profitable business as a ship-broker and chartering agent in the City of London, dealing mainly with sailings between the UK and the Baltic ports. Abbati's mother, Matilda Clotilde Peirano, was born in Genoa, Italy. Henry had an older sister, Margherita, and two younger brothers, Alfred and Bill, one of whom died in 1908, the other in 1916. The family was relatively affluent and in 1894 moved to a larger house in Highbury, London. In 1896 Abbati developed polio and had to convalesce for many months.

1901–1908 Abbati attended the boys' Catholic public school Downside, near Bath in Somerset, run by the Benedictines, and later a boys' boarding school in Bognor, West Sussex. His father's business began to run into difficulties and the family moved to a smaller house in Chiswick, London. In 1905 he had to interrupt his studies to go and work in his father's office. The family's economic circumstances grew increasingly precarious.

1909–1911 Abbati left for Argentina with very little money and he worked there for a year, probably in an import-export office. On his return he went back to work in his father's office.

1912–1918 The Balkan conflict and the closure of the Dardanelles following the First World War led to the collapse of Abbati's father's business. He found employment at three different firms, gradually improving his income. In 1918 his father died from a bout of Spanish flu.

1920–1922 In England, the post-war boom was followed by the great deflation of 1920–21 caused by the government's severe deflationary measures. Abbati observed these events closely, reaching 'the conclusion that trade depression and unemployment of both labour and capital were due to excessive saving and the withholding of purchasing power, that is, to a general buying deficiency' (1947a: 4; 1955a) and decided to write a book to set out his arguments. In 1921, after office hours, he wrote a synopsis of the book and, being a member of the Fabian Society, sent it to Sidney Webb and then, on Webb's suggestion, to J.A. Hobson. Confutation of Hobson's over-saving theory was the first step in construction of his own theory (see 1947a; 1955a).

1923 Abbati gave up business, sold the family house and began to travel abroad in France, Switzerland, Italy and Belgium. He was confident in his ability to earn money from speculation in foreign exchanges and other financial operations. In the meantime, he worked on his book, which he finished in Brussels, and remained in contact with Hobson, who encouraged him. He sent the Prologue of the book to Bernard Shaw, who replied with a note commending it.

1924 In London for a few weeks to revise the script, Abbati met Hobson several times. In August *The Unclaimed Wealth. How Money Stops Production* was published with an Introduction by Hobson (see Appendix). With the expression 'Unclaimed Wealth' Abbati meant: 'unemployed labour, unemployed capital equipment and unemployed surplus stocks of goods' (1932a: 1).[3] The reviews of the book in the British press and elsewhere were numerous (see List) and mostly favourable: among them, *The Times Literary Supplement, The Economic Review, The Star, The Manchester Guardian, The Journal of Commerce*. J.W. Scott in *The Spectator* (20 December 1924) described the *Unclaimed Wealth* as 'one of the most significant books on its theme of recent years', specifying that 'Mr Abbati is not a fool. He knows the details of what he is trying to treat'. R.B. Suthers in *The Clarion* (20 February 1925) wrote that Abbati's diagnosis 'is fresh and illuminating, sometimes crystal clear, but I cannot deny that in parts it is tough' and after some criticisms added that the reader 'will find in Mr Abbati's pages much information about the methods of money manufacture, and the inter-workings of the Monetary and Industrial systems which will well repay a tenacious perusal'. H.L. Reed, in *The American Economic Review* (no. 3, September 1925) concluded his review thus: 'But despite the brevity of the treatment in some respects, the reader will no doubt be highly charmed by the freshness and vigour with which the author carries through an affirmative analysis'. *The Economist* (30 August 1924), by contrast, entitled its review 'Economic confusion' and spoke of an 'inconsistent use of economic terminology', but in subsequent years gradually changed its view. On 24 October Abbati received a card from Keynes referring to the review of his book in *The Nation and the Athenaeum* of 27 September 1924. Keynes also invited Abbati to become a subscriber to the journal (see Abbati's letter to Robertson, 20 July 1948, Appendix). On 5 December, *The Economic Review* published a letter from Abbati, 'National debt and taxation' (see Part IV), on the deflationary effects of reducing the national debt.

1925–1926 He returned to London on several occasions to see people about his book, among them Hobson, T.E. Gregory and Sidney Webb and his wife (see 1955a). The editor of *The Economist* asked him to write a letter to the journal, which appeared on 22 November 1925. In December 1925 *The Economic*

Review published two important articles by Abbati which clarified certain essential concepts expounded in *The Unclaimed Wealth*: 'What is saved?' (see Part IV) and 'What is trade depression?'. In 1926 he began to write a Memorandum for his second book, which was intended to give more systematic development to topics treated in the first one. Arbitrage and speculation on the dollar greatly improved his financial circumstances.

1927 Abbati met Robertson in London. Robertson showed constant admiration and sympathy for Abbati[4] and engaged in enduring though intermittent correspondence with him. The Memorandum became a book by the third week in December.

1928 *The Final Buyer* was published. More complete and scientific than Abbati's first book, it attracted considerably less attention in the press: it was more difficult to read and without an introduction 'to indicate to reviewers what to say', according to Abbati.[5] However, Keynes made a significant citation of this book in a footnote to the *Treatise* (see Introduction: p.1), and Harold Barger wrote that, in this book, Abbati 'gave an analysis of the relation between savings and investment which was in many respects in advance of anything else of its kind at that time existing in the English language' (*The Economic Journal*, December 1934). On 12 September Abbati married Julia Leigh Greenwood.

1929 Abbati decided to live in Geneva, which was convenient for his work and for conducting his financial affairs in New York and elsewhere. He first occupied a flat in Quai Wilson, near the First League of Nations, and in the following year moved to 5 Square Montchoisy. His son, Tony, was born (he died in 1968). Abbati began selling his French government and other dollar bonds gradually and at a good profit, but he did not re-invest on the New York Stock Exchange. He was very 'bullish' about American industrial growth, but he realized that the market was overheated and he expected a reaction. The stock market crashed in October. Then, the Great Depression began.

1930 *The Final Buyer* was mentioned in Keynes' *Treatise*. Although Abbati was appreciative of Keynes' recognition, he thought that the way in which Keynes had presented him was not only unsatisfactory but also counterproductive (see 1947a; Abbati's letter to Robertson, 20 July 1948, Appendix). It got him nowhere, however, so Abbati decided to spread his ideas for the next three years by writing letters to the press and interested parties, publishing articles and appearing at conferences. In December he met Keynes at the latter's house in Gordon Square, London.

1931 The Great Depression gave Abbati the opportunity to expound his ideas on remedies to combat unemployment and he founded the Unclaimed Wealth Utilization Committee in Geneva. The task of this Committee was to identify 'the economic facts of fundamental importance, to interpret them correctly and to expose economic fallacies'; its purpose was to furnish businessmen, economists and statesmen with 'an independent and consistent national and international economic viewpoint and, thus, to create the necessary support for the kind of action it is advocating' (1932a: 3). The action advocated was to tackle the demand deficit provoked by the surplus of savings over investment with public works, free trade, cancellation of inter-governmental debts, a 'moratorium for taxpayers', increased imports from creditor countries, and other measures. For three consecutive years, 1931–3, almost invariably at monthly intervals, the Committee issued a series of Bulletins which were subsequently published in London in three volumes: in 1932 *The Economic Lessons of 1929–1931*, with an Introduction by T.E. Gregory (see Appendix); in 1933 *The Search for Confidence in 1932*, with an Introduction by Basil P. Blackett (see Appendix); in 1934 *Economic Readjustment in 1933*. The Bulletins conducted an extremely valuable survey of the various phases of the crisis that had begun in 1929 and of measures for stabilizing the economy that would become familiar after publication of Keynes' *General Theory*. They also contained important theoretical contributions: for instance, Bulletin no. 3 'The distinction between saving and investment' (see Appendix),[6] Bulletin no. 7 'General trade depression' (see Part III), to which Robertson's review (see below) recommended paying 'most heed', and Bulletin no. 26 'Gentlemen prefer gold II' (see Part III), which contained an anticipation of the liquidity-preference theory. In England, discussion on the trade deficit and the devaluation of sterling became increasingly insistent. The result was a huge outflow of gold from Britain, which in the autumn suspended gold payments. Abbati forcefully contested the opinion predominant in the press that the deficit in the balance of payments was excessive and that it was therefore necessary to devalue the pound. He was confident that sterling would recover when the panic was over, but the British authorities prevented the sterling exchange rate from rising. As Abbati's speculations on sterling deteriorated, he began to reinvest in first-class American shares (1955a). On 31 December he once again met Keynes at Gordon Square (see Abbati's letter to Robertson, 20 July 1948).

1932–1934 The Bulletins, and the respective books, aroused far-reaching, and in some cases enthusiastic, responses in the British and foreign press from publication of the first Bulletin (7 March 1931) onwards. In December 1932 Robertson wrote a highly favourable review of *The Economic Lessons of 1929–1931* in *The Economic Journal* (see Appendix), a review which Keynes himself had announced to Abbati by card in the previous October. Robertson, moreover, in a letter to R.F. Harrod of 24 August 1932, told him that he had reviewed Abbati's 'racy bulletins', describing them 'particularly good' on foreign investment and international capital movements (Besomi 2003). 'Toreador', in *The Statesman and Nation* of 12 December 1931, included in 'unclaimed wealth' 'unemployed labour and capital as well as [. . .] Mr Abbati's ideas'. Francis Williams, who had repeatedly discussed the

Bulletins in the *Daily Herald*, wrote in 1933 that 'Unorthodox they certainly are, but [. . .] behind their unorthodoxy lies a real grasp of the fundamental problems of economic depression and very considerable courage and power of lucid exposition in putting forward remedies' (*Daily Herald*, 14 July 1933). It was by now the general opinion that 'many of the views expressed by the Committee in 1931, which received little credence at that time, are now accepted without challenge', as one reads in the *Journal of the Royal Statistical Society* (Part I, 1933); indeed, *The Economist*, on reviewing *Economic Readjustment in 1933*, admitted that Abbati 'can now claim with great justice that, whereas in 1931 he and his enterprising committee were a voice crying in a deflationary wilderness, in 1934 they have won the day' and that almost everywhere his ideas 'have been adopted with substantial and convincing success' (9 June 1934). According to Emil Davies, Abbati's 'speciality is to present facts and proposals which are almost self-evident to an ordinary intelligent person, but become only dimly perceptible two or three years later [. . .] to some of the politicians in charge of the destinies of the nations' (*New Clarion*, 5 August 1933). While in the United States the index of business activity and the stock exchange prices plunged to catastrophic levels, with the banks near to collapse, in November 1932 the German government introduced a new economic programme. Abbati invariably commented on these events in his Bulletins and prepared *Memoranda* for the various international conferences. He maintained that the crisis was artificial, 'partly rigged by national speculators and mistakes of governments', but when Roosevelt, the newly-elected president of the United States, introduced the first measures, and in April 1933 suspended the Gold Standard, Abbati realized that the change in management of the crisis that he had so strongly advocated had finally arrived. In November 1933 he again met Keynes at Gordon Square. In 1932–3 Keynes wrote some letters to Abbati expressing appreciation of his work. In a letter dated 30 June 1932 he wrote: 'I have regularly read your bulletins with the greatest interest and a very large measure of sympathy and agreement'; in another of 10 January 1933: 'Our ideas and objects are substantially the same, and the difference is of secondary importance' (see Appendix). In this period, Abbati's financial circumstances drastically worsened, and it was not possible for a foreigner like himself to find a decent job in Geneva. He hoped for a little influential support, perhaps from Keynes himself, to find suitable employment at the Economic Section of the League of Nations. But this did not come to pass and Abbati was forced to suspend the Bulletins, whose issue had been financed by voluntary subscriptions (invariably by Robertson), and to leave Geneva for London in November 1933 (see Abbati's letter to Robertson, 20 July 1948). In December his mother died.

1935–1936 Abbati joined the staff of Govett Sons & Co., a leading financial house in London, where he was given responsibility, amongst other things, for a *Quarterly World Economic Survey* (1935–9) to be issued for the firm's

British and foreign clients.[7] He lived between London and Eastbourne. In February 1936, on behalf of his firm, Abbati travelled to Italy, on which the League of Nations had imposed sanctions in November 1935, to ascertain the truth about that country's economic situation. Abbati wrote a report entitled *Italy and the Abyssinian War* in which, despite his sincere aversion to fascism, he made a genuine attempt to be strictly impartial. He wrote that, with few exceptions, there were no visible shortages in Italy, that the debit balance of payments was less than before sanctions, that there was sufficient gold, and that the main effect of the sanctions had been to reduce opposition against the government and to intensify the national spirit. In this case too, Abbati's position was heterodox: his inquiry was an attempt to counterbalance opinions often based on insufficient information. Again for his firm, in June 1936 he wrote a report entitled *The Outlook for Interest Rates and for Stock Exchange Prices in England* in which, amongst other things, he predicted the outbreak of war within two years. In May 1936 his daughter Virginia Penelope (Joy) was born.

1939–1944 On the outbreak of the war, Abbati left his job in London and moved with his family to Exmouth. He then travelled through Italy, France, Spain and Portugal. During this time his family travelled to Wales where he eventually joined them and they all moved to Lampeter, a small town in West Wales. On his return to Britain, he was forced to give up his American dollars at 'acquisition prices', receiving around 9,000 rapidly depreciating pounds for dollars, which should have been worth 30,000 pounds. Abbati decided to invest some of this money in a farm situated about seven miles from Lampeter – Drewynt Farm, Felinfach – which he ran personally with the assistance of local farmers and an Italian prisoner of war. He thus experienced at first hand the economic problems of farmers caught between rising wage costs and prices kept artificially low, and he argued their case in the press (see Abbati's Bibliography). Henceforth support for agriculture would be one of his main concerns and he would also write an essay on the 'farming question'. Shortly before the end of the war Abbati sold the farm to the farmers working for him for the same amount that he had paid for it, so that when the war was over he could start anew.

1945 Abbati published *Towards Full Employment*, written before the appearance in 1944 of W. Beveridge's book *Full Employment in a Free Society* and the British Government's *White Paper on Employment Policy*, which he discussed, however, in the Preface. In this book Abbati again argued for government action, based on economic principles which he presumed were by now universally accepted, to neutralize the buying deficiency probable in the normal peace-time conditions of a modern economy. However, given that inflation was rising at that time, Abbati – consistently with his view that the budget should be managed to stabilize business activity – wrote a Post Script to the book in which he argued that 'at the present time there is no buying deficiency, but quite the reverse' and that, consequently, 'to-day, everything indicates the immediate need for drastic curtailment of the present excessive Government expenditure' (1945a). From the Second World War onwards, the problem of inflation became as important for Abbati as that of deflation had been in previous years, and throughout the 1950s his writings in the press were centred on the need to adjust new investments to the level of voluntary savings (see Abbati's Bibliography). Moreover, having shown that British export possibilities after the war were likely to be below the pre-war level, Abbati foresaw the need for some measures of selective control especially on the import of foodstuffs, both to prevent the creation of debit foreign balances and to protect and expand the agricultural sector.

1947   Abbati moved to 25 Colum Road in Cardiff. Reacting to a leading article in *The Times* (22 April 1946) praising Keynes after his death in April, he wrote the booklet *Lord Keynes' Central Thesis and the Concept of Unclaimed Wealth* (see Part IV) in which he claimed for himself the origin of certain fundamental concepts that the writer attributed to Keynes. This booklet was imbued with the bitterness provoked in Abbati by the fact that his role in the development of the new economics had not been acknowledged, as also emerges from his letters to Robertson. But the booklet was also an extremely valid exposition of the salient points of his theory.

1953–1960   In 1953 Abbati left his home in Cardiff, and after staying in Bournemouth, Boscombe, and Sandown on the Isle of Wight, in 1957 he settled in Eastbourne. In 1955 he wrote *The New Economic Theories and the Great Depression of 1930–1933* (see Part IV), unpublished, a lucid synthesis of his intellectual inquiries, especially in the 1930s. In 1959 he travelled through France and Switzerland to Geneva, and then to Belgium in 1960.

1964   On 23 March Abbati died in Eastbourne of cerebral thrombosis.

Notes

1 I am grateful for comments on earlier draft to Joy Abbati Yeoman and Roberto Marchionatti.
2 It is likely that his family was originally from Corsica, which had become French with the 1768 Treaty of Versailles.
3 The title page of the Bulletins that Abbati began to publish in 1931 bore the following definition: 'The Unclaimed Wealth is a surplus of goods and services made available by saving and by taxation, which, for one reason or another, is not utilized for investment nor employed for public services'.
4 See Introduction note 2; Robertson (1932); Correspondence Abbati-Robertson.
5 *The Final Buyer* and *The Unclaimed Wealth* will be discussed more thoroughly in the Introduction.
6 Signed by W. Hessling, Secretary of the Unclaimed Wealth Utilization Committee, but probably written by Abbati or largely suggested by him (see 1955a).
7 His appointment was reported in *The Times*, 12 November 1935, in the *Evening Standard*, 1 January 1936 and in *World Press News*, 16 January 1936.

Introduction[1]

Serena Di Gaspare

In the *Treatise on Money* (1930), in a footnote to chapter 12, 'A further elucidation of the distinction between savings and investment', Keynes writes:

> The notion of the distinction which I have made between savings and investment has been gradually creeping into economic literature in quite recent years. The first author to introduce it was, according to the German authorities, Ludwig Mises in his *Theorie des Geldes und der Umlaufsmittel* [. . .] published in 1912 [. . .]. Later on the idea was adopted in a more explicit form by Schumpeter, and 'forced saving' [. . .] (i.e. the difference between savings and value of investment as defined by me, though without there being attached to the idea – so far as I am aware – anything closely corresponding to the analysis of chapters 10 and 11 above) has become almost a familiar feature of the very newest German writings on money. But so far as I am concerned – and I think the same is true of most other economists of the English-speaking world – my indebtedness for clues which have set my mind working in the right direction is to Mr D. H. Robertson's *Banking Policy and the Price Level* published in 1926 [. . .]. More recently Mr Abbati's *The Final Buyer* (1928), has reached – independently I think – some substantially similar results. Mr Abbati has probably failed to make his thought fully intelligible to those who have not already found the same clue themselves. But the essence of the distinction between saving and investment is to be found in his chapter V. Moreover, by the aggregate of 'final buying', Mr Abbati means expenditure on consumption *plus* investment, and he attributes depressions to a failure of this aggregate to reach the aggregate of money incomes.
>
> (Keynes 1930a, I: 171n.)

Those who come across this footnote (see the next section and the Biography) will probably be struck by the mention of Abbati, a name unknown among eminent economists, and they may be prompted to enquire as to who he was. The same question might be asked upon reading *The Life of John Maynard Keynes* by Harrod (1951). After recalling Keynes' indebtedness to Robertson in regard to the separation between saving and investment, Harrod cites, again in a footnote, *The Final Buyer* (1928) as containing 'similar ideas' and refers to another book,

The Unclaimed Wealth (1924) 'by this interesting pioneer' (Harrod 1951 [1952]: 410n).[2] Furthermore, there is a very favourable review of another book by Abbati, *The Economic Lessons of 1929–31* (1932), written by Robertson in 1932 for *The Economic Journal* (Robertson 1932). Should the reader now decide to learn more about Abbati, he or she would find virtually nothing in the boundless literature on Keynes, pre-Keynesian theories, and more generally on theories of the economic cycle.

To tell the truth, some traces of Abbati exist in the literature: a fine article[3] written by D.J. Coppock in 1954, the four very interesting pages devoted to him by G. Mehta in his book *The Structure of the Keynesian Revolution*[4] (Mehta 1977: 73–6) and a mention by F.A. Hayek, who placed him among the 'purchasing-power theorists' with Martin and Foster and Catchings (Hayek 1932: 193) and by J.M. Clark (1950), who also reviewed *The Unclaimed Wealth* (Clark 1925). But apart from the works cited thus far,[5] the name of Abbati is almost unknown today, notwithstanding the numerous and indubitable affinities between his theory and that of Keynes.

Expounding Abbati's theory of effective demand is on the one hand straight-forward; on the other, however, it raises some difficulties. It is straightforward because the theory of effective demand, at least in its Keynesian version, is today well established, and the relative macroeconomic concepts and terms are in current use; so that they can be used to set out Abbati's arguments as well. Diffi-culties arise because in the early 1920s, when Abbati began to analyse economic facts and present his conclusions, which contrasted markedly not only with the then dominant neoclassical theory but also with the new economic cycle theories fashionable at that time, terms and concepts appropriate to his purposes were unavailable. Abbati therefore had to invent a new terminology[6] which today, as then, is certainly not conducive to understanding of his ideas. He was also a busi-nessman, did not have an academic economic education and the logic and criteria that he employed to address economic problems were different from those in use among professional economists. However, it would be a mistake to blame Abbati's eccentric and sometimes obscure language for the neglect with which his thought has been treated.[7] Any professional economist can easily follow his argu-ments, and the fact that during the 1930s Abbati enjoyed considerable popularity in the press and among bankers and businessmen shows that they can be followed even by those with only a simple idea of the problem being treated.[8]

Given that Abbati's theory is largely unknown, it is advisable to summarize it briefly before considering the merits of some of its central tenets.

The theory in synthesis

The most important feature of Abbati's thought is its anticipation of the theory of effective demand, which he developed before Keynes published his *Treatise on Money* (1930). Abbati centred his analysis on the unemployment and 'unclaimed wealth' (see Biography, note 3) consequent upon incomplete use of available productive capacity. He was not interested in the upward phase of the economic cycle, because he did not believe that depression was merely the necessary consequence of a boom; nor was he interested in monetary policy aimed at price stability and control of the cycle, because he did not believe that the economic cycle was a monetary phenomenon. These two beliefs already set Abbati at odds with the theories of the cycle then relatively widespread. To be noted, moreover, is that Abbati did not address the problem of unemployment under the promptings of the Great Depression. He did so many years before it, in fact, during the period of high unemployment that Britain, unlike the United States and most European countries, experienced in the 1920s (1947a: 4 and 1955a). This unemployment, as Patinkin acutely points out, 'did not constitute an "anomaly" or "puzzle" for the prevailing theory, which explained unemployment as the consequence of too high a wage rate'; it was the Great Depression that 'created doubts about the existing theory not only because of the persistence and worsening of unemployment, but because it constituted an anomaly for this theory' (Patinkin 1982: 18). For Abbati, the great deflation of 1920–1 also raised strong doubts concerning the existing theory, and even then he believed that reducing prices and wages did not solve the crisis but aggravated it.

According to Abbati, the level of output is determined by the level of effective demand. He therefore attributes unemployment to a deficiency of effective demand (consumption plus investment) due to the fact that the purchasing power distributed by firms to the owners of the production factors is not fully and promptly spent on the output to which they have contributed, and thus does not return to firms. This is what Abbati means when he says that 'the velocity of final buying'[9] is less than the 'velocity of production'. To put it another way, in the course of production, incomes are earned whose sum is equal to the value of the product and constitutes its potential demand; these incomes can be spent or hoarded, which means that part of saving may remain 'passive', i.e. not converted into investment. Money is created mainly by the banking system through lending to firms to finance production, and it is placed in circulation by firms at the beginning of the production cycle. This money is destroyed when the debt is repaid. Firms can also finance production through their existing liquid funds or securities. The price level is determined by the amount of goods and services offered on the market and the amount of money offered in exchange. The money that does not circulate does not contribute to price formation. It is worth quoting Abbati's next step in full:

> The circuit flow of credit money is roughly as follows: Bankers create credit money by making loans and investments. The business men to whom the money is advanced disburse it for wages, rent, interest, materials and personal expenses; and taxation thereon is disbursed in a similar manner by governments. The recipients of the money then use it as final buyers of the goods produced by the activities of the business men, who may then either repay the bankers and thus destroy the credit money, or continue to circulate it by using it to finance production as before. The point is that certain kinds of "saving" withdraw credit money from circulation in industry before it has been returned to the business men who first put it out, and the injection of new

credit money into circulation in other ways is not always sufficient to neutralize such withdrawals.

(1928: 52)

At the beginning of the production process, therefore, sufficient money to be
exchanged with the goods produced is put into circulation. If this money returns
to firms, which means that saving is equal to investment, prices are stable and
equal to costs; firms repay the banks, so that the money created is destroyed and
the money supply remains constant and equal to the cash balances desired by the
community. Other things being equal, production may resume on the same scale
in the next cycle. If, however, some of this money is removed from circulation,
i.e. is hoarded somewhere in the circuit, which means that saving exceeds investment, firms suffer losses, which they can off-set either by not repaying the banks
or by reducing their cash balances and stocks of securities, and in the next cycle
they will reduce output and employment (I shall return to this point later). As a
consequence, they also reduce the demand for credit, so that the money created by
the banking system will be less than that created in the previous cycle. For Abbati,
therefore, money is synonymous with effective demand and hoarding is synonymous with an excess of saving over investment, that is, insufficient demand.

The first signal of falling demand is a reduction in wholesale prices, to which
firms promptly react by reducing production, because both firms and workers
prefer a reduction in production to a reduction in prices and wages (1928: 66–8).
Hence a fall in demand is not necessarily followed by a decline in retail prices.
Consequently unlikely are both the Pigou effect and a transfer of consumption
from those who abstain from spending to those who do not.[10] Similarly, an
increase in demand does not necessarily imply inflation unless there is full
employment.

The crux of Abbati's analysis is that, contrary to the opinion then current, the
money that savers deposit in bank accounts or pay to financial operators in
exchange for securities – which is money withdrawn from 'circulation in
industry' – in a phase of declining demand for goods and services is likely to
remain unused, i.e. hoarded, in the absence of secure and profitable investment.
When effective demand is insufficient to absorb current production, there is no
interest rate able to stimulate investment (I shall return to also this point later).
The problem, therefore, is not so much under-consumption as the absence of a
mechanism able to remove the surplus of saving.

The remedy for unemployment is to offset the decline in effective demand with
additional effective demand. The banks are unable to fulfil this need because what
is required is not additional money but additional effective demand. Having discarded as unfeasible various types of possible compensation, which he terms
'irregular final-buying', Abbati concludes that only an increase in public spending
and appropriate tax reductions, both financed with bank loans, can furnish both
additional money and additional effective demand.

In developing the theory just outlined, Abbati profoundly innovated certain
fundamental tenets of the neoclassical theory then dominant. Despite Abbati's

scant knowledge of the academic economic literature, the fact that he constantly kept abreast of market trends both real and financial, his intuition in grasping the link between economic events, about which he was constantly very well-informed, and the international context in which he had gained his practical experience of business, nevertheless made him aware of the novelty of his arguments with respect to current theoretical positions. Abbati's main innovations, which will now be examined in more detail, consisted in reformulating the concept of saving; contesting the notion that interest rate could equalize saving and investment; and analysing the banking system from a new perspective.

Saving

In *The Unclaimed Wealth* (1924) Abbati pointed out that it is an error to define 'spending' as the effective demand for consumable goods and 'saving' as the effective demand for capital goods. This amounted to considering effective demand as equal to production. Part of saving, in fact, may be hoarded. He therefore used the term 'spending', or more often 'final buying', to denote the purchase of final commodities and services regardless of whether they are consumable or capital goods (1924a: 101). He made another important point: 'Before the steamer age', when production had not developed and the modern banking system did not exist, 'the difference between true saving and hoarding was unmistakable'. But at the time when he was writing, 'as modern wealth is hoarded it disappears!' Economy and thrift are not virtue, 'but pure and simple waste. [. . .] Parsimony, the great gospel for the creation of wealth, is negative and creates nothing' (1924a: 117–20). Purchasing power can only be truly saved when it is fully spent.

Abbati also specified that investment should be understood as a use of saving whose effect is an increase in the quantity and value of capital, in which he included capital goods, stocks of goods and skilled labour. After enumerating various uses of saving erroneously considered to be investment, he concluded that investment consisted solely in the direct and indirect purchase of new capital goods, an increase in stocks, the lending of money for these purposes, and all expenditure on training and increasing skilled labour (1925c and 1928: 52).

In *The Final Buyer*, the text cited by Keynes, Abbati provides the following succinct but exhaustive version of his concept of saving:

> To consider the different kinds of saving, therefore, we must distinguish between (i) the passive part of doing without consumable goods or certain kinds of non-productive equipment and (ii) the active part of producing commodity capital or ordering it to be produced.
>
> (1928: 49)

The passive part of saving may be voluntary, in which case Abbati calls it 'abstinence'; or it may be imposed or forced, in which case he calls it 'automatic frugality' (1928: 50). Abbati further specifies that abstaining from spending money income on consumable goods does not represent an increase in capital goods, and therefore saving, when the money 'is invested in an unproductive manner, as when hoarded or lent to a government to buy perishable goods' (1928: 49). On the other hand, if it were necessary for production factors to be shifted from the production of consumption goods to the production of capital goods, as would happen in a hypothetical situation of full employment, not even voluntary saving would be required, because forced saving would suffice. Investment is completely disjointed from voluntary saving. However, it is hoarded saving that interests Abbati, not forced saving. When commenting on Keynes' note in the *Treatise* cited at the beginning of this Introduction, in the belief that Keynes was attributing to him 'results substantially similar' to those of Robertson, Mises and Schumpeter (although it may also be that Keynes meant results similar to his own), Abbati wrote:

> First, the theories of Ludwig Mises and Schumpeter are not concerned with *hoarded* savings (which arise as a result of excessive voluntary saving), but with 'forced saving' (which takes place as a result of insufficient voluntary saving). The *hoarding* of voluntary savings and the notion of 'forced saving' involve two totally different ideas, and the idea of 'forced saving' certainly affords no clue to the concept of *hoarding*.
>
> (1947a: 15)

As regards Robertson, Abbati acknowledges[11] his very detailed analysis of hoarding in *Banking Policy and the Price Level*, but he does not think that 'this similarity justifies any suggestion that Mr. Robertson's book and mine are similar in other respects' (1947a: 15).

The reasons adduced by Abbati for excessive abstinence from consumption are manifold: an income distribution that favours people with a low propensity to consume, so that those who could spend do not do so, and those who want to spend cannot do so; economy campaigns; the taxation imposed to repay the national and foreign debt, which transfers income from the debtors, willing final buyers, to creditors, who refuse to use it for final-buying; the delay in adjusting consumption to increased income; a speculative attitude to price changes. Abbati does not give a precise definition of the dominant relationship between saving and income (nor does Keynes in the *Treatise*), and this is undoubtedly a weakness in his theory, especially when one wants to assess in quantitative terms the impact of unmade spending on output: that is, establish the extent to which output falls with a fall in effective demand.

Hoarding and liquidity preference

Hoarding has a central role in Abbati's theory. Of course, economic actors maintain 'normal' liquidity balances for convenience and precaution; the problem arises when saving exceeds the current production of capital goods. As we have seen, for Abbati hoarding comes about when a portion of current income is not spent on purchasing the current production of both consumer goods and capital goods. To use Abbati's terminology, it corresponds to the passive part of saving; or in other words, it is equivalent to the demand for money, or an excess of saving over investment. However it is defined, though, hoarding represents a lack of effective demand for goods and services which, because it results in losses for firms, induces them to reduce production and employment. It occurs mainly in the form of inactive bank deposits. But the form, cash or deposit, is irrelevant; what matters is that a flow of money blocked somewhere in the monetary circuit for some reason or other does not face a corresponding flow of goods and services on the market.

Hoarding may be undertaken by:

(a) the public, when it reduces consumption and does not use the increased saving to purchase investment goods or securities, or when an increase in income is not matched by an equal increase in spending on final goods;
(b) stockbrokers or speculators when they sell securities and abstain from using the money obtained to purchase goods, services or newly-issued securities;
(c) firms, when the revenues from the sale of goods and services that they produce, or from the securities that they sell, constitute or reconstitute monetary reserves.

As regards case (a), Abbati maintains that, whatever the reason for which consumption diminishes or does not growing sufficiently, savers will decide to purchase securities from existing operators only if their prices are sufficiently low and the prospects of ordinary shares are satisfactory. However, it is very unlikely that these circumstances will be present when effective demand is being decreased by abstinence and when money is being released by industry and trade. In these circumstances, savers deposit their savings in banks, or leave bank deposits idle, thereby shifting the burden of employing them to the banks.

> But the success of the banker in being able to do so is by no means assured, and his difficulties in this direction are enhanced to the extent in which money is being confined to deposit accounts or otherwise withheld from the pur-chase of goods and services; for, in such circumstances, the accommodation required by industry and commerce is proportionately reduced.
>
> (1925c: 540)

Hoarding by the public is therefore closely connected with the inability of banks to 'force the horse to drink', to quote Keynes.

Here Abbati's intention in particular is to confute Hobson's over-investment theory and in general the then undisputed idea that saving automatically turns into investment. According to Hobson, all the income not spent on consumption goods is used either directly or by the banks to produce investment goods, so that the effect of over-saving is over-investment, which in its turn entails an over-production of consumption goods for which a demand must be found. The fact that, in the modern economic system, when people do not spend their money they deposit it in banks reinforces this effect, because the banks are unable to pay interest on deposits if they do not use the money in some way. This is the argument which Hobson brought against Abbati when he read his synopsis in which Abbati talked of uninvested saving (see Biography). Abbati's reply was that the 'banking system did not, and could not, increase the production of new capital goods as a result of the effect on their deposits of over-saving' (1947a: 6); but thanks to his direct discussion with Hobson, Abbati realized that the crucial difficulty that his theory had to resolve was explaining exactly what happened to the excessive savings deposited in banks. It was for this reason that he minutely analysed the banking system and the nature of the interest rate. His conclusion was that the interest rate is unable to equalize saving and investment, and that when there is insufficient demand, inactive bank deposits are simply hoarded money.

However, the risk of hoarding persists even when the public does not hoard, because, as in case (b), stockbrokers may hoard in their turn. Therefore, unless the public does not buy securities relating to newly-produced capital goods, directly or indirectly lending to those who are doing so, the risk that money is blocked somewhere in the circuit is the same whether the public purchases securities or whether it leaves bank deposits idle, especially when the effective demand for goods and services, and with it economic activity, is declining. For this reason, once it is established that the public demands money for transactional and precautionary reasons, Abbati does not even investigate the public's preference between securities and liquidity: the interest rate counts for little or nothing when the economic outlook is poor; it can at most influence the choice between cash and bank deposits.

Case (b) is a classic example of liquidity preference, although it is unconnected with the interest rate. Abbati envisages, in fact, that stock exchange operators or others selling securities may exchange them for cash to be held idle, 'for they may neither wish to spend the money nor be able to find safe and profitable employment for it in industry and trade' (1928: 55). The considerations regarding case (a) naturally apply also to stock market operators, so that when the money is released by industry and trade, there may be no prices of securities that induce operators to purchase them, and no interest rate that can induce investments to increase: 'so long as the money is circulating in such stocks and shares, it is withdrawn from circulation in industry and, other things being equal, causes an equivalent stoppage in new production' (1925c: 540).

Moreover, the behaviour of stockbrokers may be governed by purely speculative motives. In Bulletin no. 26 issued in Geneva on 1 June 1933 and entitled *Gentlemen Prefer Gold. II. A Midsummer Night's Dream of 1928* (1934a: 35–48), Abbati provides a detailed description of the behaviour of the speculator who withholds liquidity in order to use it at the appropriate moment. He imagines a conference of grotesquely named multi-millionaires 'that took place somewhere, possibly in the City, or in the Champs Elysées – or even *through the ether!*'. Their goal is to achieve the maximum possible gains through liquidations of real and financial assets (by themselves provoked). The 'offensive programme' comprises three campaigns: in the first, the purpose of the speculators is to equip themselves with enormous amounts of ready cash to be used in the final campaign, and this is accomplished by quiet conversion of their assets into cash, bank deposits, short loans and first-class self-liquidating commercial loans. Also foreseen are occasional applications of the 'bull' technique to restore confidence on the market. The second campaign 'will be one of masterly inactivity'; in the third, it will be necessary to 'get into gold', provoking an increase in its price, obtain cash at discount for gold, and acquire first-class securities and property at distress prices. Only one thing could compromise the success of this colossal speculative attack: if the creditor countries converted 'in concert to the principles of war finance' and began to put additional money into circulation, increasing their public expenditure through bank loans. 'But', concludes one of the speculators, 'I think we may take it as certain that nothing, apart from a big war, would induce these governments to do anything of the sort early enough to prevent the attainment of all our objectives' (1934a: 36–45). This is a representation in speculative terms of the Great Depression,[12] but also a demonstration of Abbati's knowledge of the workings of financial markets and his awareness of the speculative nature that hoarding may assume.

It seems that Abbati's hoarding resemblance to liquidity preference can be inferred from Keynes himself, who would write in the *General Theory* that: 'The concept of *hoarding* may be regarded as a first approximation to the concept of *liquidity-preference*. Indeed if we were to substitute 'propensity to hoard' for 'hoarding', it would come to substantially the same thing' (Keynes 1936: 174). We shall return to the distinction drawn by Keynes between 'propensity to hoard' and 'hoarding' in case (c).

Before discussion of this case concludes, it should be pointed out that, for Abbati, if demand for securities outstrips supply, and stockbrokers obtain windfall gains on capital account, some of these gains may re-enter industrial circulation in the form of final-buying, and this is the only way in which, according to Abbati, the financial market can help support demand in the presence of abstinence from consumption: through partial compensation of demand for consumption goods rather than through demand for capital goods.

Case (c) warrants especial attention. When firms suffer losses because of hoarding, and therefore do not recover all the money put into circulation, there are two possibilities. First, the firms do not repay the banks. In this case, the banks find themselves with loans (to firms) on the assets side, and with deposits (of abstainers) on the liabilities side. In other words, they are creditors to firms and debtors to the abstainers for an amount equal to the losses of firms. In this case, the banks have money that is not destroyed, and that money serves to meet the demand for money by the abstainers. The money supply – equal to the money demand by abstainers, or to their hoarding – is therefore determined by the effective demand for goods and services and not their production, even less by the discretion of banks in granting loans: banks can decide how much money to *inject* into the circuit, but not how much money *remains* in the circuit, and the money that remains in the circuit is unspent money.

For Abbati, the interest rate plays a significant role neither during the creation nor the destruction of money. On the one hand, investment, and therefore the demand for financing, does not depend on the interest rate, but on the effective demand for goods and services (see the next section); on the other, banks are unable to provide or encourage the effective demand that would compensate for the lack of effective demand by abstainers and thus allow closure of the circuit. It is effective demand that determines the cash flow and the supply of money.

Second, firms can sell securities to an amount equal to their losses, securities that will be purchased by those wanting to increase their saving but not their hoarding. Firms, therefore, can cope with their losses in this way only if depositors do not hoard. This is the case considered by Keynes in the *Treatise*. Keynes wanted to show that a reduction in the prices of consumption goods, due to an increase in saving (but not in the desire to hoard) by the public, was not necessarily off-set by an increase in the prices of capital goods. That is to say, he wanted to show that losses in the consumption goods sector were not necessarily matched by gains in the capital goods sector, with all the implications of this in terms of a fall in the general price level and then in employment (Keynes 1930a and 1931).

This idea was strongly disputed by Robertson, who maintained – using an argument similar to Abbati's as outlined above (pp. 3–4) – that with an increase in saving, which is a flow of money diverted directly or indirectly from the consumption goods market to the capital goods market, prices in the latter cannot remain unchanged unless the flow is to some extent immobilized at some point – unless, that is, someone is hoarding (Robertson 1931).

But Keynes showed that even if nobody is hoarding, the prices of capital goods may remain unchanged, so that the overall level of prices may fall. How is this possible? Keynes simply hypothesises the presence of previously possessed liquid or non-liquid assets[13] in the hands of firms. Hence, if savers demand securities instead of consumption goods, firms draw from their stocks securities of an amount equal to the increase in saving and sell them to savers. One may also hypothesise that if savers, besides their saving, also increase their desire to hoard, firms may face losses by their money reserves. In the former case, there is a transfer of securities from firms to savers, and of money from savers to firms; in the latter case, there is a reduction in the cash reserves of firms, which off-sets the increase in the cash reserves of savers. This hypothesis, however, is not compatible with Keynes' assumption that the propensity to hoard is the same for everyone. In both cases, however, the losses remain in the form of a reduction in the stock of securities or cash reserves of firms, banks are repaid and the supply of money, equal to the overall demand for money, remains unchanged; but in both cases, the money withdrawn from the consumption goods market never reaches the capital goods market, with a consequent fall in the general price level.

In conclusion, Keynes argued for the independence of the prices of capital goods from those of consumption goods by introducing into the monetary circuit an external element: the already-existing stocks of money or securities that can be used to off-set possible losses. Robertson, however, continued to believe that if the prices of capital goods did not increase, this was only because someone was hoarding, and in the case just examined it was precisely the firms which were hoarding, when with the sale of securities they reconstituted the cash reserves depleted by their monetary losses (Robertson 1933). In any case, beyond questions of terminology (Robinson 1938), Robertson's position is very similar to Abbati's when he says that the prices of capital goods remain unchanged because some impediment prevents the transfer of purchasing power from the consumption goods market to the capital goods market; and this impediment, as Abbati states, is hoarding, i.e. the saving that is not invested.[14]

It is worth now highlighting some significant differences on the question of hoarding between Abbati, on one hand, and Keynes and Robertson on the other. Firstly, for Abbati, the direct effect of hoarding is an inevitable reduction in output, whereas for Robertson and Keynes in the *Treatise*, hoarding first has an effect on prices and then perhaps on output. For Robertson, for example, hoarding wasted abstinence or lacking power rather than output, since a fall in the price level provokes an unexpected increase in consumption on the part of non-abstainers (Robertson 1926: 53). As we have seen, Abbati excluded this effect. As Coppock rightly pointed out: 'Mr Abbati may fairly claim that he showed that hoarding was more likely to tax the public rather than to concede bounties of consumption' (Coppock 1954: 84). As regards Keynes, the main problem in the *Treatise* was not the level of output, but the stability of the general price level, which in its turn ensured equality between saving and investment.

Moreover, both Robertson and Keynes were of course aware that firms tend to off-set losses by reducing employment and production, but both of them believed that intervention by banks might eventually counter-balance the effect of hoarding on prices, and therefore on output. It is at this point that it is necessary to refer to the above-mentioned distinction drawn by Keynes between hoarding and the desire, or propensity, to hoard. For Keynes in the *Treatise*, an increase in hoarding means an increase in the desire to hold money as opposed to securities, and he thought that this desire could turn into effective hoarding only if the banks allowed it: 'This is why it is so important to distinguish the forces determining the quantity of hoards (which is the affair of the bankers) from the forces determining the propensity to hoard (which is the affair of the public)' (Keynes 1931: 419). In other words, the volume of hoarding is determined by the banks that are able to control saving-deposits: 'the amount of inactive deposits or hoards actually held [. . .] is determined by the banking system, since it is equal to the excess of the total bank-money created over what is required for the active deposits' (Keynes 1931: 413). Keynes believed, in fact, that there is always a price of securities that induces people to buy or sell them. If this were not so, 'it would be impossible for the banking system to expand or contract the volume of money by "open market" operations', as instead, according to Keynes, it is able to do. Keynes reiterated his position in *General Theory*: 'the amount of hoarding must be equal to the quantity of money [. . .] and the quantity of money is not determined by the public' (Keynes 1936: 174).

But an equally important issue is that Keynes at that time was convinced of the inevitable effects of the interest rate on investment, and that banks can control the interest rate. In a letter to Montagu Norman[15] of 22 May 1930 he wrote:

If we can find *no* outlet for our savings, then it would be better to save less. But this would be a counsel of despair. I am sure that there *is* an outlet for them – at an appropriate rate of interest [. . .] On the monetary and banking side [. . .] the task is to produce credit conditions which will bring down the long-term rate of interest and at the same time stimulate investing enterprise.

(Keynes 1930b: 353)

For Abbati, as we have seen, the simple non-repayment by firms of their original bank loans suffices to provide the economic system with the amount of money required by those demanding money. Abbati did not believe that banks are able to combat hoarding when effective demand is insufficient to absorb current production; nor did he believe that, in these circumstances, it is sufficient to reduce the interest rate to stimulate investment, as we shall see better in the next section.

There is a final issue on which Abbati adopted a distinctive position. He maintained that when the monetary income made available by abstinence is held idle in the banks, other things being equal, both the velocity of production and the total amount of money diminish.

The claim that maintaining idle deposits entails a reduction in the money supply is recurrent in Abbati,[16] but it would seem to be logically untenable. As Abbati well explained, the creation of credit money (an excess of deposits with respect to banks' cash reserves) does not alter the amount of cash held by banks, but only their obligation to pay cash. For simplicity, imagine that there is a just one bank. This bank grants credit to A, and with this credit A makes a payment to B. If B puts the money into the bank and leaves the deposit idle, all that changes is that now B is the owner of the deposit instead of A, while the bank's reserves and the volume of deposits have not changed.

What Abbati meant to say, however, is that when effective demand decreases and firms do not recover all the money put into circulation, in the next cycle of production they will reduce output and therefore the demand for credit to finance it; as a consequence the creation of credit money will diminish. But in this case, too, the quantity of money should remain unchanged, unless the output is reduced to below the amount that firms were able to sell in the previous cycle. For example, firms in cycle 1 will put into circulation (and the bank will create) 100; if in the end they recover 90, they repay only 90 to the bank. Therefore, credit money equal to 90 is destroyed while 10 remains in the form of deposits and corresponds to hoarding. If in cycle 2, firms reduce production, and therefore the demand for financing, to 90, the bank reduces the creation of credit money to 90, but this will add to the 10 not destroyed in cycle 1, so that the quantity of money will still be 100. The active money is reduced, but the total supply of money and the reserves/deposits ratio remain unchanged. For one to talk about a reduction in the money supply, it is necessary that in cycle 2 firms reduce their demand for loans, and banks reduce the creation of credit money, to below 90, for example to 80, even if they are able to repay 90. In this case, the quantity of money would fall to 90 (80 +10).

The fact that the fall in production in cycle 2 may be greater than the decline in effective demand during cycle 1 suggests that Abbati envisaged the operation of a mechanism very similar to the multiplier which amplifies the deflationary effects of a fall in investment consequent upon the initial fall in consumption. Abbati does not give a detailed explanation of this process, but he was certainly aware that a fall in effective demand is followed by a more than proportional fall in production (1924a: 54).

In light of the foregoing discussion, we can make better assessment of Robertson's criticism of Abbati's analysis, and we may conclude that it is not sufficiently substantiated. Robertson says that Abbati gives the impression of considering hoarded money as consisting of cash deposited in banks by abstainers, and this impression arises from the fact that, for Abbati, hoarding causes an increase in the reserves/deposits ratio which banks undergo without being able to reduce it. For Robertson, instead, hoarding consists in idle deposits, so that it does not give rise to any variation in the reserves/deposits ratio (Letter to Abbati 15 August 1948 and Robertson 1932: 613).

Of course, Abbati was convinced that hoarding takes mainly the form of idle bank deposits – this was his criticism of Hobson and the starting point of his analysis – although he sometimes spoke of cash deposited in banks. But if we admit that, as we saw in the above example, firms repay 90 in cycle 1 and in cycle 2 they demand financing for 80, then the deposits created will necessarily be less than those destroyed and, reserves remaining equal, banks will find themselves in cycle 2 with a reserves/deposits ratio greater than in cycle 1. Further, the reserve ratio of the banks may remain unchanged, 'but their discounts at the central bank, and the loans and investments of the central bank will decline; and the reserve ratio of the central bank will to that extent increase' (Letter to Robertson, 19 August 1948). Hence hoarding in the form of idle deposits may well be compatible with the increase in the reserves/deposits ratio.

Banks and the interest rate

Abbati describes in detail how in his time the Bank of England worked through its two departments (Issue and Banking), the various kinds of money, how they were created, and how money flowed to and from foreign countries, on and off the gold standard. He concentrates in particular on how bank deposits are created and on the presumed ability of banks to contract or expand credit in a closed and open economy. On the basis of what has already been said, and bearing in mind that Abbati defines as 'credit money' the excess of a bank's deposits with respect to its total reserves, these are in synthesis his main conclusions.

1   Credit money is the most important component of the money supply. The banks create it by granting loans, so that loans almost always precede deposits. Hence Abbati, like Wicksell (1898), Schumpeter (1912) and Hahn (1920), reverses the neoclassical conception according to which bank lending must be preceded by the collection of saving.[17]
2   The effective demand for credit is generated by the government in order to finance the deficit, and above all by firms to finance production and

investments, which in their turn depend on the effective demand for goods and services. Hence, 'whilst bankers are able to supply *credit money* against an *effective demand* for it, they can neither create, nor maintain in existence, any credit unless this *effective demand* exists' (1924a: 81). Nor can banks impede an expansion of credit when the effective demand is increasing. If they do so, the pressure on their reserves will be unsustainable, both because of the increase in cash withdrawals by the public, and because of the decrease in value of their securities due to the massive liquidations caused by shortage of credit. In these circumstances the velocity of money will increase and there will arise forms of credit alternative to bank credit, which, although it is the best kind of credit, is not the only one; 'consequently, in the last resort bankers have no power to contract or prevent the expansion of credit' (1924a: 83–4).

Unlike the banks, a government is, at all times, able to put as much money into circulation[18] 'as it likes merely by allowing its expenditure to exceed its revenue' (1924a: 43).

The money supply depends on the effective demand for goods and services, not on their production (1928).

3   In a gold standard regime[19] the action of the central bank is conditioned by the inflows/outflows of gold, which depend on the relative price level at home and abroad. These prices depend on the ratio between the total money supply, which in its turn depends on the effective demand, and the output available for sale on the market. Off the gold standard, the central bank's action is directly conditioned by government's decision to borrow from banks or to issue money to finance the deficit. In any case, gold standard or not, the margins for money creation available to governments are always broad, while those of banks are restricted by the demand for credit, not by the gold standard. A shortage of money to finance production occurs in only very particular cases which do not usually arise in the developed countries: 'It is not facilities for production that entrepreneurs and nations ask for to-day; all they clamour for is markets' (1924a: 25).

As regards the interest rate, Abbati entirely rejects the consolidated theory of his time. His position can be summarized as follows:

1   The interest rate depends on the demand for and the supply of loanable funds. A fall in the interest rate signals that the banks' reserves/deposits ratio is increasing. This signifies that two concomitant phenomena are occurring: people are abstaining from buying and business men are abstaining from borrowing. The idle money in the banks is simply being hoarded.

2   The bankers' control over the interest rate is limited: on a gold standard by the gold flows; off gold standard by the government's decisions about management of the national budget.

3   However, a reduction in the interest rate is not able to increase the demand for credit by business men, because this depends on the effective demand, which also determines the demand for financing of gross investments: 'both

renewals and new ventures are entirely dependent upon the *effective demand* of the public for the commodities and services to be supplied by such renewals or new ventures' (1924a: 85). Investments therefore do not depend on the interest rate.

4 The interest rate also plays a limited part in demand for credit to finance the purchase of financial activities, which is determined by conditions in the financial markets.

> The conditions in stock exchange markets consist of whether markets are 'long' or 'short', whether the prices of securities are relatively low or high as judged by their yields and prospects, whether conditions in commodity markets are such that money is being attracted into, or being turned out of, employment in industry and trade and whether, because of the monetary requirements of industry and trade or for any other reason, interest rates are high or low. [. . .] Once an article looks dear, be it any kind of commodity or security, low interest rates will not induce business men to carry any more of it than they can help; and, on the other hand, it is not the difference between 5 per cent and 10 per cent per annum that will prevent them from increasing their holdings of goods or securities that look cheap.
>
> (1928: 35)

5 A reduction in the interest rate may abate production costs, but lower production costs 'obtained by means of *reductions in the total earnings of labour, land, capital or entrepreneurs' profits reduce the effective demand to more or less the same extent as the quantity of earnings economised*' (1924a: 85).

6 Variations in the interest rate can influence the choice by the public between depositing money in banks or spending it, but this influence on the demand for money, and therefore on effective demand, is entirely negligible.

In conclusion, credit money is by far the largest component of the money supply. But the power of banks to influence the volume of loans, and therefore the level of demand for goods and services, 'is limited: by their limited power over interest rates and by the limited effects of interest rates on the extent of government borrowing and on conditions in markets, which together govern the effective demand for loans' (1928: 41).

The following passage from *The Unclaimed Wealth* well summarizes what we have seen thus far concerning banks and the interest rate in Abbati's theory of effective demand.

> It is necessary to be quite clear that money deposited in banks or circulating in a stock and share market is not *spent* on capital goods instead of consumable goods; and, in fact, is not *spent* at all, and cancels an equivalent quantity of the *credit money* of the producers whose commodities and services it should have been used to purchase. Once this is clear, there can no longer be any room for doubt that both the production of consumptive goods and the

production of capital goods are strictly determined by the positive or anticipated *effective demand* for them [. . .] It may be that there is a tendency for
the idle surplus of the rich to be pressed towards the overproduction of capital
goods in relation to the production of consumables; but it is certain that any
unwarranted check on the *effective demand* for consumable goods freezes the
whole system of production, reducing the employment and value of capital
goods. The main thing, therefore, is to ensure that it is physically possible for
the total quantity of commodities and services of every kind produced for
sale to be marketable as fast as produced without a fall in prices and the monetary losses and congestion thereby involved.

(1924a: 110–11n.)

Abbati and the theoretical debate of the 1920s

In regard to combating unemployment, in light of the discussion thus far we can
begin to exclude the instruments that for Abbati are not, and could not be, practicable: the banks, because they do not control active money, and therefore can
furnish additional money, but not additional demand; the interest rate, because its
movement balances the demand and supply of money, but not saving and investment; reduced remuneration of the production factors, particularly wages, because
this reduces production costs but also effective demand. Price reductions and
thrift are excluded by definition; indeed, as primarily responsible for depression,
they are enemies to be fought unconditionally. These beliefs place Abbati in stark
contrast not only with the dominant neo-classical orthodoxy, but also with the
new currents of thought then trying to confute it, and which are now briefly
outlined to confirm this argument.

The long crisis of 1874–96, the persistence of high unemployment rates, especially in England, and the onset of another recession towards the end of 1920,
again in England, revived analysis of business cycles. Thus the first two decades
of the twentieth century saw numerous 'theories', many of them formulated by
authors who were not economists by profession (an 'invasion by barbarians'
according to Marget), who started from rejection of Say's Law to propound a
view of the economic system at odds with the dominant theory. Abbati, therefore,
in 1924 was not alone in attacking the economic orthodoxy, but none of the theories then current reflected his thought; indeed, according to him, they were all
wrong.

In *The Final Buyer* Abbati classifies the theories most widely accepted by his
contemporaries and their criticisms into the three following groups (1928: 2–12):

1   Theories that locate the causes of recession on the productive side of busi-
     ness. A first subgroup of these theories argues that a shortage of financing
     for production comes about for some or other reason. A second subgroup
     consists of disproportionate production theories.
2   Theories that locate the cause of recession in the market mechanism. A first
     type of theory maintains that money earned by production is not enough to

pay for goods and services produced. A second type comprises the theory of over-investment.

3   Theories that maintain that general overproduction would be impossible in a barter economy.

The theories considered by Abbati largely cover the debate of his time.[20] The first group comprises the purely monetary theory of the business cycle first formulated by R. Hawtrey (1923; 1927): an expansion of credit consequent upon a cheap-money policy by banks can always engender an upward phase of the cycle, or lead the system out of depression. The upward phase is self-fuelling, but it must necessarily be brought to a halt when the credit expansion meets the limit of the gold standard. A depressive phase thus ensues, this too in constant progression, until it is halted by the banks' expansionary intervention.

This group also includes all the theories whose shared feature is a savings shortage following periods of intense investment. All the theories of savings shortage originate with Tugan-Baranovskij[21] and they are formulated in a real version and a monetary one.

The theoretical basis of the real version (Tugan-Baranovskij, Spiethoff, Cassel) is that developed by Tugan-Baranovskij to explain the alternation of periods of prosperity with ones of overproduction (or disproportion between the consumption goods and investment goods sectors). The former are periods in which capital – for which investment opportunities are ever-present – is invested rapidly until the saving funds, accumulated in previous periods for the purpose of investment, are depleted and investments cannot be undertaken at the same velocity. At this point, the production of investment goods falls below the level necessary to maintain the equilibrium between aggregate demand and aggregate supply, the consequence being a relative surplus of consumption goods.[22] The financing shortage is aggravated by the fact that the typology and the increasing volume of investments requested, investments of a non-divisible kind compatible with advanced technological development, presuppose the setting-aside of savings made in various periods.

These theorists maintain that prosperity can continue indefinitely if people abstain from excessive consumption so as to permit completion of the productive structure. However, recovery sooner or later begins, thanks to the fall in the costs of producing fixed capital caused by the depression, and even more so if this fall is accompanied by exogenous impulses, such as inventions or the cultivation of new land. To conclude, investment opportunities are always available; it is not under-consumption or over-saving that causes depression, but over-consumption and under-saving.

The monetary version of the saving shortage theory originated in large part with L. Mises and F.A. Hayek. Since it was developed mainly in the late 1920s and early 1930s, Abbati could not have known about it when he formulated his own theory. It is nevertheless considered here in order to demonstrate that Abbati's theory had nothing to do with those of Mises and Hayek.

For Hayek, disequilibrium originates from the fact that banks are able to lend money in excess of the funds deposited with them by reducing the market rate of interest below the natural rate, corresponding to the rate of return on capital. When investments exceed voluntary savings there begins a cumulative process of expansion during which the production structure enlarges and production of investment goods increases more than production of consumption goods. The expansionary phase is bound to be brought to a halt by a lack of credit to finance the rising investments, for banks cannot expand credit beyond certain limits and consumers are unwilling to forgo consumption to an extent sufficient to yield the necessary savings. The most important aspect of the crisis is that investment projects involving more indirect production structures are not feasible. At this point, equilibrium between investments and savings is restored by two mechanisms: liquidity problems induce the banks to raise the interest rate, thus reducing investments, while the fall in the relative prices of investment goods switch the production to consumption goods. Macroeconomic equilibrium is therefore substantially stable, and recessionary phases are necessary but short-lived phenomena (Hayek 1933).

Also in its monetary version, therefore, the theory's central thesis is confirmed: investment opportunities are boundless and recessions are caused by a shortage of voluntary savings. As in Hawtrey, the banks are explicitly conceived as economic institutions endowed with broad powers: lowering the interest rate sets off a boom, raising the interest rate brings the boom to a halt. Moreover, adherence to the neoclassical orthodoxy is particularly evident. If the increase in the production of investment goods is checked because it is not matched by a concomitant decrease in the production of consumption goods, this signifies that full employment is assumed. Furthermore, the interest rate is the key determinant of macroeconomic equilibrium.

The second group of theories is represented by the underconsumptionists contemporary with Abbati (Hobson, Foster and Catchings, Douglas), who started from the observation that Say's Law was not borne out by the empirical evidence.

J.A. Hobson was the most renowned representative of this group. When his first publication came out (1889), Hobson was a member of the British Liberal Party and advocated state intervention in the economy. His over-investment theory, which we have already seen, states that 'if increased thrift or caution induces people to save more in the present, they must consent to consume more in the future' (Hobson and Mummery 1889). If they do not, an overproduction of consumption goods ensues and the new capital thus created will be idle. For Hobson, therefore, saving always turns into investment. It is for this reason that problems arise.

As for why people save more, Hobson initially spoke of excessive saver prudence, which conflicted with the interest of the community – which gainsays Smith's famous maxim. In subsequent works, Hobson identified the unequal distribution of income as the prime cause of over-saving (Hobson 1922). Of particular importance for 'bad income distribution' are the formation of monopolies and the appropriation of surpluses, which place vast amounts of money in the hands of people with a low propensity to consume. Moreover, according to Hobson, the possible fall in prices due to overproduction generates a temporary increase in real income that is usually saved, while saving is scarcely sensitive to the interest rate. Hence the neoclassical readjustment mechanisms do not operate and the economy is intrinsically unstable. All these arguments were reprised by Abbati notwithstanding his critique against the assumptions of Hobson's theory.[23]

According to W. Foster and W. Catchings, general overproduction is a phenomenon typical of a monetary economy yet impossible in a barter economy; in a barter economy the size of demand is determined by supply, in a monetary economy demand is possible without it being matched by supply (Foster and Catchings 1925). For them the crucial factor is time. They point out (Foster and Catchings 1928) that the supply of consumption goods today depends on the current stock of capital, which, in its turn, is the result of saving in the past. For these authors, too, saving is always converted into investment, so that the act of saving is not accompanied by a concomitant fall in demand for consumption goods, which continue to be demanded by workers employed in the production of both consumption goods and investment goods. But the investment goods produced today will increase the production of consumption goods only in the future. It follows that current demand for consumption goods exceeds their current supply. In other words, investment is a two-edged sword; on the one hand, it immediately increases demand, on the other, it increases supply in the future. Whence 'the dilemma of thrift': saving is necessary to produce more consumption goods, but it leads to crisis. In fact, owing to the excess of demand in the consumption goods sector, there begins a period of prosperity. Subsequently, the increased supply of consumption goods requires further investments in order to create further demand for consumption goods. The spiralling process continues until the banking system is no longer able to finance new investments, so the economy is always either in an inflationary phase or a deflationary one. Foster and Catchings maintain that two conditions are necessary to prevent demand problems: (i) firms must distribute all their profits to consumers; (ii) consumers must spend all their income. Note, however, that these two conditions are not a satisfactory solution. For if consumers save, investment follows, with all the consequences seen above; if, instead, consumers spend all their incomes on consumption goods, the economy is stationary, with a net investment rate equal to zero.

The theory propounded by Major Douglas is even weaker than the previous one. Douglas argues that the economy is permanently stagnant because the production process is unable to give consumers sufficient purchasing power. The core of Douglas' theory is his well-known A + B theorem, where A denotes a firm's costs in terms of remuneration of the production factors services, and B denotes all other costs. Confusing the micro level of analysis with the macro level, Douglas claims that the total of A plus the total of B represents the market value of total output, while A represents the purchasing power of the economy. Whence derives an insufficiency of aggregate demand (Douglas 1920). In fact, Douglas wanted to say that 'there is a large amount of purchasing power which is permanently retained purely in the productive system, and never gets out into the consumers' system' (Douglas 1931), but he was unable to explain how and why.[24]

It is not possible here to conduct further analysis of the theories current in the 1920s,[25] but the foregoing brief survey enables us to draw some conclusions useful for the argument developed here.

Despite appearances, and despite the intentions of the various authors examined, the similarities among the theories belonging to the two groups prevail over their differences. The main feature shared by them is their location of crisis not in the phase when saving is converted into investment – this phase never presents problems – but in a subsequent one; for the first group of theories, the phase between the beginning of the investment process and its conclusion, for the second, the phase following the completion of investments. None of the theories envisages the possibility that crisis might be due to a lack of investment opportunities, that is, to an excess of savings over investments.

A further feature shared by the two groups of theories is the assumption of full employment, i.e. the belief that a simultaneous increase in the production of investment goods and consumption goods is untenable. For the first group, investment growth may come about without a concomitant decrease in the production of consumption goods – without, that is, an increase in voluntary savings. But in the end, if voluntary savings do not increase sufficiently (if, therefore, the production of consumption goods is not reduced), investments cannot be completed. For the second group, the starting point is an increase in voluntary savings, which coincides with a shift of production factors from the consumption goods sector to the investment goods sector. In this case, investments are completed. But there now starts the additional production of consumption goods which presupposes a reduction in voluntary savings – a reduction, that is, in the production of investment goods. (All the theories exclude production for production in the long-term. Tugan does not exclude it, but acknowledges the limits of voluntary saving.) Finally, both groups explicitly or implicitly adopt the traditional concept of banks, according to which their credit capacity is limited in the long-term by the volume of funds deposited with them, but in the short-term the banks are able to control the credit supply at will.

As we have seen, Abbati disputed both the assumption of full employment and the above-described conception of banks. In particular, according to him, the credit capacity of the banks is potentially unlimited and the banks are not able to control the credit supply. But it is especially on the fundamental question of the relationship between saving and investment that Abbati departed decisively from current theories, orthodox and heterodox: he was the first among his predecessors and contemporaries to locate with sufficient analytical support the origin of economic crisis in the phase when savings must be converted into investments. Useful for understanding of this crucial point will be the following brief survey of the saving–investment relationship.

The saving–investment relationship

The classical economists identify saving and investment by means of the wages-fund theory. Wages are paid to workers before they start to produce, and the amount of wage goods available at the beginning of the period (the wages fund) consists of the amount of output in the previous period not consumed by capitalists, i.e. their saving. Capital consists of wages advanced to workers, so that investment is equivalent to creating the wages fund. Hence it follows that at the moment when the capitalist saves, he automatically invests. In this conceptual framework, a crisis cannot be generated by the breach between saving and investment because by definition this breach does not exist. For the classical economists, a crisis can be provoked either by a falling rate of profit or by insufficient demand for consumption goods. One or the other circumstance is bound to arise when the economy moves from a steady state to growth. In the former case, Say's Law is accepted and the existence of a demand problem is denied. As Smith put it: 'What is annually saved is as regularly consumed as what is annually spent, and nearly in the same time too; but it is consumed by a different set of people' (Smith 1776: 321). In the latter case, Say's Law is rejected and the economy is regarded as suffering from chronic under-consumption because, if on the one hand the ultimate purpose of production is consumption, on the other the real wage must be maintained at the subsistence level, otherwise the surplus value will diminish. But the crisis of demand in the classicals does not arise because savings exceed investments, but because savings are always and automatically converted into investments, thus giving rise to a growing supply of consumption goods for which demand must be found.

With Marx (1895) we have the first solution for the demand problem in the version put forward by the classical under-consumptionists. The solution consists in offsetting the inevitable deficiency of demand for consumption goods (for Marx, too, wages are at subsistence level and profits are mostly saved) with an increase in demand for capital goods (means of production). The constant and systematic expansion of capital accumulation, in fact, constitutes the outlet market for increasing production. This apparently simple solution involves substantial changes to the classical conceptual framework, in particular to the definition of capital and, consequently, of investment. For Marx, capital consists not only of wage goods paid in advance to workers ('variable capital'), but also of the means of production ('constant capital'). Marx therefore gives up the wages-fund theory. He also asserts that the aim of capitalists is not consumption but profit, and therefore accumulation of capital. On this view, saving and investment are even more closely connected than they were for the classical economists; capitalists, whose sole interest is profit, tend to save the largest possible amount of their profits and to invest this saving in greater accumulation. In other words, although consumption is limited, opportunities for investment are still boundless.

However, as for the classicals so for Marx, the expansion of accumulation inevitably leads to a fall in the profit rate, and therefore to a crisis, given the insuperable limits to rising surplus value.

In Marx the possibility of demand crisis is connected with the presence of money. According to Marx, in capitalist circulation the function of money as a medium of exchange is secondary; the principal function of money is to represent wealth in its most abstract and general form. Yet implicit in the fact that money represents value *par excellence* is the risk that it may be hoarded, because capitalists prefer it to commodities as a store of value. Marx does not treat this eventuality seriously, however: given that he maintains that the purpose of capitalist production is to yield profit, once commodities, and surplus value, have been converted into money, the capitalist's drive to accumulate capital necessarily prevails over his drive to hoard. This means that, even in the presence of money, investment opportunities are boundless and the problem does not reside in the transformation of savings into investments.

With the advent of neoclassical theory, the analytical frame of reference changes radically, although it still retains numerous elements of classical thought.

It is not appropriate here to set out the tenets of the neoclassical theory. Its feature of closest relevance to our analysis is that saving and investment are taken to be distinctly separate. Investment consists in the production of capital goods, while wages are tied to labour marginal productivity. Saving and investment decisions are taken by different actors. Saving is decided by the owners of the production factors, who by furnishing the services of those factors earn incomes. Investment is decided by firms, which do not own production factors and therefore do not earn incomes. However, because saving is a loss of demand for consumption goods, while investment takes concrete form as a supply of capital goods, if the aggregate demand problem is to be prevented, a mechanism is required which equalizes savings and investments. This mechanism is the interest rate, which, on the one hand, remunerates saving and, on the other, represents the cost of financing investment. Another aspect to be borne in mind is that the supply of money (M) is an exogenous variable fixed by the central bank, while its velocity of circulation (V) is given as well, because the demand for real cash balances is given with the output level, which is given, too, at the level of full employment. As a consequence, aggregate MV determines the general price level and also the level of nominal income (Quantity Theory of Money). In sum, the neoclassical model states that saving will always be equal to investment at the current interest rate, independently of the nominal income level. Thus neoclassicals, albeit by a different route, return to the idea that there is no problem in the transformation of saving in investment.

It should be pointed out that, given full employment, voluntary saving must necessarily precede investment, because it is non-consumption that makes available the resources to use in capital goods production. However, it is also hypothesized that investment may precede a forced saving induced by a discretionary increase in the money supply by the banking system, which reduces real wages or the cost of money. A further corollary is that public spending, even if financed by bank credit, cannot supplement private spending, but can only substitute for it.

In this theoretical framework, which is the most thorough application of Say's Law, the demand problem does not arise. Possible, though, are maladjustments in the form of insufficient demand. However, for the neoclassicals these maladjustments are due solely to rigidities in markets, the labour market especially, or to erroneous movements of the market interest rate induced by the banking system, so if maladjustments occur, the only remedies available are removal of market rigidities and resumption of proper behaviour by the banks. It is implicit that the purpose of the intervention is to reduce the duration of the maladjustment, for this will in any case be spontaneously absorbed through market mechanisms.

To summarize: the classical economists and Marx, although they took different routes to do so, eliminated the 'breach' between saving and investment by defini-tion. The neoclassicals generally believed that the interest rate is able to ensure that saving is equal to investment. As regards the authors examined in the section devoted to the theoretical debate in the 1920s, none of them, despite their *a priori* rejection of Say's law, was able to break with the dominant theory on this crucial issue. In fact, they located the origin of the crisis in a phase subsequent to the one in which saving is transformed into investment – some in the phase between the beginning and conclusion of the investment process, others in the phase following completion of investments.

The remedies

Having expounded his theory and criticised current theories, Abbati addresses the problem of how to neutralize abstinence. He states that there are other kinds of final buying, which he terms 'irregular', that may offset it. They are: the final buying resulting from new gold mines or new methods of mining; that consequent on an increase in equipment and stocks by producers and distributors; that of resi-dents abroad; that of governments. Although the first two involve income pay-ments and are therefore sources of additional demand, they are to be discarded. The incidence of the first is insignificant, while the second, which consists in autonomous investment, is unlikely in the climate of decline in confidence that accompanies the fall in demand, unless there arise exogenous factors that may have a significant impact on the decisions of entrepreneurs (1928: 104–9).

As regards the 'irregular final-buying' by residents abroad, Abbati takes this into serious consideration because it was widely believed in Great Britain at Abbati's time, by both the general public and the political establishment, that economic crises could be partly or wholly neutralized by improving the foreign trade balance (1928: 65–92). Abbati was highly sceptical that a country oppressed by a large stagnant surplus of goods could rid itself of it in this manner. He justified his view by conducting long and detailed analysis of the balance of pay-ments, the foreign exchange market and various issues to do with international payments.

The crux of the entire question is that exports cannot exceed the aggregate constituted by imports minus the inflow of net incomes from abroad and minus the repayment or re-entry of capital invested abroad, when it occurs. Otherwise, appreciation of the exchange rate, or alternatively the inflow of gold, will annul the improvement in the foreign trade balance, whatever the means used to achieve it. Hence, according to Abbati, 'Owing to the enormous British capital invested abroad and the interest due to England annually in respect of it, the British exter-nal trade balance is always heavily "adverse"'. The conflict is between British capital invested abroad and British producers. A country experiencing an excess of foreign payment inflows over outflows cannot avoid an 'adverse' trade balance unless it accepts cumulating abroad assets not available at home, or incurs in losses abroad, or repays its debt to foreign creditors: 'Thus, if it is true that you cannot eat your cake and have it, it is equally true that you cannot have your cake unless you eat it' (1924a: 144).

Moreover, to increase exports it is necessary to increase imports as well:

> It is not generally appreciated that the 'Haves' must buy the work of the 'Have-nots' before the 'Have-nots' can buy from the 'Haves' [. . .] Once the 'Haves' in any country are in possession of all they require and consequently refuse to buy, for the same reason selling by them, either at home or abroad, is impossible. When the 'Haves' refuse to buy and the 'Have-nots' cannot buy, all trade stops regardless of political boundaries.
>
> (1924a: 134–5)

The same argument can be applied to the question of the enormous post-war foreign debt and of war reparations, which complicated the situation of international payments at that time. Always greatly interested in international issues, Abbati declared forcefully and repeatedly that if the creditor countries wanted the debtor countries to repay their debts, they must necessarily create the conditions for the latter to be able to do so by importing from them. The alternative for the creditor countries was to accept an exchange rate appreciation and a contraction of their foreign markets to the benefit of the debtor countries. These solutions were disliked by the creditor countries, which preferred to postpone repayment and give new money. The payment of war reparations, moreover, not only raised the insoluble problem of what should be accepted in payment (1924a: 15–21), but was entirely disadvantageous to the receiving country, which would find itself with an unsalable surplus in addition to its own, or would see its firms crowded out of the market and its trade balances worsen.

> It is claimed that Germany has paid over £500,000,000 and no doubt this is correct; but, whilst it is very debatable whether Germany is any the worse by reason of the payments made by her, the rest of the world are very much the worse for it.
>
> (1924a: 137)

Thus, whilst everyone else, including Keynes, was concerned about how much Germany was able to pay, Abbati worried about how much the creditor countries were able to receive.[26]

From what has been said, therefore, we understand that Abbati was opposed to remedying the deficit trade balance by reducing production costs in terms of income and that he considered the imposition of tariffs, exchange rate manipulation, new money to debtor countries and export credits, to be mere palliatives, as well as being harmful. It is interesting to note that Keynes instead proposed precisely these specific measures in order to increase the margin in the trade balance that would have allowed the increase in foreign investment needed to absorb excess domestic saving, namely: increasing exports by reducing production costs, reducing imports by the same means or by tariffs, more loans to borrowers so that they can purchase more exports from England (Keynes 1930b: 351).

For Abbati, therefore, an increase in foreign demand is not a viable option, so that the only sure solution to the problem of effective demand is additional demand by the government or a tax reduction[27] financed by bank loans, which can furnish both money and effective demand at the same time (1928: 121–22).

   In *The Unclaimed Wealth,* Abbati also proposed that the government should create an *ad hoc* agency to ensure the constant availability of public-sector employment, the minimum wage for which would vary with variations in the stocks of wholesalers and retailers. This would ensure that the velocity of final buying proceeded *pari passu* with the velocity of production. From *The Final Buyer* onwards, Abbati's idea of guaranteed public employment gave way to his thesis that the government should offset the deficiency of effective demand by either reducing taxes or increasing public expenditure financed by borrowing from banks. This thesis, however, had been very evident in *The Unclaimed Wealth* as well (1924a: 97–8). The notion that the public sector's role in the economy should be primarily that of neutralizing fluctuations became familiar after Keynes. But when Abbati was writing *The Unclaimed Wealth* the idea was considered bizarre, and no attempt was made to substantiate it. As Abbati wrote,

> there is no science whatever, to-day, in the manner in which taxation, borrowing and the issue of Paper Money are employed by governments; and the policies adopted are merely those which seem most expedient, taking into consideration inherited precepts, usually obsolete, and the pressure of existing political forces.
>
> (1924a: 98)

And this argument is constantly present in all his subsequent works.

   Abbati examined public intervention to stabilize the economy in regard to its principal aspects: instruments, sources of financing, methods of implementation, effects on internal and external equilibrium, and so on. These are aspects well known today and well expounded by Abbati; consequently, for reasons of space, they are not discussed in detail here. To be added is that Abbati emphatically recommended that public and private debts should not be repaid during economic recessions.

   Amongst other things, he anticipated Fisher's debt-deflation theory by pointing out that the forced liquidation of real and financial capital in order to repay debts, or also to pay taxes, depresses the value of both the capital possessed by firms and the securities possessed by banks. For all the reasons given above, budget-balancing policies in depression are entirely unjustified.

   This is not to imply that Abbati underestimated the risk of inflation; indeed, it should be stressed that he was equally firmly opposed to inflation, when, of course, the situation required it – that is, when investments exceeds voluntary savings.[28] In a letter to Edwin Cannan of 10 February 1933 Abbati wrote as follows:

> I do not think that I am such an ardent expansionist as you imagine. The Bulletins are all on that tack at the present time, because they are essentially topical and are intended to indicate the situation and the courses to be adopted [. . .] If and when the time comes to combat inflation, I shall be all out to find the villains and the heros, and shall have the strongest things to say about them. I am inclined to think that inflation is more difficult to combat than deflation, but I think that both can be combated promptly and successfully.
>
> (1933b)

And in effect, when the time came, after World War II, Abbati explicitly condemned inflationary policies and strongly advocated a reduction in public spending.[29] But since 1924 he had clearly stated that the measures which he proposed to combat deflation should be symmetrically reversed in the case of inflation.[30] At the beginning of the Great Depression, Abbati argued that preventing deflation and supporting wholesale prices were the government's most urgent tasks in that specific phase of the business cycle and he repeatedly insisted that wholesale prices should be restored to their 1926–9 level. But, as he wrote in 1933, 'We wanted wholesale commodity prices to be raised in relation to gold by means of increased buying of goods and services – by the raising of the standard of living – not by the debasing of the currencies' (1934a: 23).

The most acute commentators on Abbati's writings have recognized this important aspect of his thought. Robertson, for example, in his review of *The Economic Lessons of 1929–31*, wrote: 'Here is enough to make many people throw this book into the waste-paper basket as just one more of the pieces of crude inflationary propaganda with which the world has been flooded in recent years', but 'to treat Mr Abbati in this way would be a great mistake' (Robertson 1932: 612), and T.E. Gregory, in his Introduction to this book, thought likewise (see Appendix).

Concluding remark

There is still much to say about this interesting and still topical economist, but the purpose of this introduction has not been to furnish an exhaustive account of Abbati's complex and far-ranging thought, but more simply to bring his unjustly forgotten writings back to light.

In a letter to Abbati of 30 May 1950, F. Shirras wrote thus: 'Your *Unclaimed Wealth*, 1924 and *The Final Buyer*, 1928, not to mention the *Geneva Bulletins*, confirm me that sufficient tribute to your work has not been paid by us Keynesian Professional Economists'. This book wants to be both a tribute and a stimulus to further analysis and further historical inquiry into Abbati's work.

The original chapter numbers have been retained, which means the chapters do not number sequentially.

Notes

1 I am grateful for comments on an earlier draft to Terenzio Cozzi, Ferruccio Maggiora and Roberto Marchionatti.

2 When deciding whether or not to mention Abbati in relation to Keynes, Harrod consulted Robertson, who replied by letter that he (Robertson) was 'the worst person in the world to assess fairly the grievances of Abbati or anyone else [. . .] who thinks (as I do) that in the world's eyes too much credit has gathered round the name of one man for a set of ideas which was evolving simultaneously in many heads'. As regards Abbati he continued thus: 'I think there is no doubt that in his first book *The Unclaimed Wealth* (1924), and much more coherently in his second book *The Final Buyer* (1928), Abbati, with no academic training or backing, evolved for himself the essential thesis of "Keynesian economics", if that is taken to be the thesis that attempted saving may [. . .] go to waste in underproduction and unemployment. And that he has had very little credit from the Academic world or the general public for the fact' (Robertson 1950).

I am indebted to Daniele Besomi for bringing this letter to my attention and for making it available for me.

3 I am indebted to John Presley for having brought this article to my attention. I subsequently found the journal containing the article among Abbati's papers (see 1955a). When the article was published, Robertson wrote in a letter to Abbati on 23 February 1954 that: 'I am very glad that article has been written [. . .] I am venturing to write to Mr Coppock, whom I don't know, complimenting him on his fast-minded and scholarly approach' (Correspondence Abbati-Robertson).

4 I am grateful for citation of this book to Hirotaka Kojima of the Graduate School of Economics, University of Kyoto, who in 1995 published an article entitled 'Abbati's Theory of Effective Demand' in *Keizai Ronso (The Economic Review)*, vol. 156. The article, which I have not read, is in Japanese.

5 Abbati is also mentioned in Everyman's Encyclopaedia (1958). Coppock informs us that Abbati is also mentioned in Curtis and Townshend (1937: 78) and Brown (1940: 64).

6 See 'Notes on the use of certain terms' in *The Final Buyer*, at the end of Part II.

7 I agree with Coppock in this regard (see Coppock 1954: 87–8).

8 In a letter to Robertson dated 4 November 1932, Abbati writes: 'The fact that we handle serious and difficult problems in a manner that is sometimes somewhat flippant, leads the uninitiated to believe that we know no more about the subject than they do. We cannot alter this style because, in fact, it does enable us to get our stuff across to all sections of the public. The big economists like it as much as the business men' (Correspondence Abbati-Robertson).

9 In *The Final Buyer* the term 'effective demand', used in *The Unclaimed Wealth,* was substituted by 'final-buying' with no change of meaning.

10 See W. Hessling, *The distinction between saving and investment*, Appendix, and 1955a.

11 See also 1928: 50n.; 1955a; Correspondence Abbati-Robertson.

12 According to Abbati, speculation was only one aspect of the Great Depression, which was a consequence of a buying-deficiency. A major cause of the buying-deficiency of creditors was excessive taxation by their governments to reduce the national debt. See Bulletin no. 7 (1932a) and 1955a.

13 Matters do not change if we hypothesise that firms issue new securities.

14 In a letter to Abbati dated 15 August 1948 Robertson wrote: 'It is a curious fact that Keynes himself and his intimate disciples took a great dislike to this word [hoarding], – see the article by Mrs Robinson entitled "The Concept of Hoarding" in E.J. June 1938 (note: She uses the phrase "the fallacy of hoarding" in the "Introduction to the Theory of Employment".), so you will not impress the stricter Keynesians by claiming to have discovered "hoarding"!' (Correspondence Abbati – Robertson).

15 Governor of the Bank of England (1920–44) and Director of the Bank of International Settlements.

16 See, for instance, 1924a:37; 1928: 54–60 and 109n.; 1955a.

17 The position of E. Cannan is exemplary: 'The term "deposit" seems very appropriate as the name of the verb which we use to describe the action of placing an article with some person or institution for safe custody [. . .] It seems well to return to the nineteenth century doctrine that banks receive money from one set of people and lend it to another' (Cannan 1921: 28–35).

18 At that time also the government issued its own paper money – currency notes – which formed part of the 'monetary base'. But 'no serious government issues paper money directly for the purpose of meeting expenditure. Governments borrow the required money from banks and spend it on commodities and services, and they are forced to issue paper money in response to increased demand for cash by the public' (1924a: 96).

19 In England the gold standard was restored in 1925 at pre-war parity. It was once again suspended in September 1931.

20 In *The Unclaimed Wealth* Abbati also rapidly examines, and confutes, wages-fund theory and Malthusian population theory.

21 Tugan-Baranovskij, having attributed a theory of underconsumption to Marx, sought to demonstrate, against Marx, that underconsumption is not a problem in a capitalist economy, not even in the presence of technical progress. He thus eliminated Marx's hypothesis that the composition of capital remains constant from period to period and recast Marx's expanded reproduction scheme in order to show how production should be organized between the consumption goods and capital goods sectors in order to avoid a surplus of aggregate supply, despite the decrease in total consumption and the rapid growth of production. On demonstrating that expansion of accumulation proceeds *pari passu* with the decrease in consumption, Tugan reaches the conclusion that one single worker assisted by all the machines of the system would suffice to drive the entire production process without affecting the self-expansion process of capital (Tugan-Baranovskij 1905). Although this conclusion may appear paradoxical, there is no doubt that Tugan-Baranovskij took to its extreme consequences Marx's idea that the demand problem does not impose a structural limit on the growth of capital because a new investment can always counterbalance a reduction of consumption (see the next section). The best criticism brought against Tugan has been that by Rosa Luxemburg, according to whom Tugan's reasoning presupposed centralization or, at least, economic planning. In fact, Tugan's model does not comprise market mechanisms able to shift production factors from the consumption goods sector to the capital goods sector (Luxemburg 1913).

22 According to Spiethoff, more likely to occur is an overproduction of investment goods, which are produced yet not purchased for lack of 'free capital'.

23 It is likely that Abbati, who met Hobson several times before publication of his first book, *The Unclaimed Wealth*, discussed these issues with Hobson and was influenced by him. But it is also more likely that Hobson was influenced by Abbati. The latter declared that, in the end, Hobson 'said that he accepted my thesis. But he added that he was too old to alter what was known as his over-saving theory, which had been identified with his name for over forty years' (1947a: 6 and 1955a). Abbati also supposes that Hobson, after discussing with him the question of the 'hoarding' of bank deposits consequent on a surplus of saving, talked about it with Lavington. It was for this reason that in his *Trade Cycle*, published in 1922, Lavington 'raised the vital question of saving and of "idle" bank balances and "hoarding"' (1955a: note 1). Coppock, for his part, wrote: 'I am now convinced that the later formulations of Hobson's theory must have been influenced by Abbati's work' (Coppock 1954: 63n.).

24 Despite the inconsistency of Douglas's theory, in *The General Theory*, Chapter 23, Keynes makes frequent mention of Douglas, and although he does not include him in the 'brave army of heretics' alongside Mandeville, Malthus, Gesell and Hobson, he states that if Douglas 'had limited his B-items to the financial provision made by entrepreneurs to which no current expenditure on replacements and renewals corresponds,

he would be nearer the truth' (Keynes 1936: 371). To be noted that in this book Wicksell is mentioned only in passing, while other important contributors to the development of the new theory, among them Abbati, are entirely ignored. Robertson, in a letter to Harrod of April 1950, called Chapter 23 'an outrage' and wrote that Keynes 'found it easier to be generous to cranks than to professional economists' (Robertson 1950). (See note 2).

25 For more detailed discussion on theoretical debate in the 1920's and Abbati's criticism see Di Gaspare (2005).

26 H. Schacht, President of the Reichsbank, was of the same opinion: 'Germany can pay reparations only in so far as the world is willing and able to accept German goods. The world, however, cannot afford to take too great a quantity of these, or else the economic equilibrium of other countries will be disturbed. Hence Germany must be given an economic outlet outside the main commercial markets, if her paying capacity is to be restored'. TIME, 23 June 1924.

27 In Bulletin nos. 12 and 13 of 1932, Abbati proposed a 'Moratorium' for taxpayers in the over-deflated and gold-logged countries (1933a: 1–8).

28 Abbati was of the opinion that the bankers' action was even more limited in contrasting inflation and that fiscal policy should be used for this purpose.

29 See: Biography; Abbati's Bibliography; the Evidence submitted by Abbati to Radcliffe Committee (1957c); 1958g.

30 See Chapter XIV, 'Control of the value of the currency unit', in *The Final Buyer* (1928: 141–59) and 1924c.

Part I

The Unclaimed Wealth. How Money Stops Production (1924)

Prologue

The fruits of victory

"Now, as always, the right and just course will prove to be the most expedient."

Although we have won the war, there are important men who suggest that we shall have to forgo part of the fruits of victory owing to the inability of Germany to pay. On the other hand, great men are not lacking who insist firmly and emphatically that Germany must and shall pay every penny.

In dwelling on the alluring possibilities of indemnities, one would wish one's imagination to carry one to giddy heights that are altogether incompatible with the contemptibly material aspect of "ability to pay." Still, although only the privileged few may ignore the material when it stands in the way of the imaginary, in this matter the imaginary is something the public *mean to have*, at all events, as a mental feast. In this matter, therefore, the public may evade in its own way what only the privileged few may ignore. Why should the consideration of an indemnity be restricted to the "ability to pay" of Germany or any other finite nation? Let the conception be really a majestic one. Let us consider the possibilities of an indemnity from no less than the Devil.

Supposing that we had gained a complete and final victory over the Devil; that, in fact, we were in a position to exact from the Devil anything we cared to name; and that our interests were in the hands of three such patriotic, astute and practical men as Monsieur Careopin, Senator Ledge and Sir Edison Carr. Imagine these three gentlemen in their gravest and firmest moods, little inclined to put up with any devilish attempts at trickery; imagine the Devil facing them across the peace table, subdued and apologetic, and, in his eagerness to placate, saying:

"Gentlemen, I accept your terms in advance, no matter what they are. I will pay for reparations in full; I will pay your war bills in full; and I will pay for anything else you like in addition—nay, more, I will pay in gold, raw materials, goods or labour, or in any combination of either or all of them. Name your terms, Gentlemen, I accept them in advance."

Naturally, three such men as those representing us would be well prepared for such a situation, and they would not be likely to allow mere words and manners to influence them into anything like compassion towards such a customer as the Devil. Consequently, they would reply sternly:

"Mr. Devil, nothing that you can ever pay will be adequate reparation for our losses in men and material. Therefore, you shall pay what we like, as often as we like, and for as long as we like."

To which the Devil would reply:

"Gentlemen, what you say is just. I accept."

Thereupon the Conference is adjourned for our delegates to communicate with their respective peoples and governments regarding the nature of the first payments to be made.

Everybody would agree that payment must be either in gold or raw materials. Devilish manufactured goods would be objected to by all the industrial classes, both capitalist and labour, on the grounds that it would destroy industry and create unemployment; and devilish labour would be objected to, by moralists, because of the contaminating influence of such alien immigration, by labour, because of its harmful effect on the condition of labour generally. But raw materials would be, by no means, free from objection when people came to consider *which* raw materials, and what quantities. The agricultural classes and landowners in all countries would strongly oppose cereals, meat and foodstuffs, for if these things came from the Devil free of charge, where would they be? Further, what would be the gain? for would not whatever value the Devil delivered be so much less value produced? Cotton, America would strongly object to; coal would be equally objectionable to America and England; iron would not please America a bit more, and there would also be powerful interests both in England and France that wanted no devilish iron. England and France would like cotton, but this would so disturb the American cotton trade—so important to America—that, to avoid something verging on a *casus belli*, compromise would have to be reached, even if this mean America supplying England and France at half the price charged to American consumers on the understand that no cotton was taken from the Devil. And so it would be with all raw materials of which the consumption and value is great. It would only be raw materials of very limited consumption that could be agreed upon; and, of course, for the same reason these could only be used for negligible payments. Moreover, the general objection to all raw materials would be the same as the general objection to foodstuffs, namely: that there would be no particular gain, anyhow, because the value delivered by the Devil would be practically discounted by an equivalent reduction in the value produced. Thus, gold alone would remain. Financial experts would point out that the value of gold would diminish in proportion to the quantity delivered. If the Devil delivered to America, England and France £8,000,000,000 each, either over a short period of ten years or over a long period of two hundred years, the only effect would be so to diminish the value of gold that it would become unsuitable as the standard means of exchange.

As usual, Mr. Bottingly would solve the problem. "Britain for the Britishers," he would cry; "let America and France look after themselves. Banking accounts in favour of every responsible adult in the country must be opened forthwith, and credited with £1,000 each per annum at the Devil's expense. This can be effected through the intermedium of the Bank of England, which will debit the Devil with the total liabilities thus incurred and appoint a Special Committee to decide how it is to be made good by the Devil. This committee must have full powers over the Devil to call for anything, either foodstuffs, raw materials, manufactured goods, or gold, and to indicate the quantities of each to be delivered daily at each of the ports. In this way the indemnity obtained by the British would amount to over £20,000,000,000 per annum, and everybody would partake equally of the fruits of victory."

Naturally, there would be lacking neither foolish idealists to declaim these conditions as too hard nor weak-kneed pacifists afraid of the recommencement of hostilities; but Sir Edison Carr would only be voicing the popular sentiment when he declared that this was the *only way to make the Devil repent*; and amidst general approbation, he would sternly order the Devil to sign the Agreement to these terms.

Contrary to the expectations of many people—who agreed entirely with the opinion expressed in all the press *that the Devil could not be trusted*—the document would be duly signed. This remarkable result, due in so great part to the statesmanlike qualities of Sir Edison Carr, would be the signal for general rejoicings of a nature far out-classing anything in the past history of mankind. Whilst the soldiers and munition workers indulged in joy-riding and singing in the streets, sedate and thoughtful young men would stand on tables in *chic* restaurants and throw champagne and other things about. Even the waiters would be rejoicing, so people would have to serve themselves. "But," they would *reflect*, "what matters? Is not peace signed with a thousand a year for all?"

Towards the end of the day it would be noised about that no trains, buses, trams or taxis were running. Again people would *reflect* as they endeavoured to walk home, tired but cheery, "Is it not peace-day with a thousand a year for all?"

The next morning, no milk for breakfast, shops all shut, no trains, trams, buses or taxis, running, no answer from the telephone exchange—perhaps, not even the bank open for anybody to console themselves by procuring a cheque book or, possibly, drawing a "fiver" or so. Everybody had a thousand a year, and all small traders and employees had decided to retire.

As the day wore on, scrambling for food would begin. No food would be coming forward from the ports where it was being delivered by the Devil, so people would have to start marching to the ports. The housing problem at the ports would also become acute, seeing that there would be no question of getting labour for new construction. How the thing would end nobody can tell; but Mr. Bottingly would be shrewd enough to see that, if distribution and communication were not maintained at a reasonable cost, everybody's thousand-a-year would virtually cancel out with each other.

Of course, everybody would be exasperated at this mean trick of the Devil, and Sir Edison Carr would commence to enforce sterner measures. He would demand from the Devil two million railwaymen, one million transport workers, three million local distributors, one million skilled workers in the building trade, ten million domestic servants, and a large number of other workers of various kinds, say about eighteen to twenty million in all. Naturally, such a huge immigration of devils would be most unpleasant, but it would be the bare minimum for requirements. However, the Devil would be sternly warned that he would be held personally responsible if their behaviour was not, at all times, exemplary.

Thus we would become a nation of parasites—degenerates, flabby of mind and body, entirely dependent upon the Devil. Things would go from bad to worse. Institutions, wealth and ideals would disappear, and dissatisfaction would reign supreme. Then, perhaps, a voice would be heard:

"The gifts of Providence are bursting from the soil at your feet. Profusion awaits you in every direction—health, happiness and material wealth. Yet, you who have not learned to take the gifts of Providence desire fruits from the Devil. Health, wisdom and wealth are the gifts of Providence to those alone who deserve them and give proof of it by their works."

I The problem

[. . .]

To-day, the world is more or less continually in the throes of trade depression. Whilst factories are idle, merchant steamers laid up, warehouses full, and business men ruined or on the verge of ruin, all through lack of markets, millions of human lives are being broken up for the want of these unmarketable things. The cold hand of trade depression is felt in countries widely differing in situation, density of population, and extent of national and external debts. It is felt where there is free trade and where there is protection, where the currency is specie and where it is paper, where governments are democratic and where they are autocratic. Not in the countries lacking in material resources or in a more primitive state of development is it more intense; but where coal and power, machinery and material, are cheap and plentiful, is the struggle for existence greatest both for the marginal entrepreneur and the marginal labourer.

It is not facilities for production that entrepreneurs and nations ask for to-day; all they clamour for is markets. They must have markets at any cost. They are prepared to dump goods under cost price in a foreign country in order to find an outlet for their production. In case of need, nations will fight each other, not in order to buy more from abroad, but in order to export more—to obtain markets. To-day, perhaps America alone could produce sufficient to supply the total requirements of the whole world of food, clothing and manufactured goods. We know that, when the major part of the total able-bodied male population of Europe and America were engaged, not in production, but in destruction, the production of food and clothing, to say nothing of machinery and munitions, was as abundant as ever. Not only were the collective requirements of man supplied in normal abundance, but, in addition, Neptune was supplied abundantly and Mars superabundantly.

It is not in Brussels, the capital of a country relatively as poor in natural resources as any in Europe but more densely populated than any country in the world—it is not in Brussels that mortifying occurrences like hunger marches are to be seen. It is in London, the biggest city in the world, the capital of the greatest empire in the world, the capital of the country which produces the best coal and machinery in the world in such abundance that enormous quantities cannot be used at home, a city where dwell the owners of valuable mines and land, railways and buildings, situated in every part of the world; in the great city which, for years, has been called the clearing-house of the world, it is a common sight to see men marching in protest at the fact that their work is not wanted and that they are entitled not even to the charity that they receive. [. . .]

Man has not yet learnt properly to utilise and govern the great powers of production that have only comparatively recently been put into his hands. For thousands of years he has been forced to wrestle with nature for his subsistence, and production has been so arduous and difficult that he has come to regard as his main pre-occupation, not only production, but the manner in which to secure, at the expense of others, the largest possible share of what is produced.

The existing economic system is built upon this basis, and many of the visible results arising from it seem to justify the nature of the foundation; for workers find that wages come out of the profits of the employer or the prices paid by the consumers; entrepreneurs find that their profits consist, on the one hand, of whatever they can cut off wages and the amount paid for materials, and on the other hand, of the money they secure from consumers by their sales; and merchants all know that their profits consist of squeezing down prices when they buy and "bulling" them up when they sell. The conclusion arising from these facts seems to indicate that what is one man's gain is necessarily another man's loss.

This conclusion, before the Coal Age, was very near the truth, if not the bare truth itself; and it has been hammered so deeply into man's senses that he can hardly be brought to believe that things have altered. Things, nevertheless, have totally altered. To-day, if we understand our world aright, increased consumption and utilisation of commodities and services, as a whole, would go hand in hand with increased profits of entrepreneurs and increased wages of workers; and lordly mansions could grow up freely whilst garden villas take the place of slums.

No doubt it will be objected that such statements are inconsistent with each other; that higher wages are only consistent with higher prices, not with increased profits, although increased profits might be followed by higher wages; that wages are always limited by the quantity of capital available for paying wages as well as by the Malthusian Theory that population tends to outrun subsistence; and that the only way to higher profits is by increased production.

So far as the limitation of wages by available capital is concerned, known as the Wages Fund Theory, it cannot be reconciled with the fact that, as a rule, when stocks available for purposes of production and consumption are greatest, employment and wages are least. The fact is that the demand for labour and the wages paid to labour are dependent upon very different considerations to a so-called Wages Fund.

The Malthusian Theory, perhaps, requires more attention than the Wage Fund Theory in consideration of the new prominence given to it by certain economic writers. The weakness of the theory is that there is no evidence of population outgrowing subsistence. As a matter of fact, in the more densely populated places we find that the growth of culture is a more potent check on the increase of population than the lack of subsistence. It is not implied that heavy mortality, particularly infantile mortality, and emigration does not arise from lack of subsistence—insufficient food, clothing and overcrowding; but it can be affirmed that the lack of subsistence is hardly ever due to a shortage, either in the world, or at the point where the mortality and emigration takes place, and that it is due to defective distribution accompanied by the complementary stoppage in the producing machine. It is, moreover, safe to say that mortality and emigration from lack of subsistence are frequently greatest at the time when, and at the place where, food, clothing and housing are most plentiful and cheapest.

It is contended that, for some time past, the wheat and other harvests have not kept pace with the populations of countries consuming these crops. Whether correct or not, it is a contention that has always been made ever since the time of Malthus. The only test of it is whether, on an average, people are less nourished, clothed or housed than previously. Allowing, for instance, that less wheat per head of population is consumed to-day, can it be shown that this is not more than counterbalanced by the consumption of more meat or other foods? Allowing, even, that the world's population, or the population of any country, is, in fact, on an average, less nourished, clothed and housed than previously, this could not be accounted for by any theoretical diminishing returns of power. Let the diminishing returns of the modern application of power be proved before any effects are attributed to it. As a matter of fact, all the evidence is directly and strongly to the contrary. The returns of power, as a result of labour-saving inventions and organisations, are at present heavily increasing. All the symptoms in connection with the approach of trade depression, with trade depression at its crisis, and in connection with the recovery from trade depression, point to maldistribution of production arising from *increasing* returns of power, and resulting in the displacement of the bargaining power of labour for its right to consume as fast as it produces.

Neither can it be effectively maintained that the overproduction of manufactured goods, or even capital goods, takes place at the expense of under-production of foodstuffs and raw materials. To start with, manufactured goods of all kinds can only be overproduced to the extent in which raw materials are overproduced; whilst, as regards the production of foodstuffs, producers rightly look upon the continuous abundance of the total supply in relation to the *effective demand* as the sole cause of their difficulties, their production being restricted exclusively by the lowness of prices arising from difficulties of marketing. Further, if it were true that foodstuffs and raw materials were under-produced in relation to manufactured goods, the profits and wages on the production of the former would be proportionately greater than on the latter. There is no evidence whatever of this and, in fact, it cannot be possible at a time when there are so many energetic and capable young men only too anxious to make a living even in the desert, and when there are millions of acres of uncultivated fertile land in the world. In industry, agriculture and mining, alike, there is nothing for the newcomer to cut at, under present conditions. There are marginal producers in all these trades, there are producers in privileged positions in all these trades, and, in all of them, maximum production is miles away. No more of anything can be continuously produced than the quantity for which the demand is effective. No less is continuously produced, either; for, the smallest diminution in the supply of anything in relation to the *effective demand* for it, causes a rise in its exchange value together with an extension of the margin of production of that particular commodity. We hear the perpetual cry of the money merchant and the consumer for increased production; but we must side with the producer who would willingly produce more than he does, but cannot afford to produce more than that quantity for which he can obtain fair value in exchange.

It is not asserted that there are no places where local exhaustion of natural resources or changing world conditions prevent an increase, or cause a reduction, in the population. Neither is it disputed that there is a point at which the increase of the world's population can go no further; but it is urged that we are so remotely far from this point at present that there is no more justification for considering the available supply of subsistence than the available supply of fresh air. If we look ahead, our main concern is the supply of coal, oil, or substitutes for the abundant production of power. Given this, combined with organisation and distribution, the growth of culture is sufficient to prevent posterity ever being faced with the problem of outrunning the world's potential supplies of subsistence.

Having dealt with the Wages Fund and Malthusian theories, we may agree that the only way to higher wages and increased profits is by increased production; but it remains to be seen why this increased production does not take place, and in what manner it can take place, in the existing economic system.

This is our problem. Economic science must find the correct theory of cause which, itself, indicates the correct remedy; for, until this be done, industrial balance will be at the mercy of every fallacy resulting from conflicting interests and political jobbery, and men and women shall pay the penalty with sorrow and death.

II The limits of production

The production and distribution of commodities and services in a State are only necessarily limited by its natural resources, man power and potential means of development; but the extent in which these resources are actually employed, and the efficiency with which they are employed, are determined by the extent of existing incentives for production.

Apart from the negligible quantity of production that takes place in the spare time of individuals who have taken up "hobbies," incentives for production arise from the *effective demand*, and the expectation of an *effective demand*, for commodities and services.

It must be noted that production includes not only the services rendered by labour and capital in actual vegetable, mineral and industrial production, but it also includes the services rendered by labour and capital in the distribution of every kind of commodity and service for purposes of production, final consumption and deferred utilisation, of all commodities and services.

It is generally taken for granted that the extent of the *effective demand* for commodities and services is determined by, and equal to, production; or, in other words, that the total income earned by production creates an *effective demand* for an equal quantity of commodities and services in some form or another. Such a conception of the existing economic system is not consistent with the facts.

It is quite correctly argued that the greater the quantity of commodities and services continuously produced in relation to the population, the greater will be the total continuous purchasing power of everybody individually and collectively. It is, further, correctly argued that the money earned by labour, land, capital, entrepreneurs and governments, represents the total amount of money continuously earned by all factors and parties, irrespective of the manner in which it is divided among them, in the continuous production of commodities and services (presumably excluding monetary specie); that these total earnings are determined by the prices which the commodities and services in question continuously realise; and, consequently, the total amount of money used to *demand effectively*, or *spent*, must be continuously equal to the total amount of money earned by the production of commodities and services (presumably excluding monetary specie).

From this, however, it is erroneously believed that the total amount of money continuously earned is all used, in one form or another, to *demand effectively* all the commodities and services produced.

If the theory that the extent of the *effective demand* is determined by, and equal to, the production of commodities and services were correct for all existing conditions, an expansion of the *effective demand* would always take place in proportion to any increase in production, and the limit of expansion of the *effective demand* in a State would only be determined by its natural resources, man power and potential means of development. Incentives for production would, thus, always exist in a tangible form to the same extent as material, man power and method, and the State would rapidly proceed to its fullest development. In fact, were it not for the human factors of natural lethargy[1] both in production and consumption the world might, with the present powerful labour-saving machinery and methods, proceed to its fullest development so rapidly that its known resources in coal and oil would become exhausted far too quickly, and before they could be replaced by science, if, indeed, science ever does find a substitute for coal and oil. If, however, the expansion of the *effective demand* in a State is limited by narrower factors than those mentioned, then production and development in the State are also limited by these narrower factors.

The arguments put forward in support of the theory that the extent of the *effective demand* is determined by, and equal to, the production of commodities and services, are correct as far as they go; but they do not reach the crux of the question which is involved in the manner in which the purchasing power, or value in exchange, of commodities and services is governed by their utilisation, and in the monetary system.

III Purchasing power

Let us be quite clear about the meaning of the expression "purchasing power." It is customary to use this expression in reference to the quantity of money that is available for buying. For our purpose, however, this use of the expression is inconvenient. The different forms of money, and the laws which govern the quantities of each, will be dealt with separately and fully in later chapters. Meantime it is necessary to make some general observations regarding the power to purchase in relation to the production of commodities and services without the question of prices and, consequently, monetary prices being involved. For our purpose, then, anybody who owns anything that can be exchanged for anything else possesses purchasing power. The thing or things owned may be capital or income, including payment for services, and may be either in the form of money or in the form of commodities.

The extent of purchasing power depends not merely upon the quantity of the thing or things owned, but upon their market value in relation to other commodities and services. For example, if the thing owned is money, the purchasing power of £100 may be greater after a fall in prices than £120 was before the fall in prices; or, on the other hand, after a rise in prices £100 might purchase less than £80 before the rise. Similarly, the purchasing power of a hundred head of cattle would vary as the market value of other commodities and services rises or falls in relation to cattle.

The market value of commodities and services and money in relation to each other depends upon the extent of the entire supply of each and the manner in which it is being utilised; for every subjection of the use of any supply to a lower utility affects its purchasing power in accordance with the law of diminishing utility.

Whatever the extent and manner in which the supplies of the different commodities and services are utilised, and their market value in relation to each other, theoretically they are all exchangeable with each other, and, therefore, the greater the quantity of commodities and services produced in relation to the number of people, the greater is the purchasing power per head of population.

Nevertheless, where money exists the total purchasing power theoretically arising from the total production of commodities and services for sale cannot actually purchase these same commodities and services unless and until they are all ready for sale *at the best prices obtainable in money* from buyers. In practice, those who have sold, or are able to sell, their commodities and services satisfactorily for money, and whose purchasing power is thus converted, or readily convertible, into money, are by no means always disposed to employ it in buying those commodities and services which, failing the existence of money, they would have had to have taken in exchange for their own. Further, in the case of an increased quantity of commodities and services, buyers for final consumption and deferred utilisation do not readily buy larger quantities than usual unless they can get a reduction in the price, whilst producers and distributors do not readily sell supplies at reduced prices. Thus, in any case, some delay must occur before the theoretic additional purchasing power arising from increased production is, in fact, used for purchasing. The delay, however, affecting the sale of the increased supply of commodities and services also affects the whole supply; and, as a result, the production of new supplies diminishes to an extent proportionate to the difficulties of marketing. Thus, the additional purchasing power arising from increased production is usually stillborn, and the damage does not always end with this loss.

Manufacturers and merchants know by experience, for which most of them have paid heavily, that a fall in wholesale prices means losses to them. They always have a certain quantity of commodities in course of production, in transit or in stock, and this quantity is based upon estimates of the *effective demand* at a reasonable price. Suddenly the market breaks and buyers withdraw. The break is induced by the inevitable outrunning of production over the *effective demand*. The position may be held for a time by manufacturers refusing to reduce their prices and by merchants holding on to stocks and taking over the stocks of weaker holders; but the longer it is stayed the worse it is when it does come, for it finds the market overloaded with stock, and bankers tired and nervous of advances made upon it. Severe liquidation then sets in, accompanied by stop-loss selling and bankers calling in loans. Fortunes are lost and large firms smashed.

It will be objected that these manufacturers and merchants brought it upon themselves by overtrading; that the manufacturers produced too much and the merchants bought too much. Such an argument is "back-jobbing." If the manufacturer and merchant must not produce or buy more than their clients require, neither must they produce or buy less—or they lose their clients. This is the whole essence of business, but it is not so easy as it seems. If *all* the manufacturers and merchants had produced and bought less, there would have been a shortage, and prices would have gone up instead of down; and if *some* of the manufacturers and merchants had produced and bought less, prices might have remained steady, but those who had produced or bought with least restraint would score at the expense of those who had been more prudent. The manufacturer and the merchant must produce and buy for the *effective demand* to the best of their ability to estimate it, and the better it looks and the greater the confidence it creates, the more is it urged upon them to do their share. They must follow the market and produce and buy with the rest; and, together with the rest, they must sooner or later bring about the downfall of the market, each one endeavouring not to be the hindermost that are taken by the devil. It is common knowledge that this sort of thing happens time after time in all wholesale markets. Every time it happens the folly of it is apparent, nevertheless, again and again everybody is dragged in. Natural judgment, long experience, prudence bought and paid for by many a hard hit, unlimited financial support, all go for little more than mere survival. There is no room for any fools on the wholesale markets, and it is only a matter of time for the cleverest and luckiest to get caught. Unless they retire in time, "those who live by the sword shall die by the sword."

It is important to notice that this argument applies as much to capital goods, such as tools, machinery, factories, and those things by which transport of every kind is effected, as it does to commodities for final consumption. The use of capital goods by the producers, and the resulting *effective demand* for them, is strictly in accordance with the quantity of commodities for final consumption which are, rightly or wrongly, being produced. It is an error to believe that, under present conditions, the quantity of capital goods produced and the extent in which they are kept in repair varies inversely as voluntary abstinence by the public in the consumption of commodities for final consumption. The producer can always secure sufficient capital goods for the production of commodities for final consumption, for which a market at a reasonably profitable price is believed to exist; but the consumption of the latter goods is generally disappointing in the end. The cause of this failure to consume will be dealt with presently; meantime, it must be emphasised that it is not due to over-production of capital goods taking place *at the expense* of the production of consumable goods, for, as a matter of fact, the continuous over-production of all capital goods in the right proportion to each other, if pressed to the limits of raw materials, means of production and man power, would ensure the same quantity of employment for these capital goods as if they were being used to produce commodities for final consumption.

One hears talk of committees of producers and consumers being appointed to decide what commodities should be produced and the quantities of each; but if there is anybody who could nominate a committee capable of this, "the world is his and all that's in it." It is quite unnecessary for such a person to wait for his party to get into power before he starts his work of elevating society. Let the committee show its ability on the wheat and cotton markets, where statistics of production and consumption all over the world have been compiled in a very complete manner for many years past; and, if the people on the committee are really as clever as they think, they can soon make enough to buy all those whom they cannot convince.

Thus, whatever the increase in the quantity of commodities and services produced and the increased purchasing power they theoretically represent, should a fall in prices take place either as a result of failure to utilise fully the entire supply or for any other reason, those who had produced most would not necessarily be gainers. The prices of commodities and services would not all have fallen proportionately to the same extent, so that the only gainers would be those who bought when prices had fallen most and sold when prices had fallen least. Those who had produced any commodity the total quantity of which had been increased in relation to that of other commodities and services, would probably find that the price at which they had to sell had fallen most; and in this case they would be losers not only in actual money but relatively, also, in commodities and services.

In practice, therefore, under existing conditions, it is suicidal for any individual or company to attempt to increase the total quantity of any particular commodity; and not only does every business man shun such a proceeding, but he endeavours to produce or buy only those commodities or services of which there is rather a shortage in the total supply.

IV The monetary system

Enough has been said to show that the use of money causes certain delays in the manner in which commodities and services are exchanged and circulated, which delays react upon the value of existing supplies in the market and upon the production of further supplies. It is not pretended that these delays and their reactions upon production would not be greater without any monetary system at all; but it is necessary to ascertain whether these delays are really inevitable or not, and this can only be done by an exact understanding of the manner in which they are caused by the monetary system.

In a modern state the *effective demand* normally operates through the monetary system, for people can only demand commodities and services effectively by giving money for them. Thus, unless the total supply of *cash* and *credit money* *contracts* and *expands* at all times in a manner proportionate to the production of commodities and services, the quantity of them *effectively demanded* cannot *contract* and *expand* in the same manner as the quantity produced without a rise or fall in the general price level. These variations in the price level, however, do not give the *effective demand* the required elasticity.

Let us consider separately, for a moment: (*a*) A continuous *rise* in the general level of prices accompanied by a *contraction* in the *effective demand*; (*b*) a continuous *rise* in the general level of prices accompanied by an *expansion* in the *effective demand*; (*c*) a continuous *fall* in the general price level accompanied by an *expansion* in the *effective demand*; and, (*d*) a continuous *fall* in the general level of prices accompanied by a *contraction* in the *effective demand*.

(*a*) A continuous *rise* in the general level of prices accompanied by a *contraction* in the *effective demand* is an occurrence which is practically limited to States of which the natural resources are being exhausted, or where production is restricted or over-penalised in some way or another. It is rather an abnormal occurrence which carries its own remedy or lack of remedy in a very obvious manner.

(*b*) A continuous *rise* in the general level of prices accompanied by an *expansion* in the *effective demand* indicates that the total supply of *cash* and *credit money* is *expanding* in a manner proportionately more rapid than the production of commodities and services for sale. In such circumstances production is meeting with no impediment from the monetary system, and, other things equal, is taking place to an extent proportionate to human inclination to develop natural resources. We must observe, however, that such an *expansion* in the total supply of *cash* and *credit money* can only be due to continuous excessive borrowing or issue of Paper Money by a government and, in certain circumstances,[2] in countries where the issue of Paper Money is not restricted to the government, by the issue of Paper Money by banks; and we must also observe that prices cannot rise for ever to any perceptible extent without destroying the currency concerned as a standard and stable means of measuring and exchanging value and wealth.

(*c*) A continuous *fall* in the general price level accompanied by an *expansion* in the *effective demand* can only take place gradually over long periods in two ways.

(1) By a reduction in the cost of production arising from progress in the arts of production and distribution. Notice that lower costs of production obtained by means of reductions in the total monetary earnings of labour, land, capital or entrepreneurs' profits, other things equal, do not cause an *expansion* in the *effective demand*, but reduce the *effective demand* to more or less the same extent as the quantity of earnings economised.

(2) By a permanent rise in the value of money due to the total quantity of *cash* and *credit money* having become permanently smaller in proportion to the total quantity of commodities and services for sale. Such a rise in the value of money is always resisted, and rightly so, by producers and distributors, who are losers thereby through no fault of their own. We know that, whilst prices are visibly moving down, an *expansion* in the *effective demand* never takes place owing to the disinclination of both buyers and sellers to operate, production and distribution are meanwhile slowed down until either the quantity of commodities and services for sale has been reduced to a point which enables producers to hold their own against consumers and money merchants, or until producers and distributors have cut all their losses, and prices are on a lower basis all round.[3]

A *rise* in the general price level accompanied either by a *contraction* or an *expansion* in the *effective demand* and a *fall* in the general price level accompanied by an *expansion* in the *effective demand*, are not the main subject of our enquiry. What we must examine closely is a *fall* in the general level of prices accompanied by a *contraction* in the *effective demand*, for this is trade depression as we know it so well. Prices falling through abundance of supplies of commodities and services; but the *effective demand* diminishing because consumers are either unable or unwilling to buy.

A rise in the general level of prices may be a useful method of checking the rate of consumption when required, but it does not necessarily do so. During the great world war the only check on consumption was the rate of production, not the price level; and after the war in many countries the only check on consumption was home production plus what could be borrowed from abroad. No existing monetary system has yet stood up to man's fixed determination to consume all there is to consume, when the determination to do so regardless of price exists. Normally, however, this aspect of the matter does not arise.

The aspect that does arise potently, and is more or less always with us, is the difficulty of marketing the production of commodities and services as fast as it takes place, and the fact that a fall in the price level, so far as it adjusts things, does so, not by increasing consumption, but merely by holding back the production of further supplies.

Briefly, then, the monetary system is such that the total quantity of commodities and services produced and distributed for sale cannot be continuously marketed after any increase in the total quantity continuously produced unless, either the *expansion* of the total supply of *cash* and *credit money* is continuously maintained to the same extent, or, unless the total monetary value of the increased supply of commodities and services continuously produced for sale is reduced in a manner proportionate to the total value of the existing supply of *cash* and *credit money* by means of a fall in prices. If, however, a fall in the price level merely holds back production instead of increasing the *effective demand*, the only alternative is for the *expansion* of the total supply of *cash* and *credit money* to be governed by, and maintained continuously in the same proportion to, the total supply of commodities continuously produced for sale; for, if this *expansion* is governed by narrower factors, the *expansion* of the *effective demand* is narrowed to the same extent[4] together with production and development in the area affected.

We must, therefore, examine the nature of the total supply of *cash* and *credit money* in order to ascertain whether its *expansion* and *contraction* is governed by narrower factors than variations in the rate of production and distribution.

V   The supply of money

The total supply of money consists of the following *cash* and *credit money*:

(1) Gold and silver coin and bullion;
(2) *Credit money*, or money arising from the mode in which the same cash functions in several operations simultaneously by means of banks;
(3) Paper Money, or supplementary cash issued by Governments (and sometimes by banks).

Although, except for international purposes, the proper function of paper money is the same as gold and silver coin and bullion, it is taken after *credit money* in order the better to explain its nature in relation to the latter.

Before examining these three classes of money, it must be pointed out that variations in the rapidity with which money is made to function or circulate are equivalent to *contractions* and *expansions* in the total supply of *cash* and *credit money*. Money may be used, either by the *cash* itself changing hands every time a transaction takes place, or by means of the cheque system, which amounts to leaving the actual *cash* in a bank which pays, or guarantees payment, to whomsoever the final payment is due; but in either case, the same money may be used more or less frequently during a given time. There is, however, a limit to the quantity and value of commodities and services that can be traded by the same money in a given time. In the first place, in any one transaction the value of the money must be as great as the value of the commodities and services traded; and, in the second place, the limit is determined by the maximum rapidity with which it is possible for *cash* to change hands or cheques to be cleared.

These variations in the rapidity of circulation of money do not necessarily take place harmoniously with variations in the quantities of commodities and services produced for sale. An increase in the rapidity of circulation of money only takes place because of an increase in the *effective demand* for commodities and services; but an increase in the production of commodities and services, whether due to an actual increase in the *effective demand* or to the expectation of such an increase, may be followed by buyers subsequently waiting for a fall in prices or refusing to buy at all. Therefore, the rapidity of circulation of money may even diminish after an increase in the production of commodities and services for sale.

We can therefore state that:

The rapidity of circulation of money varies as the effective demand for commodities and services and not as their production.[5]

[. . .]

VII   Credit money

or Money arising from the mode in which the same cash functions in several operations simultaneously by means of banks

[...]

Bankers must keep their eyes fixed on their *cash* reserves and endeavour to keep them in the right ratio to their obligations on deposit accounts, i.e. to the quantity of *credit money*. The means at their disposal are: in respect of *cash* reserves, to adjust their borrowing rate or deposit rate at the required level to induce the public and the foreigner to part with more or less *cash*; and, in respect of obligations on deposit accounts, to adjust their lending rates at the required level to discourage or induce more or less borrowing.

As already stated, however, powerful as these means are in the hands of bankers, in the last resort their salvation does not lie in their own hands. In the last resort, bankers can neither prevent people from depositing all their *cash* in the banks and refusing to do any borrowing; nor can they prevent people making a simultaneous call for all the *cash* due to them resulting in a general suspension of payments; and they cannot even prevent people from borrowing in other ways virtually all the credit for which they are able to give proper security.

Obviously, bankers can neither prevent people who have *cash* from depositing it in the banks, nor force people able to give proper security to borrow—and there is no question of a loan from bankers without proper security. Thus, whilst bankers are able to supply *credit money* against an *effective demand* for it, they can neither create, nor maintain in existence, any credit unless this *effective demand* exists.

It is equally certain that bankers cannot even prevent the creation of credit by refusing to lend, or by any other means. In order to test the matter, let us consider an extreme hypothetical situation in which all the bankers, for their own ends or for some misguided motive, arranged among themselves to call in and permanently reduce the total quantity of loans by 20 per cent., and that they attempted this at a time when the *effective demand* of the public for commodities and services was steadily increasing and when, consequently, the *effective demand* for loans was steadily increasing.

The immediate effects of this would, naturally, be sufficiently drastic, as stocks in the hands of all traders financed by bankers would have to be reduced by 20 per cent. The retailers would not suffer much, for they would sell practically the same quantities as before, only more on a *cash* basis, and those dealing in non-perishable goods who carry stock, more or less, on credit would be forced to replenish them in smaller quantities and more frequently. The stocks in the hands of importers, manufacturers and wholesale merchants, however, would suffer a temporary congestion on the reduction of the replenishing orders from retailers, and this congestion would, no doubt, cause a temporary fall in wholesale prices and a reduction in further supplies. It would only be very temporary, for the next orders from the retailers who were unable to take the usual quantity on the last occasion would come in quicker than usual. Nevertheless, importers, manufacturers and wholesale merchants would be unable to renew their own supplies in as large quantities as usual unless a fall in prices enabled them to buy the same quantities for 20 per cent. less money, or unless the shortage of *credit money* could be replaced.

If, in fact, prices did fall sufficiently rapidly for importers, manufacturers and wholesale merchants to replace their stocks fully without any check, the contraction of credit aimed at by the bankers would have been successfully effected, at any rate, for a certain time. This, however, could not possibly take place at a time when the public were firm buyers of goods the purchase of which had, perhaps, been deferred too long; and it could not take place sufficiently rapidly to obviate a check in the importation and production of new supplies. Thus, with a shortage ahead, events would be moving in the direction of a rise in prices. Further, if the public remained firm buyers and the retailers were forced to insist on a greater proportion of *cash* payments from the public, the latter would have to increase their calls upon the *cash* reserves of the bankers. In fact, the bankers might find the public knocking at their doors in a manner which threatened their very existence; for, contraction of credit or not, the bankers have legal obligations to pay the public at least three times as much *cash* as exists. Meantime, heavy liquidation in securities brought about by the shortage of money might pull down values to such an extent that shrinkage in the value of securities held by bankers might be as rapid as the shrinkage in their *cash* reserves.

There is not the least doubt that an argument in which the public refused to stop buying and the bankers refused to supply *credit money*, would end, so far as the bankers are concerned, in a manner both "short and sweet". The argument, however, might not necessarily reach its logical conclusion; for the shortage of money could be partly mitigated by a more rapid use of *cash* by the public and partly replaced by a more extensive credit system growing up among traders themselves. The fierce demand for *cash* under circumstances of the sort stated, and the resulting high rate of interest that would be obtainable for the use of it, would keep all *cash* in rapid and continuous circulation. The public would lend without delay any *cash* that they did not wish to spend immediately; and, in any case, the *cash* would be rushed by retailers back to wholesalers, manufacturers, and back to the public again. For larger payments, bills drawn by one first-class firm and accepted by another, would eventually be accepted and circulated freely instead of *cash*—of course, at a discount; and even post-dated cheques would in certain cases be accepted instead of *cash*.

Thus, bankers' *credit money*, although the best kind of credit, is not the only kind of credit; and, consequently, in the last resort bankers have no power to contract or prevent the expansion of credit. Their position in relation to credit is purely that of suppliers, and the only control they have over their supplies is that obtained by *inducing* the public and the foreigner to deposit more, or less, *cash* with them, and to borrow more, or less, money from them.

As credit is not created by the banks, neither is it created by the borrowers. Borrowing cannot take place continuously unless the money borrowed can be, and is, employed profitably; for, otherwise, those able to give proper security are not able to do so for long. On the other hand, as we have seen, nothing can prevent those able to give proper security from borrowing continuously when they can, and do, employ loans profitably. Hence, both the power to borrow and the actual amount borrowed, subject to the limit imposed by the existing quantity of *cash* in gold and Paper Money, depends upon the total quantity of money that can be employed profitably, and this, in turn, depends upon the *effective demand* for commodities and services.

Among the factors which govern the rate of final consumption and deferred utilisation of commodities and services, and the corresponding *effective demand*, is the *inducement* which bankers are able to offer the public to put *cash* into bankers' *cash* reserves instead of spending it on commodities and services. *The extent to which money is saved and kept on deposit in banks instead of being spent on commodities and services for final consumption or deferred utilisation determines, on the one hand, the quantity of bankers' cash reserves, and, on the other hand, the effective demand for loans together with the eventual quantity of credit money.*

Notice that a fall in bankers' rates for granting accommodation to traders, although it may lower the cost of production and the general price level, does not cause an increase in the *effective demand* either for commodities and services or for loans; for, a fall in the general price level, other things equal, *reduces the total monetary income earned*, and lower costs of production obtained by means of *reductions in the total earnings of labour, land, capital or entrepreneurs' profits reduce the effective demand to more or less the same extent as the quantity of earnings economised.* It is true that entrepreneurs and companies, other things equal, are influenced by the monetary situation as to the moment they choose to come in as buyers for commodities for deferred utilisation, either in respect of renewals or entirely new ventures. Nevertheless, so far as loans for this purpose are concerned, it is only a question of finding the most favourable moment from all points of view; for, both renewals and new ventures are entirely dependent upon the *effective demand* of the public for the commodities and services to be supplied by such renewals or new ventures. The only manner, therefore, in which variations in the rate of interest on money can influence the *effective demand*, either for commodities and services or for loans, is by the effect of its inducement on the public to *spend* more or less money on commodities and services for final consumption or deferred utilisation. It is doubtful whether normal variations in the rate of interest obtainable by the public for their monetary "savings" has any measurable influence in stabilising the *effective demand*. So far as bankers' deposit rates are concerned, they vary normally between about 1½ per cent. and

3 per cent.; whilst, variations in the prices of "guilt-edged", and other first-class securities, resulting from variations in the monetary situation do not alter the yields to more than about 1 per cent. Such small variations cannot have much effect in altering the proportion of the money not spent to the money spent.

The manner in which bankers' power to supply *credit money* is limited by the existing supply of *cash* in gold and Paper Money is examined, later, in relation to the issue of Paper Money. For the moment, however, it must be remarked that, at any time, when the total supply of *credit money* is not expanded to the fullest extent that is consistent with safety in relation to *cash* reserves in the banks, any further *cash* left by the public on deposit in the banks does not in any way increase the quantity of *credit money* supplied by them. Whenever bankers' *cash* reserves are not being used up to the hilt, or, in other words, whenever the ratio of *cash* reserves to *credit money* in the banks is unnecessarily high, any increase in the *cash* reserves without a proportionate increase in the *effective demand* for *credit money* merely reduces the rate of interest on money. Notice, also, that proportionate increase in *credit money* to *cash* must be at least as three to one; but, in any case, the *effective demand* for credit cannot increase at all at a time when the total amount of money being spent on commodities and services is being reduced.

Credit, therefore, is created and destroyed by those social, political and commercial factors which govern the rate of production of commodities and services for sale, and the rate of their final consumption and deferred utilisation; and, subject to prices being unaltered and to the limit on the total quantity of *credit money* imposed by the existing quantity of *cash*, the total quantity of *credit money* is, at all times, the monetary measure of *active total utility* or true wealth.

Although the supply of *credit money* may vary within the limits already explained in relation to the supply of *cash*, these variations do not necessarily take place harmoniously with variations in the quantities of commodities and services produced for sale. An increase in the quantity of *credit money* takes place as a result of an increased *effective demand* for money by the public arising from an increase in the *effective demand* for commodities and services—and this is almost invariably accompanied by increased production. But an increase in the production of commodities and services for sale, whether it takes place as the result of an actual increase in the *effective demand* or merely as the result of the expectation of such an increase, may be followed by those in possession of the money waiting for a fall in prices, or refusing absolutely to buy commodities and services of any kind or to lend money to anybody else to use in this manner. The extent to which the *effective demand* is thereby reduced correspondingly reduces the supply of *credit money*; and, hence, the supply of *credit money* may even diminish eventually[6] as the result of an increase in the production of commodities and services for sale. We can therefore state:

That the supply of credit money, subject to the manner in which it is limited by the supply of cash, varies as the effective demand for commodities and services and not as their production.

VIII   Paper money

or Supplementary cash issued by governments

Whatever the arguments in favour of classifying Paper Money as a sort of credit, it is not in the same class as the bankers' *credit money* which has been fully described in the last chapter. Bankers' *credit money* is the legal obligation of bankers to pay *cash*; whilst, Paper Money *is*, itself, the *cash* whereby bankers can legally carry out their obligations in this respect. Thus, whatever the backing of Paper Money, it is as truly *cash* as gold, in relation to *credit money*.

Paper Money is the most important factor in the monetary question; for, owing to the fact that the supply of gold is relatively constant and the supply of *credit money* is dependent on *cash* reserves, variations in the maximum possible supply of *cash* and *credit money* is governed by variations in the quantity of Paper Money issued. In the correct use of the issue of Paper Money by governments lies the key to the economic machine.

The backing of Paper Money, which is supposed to guarantee its value, may consist mainly of gold or mainly of securities. For example, in England there are two kinds of Paper Money: Bank of England Notes and Currency Notes.

[. . .]

The backing of Paper Money may be gold, Government securities, or mortgages on land or industry; but, as a matter of fact, the backing is more or less humbug. The value of Paper Money in relation to commodities and services is not affected by its backing, but by the total supply of *cash* and *credit money* available as means of payment in relation to the total quantity of commodities and services which are effectively traded. The public must have *cash* as a means of payment, and bankers must have *cash* as legal tender against their obligations to pay *cash*; and the value of a unit of *cash* in Paper Money, whatever its backing, is always proportionate to the ratio of the total supply of *cash* and *credit money* to the total quantity of commodities and services traded.

The supply of Paper Money does not necessarily vary harmoniously with the production of commodities and services. Paper Money is issued by governments in order to enable bankers to avoid a general suspension of payments in moments when the public, actuated either by panic or desire to ensure the safety of its money, or by the necessity for more *cash* for circulation, is calling for *cash* in excess of *cash* reserves in the banks.

In the days of gold payments a general run on the banks arising from panic on the part of the public was a very real danger; but with Paper Money as legal tender *cash*, the public know that their money is no safer in their pockets than in the banks. Nevertheless, should the public insist on *cash* payments by the bankers to the full extent of their legal obligations, the Government would, undoubtedly, step in and supply the bankers with additional Paper Money against their lodging the required securities. In a case of this sort, the increase in the supply of Paper Money so obtained would have nothing to do with any variation in the production of commodities and services, and, other things equal, would be cancelled as soon as the panic was over.

On the other hand, when the public is calling for *cash* in excess of bankers' *cash* reserves because it requires more *cash* for circulation, this is due, not to increased production of commodities and services, but to an increase in the *effective demand* for commodities and services.

Both cases are well illustrated by events in England since August 1914. When the war broke out, Currency Notes were, at first, issued to satisfy the demand for *cash* arising from panic on the part of the public; but during the period between 1916 and 1920, the continual increase in the issue of Currency Notes was due to the continual increase in the public demand for *cash* for circulation arising from the pressure of the *effective demand* for commodities and services over the rate of production. As a matter of fact, the quantity of commodities and services for which there were effective buyers was in excess of the actual and potential rate of production; and the monetary reconciliation between the quantities of commodities and services *effectively demanded* and the quantities available only took place, in part through Government control of consumption, and in part through strong rises in the price level. Such a situation only arose because all governments were keen buyers of all the commodities and services that could be produced, and they did not wish their efforts to obtain supplies to be embarrassed by any financial considerations. The quantity of Paper Money issued, for instance, might have been so limited that the total supply of *cash* and *credit money* remained continuously in the same proportion to the total quantity of commodities and services traded. It seems tolerably certain that, had the principal allied governments adopted the same monetary policy, the public demand for *cash* in excess of the quantity required to trade the fullest actual and potential supplies of commodities and services without a permanent rise in the general price level, could have been successfully met by a more or less severe rise in the rate of interest for money instead of by the issue of additional *cash*. Of course, if this had been done, part of the incentive to produce rapidly arising from the more or less illusory advantage of higher prices would have been lost to producers.

No serious government issues Paper Money directly for the purpose of meeting expenditure. Governments borrow the required money from bankers and spend it on commodities and services, and they are then forced to issue Paper Money in response to increased demand for *cash* by the public. Every such loan creates a deposit of *credit money* in favour of government employees, contractors, etc., as well as an *effective demand* for new loans by the public for any necessary increase in the quantity of *credit money* to finance an increased volume of production and trade; bankers then require more *cash* to meet increased calls by the public, and the governments are then obliged to issue the necessary *cash* in order to avoid a general suspension of payments by bankers.

We can therefore state that:

The supply of Paper Money varies as the effective demand for commodities and services and not as their production.

Nevertheless, although serious governments only issue Paper Money in response to *effective demands* for additional *cash* by the public, the governments are not only almost entirely responsible for whatever the public demands for *cash* happen to be, but they can effectively control it.

By increased taxation, governments can directly reduce the quantity of money spent by the public on commodities and services for both final consumption and deferred utilisation; and the same results can be obtained indirectly by governments squeezing bankers' *cash* reserves of Paper Money and forcing up the rate of interest. In this manner, the reduced *effective demand* for commodities and services reduces the *effective demand* by traders for loans to finance trade, together with the quantity of *credit money* on deposit in banks, and the calls by the public on bankers' *cash* reserves.

On the other hand, by increased borrowing from bankers for the purpose of expenditure, governments can directly increase the quantity of money spent on commodities and services for final consumption and deferred utilisation; and the same results can be encouraged indirectly by governments freely supplying bankers with Paper Money for their *cash* reserves, against the deposit by them of securities, and thus forcing down the rate of interest for money.

Government expenditure remaining unaltered, increased borrowing by a government relieves taxation, and vice versa. But, at any time, when a government finds that the total supply of *cash* and *credit money* is insufficient to trade the total supply of commodities and services for sale without a fall in prices, and that further production is thereby being held up, it can increase its expenditure by the extension and improvement of public works. In circumstances of this sort it is the duty of a government to increase expenditure without increasing taxation; for the increased expenditure will not only supply the additional quantity of *cash* and *credit money* to avoid undeserved losses to traders, but it will enable private production and enterprise to continue normally, and thereby the private wealth of the nation as well as its wealth in public works will be increased.

This interesting point will be referred to again in the proper place. Meantime, there is no science whatever, to-day, in the manner in which taxation, borrowing and the issue of Paper Money, are employed by governments; and the policies adopted are merely those which seem most expedient, taking into consideration inherited precepts, usually obsolete, and the pressure of existing political forces.

We have, therefore, the following facts regarding the *expansion* and *contraction* of the total supply of *cash* and *credit money*.

The rapidity of circulation of money varies as the *effective demand* for commodities and services and not as their production; the world supply of gold coin and bullion is relatively constant, but the supply in a State varies as the relative supplies of Paper Money and *credit money* and not as the production of commodities and services; and the supplies of *credit money* and Paper Money vary as the *effective demand* for commodities and services and not as their production. Therefore:

The total supply of cash and credit money expands and contracts as the effective demand for commodities and services and not as their production.

IX Saving

Seeing that the total supply of *cash* and *credit money* expands and contracts, not as the production of commodities and services, but as the *effective demand* for them, it is not surprising that the proportion of the total supply of money to the total supply of commodities and services[7] for sale varies considerably. Nevertheless, as our examination of *purchasing power* has shown, whenever the total supply of *cash* and *credit money* fails to expand in a manner at all times proportionate to the total supply of commodities and services for sale, they cannot all be marketed unless their total value is correspondingly reduced by a fall in the price level.

As a matter of fact, under existing conditions, although the total supply of *cash* and *credit money* may for a time *expand* to the same, or even to a greater, extent in proportion to any increase in the production and total supply of commodities and services for sale, it must invariably without much delay ultimately fail to attain or maintain an expansion proportionately as great.

The expansion of the total supply of *cash* and *credit money* does take place in a manner at all times proportionate to the production and total supply of commodities and services for sale, provided the total amount of money continuously *earned* (gross earnings) in the production of commodities and services by labour, land, capital, entrepreneurs and governments is all *continuously spent*[8] on commodities and services. Whilst we can agree that the total amount of money *spent* on such commodities and services creates an equal total quantity of gross monetary *earnings* by labour, land, capital, entrepreneurs and governments,[9] we cannot agree that there are no monetary *earnings* apart from those arising from money *spent*, nor can we agree that the total monetary *earnings* determines either the maximum or the minimum of the total amount of money *spent*.

The money *earned* by the production of monetary specie does not consist of any money *spent*. An individual or a company producing gold which can be tested, weighed and officially stamped, or coined, into official money, *earns* money that has not been previously *spent*.

It is true that the gross amount of money *earned* by the production of gold is *spent* in whole or in part by the miners, mine-owners and those earning or receiving money directly from the gold-mining industry; but the amount so *spent* is offset by a further quantity of gross *earnings* in favour of those on whose commodities and services it is *spent*.

Thus, the gross amount of money *earned* by the production of gold, unlike that earned by the production of commodities and services, is *additional* to the existing quantity of money and in no way dependent upon or offset by money previously *spent*.

Furthermore, the gross amount of money *earned* by the production of gold is not necessarily *all spent* by those into whose possession it happens to get. We know that gold can be hoarded and, under primitive conditions, is hoarded; and we know that, under modern conditions, the *cash* and *credit money* obtained in exchange for newly produced gold can be placed on deposit in a bank or made to circulate in a bond market instead of being spent on commodities and services.

In order to understand the matter more clearly, let us disregard, for the moment, new supplies of *cash* and *credit money*, and the manner in which monetary specie and money are permanently withdrawn from use as money; and let the total quantity of every kind of money be regarded as invariable and represented by $100x$.

The amount continuously earned will be admittedly equal to the amount continuously spent, regardless of the rapidity with which transactions are taking place and the money changing hands between buyers and sellers. This rapidity will be determined by how soon after each transaction the sellers who have received the money decide to spend it again; for, evidently, those who have parted with the money in exchange for commodities and services cannot bring about any new transactions until those who have got the money wish to do so. As a matter of fact, those who have got the money normally, control the situation. They can take their own time as regards new transactions; and the pace at which they spend money will, in like manner, adjust the pace of money again being earned.

Should those who have, together, got all the money at any time, suddenly lock up $10x$ and spend freely only up to $90x$, money earned will exceed money spent to this extent; but the total amount of money earned from that time will be equal to the total amount of money spent; and, although it will only be possible for transactions to take place simultaneously up to a value not exceeding $90x$, the total amount of money spent and earned in a given time will be determined by the rapidity with which transactions follow each other.

Should the locked up money represented by $10x$ then be lent to others to spend, money spent will then exceed money earned to this extent; but the total amount of money earned from that time will be equal to the total amount of money spent; and, although transactions could then take place up to the full $100x$, as before, the total amount of money spent and earned in a given time will be determined by the rapidity with which transactions follow each other.

It must be remarked that the total amount of money spent and earned in a given time may be greater when $90x$ is circulating rapidly than when $100x$ is circulating slowly, or equal when $100x$ is circulating 10 per cent. less rapidly than $90x$; and that, in all cases, it is the spenders of the money after the last transactions who make the pace and thereby determine the total earnings and continuous earnings of money.

Now let us suppose that, to this fixed quantity of money represented by $100x$, new money is added by the production of fresh supplies of gold to the value of $6x$. Then, to the total quantity of money that was being spent and earned before the new gold was produced, must be added 6*x*, the value of the new money earned. Some of this 6*x* will inevitably be spent by miners, mine-owners and others who earn or receive it; but any amount so spent is offset by a further equal quantity of earnings in favour of those on whose commodities and services the money is spent. Therefore, whatever portion of 6*x* is spent, the total amount of money earned will exceed the total amount spent by 6*x* during the time in which the 6*x* is being earned by the production of gold.

Therefore, so far as gold is concerned, the gross amount of money *earned* by the production of gold is not necessarily *all spent* on commodities and services either before or after it is so *earned*, but the total quantity of money has been increased and is being increased to the extent in which money so *earned* is *spent*; and, in any case, the total amount of money continuously *earned*, other things equal, exceeds the total amount of money continuously *spent* to the extent of the gross amount of money continuously *earned* by the production of gold.

As regards *credit money*, not only are the total monetary *earnings* arising from the money *spent* on commodities and services not necessarily *spent* again, but the total amount *spent* is not necessarily *earned* before it is *spent*.

Credit money only comes into existence by being borrowed and *spent* on commodities and services for final consumption or deferred utilisation when, for the first time, it is simultaneously *earned* by the factors of production (together with taxation for the governments). Once *earned*, it only continues in existence provided it is again *spent* by some people and simultaneously *earned* by others, and so on. As soon, however, as the last people who *earn* it fail, either to *spend* it themselves or to lend it to other people to *spend*, it is cancelled; for, in effect, the failure to *spend credit money* on commodities and services for final consumption or deferred utilisation reduces the total amount of money lent to the public by bankers, and every loan from a banker creates a deposit of *credit money*, and every repayment of a loan from a banker destroys a deposit of *credit money*.

Both *cash* and *credit money*, when not *spent* on commodities and services for final consumption or deferred utilisation, must either be locked up or, sooner or later, directly or indirectly, be placed on deposit in banks. If it is invested in a new company or in a company increasing its capital, it is *spent* on commodities and services, with the exception of what may happen to any money corresponding to the promoting profits; but, if it is used to purchase shares of an existing company, or bonds, once or repeatedly, the last seller of the shares, or bonds, must lock it up or keep it in a bank, if he does not *spend* it on commodities and services.

The total supply of *cash* and *credit money* is, other things equal, reduced by any money that is kept on deposit in banks by the public instead of being *spent* on commodities and services for final consumption or deferred utilisation. Such money does nothing to create any *effective demand* for loans from the banks; but, other things equal, any *cash* deposited in banks by the public increases the total *cash* reserves of bankers when, other things equal, such an increase is not required by the bankers, and in the case of gold payments the equivalent gold goes abroad, or, otherwise, the equivalent Paper Money is cancelled.

On the other hand, any gross monetary *earnings* from the production of commodities and services, unless again *spent* on commodities and services, other things equal, brings about a proportionate fall in the price level together with corresponding monetary losses to traders and the cancellation of an equal quantity of *credit money*.

In the case of trade being so brisk that the public is calling for *cash* in excess of bankers' cash reserves, that the capacity of bankers to supply *credit money* is fully engaged, and that the total supply of *credit money* is, consequently, at its fullest *expansion*, it is true that keeping money in banks instead of *spending* it does relieve pressure upon the *cash* reserves of bankers enabling them to supply, on easier terms, *credit money* that may be required to finance the production of commodities for deferred utilisation such as buildings, machinery, factories, and even works of art. Nevertheless, in such cases, the abstinence from *spending* money on commodities and services on the part of the public and the retaining of the money on deposit in banks by them, is not the only means of financing the production of more urgently required commodities for deferred utilisation. The commodities and services for which the *effective demand* is strongest, whether for final consumption or deferred utilisation, are the commodities and services most profitable to produce; and, consequently, effective borrowers in respect of this production are in a position to make the highest bids for the available supply of *cash* and *credit money*. When, at any time, potential production is unable to cope simultaneously with the building of a certain number of railways, factories, steamers and houses, together with the production of a certain quantity of food and clothing, the respective quantities of each for which the *effective demand* is strongest automatically secure the required proportions of the available supply of *cash* and *credit money*; and the measure of the quantities of each for which the *effective demand* is strongest depends upon the physical, mental and moral condition of the people.

It is preferable for people to bid for their requirements from the general stock of existing and producible commodities and services than for them to be cajoled into buying what they do not want or, with self-satisfied virtue, breaking the hearts of the producers by refusing to buy at all.

As a matter of fact, the contingency of the total supply of *cash* and *credit money* being at its fullest *expansion* never worried[10] anybody even in the days of gold payments when bankers' *cash* reserves really meant something in a more or less vital manner. To-day, with the proper use of Paper Money, the maximum *expansion* of the total supply of *cash* and *credit money* need only be reached when the rate of production is in danger of lagging behind the rate of consumption, and when further *expansion* in the supply of money as well as consumption of commodities and services must be checked by dearer money and, in case of need, increased taxation.

During the last war there is no doubt that production was not keeping pace with consumption, in so far as railways, buildings and roads, and most commodities for deferred utilisation, were not being kept in proper repair or being renewed; and for this reason the continuous *expansion* of the quantity of *credit money* that was permitted damaged, more or less proportionately, the values of the units of the currencies concerned. It is common knowledge, however, that considerable stock of every kind and class of commodities had accumulated in America and England and most other countries during the period between the end of the war and April 1920, when the Bank Rate was raised to 7 per cent; and consequently any further *expansion* of *credit money* that took place during this period in all countries, with the exception of Central and Eastern Europe, was more than backed by the increase in the total quantity of commodity and services for sale. In Central and Eastern European countries, owing to political exigencies, the inflation of the currencies soon began to outstrip, with greater or lesser rapidity, increases in the quantities of commodities and services for sale; but, almost everywhere else, particularly in America and England, the accumulation of stocks became so great, and the growing inclination to wait for a fall in prices became so pronounced that, even if money had become cheaper, a heavy fall in the price level would have been inevitable unless the Government had forced the right quantity of *credit money* into circulation by meeting expenditure on borrowed money instead of by taxation. As a matter of fact, the Government adopted the reverse policy with the disastrous results that we have seen. The policy of severe restriction of *credit money* adopted by the Government might have been useful before the heavy accumulation of stock had taken place. Undoubtedly something could have been done to prevent the production of supplies which were merely to be held by speculators instead of consumed by the public as fast as produced; and, undoubtedly, without the assistance of the banks, speculators could never have held such large stocks. Nevertheless, the feeling of optimism after the armistice was so strong, and men who had done nothing for four years were so eager to get busy, that it is doubtful whether finance would have been strong enough to oppose them in their determination to produce, and demand production, at any price. However, once the stocks existed, not only deflation should not have been attempted, but it should have been prevented, as far as possible, by the Government forcing *credit money* into circulation in the manner stated above.

To-day, at any rate in the coal countries, the usual position is that the *effective demand* for commodities and services is never as great as the supply for sale; and the same may be said of the coal countries in peace time from practically commencement of the steam era. Henry George noted it about fifty years ago when he wrote *Progress and Poverty*. It may be inferred, by deduction, from symptoms of "The Problem" stated in the first chapter; it is a matter of common experience to all traders; it is confirmed by the fact that a contraction of the *effective demand* is almost invariably accompanied by a fall in prices resulting from abundant production; and it remains to be shown how it accounts for all economic phenomena, e.g. unemployment and trade depression at a time when commodities and services of every kind are most abundant, the desire of all countries to increase their exports and protect themselves against imports, and the general inability of creditor countries to receive payments from debtor countries of indemnities and international debts on a large scale. In such circumstances keeping money in banks instead of spending it, not only saves nothing,[11] but it wastes things that are actually produced and ready for use and prevents the further production of similar things.

In view, therefore, of existing conditions whereby quantities of *credit money* are continually cancelled as a result of saving, and, whereby, in any case, the *expansion* of *credit money* is limited arbitrarily by the total supply of *cash* in a manner bearing no relation whatever to the production of commodities and services, any *expansion* in the total supply of *cash* and *credit money* must invariably without much delay fail to attain or maintain an *expansion* proportionately as great as the total supply of commodities and services for sale.

X Saving and the utilisation of purchasing power

We have remarked, when considering the nature of Purchasing Power, that the market value of commodities and services and money in relation to each other depends upon the extent of the entire supply of each and the manner in which it is being *utilised*, and that every subjection of the use of any supply to a lower utility affects its purchasing power in accordance with the law of diminishing utility.

We have seen, also, that whenever the total supply of *cash* and *credit money* fails to *expand* in a manner at all times proportionate to the production and total supply of commodities and services for sale, they cannot all be marketed unless their total value is correspondingly reduced by a fall in the price level.

On the other hand, our examination of the monetary system shows that the *expansion* of the total supply of *cash* and *credit money* is only, at all times, proportionate to the production and total supply of commodities and services for sale, provided the total amount of money continuously *earned* in production by labour, land, capital, enterpreneurs and governments, or an equal quantity of money, is *all spent* on commodities and services for final consumption or deferred utilisation as fast as it is *earned*.

Therefore, the total continuous purchasing power or income arising from, or *earned* by, production can only be *utilised* provided it is *all spent* on commodities and services as fast as it is *earned* or received.

The nature of the commodities and services on which the total continuous purchasing power or income is *spent*, and whether *spending* money in any particular manner is a "wicked waste," are questions beside the point. The point is that any income, in being *spent* on commodities and services as fast as *earned*, is actually *utilised* to *demand effectively*. It may be *spent* on anything for final consumption, from degenerating drugs to healthy food and exercise; or it may be *spent* on anything for deferred utilisation, from pictures and ornaments of art to necessary furniture, or from special machinery for the production of a patent medicine for prize rats to a necessary farm, factory or railway; but purchasing power is *utilised* so long as it is *spent* on commodities and services as fast as it is *earned* or received. Those from whom the wasteful or useful commodities and services have been bought can employ the purchasing power so *earned* in any way that suits them. Purchasing power *earned* directly or indirectly by the sale of a degenerating drug may be *utilised* to maintain the widowed mother of a growing future inventor, or it may be *utilised* to buy a cottage which eventually keeps somebody off the poor rates.

Notice that the total monetary income arising from all sources in production can trade all the commodities and services produced for sale without a fall in the price level provided it is *all spent* as fast as it is *earned* or received; and that this is so regardless of whether the commodities and services are for final consumption, or for deferred utilisation in the form of new capital commodities. Naturally, it is not possible for producers to estimate always the exact quantity of each commodity that will be *demanded effectively* at the same price; but, a rise in prices in respect of under-stocked commodities and a fall in prices in respect of overstocked commodities, would continually reconcile the quantity of each commodity in stock to the quantity of money used to demand it effectively, and simultaneously adjust the quantities further produced; and, any loss or hardship to producers in respect of a relatively over-stocked commodity would be balanced by an increased gain to producers in respect of commodities, the quantities in stock of which were relatively less plentiful.

The extent in which the total purchasing power continuously *earned*, or the total income, is *utilised*, varies according to the manner in which it is distributed; for anybody receiving continuously purchasing power or income in excess of what they are obliged to *utilise*, by *spending* as fast as they receive it on commodities and services for final consumption or deferred utilisation, may be unwilling to do so with *all* of it.

The poorer working classes are forced to *utilise* all, or nearly all, their continuous purchasing power or income; for it is so small that they can hardly do with less commodities and services than it enables them to buy. Consequently, any variations in the continuous purchasing power or income received by the great mass of people causes almost like variations in the extent in which it is *utilised*. Rich people, however, often receive more continuous purchasing power or income than they are obliged to *utilise*. Such people are in a position to choose between *spending* it on commodities and services for final consumption or deferred utilisation, or not *spending* it at all; and, at any rate, they may wish to "*save*" some of it.

People receiving continuously purchasing power or income in excess of what they are obliged to *utilise*, can *utilise* it fully, so far as the objective economic system is concerned, by *spending* it as fast as they receive it on any kind of commodities and services; but, so far as they themselves are concerned, the subjective *utility* secured by them can be varied and determined by judicious choice of the nature of the commodities and services on which it is *spent* for final consumption or deferred utilisation. If the subjective *utility* required is final consumption, it can be bought with a bottle of whisky, bread and cheese, or a new hat; and if deferred utilisation is required, it can be bought with a motor lorry or a factory; but whether the subjective *utility* so obtained is positive or negative is another matter, for what is medicine to some is poison to others.

Continuous purchasing power or income *spent* as fast as received on commodities and services capable of gradual or continual use, or for deferred utilisation, is *truly saved* as well as *utilised*.

On the other hand, continuous purchasing power or income, the deferred utilisation of which is secured by the acquisition of shares of existing companies, or bonds, or by being lent to individuals or bankers, is not necessarily *utilised*; for, those who thus receive it, or obtain the use of it, do not necessarily[12] *spend* it themselves, or cause it to be *spent*, on commodities and services for final consumption or deferred utilisation, nor is material delay necessarily avoided should it be so *spent*. Further, even when it is *utilised* by those who thus obtain the use of it and is spent without material delay on commodities and services, the *utility* so gained by the objective economic system is cancelled[13] should, at any time, the commodities and services in question, or equivalent commodities and services, be thrown on to the market in order to withdraw money to buy back the bonds or repay the lenders.

Continuous purchasing power or income may be *utilised* subjectively by the creation of a debt or lien on future production; but, unless *spent* on commodities and services for final consumption or deferred utilisation, nothing whatever is, in fact, saved.

Before the steamer age, when the division of labour was relatively in its infancy, when production was difficult and the modern banking system non-existent, the difference between true saving and hoarding was unmistakable.

The only way to save was by producing commodities of a durable kind, such as primitive labour-saving devices, objects of art, or buildings. In order to produce such things it was absolutely essential to observe economy in the consumption of perishable commodities. When man abstained more than necessary from the consumption of perishable commodities, he did so because he wanted to save the time to produce a plough, sword, cottage, or even a castle or a church. When he wanted none of these or any other enduring commodities, he observed no more abstinence in the consumption of perishables than was necessary to save undue fatigue. The possibilities of investing in trading companies or putting money on deposit in banks are more or less recent privileges for the thrifty. It is true that the Jews did a certain amount of money lending, but this method of saving was by no means open to everybody and was somewhat precarious. The only other means of saving was that of hoarding valuable metals and stones. The effect of thrift then was: to produce labour-saving appliances, objects of art and buildings; to save effort; and to hoard precious metals and stones.

As a result of these restrictions in the mode of saving open to our ancestors, in spite of the extreme poverty of the means at their disposal for purposes of production, they have left us a noble heritage of fine buildings and works of art. There are relatively few buildings put up in modern times that compare with the ancient buildings of Babylonia and Egypt and, later, those of Greece and Rome, or the churches and castles of the Middle Ages. What have we done in modern times that we can show for our enormous resources in power and material, division of labour and science? Even the sky-scrapers of New York are rather the reflexion of lack of building space on Manhattan Island than of spiritual and mental greatness in the modern mind.

London is a richer city than Paris; but the British may well envy the broad streets of Paris and the ample and uniform size and construction of its buildings. The resources of England to-day are greater than they were a quarter of a century ago, yet all the big hotels in England were not built during the last twenty-five years. To-day, the British effort in the building line mainly consists of badly built suburban houses; and even the spacious well-designed villa of the successful business man is not to be compared with the older homes of English gentlemen.

Compare Brussels with Cardiff or Newcastle. Is Brussels the richer city? or where do the great coal cities hide their wealth? One cannot believe that they are the centres of the famous British coal areas which daily pour forth energy untold in the history of man—energy by means of which millions of people and millions of tons of material are carried long distances over land and water at high speeds, and by means of which nations have grown into existence on the far sides of the earth. By what maniac rule must men starve, and women sell themselves for a pittance, in these cities as elsewhere.

If the rich are richer than ever, where does the wealth go? If by our thrift we save something more than effort, where is this saving? In spite of our fondness of export, we cannot export it because all nations love export and "favourable" trade balances as much as ourselves.

The increased effectiveness of labour arising from progress in modern times has served, not to increase the welfare of man, but merely to swell his numbers. As modern wealth is hoarded it disappears!

We hear a good deal about the virtue of economy and thrift, but when it consists of abstaining from the utilisation or proper consumption of things that exist and, incidentally, their component parts, then it is no virtue but pure and simple waste. On the other hand, virtue or no virtue, one cannot use or consume things that do not exist, or of which the supply is so small and the price so high that they are beyond one's reach. Whilst the things that are not available for use take care of themselves, the things that *are available* for use ought to be used, and it is for man to see that they are properly used. Either way, economy and thrift are not in the picture. Parsimony, the great gospel for the creation of wealth, is negative and creates nothing.

This does not mean that there is no virtue in abstaining from the use of one thing in order to be able to use more of another. Nor does it mean, in circumstances such as war, when labour is restricted to the quantity of labour not employed in the fighting machines, when consumption is swelled to the limit almost of man's energy to consume, and when, consequently, the monetary system fails to function as a control of production and consumption, that there is no advantage in voluntary or compulsory economy in the use of commodities and services in certain forms in order to increase the supply of them in other forms. What it means is that, whilst the *effective demand* for commodities and services for final consumption and deferred utilisation cannot be continuously greater than production and purchasing power, any purchasing power for any reason not fully utilised disappears.

Those who think they save anything by merely abstaining from spending, save nothing; but they do gain an option on the labour and lives of all others who are unable to do likewise, and humanity feels that this is what really happens. Further, if everybody were able and willing to save in this manner, the options so gained would cancel each other without leaving a trace.

Purchasing power, whether it is derived from any sort of wages, rent, interest or profit, can only be truly saved when it is fully utilised by being *all spent* without delay on those things that maintain human life in its highest form. It must be all spent not merely on bare necessities of food, clothing and shelter, but upon luxuries, art and education; and by being so spent it creates automatically that quantity of labour-saving machinery and plant that is required for the purpose. It is only by *spending* money that humanity can grow in number, beauty and greatness, and only in this way is anything truly saved.

XII   The abuse of surplus

Where all factors of production are unlimited and subject to free competition, consumers and producers obtain their exact quota of the respective kinds of *surplus*; and in this manner a proper balance would probably be maintained between production and consumption. Although *surplus* when justly distributed is not necessarily fully *utilised*, it cannot be fully *utilised* unless it is justly distributed. The final consumption and deferred utilisation of commodities and services must take place as fast as their production, and in exact proportion to it; otherwise there appears, instead of *consumers' surplus*, a stagnant surplus that is not even exportable.

An exportable surplus is exportable in so far as it consists of a surplus of supplies available for exchange with, and in payment of, supplies in stronger demand. In so far as a surplus is exportable and there exists an *effective demand* for supplies in exchange, such a surplus is subject to continuous liquidation and consequently never appears as a surplus. When, however, there is no *effective demand* for the surplus itself, nor for other supplies in exchange, you get an unexportable surplus. Great Britain, America and Germany before the war were commonly loaded with unexportable surpluses. To avoid the evil consequences of unexportable surpluses upon both master and man, dumping or even partial destruction of surpluses has been resorted to; and "protection" from the surpluses of other nations is commonly demanded.

The absurdity of such a situation is palpable. Millions in want of the barest necessities of life; but producers and labour asking for protection against the necessary supplies, lest their own purchasing power disappears as well and they, themselves, go to swell the crowd of millions in distress.

This state of affairs is quite a common one. It is called "trade depression," and is explained by politicians, economists and business men in all sorts of ways. Henry George wrote that it was attributed by different schools of thought both to overproduction and overconsumption; and he asks, "While the great masses of men want more wealth than they can get, and while they are willing to give for it that which is the basis of raw material and wealth—their labour—how can there be overproduction?" As for overconsumption, so far as England is concerned, the pre-war average weekly wage of ten millions of men was 25s. 9d., and five million and a half women 10s. 11d.[14]

In the spring of 1919, Sir Richard Vassar Smith stated publicly that the country (England) had been living on its capital, and that the only way to put things right was by economy and increased production. About a month later, Lord Milner stated in the House of Lords that, apart from a certain depreciation on railways, roads and buildings, the actual wealth of the country had not diminished since 1914, and that the National Debt, whilst an embarrassment to the Government, was no liability to the country. In any case, since then we have had both the increased production and the economy,—the majority of people having been forced to economise; but "the last state is worse than the first." We are now told by British experts that the trouble lies with the depreciated foreign currencies which is stopping the export trade upon which England is so dependent. American experts agree that the trade depression is due to the depreciated foreign currencies, but it is the depreciation of Sterling and its effect upon the American export trade that they have in mind as much as anything. Nevertheless, when Sterling improves in relation to dollars, other currencies are further depreciated in relation to Sterling. On the other hand, an important section of French opinion says that England has caused the depreciation of the Franc in order to make France pay more dearly for British commodities, just as a certain section of Britishers complain of America having knocked Sterling below the Dollar parity in order to squeeze more out of England for American cotton, wheat, etc.

The difficulty of exporting or otherwise getting rid of stocks is also put down to high prices. Whilst producers show that prices must go up to enable production (of their commodities) to take place without losses—let alone profit, the same people insist that prices must come down where other commodities are concerned. Everybody wants high prices as sellers but low prices as buyers. "Unbiassed" individuals with an eye on the export trade and cheaper production as the means to secure it, call for the return to an "economic" price level—whatever that means; but these individuals will not admit that any export trade in competition with export by their own country helps to alleviate the trade depression. If they are English they are convinced that it is increased export by England that is the means to the end so far as England is concerned; and if they are Americans they are convinced that increased exports by America is the means to the end for America. Far from being willing to assist the European export trade, America, the enormous creditor of Europe, wants "protection" from the only manner in which she can receive payment from Europe. She wants protection from the sale of European goods in her home market, and would like it also in her foreign markets. England, likewise, wants protection from the receipt of the German indemnity. England is willing to cancel old debts or even grant further loans to all foreign debtors rather than receive other than book payments for the amounts already owed. America was also willing to grant further loans to its foreign debtors, but Mr. Hoover pointed out that further loans to Europe to buy American goods was merely a tax on the whole country for the benefit of the exporters.

Mr. Lloyd George, looking at the debacle, said that it is the sort of thing that always happens after a big war, and gave data to that effect.

As a matter of fact, this sort of talk is miles away from the real issue. It is not generally appreciated that the "Haves" must buy the work of the "Have-nots" before the "Have-nots" can buy from the "Haves," and that lending is only putting off the issue; that if the creditor countries are unable or unwilling to buy or import from the debtor countries, still less are the debtor countries able or willing to buy or import from the creditor countries; and that the inability of the creditor countries to buy is due to the disproportion between "Haves" and "Have-nots" in these countries, the "Haves" *being unwilling to buy because they already possess far more than they can utilise, and the* "Have-nots" *being unable to buy*. The "Haves" of America can only sell provided there are other people in America who are able to buy from them directly or indirectly. *Selling abroad,—exporting—by America is impracticable unless there are people in America able and willing to buy goods imported in exchange for those exported*. Once the "Haves" in any country are in possession of all they require and consequently refuse to buy, for that same reason, selling by them, either at home or abroad, is impossible. *When the "Haves" refuse to buy and the "Have-nots" cannot buy, all trade stops regardless of political boundaries.*

The present trade depression, like every trade depression, as well as the German indemnity and international debt muddles, are due to a defective system of distribution. The defect is small as compared with the whole system; but it ruins the whole system just as a sparking plug missing fire ruins the running of a fine motor engine.

The defect is that workers are not receiving their just share of *consumers' surplus*. The purchasing power or income that producers together receive for their work is insufficient to keep the objective economic system running. The workers produce more than they are allowed to consume; and although those who have wrongfully secured the legal right to enjoy this *consumers' surplus* may use some of it for final consumption or deferred utilisation of commodities and services, a colossal quantity of it is held up by them and never utilised so far as the objective economic system is concerned. In so far as it is not utilised for the final consumption or deferred utilisation of commodities and services, it mainly accumulates towards a stagnant surplus, to the particular disadvantage of all grades and kinds of producers, and to the general disadvantage of humanity which becomes a spectator of its cancellation, or belated gradual consumption, at the cost of misery and death of the poor and at the expense of those who, for their own reasons, *refuse*[15] *to utilise it* properly. Moreover, those who have the power to buy in excess of their requirements, when they employ this power, usually only buy what is scarce; and, therefore, whenever there is a visible surplus of any sort the trade machine cannot function properly.

The Abuse of Surplus in Relation to Indemnities.—The German indemnity muddle arises from an attempt on the part of the victors to appropriate the *consumers' surplus* of the German people; and, as a result, the whole of it vanishes in accordance with the law of *consumers' surplus*.

The payments can, in effect, only be received by the victors through the proceeds of the sale of German goods in the countries of the victors or in the foreign markets of the victors. But those who have the reserves of purchasing power in these countries refuse to buy the goods because they do not require them; and those who have no reserves of purchasing power, lose whatever purchasing power they have to the extent in which German payment consignments deprive them of their employment.

It is claimed that Germany has paid over £500,000,000, and no doubt this is correct; but, whilst it is very debatable whether Germany is any the worse by reason of the payments made by her, the rest of the world are very much the worse for it.

[. . .]

Thus, the net amount received by the victors was only £212,000,000. Nevertheless, when the payments are considered from the point of view of the receivers, the whole lot together are worse than valueless.

The deliveries in kind, so far as England is concerned, were a real disaster. The £20,000,000 of German shipping would have been much better at the bottom of the sea from the point of the British shipbuilding and shipping trade, and whatever advantage consumers got from lower freights they lost by lower wages and lower profits or actual losses. Had the victors paid for the £161,000,000 miscellaneous deliveries in kind received from Germany, their production and exports would have been increased *at least* by this amount; or, had they not received the deliveries in kind at all, their home production and earnings thereon, with the exception perhaps of coal, would have been increased *at least* by this amount. Coal we may allow as a real payment, but even coal is extremely debatable, and full of proviso and exception. It is no exaggeration to say "at least," for deliveries in kind have turned the trade machine upside down.

As for cash payments, they consist of part of the profits made by the sale of German marks. Thousands of millions of German marks were sold to the world at what proved to be wonderful prices. Everybody, all the world over, bought German marks hand over fist. Every section of society bought, from the biggest bankers to the smallest newspaper boys. They were as hungry for German marks in Yokohama, Singapore, Valparaiso, and even Paraguay, as they were in London, Paris and New York. Everybody wanted to become millionaires. On the other hand, had no cash profits been made by somebody on German marks, there would have been no cash to pay—unless German exports of commodities and services had been further increased or the exports of the victors to Germany reduced. Even if the necessary gold had been miraculously showered into Germany, the cash so created would have been almost valueless.

Property ceded by Germany is valued at £127,000,000; but who does that make any richer in the victor countries? When all is above board, ceded property is more a question for the politician than the financier; but, when all is not above board, the financiers of the country ceding the property can do as well out of it as anybody else.

We know that Germany had made payments to the value of over £400,000,000 at the time when the economic position of the world became equivalent to a *refusal to receive* further payments on the part of the victors. Only then did the payments cease, and only then did the serious troubles of Germany begin; for up to that time she had paid her way by increased production. But once the victors were refusing to receive the payments, Germany was helpless; and, only when M. Poincaré pranced into the Ruhr, she started to crumple up. On the other hand, the receipt of the payments actually made were not merely of no value to the victors, even as an offset to the expenditure on the armies of occupation, but they were a disaster to the victors.

The essential causes of non-payment are neither "International Interdependence" nor "Inability of Germany to pay"; but *inability of the victors to receive.*

The enormous production that took place in England during the war, in spite of the fact that one-seventh of the population—and the most effective seventh—were under arms, gives some idea of potential production in the coal countries to-day. Given proper incentives, Germany could produce a far greater quantity of commodities and services of every class than is thought possible; and from such increased production, given *ability of victors to receive*, she could rapidly pay the indemnity. The proper incentives, however, are the very last things that the victors wish her to have; because, whatever form these incentive take, they would cause Germany to create colossal assets for herself in addition to any payments made.

The non-payment by Germany of the amount demanded by the victors is largely put down to some phenomenal adroitness on the part of the Germans, who seem widely to be attributed with the power of thinking with superhuman accuracy and imagination as well as collectively, harmoniously and simultaneously—the whole 70,000,000 of them.

One is so often asked by those who look upon the so-called "trickery" of Germany as equivalent to a fundamental force, how France paid in 1870. The reply is that, then as now, the payment of an indemnity up to £200,000,000 or £300,000,000 by one big nation to another costs the victims nothing to pay and the victors quite a lot to receive. Between 1870 and 1880, trade was never better and prosperity never greater in France; whilst in Germany, with the exception of a short period in 1872, things were never worse. Bismarck, speaking in the Reichstag in 1879, said:

> "We see that France has managed to face the actual financial difficulties of the civilised world with greater success than ourselves . . . and, as a matter of fact, the French are complaining less of the hard times."

And again in 1881 he said:

> "About 1877 I began to remark for the first time the general and growing situation of insolvency of Germany in contrast with the situation in France; and I observed the closing of factories and the general decline of welfare and the worsening of the conditions of the labour classes and business men together with a disastrous state of affairs."

There were thousands of unemployed, and in the winter of 1876–77 things became so bad that it was necessary for moving kitchens and factories to be opened by the State.[16]

Whilst millions of money were flowing from France into Germany, the latter was suffering a serious financial crisis; and the influx of money had so little effect in generally strengthening the position of German trade and finance that twelve months after the final payment the bank rate was higher in Berlin than in Paris. Between the years 1872 and 1877 the money on deposit in banks in Germany was reduced by about 20 per cent.; but in France the deposits during the same period increased by about 20 per cent. Further, during the years 1872 and 1873 the emigration from Germany was greater in relation to the total population than it had ever been, the figures for 1872 being 154,000, and for 1873 134,000, as against 70,000 in 1869.

Hans Blum directly attributed to the indemnity the series of crises between 1873 and 1880, and describes the situation in Germany as an explosive exit of prosperity and the ruin of thousands and thousands.[17]

The explanation is that the ratio of gold to the total quantity of commodities and services for sale in Germany went up, putting up the price level in Germany accordingly; whilst the reverse occurred in France. Thus French commodities and services had a selling advantage in all markets both inside and outside Germany; and to the extent in which French commodities and services displaced those of Germany the latter was forced to become a nonproducer. No gold need actually have left France at all. The mere earmarking of it for payments to Germany had the same effect on the relative commodity values of gold in France and Germany; and whether any gold actually went from France to Germany, it came back as fast as it went. In fact, it came back faster; for the export trade of France established a definite advance at the expense of Germany, and some of the gold which was thus being bought by France for payment to Germany, eventually came to rest in France after the last payment had been effected. France increased the production of commodities and services, and effected the payments by the transfer to Germany, and German markets abroad, of this increased production together with other commodities and services which, in any case, would have been accumulating towards a stagnant surplus. France was no loser because she paid away a surplus of something for which there was no market in France; in fact, France appears to have benefited by the enforced relief to her wealth digestive organs. Germany, however, was quite incapable of digesting the stagnant surplus of France as well as her own, and in attempting to do so she got what she deserved.

Who really paid the indemnity?

The Abuse of Surplus in Relation to International Debts.—When it comes to international debts that are too large to be lost in the ordinary international trade balances, the same problem presents itself in a manner large enough openly to flog and mock mankind. France and Italy prefer the mocking to the flogging; and they lie low when confronted with their international debts, or they change the subject to "reparations." The British cannot pay the debt to the United States, and have funded it for deferred payment; but it remains to be seen whether, thereby, England or America escape both the mocking and the flogging.

Whilst optimists in America and pessimists in England believe that something is going to be obtained from England to the advantage of America, the reality is that any extent to which the debt is reduced must, under existing conditions, be at the expense of American trade. The only means by which any payments can be made to America, under existing conditions, arise from the displacement of

American commodities and services in the world's markets, from money spent by American tourists abroad, and from losses by exchange operators in America on the purchase of foreign currencies. The shipment to America of British gold profits on the Rand mines helps to reduce the total foreign debts to America, as a State, provided the American foreign trade balance remains unaffected thereby; but, as a matter of fact, the import of this gold into America must tend to diminish the proportion of American exports in relation to imports, for, other things equal, it increases the ratio of the total supply of *cash* and *credit money* to the total supply of commodities and services for sale, thereby causing a rise[18] in the general price level which would turn away more or less foreign buyers.

Owing to the enormous British capital invested abroad, and the interest due to England annually in respect of it, the British external trade balance is always heavily "adverse." What the British receive as interest on capital invested abroad must necessarily be in excess of the value of the commodities and services exported by them. The conflict is between British capital invested abroad and British producers; and only a certain compromise is reached by a quantity of the interest due from abroad on such capital being reinvested abroad in the form of British commodities and services that are exported for deferred utilisation abroad as capital. The foreign trade balance, nevertheless, is heavily "adverse"; and will remain so unless the British capitalist is content never to bring home his capital or the interest on it. Thus, if it is true that you cannot eat your cake and have it, it is equally true that you cannot have your cake unless you eat it.

So much for actual payments by the British Government to the United States; but as regards the mere action of funding the debt, whether it is large scale muddle or not, its significance may be interpreted in different ways. Whether it indicates honesty on the part of the British or hardness on the part of the Americans, or the madness of both, so far as the British are concerned, there is some method in their madness inasmuch as they know that they will gain in trade by any payments made. On the other hand, when the British public are told that the payment of the debt means an additional sixpence in the pound on the income tax, one discovers there is not so much method in it as one would, at first, suppose.

Taxation or increased taxation in England does not increase the production of commodities and services in England, nor the British export trade, nor the total quantity of cash and credit money available in England for payments. On the contrary, taxation for the purpose of repaying loans restricts production and creates unemployment by contracting the total quantity of *credit money*, dragging down the price level and reducing the total monetary income spent. Allowing even that taxation, by lowering the standard of living, can reduce imports without any proportionate loss to the export trade, is this what is aimed at? If so, how can it be accomplished whilst the really ruthless elimination of all those incapable of living at a lower standard is prevented by unemployment relief? The debt to America is a foreign debt to be paid in gold or dollars; and taxation in England does not help the British public to get either of them.

Of course, Sterling is needed by the British Government to buy the gold and dollars, and taxation transfers Sterling from the public to the Government; but an infinity of Sterling would not buy any more gold or dollars that those who possess the gold and the dollars wish to sell for Sterling. Assuming that the British Government did obtain sufficient Sterling, and that it was accepted in America as payment for the necessary gold and dollars to settle the debt regardless of the British external trade balance; even then, somebody in England would be holding at the disposal of, or owing, somebody in America that much Sterling. Neverthe-less, sooner or later the Americans must find out that Sterling balances in England are of no value to them unless they spend the money outside America, or unless the money is used to displace American commodities and services by British commodities and services in the world's markets. If the Americans did use the money in this way, the expansion of British trade would be so great that the British Government would get sufficient Sterling from the public without any increase in the rate of taxation; but if the Americans are never going to use the Sterling in the only effective manner open to them, the guarantee of the British Government to supply it as, and when, required is sufficient. To drag Sterling out of the hands of the public by taxation merely to sell it directly or indirectly to speculators on the London—New York exchange, is an attack on the life of British currency and British trade which brings no profit even to the Americans.

By transferring to America the stagnant surplus that is continually overhanging in England, the debt to the United States could be paid quickly and easily; but America has a still greater stagnant surplus of her own which she cannot afford to increase by a more "adverse" trade balance.

As a matter of fact, under existing conditions, the only manner in which a sub-stantial portion of the European debts to America could be settled is if America became engaged in a big war. Then, other things equal, neutral European count-ries would do as well by supplying America with munitions in settlement of debts as America did by supplying European countries with munitions on credit.

The Abuse of Surplus in Relation to National Debts.—The pledging of posterity by governments for the purpose of national or international loans, is a proceeding that is almost invariably unjustifiable; but it is resorted to with amazing freedom by all governments from the most corrupt to the most honest. In fact, it is the most honest governments that adopt it most freely, for the more corrupt ones get less opportunity. Very serious, solid and sound prime ministers and ministers of finance come forward in times of national stress and emergency and point out that, as pos-terity is as much interested in the defence of the country as anybody living, posterity must bear part of the cost of a war in progress. People believe, to-day, that by debit-ing posterity with the war loans, some of the burden of the war is lifted off the shoulders of the people living during the war. Nevertheless, the fact is that a war can only be paid for by wealth created prior to or during a war. Every hour's work that was required during the last great war was paid for at the time, and, excluding what was borrowed from abroad, practically the whole of the material that was required during the war was produced by labour at the time. Some material, of course, had to be advanced initially before war production got into full swing; but it was relatively a minute proportion of the total quantity used, and most of it was repaid before the war ended. Let us be quite clear about the capital and wealth that is supposed to have been advanced during the war and not repaid. When any capital or wealth in a country is consumed and not replaced, the country remains with that much less capital and wealth; nevertheless, the position in England when the war ended was that a certain quantity of foreign bonds and shares previously owned in England had been transferred to and sold in America, but, apart from this and a certain depreciation on railways, roads and buildings, the actual wealth of the country had not diminished since 1914.[19] As a matter of fact, a country can never consume anything materially in excess[20] of what it is able to produce and replace continuously; but even allowing that this does take place during a war, what claims for repayment by posterity have those who advanced what they themselves alone possessed and what they must have lost, together with a lot more, had they not advanced it? Their claim can, in justice, only be that the burden should be divided among each of them in proportion to what each possessed at the time when it was all endangered. Certainly, those who possessed nothing but who fought in order that the possessors of property should continue to retain it, cannot justly be asked to pay for the material used by them in the fight.

As for their descendants and posterity, if they had been debited with a million tons of flesh or the moon, instead of millions of pounds, there would have been just as much material and money for the war, and, the financial position would probably not be thought so badly of as it is to-day, in spite of the fact that neither the flesh nor the moon are at all accessible to financiers. As it is, the lower the standard of living is dragged by taxation, the less will be the value of what the governments and its creditors positively receive.

The pledging of posterity by governments for the purpose of national loans, when it causes an *expansion* in the total quantity of *cash* and *credit money* that is not accompanied by a corresponding increase in the production and total supply of commodities and services for sale, neither creates nor advances anything; but it destroys *consumers' surplus* to the extent in which it transfers purchasing power from those who wish to *utilise* it to those who do not.

The pledging of posterity is only permissible for purposes of national loans in order that the *expansion* of the total supply of *cash* and *credit money* may be maintained in proportion to an increase in the total supply of commodities and services for sale. Moreover, the total supply of *cash* and *credit money* must always be maintained in the same proportion to the total supply of commodities and services for sale; and it should be the chief function of government in a modern State to pledge the present and future assets of the State for this purpose whether the government requires the money or not, and to find a means of employing it if necessary. This should be the main use of governments; and it is the only use of the power to pledge by governments, anything else being an abuse, no matter what the circumstances.[21]

The Common Denominator of Stagnant Surplus.—Individually, nationally and internationally, all modern economic evils arise from the wrongful distribution of purchasing power, whereby, those who, together, possess the major part of it fail to *utilise* it fully by the purchase of commodities and services for sale. Their fantastic efforts and wild hopes to enjoy their cake without eating it simply amount to each trying to gain an advantage over the others by consuming a smaller proportion of his purchasing power and feeding on the price losses of the others. When those who, together, possess everything wish to sell more than they buy, and they all seek to cut each other's prices—and throats—in order to do so, it is not surprising that a vast number of throats are cut and that *consumers' surplus* disappears from such miserable surroundings.

When stocks are in excess of the demand for them, and when America and England are unable to export, to receive foreign payments of debts and to receive the German indemnity, this is all due to the inability of the former countries to buy and use sufficient of their home produce, or sufficient foreign produce in exchange for exports, and it forces a depreciation in the currencies of the countries from which sufficient has not been bought. The whole arises from the abuse of *surplus* by monopolies and governments, resulting in the refusal to buy on the part of those who have wrongfully become the possessors of the right to enjoy the *surplus*, and the inability to buy on the part of those from whom the *surplus* has been mis-appropriated.

As a matter of fact, the principles on which the existing economic system is run are inimical to each other; and, it is only because humanity is too weak to be thorough, that this fact does not make itself felt in a manner clear to all. The rigorous application of abstinence in the final consumption and deferred utilisation of commodities and services, together with its full effects, is averted by the dissipation of part of this abstinence; for part of the money not used to buy the employment of the workers is eventually used to subscribe charity and doles to them, and part of it is dissipated in vice by the friends and relations of the virtuous abstainers whose demands or requests they have not the strength to deny. If this dissipation of abstinence were rigorously eliminated together with the employment which it maintains, more workers would be thrown out of work; and, with the rigorous elimination of what they were consuming, yet a further batch would become unemployed; and so on, until production was reduced to a point at which any sort of voluntary abstinence became impossible.

The power to enjoy *consumers' surplus* wrongfully, is dependent upon a sufficient quantity of it being held up and wasted, and the effective demand for labour being so restricted that the market price of labour is held below the level at which *consumers' surplus* begins. The quantity of *consumers' surplus* thus wrongfully gained by some, however, is nothing like as great as the quantity that is needlessly lost by all, from the humblest labourer at the subsistence wage to the master entrepreneur with the knife of competition continually against him for the needlessly limited demand.

On the other hand:

If all those who together, rightly or wrongly, possess the legal right to enjoy the total consumers' surplus attempt to do so simultaneously by the final consumption or deferred utilisation of commodities and services, sufficient competition for labour and production will ensue to enable workers and others to obtain the power to enjoy such consumers' surplus as rightly and justly accrues to them.

XIV   The inefficacy of currently proposed remedies

The defects from which the existing economic system is suffering have now been diagnosed, but before proceeding to outline the remedy which the diagnosis, itself, suggests, we shall run through the principal ideas held on the matter and the currently proposed remedies.

Firstly, there are those who see the trouble in the dissipation of wealth by governments and individuals. They call for reduced taxation by means of greater economy in government, and reduction of government debts by cancellation or Capital Levy; and they would like to abolish the middle man and prohibit speculation.

Greater Economy in Government.—A lot has been said about true and false economy, but these are not questions that we need go into. Greater economy in government is mainly advocated by the vested interests which are alive to the evils of over-taxation but do not wish government debts to be touched. When a country is consuming more than it is able to produce, economy is the remedy; but when a country is well stocked with commodities accompanied with large numbers of unemployed, greater economy in government fails because the evil resulting from the diminished *effective demand* of those who are supposed to be "wasting" is not compensated for by any reduced taxation. "Stop the waste" campaigns are useless at the best, in such circumstances, and are very unjust and cruel in application.

Reduction of Government Debts by Cancellation or by a Capital Levy.—The advocates of this are mainly those who are in the opposite camp to that of the vested interests. They believe that, by means of the government debts, the vested interests get a larger proportion of the total production of a country at the expense of labour than would otherwise be the case. It is, also, believed that the taxation required to pay the interest and sinking funds, by increasing the cost of production, reacts against the export trade. For the rest, they know the war debts are unjust and they do not like them; but they have a very hazy idea of the effect of government debts on the economic system.

In the first place, nobody can tell what would be the effect of the cessation of distribution of interest by governments; but, at all events, as regards England, it would not be surprising if the *effective demand* were not, thereby, substantially reduced. It is a question of whether the people from whom the money is taken by taxation would *spend* more of it on commodities and services for final consumption and deferred utilisation than those people do, now, who receive it from the Government as interest on the National Debt. It is quite likely that the former would *spend* less of it in order to "save," if it remained in their hands; whilst those to whom it is now distributed by the Government treat it as income and probably *spend* it all. Allowing, however, that the same amount is *spent* on commodities and services in either case, other things equal, the *effective demand* would not be increased by the cessation of the distribution of the interest; and, consequently, there could be no increase in production for the home market, nor could there be any increase for the export trade, for we have seen that this, other things equal, is dependent upon the value of commodities and services imported, without which exports cannot be paid for.

When it comes to a Capital Levy, one may well exclaim: "What! again?"

A Capital Levy took place during the war on all money and bonds or shares of fixed monetary value; for the rise in the price level resulting from monetary inflation was a levy in favour of the State on the value of all such monetary capital, and it was also a levy on wages wherever wages were not rising as fast as prices. Although there is really nothing controversial about this statement, the effect of inflation may, briefly, be described.

Inflation is an *expansion*[22] in the total supply of *cash* and *credit money* unaccompanied by a proportionate increase in the total supply of commodities and services for sale. It can take place as the result of the public being anxious to buy commodities and services for final consumption or deferred utilisation more rapidly than they are being produced and offered for sale, causing rising prices and recourse to bankers for increased supplies of *credit money*; but it is unusual for any perceptible inflation to be caused in this manner. Inflation in the aggravated form we are accustomed to connect with the word is due to government expenditure of money, together with the total expenditure of money by the public, taking place more rapidly than the production and supply offered for sale of commodities and services: and this is due to failure on the part of governments, either to limit adequately their own expenditure of money, or to limit adequately the total expenditure of money by the public by sufficient taxation. If, for the purpose of war or for any other reason, a government wishes to increase its continuous purchases of commodities and services for final consumption and deferred utilisation in such manner that these, together with the continuous purchases of the public, are in excess of continuous production and supply for sale, it can only do so (excluding what can be borrowed from abroad) provided the purchases of the public are correspondingly reduced. A government can reduce the quantity of purchases by the public firstly: by imposing heavier taxation upon it, and secondly: by bidding higher prices for the available commodities and services for sale, paying for them by borrowed money, causing a general recourse to bankers for increased supplies of *credit money*, and supplying any additional *cash* that may be required by bankers to meet their increased obligations to depositors of *credit money*. The latter method is monetary inflation. The rise in prices, however, by diminishing the purchasing power of monetary units, inflicts losses on all holders of, and on all those with claims to, fixed quantities of monetary units. Nevertheless, a large portion of people are able to gain by the rise in prices more or less as much as they lose in the reduced value of any monetary units they hold or have claims to. Speculators for a rise gain by a rise pretty well in proportion to what they stake; and merchants and manufacturers, on the whole, gain more than they lose. Wage-earners usually lose; but they do not necessarily lose, for both their bargaining power and the effectiveness of their labour might, eventually, be increased in the case of an increased volume of trade resulting from a rise in prices. Those who have contracted to pay fixed quantities of monetary units at deferred dates, and whose revenues are derived directly or indirectly from trading commodities and services, are gainers; for, their monetary obligations or debts correspond to a smaller quantity of their stock in trade than before the rise. After a rise in prices, other things equal, the revenue in monetary units obtained by a government from taxation on trade, and the profits on trade, is greater, although the commodity value of this increased monetary revenue remains unchanged; for taxation is only on monetary values irrespective of volume, weight and quality. In effect, therefore, a rise in prices causes the commodity value of government debts to be reduced, whilst, not only it does not necessarily cause any reduction in the commodity value of revenue, but it might cause, by improving trade, an increase in the commodity value of revenue. Hence, inflation does reduce government debt at the expense of certain classes, and may, therefore, be regarded as a levy upon both their capital and income.

In England, when the highest point of inflation after the war had been reached, had the currency been officially divorced or devalued from the supposed gold standard and gradually stabilised with a new gold standard compatible with the gold resources of the country, all would have been well in the matter. The holders of money and fixed interest bearing bonds, however, made a fierce attack, resulting in another Capital Levy that took place towards the end of 1920 and 1921 on all capital in the form of commodities and services for final consumption and deferred utilisation. As a result of the buyers' strike and monetary deflation that took place, a levy was made on all commodity capital in favour of the holders of monetary capital; and by means of this Capital Levy the National Debt was more than doubled in terms of commodities and services by the fall in the price level. Nevertheless, as usual, producers could not, and cannot, pay in commodities and services because the necessary markets are lacking. The quantity of commodities and services required to pay the debt were not, and are not, wanted by those who have the money; and so payment from producers is not acceptable in commodities and services, and the reduced *effective demand* of the victims of the fall in prices renders it still less acceptable in this form. Thus, whilst individuals score at the expense of each other, the State suffers.

How do those who are calling for a Capital Levy want to reduce the Government Debt? Do they admit that the debt is due to be repaid in gold, and do they want to reduce the quantity of gold due by means of a Capital Levy, without altering the present price level of commodities and services? If so, this is impracticable on the face of it. As a considerable part of the Government Debt, as well as other securities on which the levy would be made, are either direct loans from bankers or stand as security for loans from bankers, and, as *every repayment of a loan to a banker destroys a deposit of credit money*, the quantity of capital appropriated in this respect by the levy must proportionately reduce the total quantity of *credit money* and lower, proportionately, the price level. On the other hand, any war loan or bonds, *cash* or *credit money*, taken from the public by the Levy, or in any other way, and not returned to it by Government expenditure on commodities and services will, to a greater or less extent—probably to a proportionate extent—reduce the *effective demand* for commodities and services together with the *effective demand* for bankers' loans; and, therefore, the total quantity of *credit money* will be proportionately reduced and the price level proportionately lowered. It is argued that there would be no deflation because, although the Government would pay its debts by means of the Levy, those to whom the money is paid would use it in trade. This is a fallacy arising from a fallacious idea of the nature of credit. As shown in Chapter VII, effective borrowers for trade or for any other purpose can always borrow; but, so far as trade is concerned, it is only the *effective demand* for commodities and services that creates effective borrowers. The Capital Levy would not create any effective borrowers except those who required to borrow in order to pay the Levy; and such people, whether they borrowed from the Government by getting an extension of time for payment, or whether they were considered good enough for a banker's loan on the usual terms, the moment they repaid the loan, either to the Government or to the bankers, so much *credit money* would be cancelled.

If it is agreed that deflation, to-day, has already gone further than is warranted by the extent of the National Debt, it may also be admitted that the extent of the deflation arising from a Capital Levy of Government gold obligations, and stocks and shares of companies, would be proportionately less severe. That is to say, if the total quantity of *cash* and *credit money* in the country is, to-day, unwarrantably small in relation to the Government's debt to the nation, which would be the case if people are spending money too sparingly in relation to the rate at which they are receiving interest from the Government and earning it, the reduction of the National Debt by means of the Levy would not reduce the *effective demand* for commodities and services and, consequently, the total quantity of *cash* and *credit money*, to a proportionate extent. Probably, owing to the heavy taxation for the purpose of reduction of debt that has been going on together with the normal disposition of the public to spend less than it earns, the *effective demand* to-day is more than abnormally low.

However, nobody can say how a Capital Levy of this class would end; but in any case, if the commodity value of gold is increased as fast as the quantity of gold to the debit of the Government is reduced, where is the advantage? It cannot even be argued that, once the quantity of gold to the debit of the Government is reduced, the commodity value of gold could then be reduced by a rise in prices; because the price level could only be deliberately[23] raised by means of inflation from Government borrowing, in which case the debt would again be increased to an extent proportionate with the degree to which the price level is raised.

Thus, the quantity of gold for which the Government is a debtor can neither be increased nor reduced without altering the price level, probably, to a proportionate extent.

Another way of looking at it is that the Government would not attempt to collect the Capital Levy in money, but would be satisfied to remain, on the one hand, the creditor of those from whom the levy is due, and on the other hand, the debtor of the same people as she is at present. Even this does not stand; for the largest present creditors of the Government would be heavily liable for the Levy, so that the Debt and the Levy would unavoidably cancel in such cases; whilst those who remained debtors of the Government because they could not pay would not be good debtors. Thus, deflation would be mostly unavoidable in respect of those who could pay, and the rest would be virtually in the same position as ordinary taxpayers with an additional tax in respect of the interest on their debt to the government. Nevertheless, *a Capital Levy accompanied by nationalisation of land and railways would enable the State to become the owner of land and railways without altering the National Debt; and, consequently, in these circumstances there would be no deflation or alteration in the price level provided the revenue on the increased capital of the State were used to demand effectively to the same extent as if it had remained in private hands.*

The only other alternative is to treat the debt for what it is, namely: a debt contracted and repayable in a depreciated currency. The matter involves neither higher mathematics nor great accountancy, but is merely a matter of common sense.

The government is supposed to owe a quantity of *gold* ludicrously in excess of the quantity of *gold* that can be paid. Commodities and services cannot be substituted as the means of repayment. If you agree that you owe *more gold than exists*, a whole universe of commodities and services levied on earth and in the heavens would bring you no nearer settling the debt. The only thing to do is to settle on the basis of what quantity of gold the country can pay, and can be reasonably expected to pay. The currency must be officially divorced or devalued from its supposed present gold standard, and freely allowed to find its own level in relation to commodities and services and the dollar. If, as may well be believed, deflation has gone too far in England and Sterling stands much too high in relation to commodities and services and the dollar, the issue must be faced and a rise in the price level must be encouraged by means of inflation. Thus, by a stroke of the pen your Capital Levy is effected right through every kind of capital.[24] The commodity value of the National Debt can be halved by means of a rise in prices in the existing currency; and the depreciation of the currency would bring about an increase in the *effective demand* for commodities and services from both home and foreign markets.

In any case, whether the issue regarding the true value of the currency in relation to the National Debt is faced or not, and regardless of any attempts to put the Debt on a par with the prewar commodity value of gold, it must sooner or later drop to a reasonable value[25] in relation to commodities and services. Either the concentration of gold in America will eventually force down the commodity value of gold with, other things equal, a corresponding rise in the price level of commodities and services all over the world; or the currency in which the Debt is due will depreciate to the extent in which the Government is forced, by an excessively low price level, to meet expenditure by inflation through the partial failure of taxation. Either way, the price level must rise and the National Debt must come to a reasonable level in relation to commodities and services. However hard, and however long, the wriggle, in the end, two and two will be found to make exactly four—meantime the delay is costing lives.

Abolition of the Middleman.—The grievance against the middlemen arises from the fact that both the producer and the consumer covet the profit made by him. The middleman is an essential factor in production. Buying by the wholesale dealer of stocks, some of which he may not, and frequently does not, sell, enables the manufacturer to produce a good variety of supplies in sufficiently large quantities to keep the cost of production low. Buying by the retailer from the wholesaler enables the latter to give the necessary orders to the different manufacturers. If the wholesaler and possibly the retailer are abolished, the new system of distribution would have to charge prices adequate to cover central and local management, transport, rent, insurance, interest and, last but not least, loss on unsaleable stock. Prices would be no lower, but the choice would be much more limited. In fact, if the middleman is unnecessary, why have manufacturers no other arrangements for marketing whereby they could secure his profit for themselves? Further, allowing that economies could be effected, and there is ground for thinking his multiplication and his charges in certain cases excessive, this would cause a reduction in the *effective demand* in proportion to the number of people who thereby became unemployed or emigrated.

It is true that if the profits formerly made by the displaced middlemen are received by producers as additional wages and profits and by consumers in lower prices, the *effective demand* would not necessarily be reduced; nevertheless, under existing conditions, competition would always level the remuneration of producers down to a basis starting from mere subsistence of marginal producers.

Prohibition of Speculation.—Contrary to what is generally believed, speculation tends to minimise fluctuation. Speculation does not include monopolisation or attempts, either successful or unsuccessful, to "corner" any supply.

As a matter of fact, attempts to "corner" a supply by means of speculation are made about "once in a blue moon"; for the odds are heavily against success, the penalty for failure is of the severest kind, and unlimited capital is required. Apart from such attempts to "corner" a supply, prices cannot be deliberately rocked in a direction opposite to that which in the long run is compatible with production and consumption, or, in the case of securities, compatible with intrinsic worth in relation to other securities. It is true that, sometimes, in narrow markets, when buyers and sellers are indisposed to meet each other, it is possible to bluff a few isolated buyers or sellers into paying or accepting unwarrantable prices. A powerful operator wishing to buy on such a market might come in and start selling; and he would not have to sell much, and perhaps not at all, in order to frighten an anxious seller into offering stuff at a lower price. Such cheap stuff would be snapped up immediately, and the next dealing would quickly throw off the effect of the lower prices accepted in these conditions. Of course, anybody with rather a larger book than he feels he can afford to carry can be bluffed, particularly as buyers and sellers are dealing through brokers who do not disclose the names of their principals. A narrow market can be made to look weak or strong by a clever operator. Further, at times when speculators are overloaded one way or another the market is very sensitive to any news, and the jumpy state of the nerves of the operators are reflected by jumpy price fluctuations. These fluctuations, however, are only of a minor sort; they only amount to imaginary variations in bargaining power, and they do not affect the general trend of prices over several months. Neither do they affect the producer or the consumer, for wholesale sellers and wholesale distributors cannot remain in business unless they are very skilful in making good average prices over the longer periods. In fact they are so skilful that they frequently beat the speculator at his own game, picking him up when he makes mistakes. However, it is the endeavour of everybody to operate in a manner compatible with the real facts, for anything else entails losses in the long run.

Aggravation does take place, both in daily fluctuations, and in fluctuations over longer periods; but this is due, not to deliberate manipulations of speculators, but to the fact that traders are afraid to buy on falling markets and sell on rising markets. Everybody knows by experience that, to operate for a reaction too early before the turning point is reached, entails losses. The speculator, however, is forced to exercise better judgment and to act before the wholesale sellers and the wholesale buyers for distribution, otherwise there is no room for him to live on the market; and it is just this enforced earliness of action of the speculator that helps to minimise fluctuations.

The speculator is the man who steps into the breach at times when there is an abnormal excess of commodities and services offered, or an abnormal excess of them demanded effectively. Both in the distribution of raw materials and in the exchange of securities, it frequently occurs that actual holders obstinately refuse to sell when buyers most require to buy, and vice versa. The speculator is the buffer that takes up the pressure from the buyer when the holder of the stock is intractable; and, vice versa, he is the buffer that takes up the pressure from the holder of the stock who is anxious to sell when the buyer is intractable. When the speculator anticipates a particularly heavy supply, he starts selling in blank at buyers' prices sufficiently early to get the stock digested gradually, and thus he prevents the debacle that would occur if the whole supply were held at the normal price until the abnormal quantity came forward in a lump. On the other hand, he anticipates a shortage, and forces a restriction in buying for consumption by buying part of the supply himself sufficiently early to create a reserve to carry the short supply over the required period. Of course, speculators are not always right, and opposite views are continually taken by them; but those who are able to remain in business must be more often right than wrong. Therefore, the anticipations of speculators, collectively, justify their operations which help to minimise fluctuations.

To abolish the Stock Exchange, for instance, would put the sale and purchase of securities on such a basis that genuine buyers would always be forced to pay fancy prices to induce somebody to sell, and genuine sellers would have to accept knock-out prices to induce somebody to buy. Lack of coincidence between genuine buyers and sellers would, in any case, be the cause of wide fluctuations;

whilst, on the Stock Exchange, there is frequently ¼ per cent. difference between sale and purchase prices of stock.

A Commission appointed in the United States to examine the question, reported favourably upon speculation from the point of view of the State.

Secondly, there are those who see the trouble in unemployment. Some of them call for various Credit Schemes and others for Protection and Small Holdings.

Credit Schemes.—Some see the failure of the export trade and unemployment as the result of lack of buying power on the part of the foreigner, and propose government credit for the foreigner to buy home commodities. The British Government did authorise a scheme of this sort, but it was inevitably a failure. Either the foreign borrower is good for the money or he is not, and when the bankers do not think he is good enough they are better judges than the Government. To lend money to the foreigner on anything but bankers' business terms in order to favour the British export trade, simply amounts to taking money out of the pocket of the public and putting it into pockets of British exporters and foreign importers. Mr. Hoover pointed out this fact when American exporters were calling for foreign credits.

Further, whether the foreigner is good for the proposed credits or not, if these credits are in respect of potential increased production in the lending country, why the eagerness to allow the use of it to foreigners rather than utilise it at home?

Credit Schemes in favour of the home trade are also called for; and these are more justifiable than foreign credit schemes because, not only is the *effective demand* increased, but the commodities remain in the country. The weak point about this idea is that good borrowers can always obtain as much credit as they require from the banks, but do not want it unless trade is good. Credit to a private concern for the purpose of production is an absurdity when the *effective demand* at profitable prices is lacking; and no good borrower wants to borrow in such circumstances.

Any *credit money* issued under a credit scheme, whether issued on the understanding that it is to be wholly spent on production or whether issued directly to labour as wages, other things equal, will be proportionately reduced to the extent in which any portion of it comes to rest on deposit in banks or gets into circulation in a stock and share market. It is true that more or less loosely granted credits might stimulate an *expansion* in the *effective demand* for commodities and services causing a corresponding *expansion* in the total supply of *cash* and *credit money*. Under existing conditions, however, this *expansion* could not be maintained for long. Sooner or later substantial portions of the capital and income created by the new prosperity would be absorbed by monopolies raising prices, and this, together with the normal public "saving" policy, would cause production to outrun the *effective demand*. Pressure to sell on glutted markets would then cause a collapse[26] in all values on the security of which the *credit money* had been granted, leaving those to whom it was issued bad debtors of the State, and creating a lien on future production in favour of those who had brought it to a standstill in the banks.

[. . .]

Notes to Part I

1 In a world in which labour-saving machinery were all powerful and the *effective demand* for production at all times equal to production, human lethargy would be a valuable quality for preventing the rapid exhaustion of the world's mineral resources.

2 A government is, at all times, able to put as much paper money into circulation as it likes merely by allowing its expenditure to exceed its revenue; but banks cannot put more paper money into circulation than is called for by the public. This matter is fully discussed later.

3 The quantity theory of money is, here, envolved. This theory is well explained by J. M. Keynes in a *Tract on Monetary Reform*. We are, however, about to refute the idea that seems current among modern monetary experts that the total quantity of money and credit is governed by bankers or that it is possible for them to execute absolute control over it by means of some central national or international banking institution.

4 It will be shown later that the total supply of *credit money*, in fact, varies as the *effective demand*; and, thus, although there can never be a positive deficiency of *credit money* in relation to the *effective demand*, it is wrong to assume that there is not frequently a deficiency of both *credit money* and *effective demand* in relation to production and potential production. It will, further, be shown that the total supply of *cash* sets a limit to the *expansion* of *credit money*; and, consequently, there can be a positive deficiency of *cash* in relation to potential production causing a dragging effect on prices and production. All this will become clearer as we proceed.

5 So far as *cash* is concerned, its rapidity of circulation is also affected by the supply of gold and Paper Money available as *cash*; but, as regards *credit money*, it will be shown later that no more *credit money* exists, at any time, than is being actually used or circulated.

6 As a rule, increased *effective demand* is accompanied by both increased production and by *expansion* in the supply of *credit money*; but on the exceptional occasions when increased *effective demand* and falling prices accompany each other (ref. p. 44), an *expansion* in the supply of *credit money* might be absent in spite of increased production. In this case, as in all cases, if subsequently the *effective demand* fails to keep pace with production the supply of *credit money* will proportionately contract; for, there would be less trade at the same, or lower, prices, together with a reduction in the effective demand for loans by the public. The fact, sometimes disputed, that the *effective demand* frequently fails to keep pace with production, and the exact manner in which this takes place, is fully examined in a later chapter.

7 Commodities and services for final consumption and deferred utilisation.

8 "Spending" is the term commonly used as equivalent to *effective demand* for consumable goods, and "saving" is commonly used as equivalent to *effective demand* for non-consumable or capital goods; but, as is shown, money may be withheld from either of these uses by certain forms of hoarding, and such money is regarded as "saved." This,

however, is ambiguous and inconvenient. For our purpose, money is considered as *spent* regardless of the nature of the commodities and services on which it is spent and regardless of whether they are consumable or capital goods. The real nature of the saving of money is reserved for examination in the next chapter. Our present object is to cut away the belief that the total amount of money *spent*, or the *effective demand*, is equal to production.

9   It is generally taken for granted that the total income earned by production creates an effective demand for an equal quantity of commodities and services in some form or another. Ref. Ch. II.

10   The Bank Rate may be regarded as the best index of the position of the *expansion* of *credit money* in relation to bankers' *cash* reserves. Any Bank Rate under 7 per cent. or 8 per cent. cannot be regarded as indicating anxiety on the part of bankers in this respect. Prior to 1914, the Bank Rate was normally below 5 per cent., it has seldom touched 6 per cent., and during the last 100 years it has only reached 10 per cent. twice, and on these occasions the cause was political.

11   It is necessary to be quite clear that money deposited in banks or circulating in a stock and share market is not *spent* on capital goods instead of consumable goods; and, in fact, is not *spent* at all, and cancels an equivalent quantity of the *credit money* of the producers whose commodities and services it should have been used to purchase. Once this is clear, there can no longer be any room for doubt that both the production of consumptive goods and the production of capital goods are strictly determined by the positive or anticipated *effective demand* for them. Thus, the proportion of consumptive goods produced to capital goods produced automatically adjusts itself in the same manner as the proportions of the quantities of the different kinds of consumptive goods are automatically adjusted, and the proportions of the quantities of the different kinds of capital goods are automatically adjusted, to suit public requirements. It may be that there is a tendency for the idle surplus of the rich to be pressed towards the overproduction of capital goods in relation to the production of consumables; but it is certain that any unwarranted check on the *effective demand* for consumable goods freezes the whole system of production, reducing the employment and value of capital goods. The main thing, therefore, is to ensure that it is physically possible for the total quantity of commodities and services of every kind produced for sale to be marketable as fast as produced without a fall in prices and the monetary losses and congestion thereby involved.

12   Money received and held on deposit by bankers, also money borrowed for the purpose of settling pressing debts or repaying maturing loans, is not *spent*. Nor does the settlement of an old debt or the repayment of a loan necessarily cause more money to be *spent* than would otherwise be the case.

13   Second-hand commodities coming on to the market for sale cause an increase in the total quantity of commodities and services for sale without any corresponding increase in the total quantity of money. Other things equal, therefore, the sale of these second-hand commodities draws off some of the money that has been earned by new production, all of which money is necessary for the marketing of this new production without a fall in prices. Of course, if the money realised from the sale of the second-hand goods is used for the purchase of new ones, this does not apply; but our proposition, here, is that the money is to be used to buy bonds or repay lenders.

14   Sidney Webb, *New Statesman*, May 10, 1913.

15   They cannot use it for investment on capital goods because all the productive power that can be employed to supply the *effective demand* for consumables already exists. They could use it for more luxuries and it would be better if they did—particularly on luxuries for gradual and deferred utilisation.

16   Ref. *Die Wirtschafts Finanz und Sozialreform im Deutchen Reich*. Leipzig, 1882.

17   Ref. *The Great Illusion*, by Norman Angell, for further data.

18   Although a large portion of the gold in America is kept functionless by the Government, and is not allowed to form a basis either for paper money or *credit money*,

it is generally agreed that the present price level in America is higher than pre-war owing to the accumulation of gold there.

19 Ref. Speech Lord Milner, House of Lords, spring 1919.

20 It is true that borrowing from abroad can take place to an extent compatible with the resources of a wealthy ally; but, otherwise, the power to borrow from abroad of the wealthiest countries is limited, particularly when they are at war.

21 A loan from abroad might be justifiable, in certain urgent cases, in order to obtain essential material from abroad which cannot be paid for at once; a loan from abroad, however, other things equal, is unlikely to cause any variation, at home, in the *effective demand* and in the total supply of *cash* and *credit money*, but, should it do so in a manner not proportionate to the total supply of commodities and services for sale, this must be counteracted by a proportionate variation in the national debt.

22 An increase in the total supply of money, when it consists exclusively of an increased quantity of gold, is not regarded as inflation.

23 The public, by increasing its *effective demand* more rapidly than production and supply of commodities and services for sale, could bring about inflation without any Government borrowing. There are no instances, however, of inflation ever having been carried to an appreciable degree in this manner: and there is no reason to suppose that it would occur after deflation resulting from the Capital Levy.

24 J. M. Keynes, in *A Tract on Monetary Reform*, favours a direct levy on all forms of capital in preference to a levy by inflation, on the ground that the former is the scientific method. Whatever the merits of the direct levy, its scientific qualities are by no means striking. Apart from the fact that the valuation of wealth and capital at any time, either at the market price or at the cost price, involves gains or losses according to whether the values of the different forms of property and commodities have gone up or down, the method of valuation could not be carried out with uniformity, and would vary considerably at different places according to the personality of the valuers;—and even in the same localities, the arbitrary fixing of values could not be uniform. The mere likelihood of such a thing being passed into law would bring out sellers and hold back buyers, causing an alteration in values. Considerable evasion would also take place, and the cost would be enormous. The levy by inflation, on the other hand, is only unjustly heavy on those whose capital or income is mainly composed of fixed amounts of money and claims to money. It would be a relatively simple matter to allow such people to prove the quantity of money and claims to money they possessed at the time fixed upon for inflation to commence, and allow them all compensation on a fixed scale.

25 A reasonable commodity value of the National Debt would result from a price level at which the Government is able continuously to meet expenditure without further borrowing and without the rate of taxation being heavy enough to act as a factor towards deflation.

26 The only way to avoid this is by the continuous maintenance of the right volume of *effective demand*, in case of need, by the government. A suggestion for this purpose is outlined in Ch. XV.

Part II
The Final Buyer (1928)

I   Introductory (1927)

Although the major fluctuations in general productive activity, which constitute what is known as the trade cycle, have been the subject of long and careful observation, and although a great deal of knowledge about these variations is now in black and white, the matter is in some ways obscured by certain notions such as periodicity, and those who demand a complete statement of cause and effect must expect to hear much that is conflicting and much that is vague. As for the less obvious or minor fluctuations in general productive activity, one does not hear much about them—except from business men—for academical men do not seem to think that there is any special lesson in these minor fluctuations.

Again, on the theory that depressions not merely follow, but are *caused* by booms, there is a tendency in certain financial as well as academic quarters to look with almost as much disfavour upon the boom parts of these general fluctuations in productive activity as upon the depression parts. Yet even those who completely accept the theory that booms necessarily cause depressions must admit that the irreconcilable enemy lies in the depressions, and that the most they can accuse the booms of is fostering the enemy.

Our inquiry, then, is concerned with the causes of minor and major fluctuations in general productive activity, and in particular with the causes of the depression parts of these fluctuations—which we shall call "general trade depression."

We shall first glance at the theories regarding the causes of general trade depression which singly and in combination constitute special features of the ground it is proposed to work through. In one class may be placed the theories which find the causes of general trade depression on the productive side of business, consisting of (1) theories to the effect that, for one reason or another, enough money is not always available for financing production, and (2) theories which attribute decreased production in general to disproportionate production of particular kinds of goods in relation to each other. In another class may be placed the theories which find the causes of general trade depression on the marketing side of business, consisting of (3) theories to the effect that, for one reason or another, the process of production does not distribute enough money to final buyers[1] for them to buy the product at prices that cover costs plus profits; (4) theories to the effect that the money distributed to final buyers by the process of production is not used by them for taking the right kinds of goods, or enough goods in general, off the market—namely, (*a*) some of the said money is used for excessively increasing the quantity of productive equipment and stocks of goods of all kinds, or (*b*) some of it is entirely withdrawn from circulation; and (5) the theory that general over-production of goods is only possible in relation to the money which final buyers offer in exchange for goods, and that in a barter economy the actual general effective demand, or the actual velocity of final-buying, must always be equal to the actual velocity of production. The following observations must be made on these five kinds of theories:

(1) Without attempting to put the case for those who contend that enough money is not always available for financing production, it must be urged that a country may be fairly said to be suffering from a shortage of money for production when, for instance, its position is as follows: It is operating on a strict gold standard, and its bank credit is fully expanded in relation to its gold supplies. It is a debtor country and has to make regular payments to countries abroad. It cannot make the payments in question without decreasing its gold supplies and incidentally its bank credit, because countries abroad refuse to increase the money value of their imports from it, because it cannot decrease its imports from them without suffering from insufficient raw materials, and because it cannot borrow the required amount of money abroad.[2] At the same time it must be remembered that, even when for any reason there is a decrease in the quantity of money in relation to the quantity of goods and services for sale, there will always be enough money for all productive purposes provided producers and distributors of raw or semi-raw goods are willing promptly to accept proportionately lower money prices, provided workers are willing promptly to accept proportionately lower money wages, and provided buyers are willing promptly to buy at the proportionately lower prices without attempting to squeeze sellers excessively. The trouble is that such amiable and accommodating behaviour on the part of producers, distributors, workers and buyers is not to be expected and is quite impracticable, for more reasons than one.

In the case of the richer countries, we know from experience that there is normally no difficulty for the right kind of business men to arrange for the financing of the right kind of business. Foster and Catchings say that there is never any shortage of money for production;[3] which is true of conditions in the United States since the institution of the Federal Reserve System, and also of conditions in England for many years past.[4]

(2) As regards disproportionate production of particular kinds of goods in relation to each other, it is fairly obvious that a shortage of any particular commodity in general use, whether it (the shortage) is due to human error or design or to elements beyond human control, may cause more or less depression in the particular trades affected, or even more or less general trade depression. For, in the case of a raw material, decreased production must occur in all trades affected by the shortage; and in the case of a commodity in general use, when the shortage causes a rise in the price-level that is resisted by buyers reducing their general purchases, more or less general trade depression will result. It is even more obvious that a glut in the supply of any particular commodity, whatever the cause, will result in more or less depression in the trade or trades engaged in the production of the

commodity in question. At all events, it is beyond controversy that industries in which production has been disprotionately great are, sooner or later and in one way or another, checked until the production of other kinds of goods catches up.

Owing to the impossibility of knowing in advance either to what extent harvests are going to be affected by such things as weather conditions and insects, or to what extent final buying is going to be affected by such things as politics and fashions, Disproportionate Production is an evil which one must not expect to banish entirely. But it is an evil which business men, by means of increased equipment and financial facilities for storing stocks of goods, by means of more numerous and wider option markets whereby producers and distributors can freely hedge against price fluctuations, and by means of efforts to eliminate the wilder kinds of competition, have got well in hand.

However, Disproportionate Production is quite frequently put forward by the economist to explain not only depression in particular trades, but also general trade depression; and if recently his pretensions in this respect have been more reasonable, it is only because he has been very busy—perhaps at the instance of the cartelist, eager either to restrict or to "rationalize" production—in the arraignment of certain malefactors,[5] to wit, Import and Export Barriers and Restrictions, which amongst their other offences are impediments to the satisfaction of the international desires of the cartelist. Anyhow, one may well be tempted to regard Disproportionate Production as the over-worked general servant of the economist, as well as the friend used by the cartelist to justify cartelization.

The fact is that enough distinction is not made between, on the one hand, Disproportionate Production, and, on the other, the far worse evil of maladjustment between the velocity of final-buying and the velocity of production—the evil of maladjustment between aggregate final-buying of all goods and services in general and aggregate production of all goods and services in general—of final buyers as a whole, either pressing to buy goods and services in general faster than producers and workers are willing and able to produce, or refusing to buy goods and services in general as fast as producers and workers are willing and able to produce—of inflation and all its consequences when final buyers are too active, or deflation and resistance to lower prices when they are too passive. Although this maladjustment between the velocity of final-buying and the velocity of production may sometimes be started by Disproportionate Production, the two are quite distinct economic occurrences. At all events a sharp distinction is, here, made between them, for, leaving Disproportionate Production to business men and others, we shall concentrate on the said general maladjustment, which—it is here urged—constitutes the primary problem.

Before we go on to the remaining three of the five kinds of theories named a few pages back regarding the causes of general trade depression—the three concerned with the marketing side of business or the different aspects of the question of an inadequate velocity of final-buying—it is desirable that some further observations be made on this all-important subject of adjustment and maladjustment between the velocity of final-buying and the velocity of production.

Since practically everything produced is sooner or later sold to final buyers, the following must be true in the case of a self-contained area: the *average* velocity of final-buying is equal to the *average* velocity of production; the *actual* velocity of final-buying at a time when stocks of goods are being increased is less than the *actual* velocity of production; and the *actual* velocity of final-buying at a time when stocks of goods are being decreased is greater than the *actual* velocity of production. In short, the velocities of production and final-buying, acting and reacting on each other and on stocks of goods, fluctuate freely in relation to each other above and below the same *average* velocity. The mode and extent of this action and reaction are considered later; but it is urged here that, whatever the possibilities of productive resources—the natural resources of the earth, the natural and acquired desires and capabilities of mankind, and the quantity and kinds of productive equipment—no production takes place without incentives, and that incentives to production only build up in the modern economic system through final-buying. In these circumstances, an inquiry into the question of adjustment or maladjustment between the velocity of final-buying and the velocity of production does not involve an inquiry into productive possibilities, nor yet into the extent of ready productive capacity at any time. Thus, our particular object is to examine the variations in the velocity of final-buying, and to ascertain the nature, causes and effects of both an excessive, and an inadequate, velocity of final-buying—especially the causes of an inadequate velocity of final-buying and the checks thus administered to the velocity of production.

For those who know what is going on in the business world it requires little effort to see that neither an excessive velocity of final-buying nor attempts to increase it excessively are frequent occurrences, that the cause of any such actual or attempted excessive general final-buying is almost invariably a war or catastrophe, and that the effects are currency depreciation. But when it comes to the question of an inadequate velocity of final-buying—which, it is here urged, is what produces and workers have to contend with more often than not—all kinds of considerations of the most difficult order are involved.

Let us now proceed with the three kinds of theories regarding the causes of general trade depression on the marketing side of business:

(3) The contention that the process of production does not distribute enough money to final buyers for them to buy the product at prices which cover costs plus profits, is one which will be identified with the name of Major Douglas,[6] and, although it has many adherents, including, notably, Messrs. Foster and Catchings,[7] it does not stand inspection.

Notwithstanding all these gentlemen say, the fact remains that the process of production (and bringing to market) causes producers and distributors to disburse wages, rent, interest, the cost of materials, *and the amount of their own personal expenses*, in money *before* the goods they produce and handle come to market, and regardless of whether the goods in question are sold or not, whether the producers and distributors in question are making profits or losses, or whether their outlay and disbursements of money are effected by means of loans from bankers or by means of their own cash in hand and bank balances. It is, in fact, the money disbursed for the personal expenses of producers and distributors to-day which, other things being equal, corresponds as a whole to their money profits of to-morrow. Thus, when total output of goods and services declines in relation to total money disbursements by producers and distributors, they must in the aggregate sell at higher money prices, to obviate their total money disbursements exceeding their total money receipts; and, vice versa, when total output of goods and services increases in relation to total money disbursements by producers and distributors, they can in the aggregate sell at lower money prices without causing their total money disbursements to exceed their total money receipts. The total quantity of money, therefore, disbursed by producers and distributors for both their businesses and their private purposes is always enough to enable final buyers to buy all the goods and services produced—and to buy them at prices which in the aggregate are high enough to render the total money receipts of producers and distributors greater than their total business disbursements. But—here is the rub—final buyers, although able, may be far from willing to buy enough in quantity and to pay high enough prices.

The truth is that frequently—particularly at a time when the actual or potential productive output per unit of labour is, for any reason, increasing—buyers are not disposed to buy adequately at adequate prices for the total money receipts of producers and distributors to exceed their total business disbursements; and that final buyers of durable kinds of equipment prefer to wait, if they can, whenever there is any prospect, for one reason or another, of prices being stabilized at a lower level.

(4a) For years past J. A. Hobson, starting from the basis that purchasing power is equal to production, and assuming that in a modern State the hoarding of money may be regarded as negligible, has urged that, when money income is not used for the final-buying of consumable goods, it is directly or indirectly invested or caused to be invested by the savers in increased productive equipment and stocks of goods; and that, thus, the practice of saving, carried beyond certain limits, causes over-production of the said equipment, and creation of excessively large stocks of goods, in relation to consumption.

The influence of Hobson in this respect is more or less pronounced in quite a few after-war works on the subject, and it is, perhaps, of particular interest to note the line taken by P. W. Martin, and endorsed by Foster and Catchings. Mr. Martin writes:

> "Provided that industry distributes in wages, dividends, etc., as much as it charges in prices, and provided that these wages and dividends are all used to pay these prices, obviously everything that is made will be bought. But if part of this purchasing power is used *not to buy goods but to induce the production of more goods*, it is obvious that more goods will be produced than there is purchasing power available to buy them."[8]

He, in fact, urges, *first*, that industry does not distribute in wages and dividends as much as it charges in prices, and, *second*, that even what is distributed in wages and dividends is not all used for final-buying,[9] some of it being used to induce the production of more goods. Messers. Foster and Catchings bring an impressive volume of statistical evidence to show the large proportion of profits that are not distributed in dividends, and are converted into reserve funds or used as working capital for increased production, by businesses in the United States.[10] Without going into the ways in which this theme is developed by the respective writers, it is worth noting that they appear to start off with the Hobsonian theory already referred to—namely, that when money income is not used for the final-buying of consumable goods, it is directly or indirectly invested or caused to be invested by the savers in increased productive equipment and stocks of goods.

Whilst we must fully agree that frequently the velocity of production is greater than the velocity of final-buying, due to insufficient general final-buying by the recipients of wages, rent, interest and profits, we must carefully note that, at a time when ample quantities of equipment and stocks of goods are known to exist, producers and distributors as a whole do not borrow or use part of their profits to finance increased production, and, far from increasing their output, they reduce it. What, then, is done with the money?

(4b) It must be emphasised that under-consumption and insufficient general final-buying do not "induce the production of more goods," but cause decreased production, together with both a decrease in the volume of bank loans for financing production and a decrease in the quantity of money distributed to final buyers by producers. It must be urged, in fact, that, *at a time when ready productive capacity is not fully engaged*, holding money income on deposit in banks instead of using it for final-buying is virtually hoarding it, in that such behaviour at such a time causes a decrease, and not an increase, in both the velocity of production and the quantity of money.

(5) Although we may agree that the existence of money readily renders possible a general over-production of goods in relation to the money which consumers offer in exchange for goods, we cannot agree that, in a barter economy, the actual general effective demand, or the actual velocity of final-buying, at any time must necessarily be equal to the actual velocity of production.

The crux of the whole question is to be found in how wealth and income are distributed and how they are employed by the owners or recipients. If the aggregate wealth and the aggregate income, either in money or in goods, of some people are greater than what they are employing for their own consumption or use, they must either lend the excess to others, or they must maintain or store it themselves. But there is a limit to the quantity of money or goods that can be safely and profitably lent; and, as a matter of fact, the number of reliable borrowers will decrease as the result of excessive abstinence on the part of the lenders, particularly if the latter decline either to buy goods or to accept payments in kind. Thus, as the result of excessive abstinence, a time must sooner or later come when unused equipment, stocks of goods of every kind and money (where money is in use), in the hands of lenders, savers and capitalists reach the maximum that can be maintained without excessive losses in respect of deterioration and excessive costs in respect of warehousing. When this happens, the lenders, savers and capitalists will shun the maintenance and storage of all those kinds of goods that can be freely and abundantly produced, particularly the more perishable kinds; and they will seek to exchange all such kinds of goods they have to spare for kinds of goods that are most limited in quantity by nature, most durable and most easily handled. In these circumstances, where a barter economy exists, the entry of a money economy is observable, the scarce, durable and easily handled goods constituting the money; and, at all events, there will be a fall in market values of perishable and plentiful goods in relation to scarce, durable and easily handled goods, and production will be curtailed in most trades. Thus, barter economy or not, once all land, equipment, stocks of goods and money (where money is in use) belong to fewer people than are willing to employ, utilize or consume them all, and incidentally all reliable borrowers have ceased borrowing, the services of a certain number of workers will be dispensed with until, somehow, the situation alters.

In effect, then, we cannot be satisfied with all that is said about (1) shortage of money for production, (2) disproportionate production of different kinds of goods, (3) failure of the process of production to distribute enough money to final buyers, (4a) over-production of productive equipment and stocks of goods in relation to consumption, and (5) the special merits of a barter economy as regards the relationship of final-buying to production. As a matter of fact, no complete understanding of the nature and importance of any of the above questions is possible without reference to the different aspects of the theory (4b) that large amounts of money distributed to final buyers by the process of production are, in certain circumstances and in effect, not used for the final-buying of anything at all, but entirely withdrawn from circulation. In a word, if it is a fact that final buyers can at any time—and frequently do, voluntarily and deliberately—decrease the velocity of final-buying in relation to the velocity of production, and if it is a fact that such a decrease in the velocity of final-buying sooner or later entails a corresponding decrease in the velocity of production, this would account for general trade depression at a time when materials, equipment and labour are plentiful.

Anybody looking for employment, whether ordinary, humble and content just to live, or capable, energetic and ambitious, may spend weeks, months, and even years, hearing that trade is slack and that employers are over-equipped and over-staffed for the business they have to do. And anybody, whether dependent upon employment or the owner of a business, may reasonably come to the conclusion that, although both the resources of the earth and the possibilities of productive equipment are far from fully developed, and although too often there are large quantities of food, materials and productive equipment awaiting consumption and utilization—immobilized only by absence of buyers—vast potentialities in men and women are continuously being stifled by lack of opportunity. To those who, before the World War, vaguely suspected that there must be something artificial rather than inevitable about these conditions, the magnitude of war-productive achievement, and the marvellous manner in which young and old quickly rose to the occasion in skill and sense of responsibility, came as practical confirmation.

The same conclusion is suggested by observation of the process of deflation in England and the United States from the autumn of 1920 to about the end of 1921. In those days of abundant quantities of goods pressing on glutted markets, the cry was for lower prices, lower money wages and economy. In spite of the fact that every fall in the money earnings of capital and labour correspondingly reduced the quantity of money in the hands of final buyers, and that the fear or expectation of still lower price-levels retarded and reduced production, it was blindly[11] urged that lower prices were necessary to make it possible to sell a larger quantity of goods. And the anxious calls for economy to be heard on all sides sounded strange whilst the war-time performance of women, children, and men unfit for military service was still fresh in the memory, and whilst the mind was still in wonder at the quantity of equipment which was then produced and utilized and the quantities of goods which were consumed by civilians and soldiers, destroyed in the battle-fields and lost at sea. On the other hand, in France, Germany and Italy, where the cry for lower prices, lower money wages and economy was drowned by noises of another kind, and where inflation was present and in some cases ran amuck, there was at all events no general trade depression, and on the whole production, con-sumption, and utilization of both consumable goods and equipment surpassed all records. But all nations have, for one reason or another, since joined in the game of deflation more or less fiercely, and one may have observed everywhere decreased final-buying forcing down prices, piling up the commodity values of public debts, and causing production to wane; whilst the way in which conflicts between capitalists and workers, and confused economic convictions, have been dragging down the standard of living of certain classes is alarming and mortifying.

Part I. consists of an inquiry into the causes and effects of maladjustment between the velocity of final-buying and the velocity of production, in which an attempt is made to outline briefly the essential features of all the elements of the subject, to show the relation of each to the whole, and to indicate the kinds of control exerted and capable of being exerted by the human factor at the different points. Part II. consists of a series of essays on current economic problems,[12] the object of which is partly to illustrate and amplify, and partly to corroborate, the principles set out in Part I. A few of the terms used are innovations, and a certain number are mutually exclusive, but they all—it is hoped—readily suggest their meaning; and at all events there are notes on their use at the end of the book to which the reader can refer.

After examining the monetary system, the purchasing power of final buyers, the nature and effects of saving, and the different kinds of final buyers and their behaviour, we arrive at the following principal conclusions:

That the possibilities of monetary technique are such that there is no insuper-able reason why the velocity of production should ever be held back by a shortage of money.

That, when money is placed or held on deposit in banks instead of being used for final-buying, the final-buying thus omitted by the owners of the money is not necessarily replaced by increased final-buying by borrowers; for the effective demand for loans for financing new productive equipment and stocks of goods tends to vary as the extent of final-buying by the recipients of money income and the owners of money capital.

That maladjustment between the velocity of final-buying and the velocity of production is aggravated as often as it is neutralized by variations in the extent of final-buying of governments, and by variations in the extent of final-buying resulting from the activities of producers and distributors. That the extent of final-buying by countries abroad from the home country, contrary to all hopes, must be expected to decrease and aggravate, as often as it increases and neutralizes, an inadequate home velocity of final-buying; because, amongst other things, international payments and movements of money always have it their own way either with price-levels or with foreign-exchange rates, and always have it their own way with foreign trade balances,[13] quite regardless of import and export restrictions and barriers. That, in these circumstances, continuous minor and major maladjustments between the velocity of final-buying and the velocity of production are to be expected.

And, in connection with individual, national and international debts, that, subject to no effective intervention by governments, those able to buy can as a whole at any time bring about either more or less inflation or more or less deflation. In fact, they can bring about a state of affairs in which the effective demand for goods and services is of a frenzied order, and in which the bond-holder goes to the wall; or, on the other hand, by means of excessive abstinence and insufficient final-buying, they can hold the great possibilities of our time down to a paltry level, and enable the bond-holder idly to profit by the desperate competition to sell goods and services which these conditions impose upon producers and workers.

Finally, we find that, not only does the velocity of final-buying largely determine the proportion in which the product of industry is divided between those actively engaged in industry on the one hand, and bond-holders on the other, but it also largely determines all economic positions between the extremes of inflation and deflation. For prices, the quantity and nature of goods produced, employment of labour, the volume of bankers' investments and loans, together with the quantity of money, the quantity and nature of foreign investments, the nature and effects of international debt settlements and other international payments, and the foreign exchange value of currencies, all turn on how the multitude of large and small final buyers settle the question: *to buy or not to buy?*

Perhaps somewhere between the extremes of inflation and deflation a position exists in which creative and productive energy displaces gold as the economic god! Who knows? But at all events it is certain that, if general trade depression is to be eliminated, intelligent regulation of the velocity of final-buying is indispensable.

II The potential supply of money

Money may be divided into two classes: (1) Cash and (2) Credit Money.

1 Cash

Cash consists of gold and silver coin and bullion and all forms of metallic or paper money that are legal tender.

i *Gold and silver coin and bullion*

The total quantity of gold and silver in the world used as cash varies to the extent that new metal comes from the mines, and to the extent that more or less of it is used for commercial purposes or hoarded by individuals, but such variations are relatively small, and usually gradual.

The quantity of gold and silver[14] used as money in a particular country is governed, as we shall see in later chapters, by its monetary policy, its foreign trade balances, and inward and outward transfers of money income and money capital.

ii *Paper money*

All forms of banknotes—whether legal tender or not—and currency notes are usually called paper money. But the quantity of paper money that is not legal tender is nowadays negligible in the more advanced countries. Legal-tender paper money may be issued in respect of and against gold or standard metal held by the issuing institution, or against only a partial or even no backing of this kind—any quantity of it so issued in excess of or without a standard metal backing being, as a rule, backed by government securities or first-class bonds of some kind, and being known as the fiduciary issue. However, whenever anything—no matter how valuable and safe—other than the standard metal is used as a backing for the issue of legal-tender paper money, additional cash is created. Such additional cash will be referred to in this volume as "fiduciary paper money," and the general term "paper money," being usually too vague for our purpose, will be avoided.

Although banknotes which are not legal tender may be classed as a kind of credit money, fiduciary paper money which is legal tender functions for the internal purposes of a country in the same manner as cash in gold, and, as we shall see in Chapter XIV, neither its internal commodity value nor its value on the foreign exchange market depreciates when the supply of it is properly regulated in relation to production of goods and services.

With few exceptions, the issue of fiduciary paper money in any country takes place through a bank, usually the national or central bank, which only pays it out on demand to its depositors or to people who are entitled to demand cash payments from it. In other words, the public, the clearing banks and the government can only obtain fiduciary paper money either by drawing against deposits that they have at the central bank, or by borrowing money from it.

In no case can the total quantity of cash, whether gold or fiduciary paper money, demanded of the central or issuing bank exceed the total deposits in its books; and as these deposits originate from gold that has been either deposited with it or bought by it, and from its own investments and loans, it can limit the total deposits in its books in excess of gold held by it, and incidentally the total quantity of fiduciary paper money that it may be called upon to issue, by limiting its own investments and loans. In this way the central or issuing bank is able to limit the issue of fiduciary paper money to any maximum decided upon.

It is true that, when additional supplies of fiduciary paper money are available without difficulty from the government, the public may become abnormally anxious to obtain loans from bankers to buy goods and services and foreign currencies, and the bankers not only may lend more freely than is justified by the velocity of production, but may also themselves unduly enlarge their investments and holdings of foreign currencies. Further, the central or issuing bank cannot usually, in practice, refuse loans to the government, and when such loans create demands for cash which cannot be met without exceeding the existing legal maximum issue of fiduciary paper money, the legal maximum must be raised by the government. Nevertheless, neither the public nor the government can cause an expansion in the quantity of fiduciary paper money without the co-operation of the bank that may be entrusted with its sole issue.

iii *Reserves*

This is the name given by bankers to their cash in hand and the money that they hold on demand or time deposit at the central bank, and sometimes at other banks. A distinction must, however, be made between a banker's cash in hand and amounts of money held to his credit in another bank—which latter are called his "balances with other banks."

The point to be noted is that although balances held by a banker in other banks figure as reserves in his own books, they figure as deposits in the books of the other banks, and deposits may only consist of cash in part. Reserves consisting of balances with other banks, in fact, originate in the same manner as deposits, as will be seen when we come to consider the nature of credit money.

iv *The power of bankers over variations in the quantity of cash in their hands*

All the banks in the world can only increase the total quantity of cash in their hands simultaneously, either by inducing the public to retain less cash outside the banks, or by obtaining the permission or assistance of governments to increase the issue of fiduciary paper money. All the banks in one country, however, can simultaneously increase the total quantity of cash in their hands, not only by inducing the public to deposit more cash in the banks and by increasing or obtaining an increase in the issue of fiduciary paper money, but also by borrowing gold from abroad. Whilst, in the case of a single bank, in addition to all the preceding means of obtaining increased supplies of cash, it can borrow from other banks, and also it can obtain cash from other banks to the extent that it can obtain depositors and deposits.

It is important to remark that, although the mode of obtaining the use of cash by means of depositors is scarcely within the control of the bank itself, it is, from a banker's point of view, by far the most profitable and the best. In the first place, it is much the cheapest way in which a banker's cash supplies are obtained. In the second place, without depositors a banker neither possesses the power to create credit nor can he profit by the creation of credit by other bankers. For a loan granted by a banker who has no depositors can only be a simple payment out of his own cash resources, whilst investments and loans made by other bankers bring no cash his way. But when a banker has depositors, investments and loans made by him frequently involve, directly or indirectly, payments to his own depositors, which cause little or no loss to his cash resources; whilst money in respect of investments and loans made by other bankers is frequently paid to his depositors, and to that extent both the deposits in his books and his cash resources are increased. However, this will be made clearer in the next few pages on credit money and the process by which it is created.

2 Credit money

i *Deposits*

The money which stands in the books of a bank to the credit of its clients is called its deposits, and the excess of total bankers' deposits over the total quantity of cash in their hands we shall call "credit money."

The minimum proportion of reserves to deposits which bankers maintain is fixed by law in some countries, and in others it is a matter of convention amongst the bankers themselves. In England it is customary for the clearing banks to maintain the proportion of their reserves to the deposits in their books at not less than 10 per cent. But, as a substantial part of their reserves consist of balances with the Bank of England—where they figure as deposits—and as the proportion of cash to deposits maintained by the Bank of England has in recent years varied widely around 25 per cent., the proportion of the total quantity of cash held by the whole banking system in England to its total deposits is always considerably less than

10 per cent. However, no pretence is made anywhere that bankers' deposits represent the quantity of cash either in the banks or in existence. Bankers' deposits, in fact, mainly consist of credit money, and are built up partly with cash, but mainly as the result of the creation of credit by the bankers themselves when they make investments and loans. For illustration, below is a representative combined balance sheet of the liabilities and assets of the ten London clearing banks, with deposits reduced to 100 and the other items in percentages of deposits to the nearest integer.

Liabilities.		*Assets.*	
Capital, etc. . . .	8	Cash on hand and balances	
Deposits and Acceptances	100	with Bank of England.	12
		Money in transit and at	
		call	11
		Investments . . .	17
		Loans	68
	108		108

Let us glance at the way in which credits become deposits. It is when bankers make either investments or loans, and provided the money is sooner or later deposited with them, that they create deposits of credit money. The first effect of a banker making an investment or a loan is to cause his assets in respect of the said items to be increased, and in respect of reserves to be decreased, by the amount in question—but his total assets remain unaltered and his liabilities entirely unaffected. The money, however, if it is drawn out of this bank, is, usually, almost immediately paid by the recipients or sub-recipients into the same or other banks; and both the liabilities in respect of deposits and the assets in respect of reserves of the bank or banks where the money eventually remains on deposit are increased by the amount in question. In effect, the monetary position after an investment or a loan made by a banker is as follows:

First, the total quantity of bank reserves remains unaltered by the transfer of reserves from one bank to another.

Second, the deposits in the books of a banker, being his liabilities, are not affected by any reserves he pays away in respect of investments or loans made by him; whilst his assets are not affected as to quantity, but only as to class, investments and loans increasing to the extent that reserves are decreased.

Third, when, after a banker has made an investment or loan, the money in question is at once deposited with him, his reserves remain unaltered whilst the newly-created investments or loans appear and figure as assets, and the newly-created deposits appear and figure as liabilities, in his books. But when the money in question is sooner or later deposited with other banks, to that extent his reserves are decreased and the reserves of the other banks increased, whilst the creation of additional investments and loans in his books (assets which take the place of his lost reserves) is followed by the creation of additional deposits in the books of the other banks (liabilities which offset their newly-obtained reserves).

Fourth, to the extent that the public as a whole retains outside the banks any money paid to it by bankers in respect of investments or loans made by them, the creation of deposits of credit money is to that extent prevented. But the public does not normally behave in this manner to any appreciable extent, and, whenever there is any tendency for such a thing to happen, the bankers at once restrict their investments and loans and do what they can to attract deposits of cash from the public.

Thus, investments and loans made by bankers create deposits, and, conversely, it may be shown that the liquidation of investments and loans by bankers reduces deposits. In principle, therefore, it may be said that every investment or loan made by a banker creates a deposit, and every liquidation of an investment or a loan destroys a deposit.

ii *The capacity of bankers to create credit money*

First, an ordinary deposit bank or clearing bank cannot make investments and loans relatively more freely than the other competing banks, for if it attempts to do so its reserves start draining out into the other banks. It is inevitable that, whatever the total volume of bankers' investments and loans being made in relation to total bankers' reserves at any time, all the competing banks must adhere to about the same proportion, for only on this condition are the reserves paid away by each bank replaced in each bank. But, apart from laws or customs regulating reserves, the competing banks can, together, greatly increase the proportion of their investments and loans to their reserves—and, thereby, reduce the proportion of their reserves to their deposits—without imperilling their ability to meet the cash demands of the public upon them.

Second, where there is a central or national bank in which a large quantity of the reserves of the deposit banks are held, it normally controls the proportion of the total quantity of cash to total deposits in the banking system of the country— and it is in the best of positions to do so. A central bank, like a deposit bank, creates deposits of credit money every time it makes an investment or a loan, but, unlike a deposit bank, it hardly ever parts with any substantial quantity of reserves as the result. An investment or a loan made by a deposit bank, as we have seen, frequently creates deposits in the books of other banks, and it has to transfer reserves to these other banks. But an investment or a loan made by a central bank almost invariably creates a deposit in its own books; for, whether the money is kept on deposit at the central bank by the recipients or whether they pay it into other banks, it almost invariably ends up as deposits to the credit of bankers or others in the books of the central bank. Deposits of credit money so created by the central bank, and standing in its books to the credit of the deposit banks, constitute reserves for the said deposit banks which they can use as a basis for making investments and loans, and incidentally, further deposits of credit money. Vice versa, the liquidation by the central bank of investments and loans made by it destroys deposits in its own books to about the same extent, and reduces the capacity of the deposit banks to create credit money to a much greater extent.

Third, the capacity of a whole banking system to create credit money only ends when the proportion of total deposits to total reserves of all the banks taken together—including the central bank—is up to the maximum permitted by the law or custom of the country; or when the power of the banks to increase their reserves, either by attracting cash from the public, borrowing gold or gold currencies from abroad, or obtaining paper money or the right to issue paper money from the government, is exhausted. Taking into consideration possibilities in connection with the issue of fiduciary paper money, and the fact that government policy and action in this respect are largely determined by banking influence, the capacity of a whole banking system to create credit money is at all times more or less vast, and is, subject to government co-operation, in the last resort only limited by the question of currency depreciation.[15]

It is just the question of currency appreciation and depreciation which is the crucial one in monetary technique, but it must be left for later chapters. For the moment all that is attempted is to ascertain the capacity of bankers to supply monetary units, and to show that there is no insuperable reason why the monetary instrument should ever hold back the velocity of production, either directly through a shortage of money for production, or indirectly by causing the velocity of final-buying to lag behind the velocity of production or behind ready productive capacity.

Note

The expressions: *cash, fiduciary paper money, bankers' balances with other banks, reserves*, and *deposits*, used in this chapter, are placed, with their meanings, in the notes on the use of terms at the end of the book [see end of Part II] for reference at any time.

III The quantity of money

The total quantity of money at any time consists of the total quantity of cash that is in the hands of the public outside the banks plus the total deposits of cash and credit money with the banks. The overwhelming proportions of the quantity of credit money in relation to the quantity of cash in the advanced countries must be emphasized. In England, for instance, as already shown, only about 12 per cent of the deposit of the clearing banks consists of reserves, and of these reserves only a part consists of cash, the other part being merely deposits of credit money at the Bank of England.

1 Determining factors of the quantity of money

Although, as we have seen, it is possible for the quantity of cash to vary vastly, normally this does not occur. But taking the quantity of cash as constant, the total quantity of money still varies vastly, according to how much of the total quantity of cash is held in the banks, and according to the proportion that the total quantity of cash held in the banks bears to total deposits. It must not be assumed, however, that the greater the proportion of the total quantity of cash held in the banks to the total quantity held outside, the greater is the total quantity of deposits. When trade is good, for instance, we usually find that the public requires more cash for hand-to-hand circulation, which is therefore drawn out of the banks; but, at the same time, we must expect to find the total quantity of deposits also increasing. In other words, whilst deposits of cash with the banks decrease to the extent that cash is withdrawn by the public, investments and loans may increase to such an extent that deposits of credit money may increase more than reserves decrease. We must therefore inquire to what extent the total quantity of money is governed by the quantity of cash held in the banks, and to what extent it is governed by the condition of industry and trade.

It is the business of bankers to maintain their investments and loans as large as possible, possibilities in this respect being limited, on the one hand, by the absolute or technical limits to their reserves, and, on the other, by the limits to the possibilities of making safe and profitable investments and loans, or sometimes even by considerations regarding obviating currency depreciation. But whilst, as already indicated, the question of reserves is largely a question of monetary technique, and, subject to government cooperation, presents no insuperable impediment to an unlimited volume of bankers' investments and loans and an unlimited expansion in the quantity of credit money, we shall see that the quantity of credit money that can be put into investments and loans by bankers, both profitably to them and without currency depreciation, is always strictly limited by conditions arising from the behaviour of the public and the government of the country.

Setting aside for the moment the question of currency depreciation, certain prominent monetary experts urge: first, that bankers can inject into, or withdraw from, circulation as much credit money as they like by buying or selling securities;[16] and second, that they can increase or decrease to any desired extent the total volume of bank loans outstanding by altering interest rates. As a matter of fact, apart from the large amount of discussion which has taken place in most countries on the subject, in 1926 a bill was introduced in the United States advocating that the powers of the Federal Reserve System should be used for this purpose. But Governor Benjamin Strong, of the New York Federal Reserve Bank, testifying on the bill before the House Committee, indicated his doubts that it would accomplish the stabilization sought, and stated that it charged the Federal Reserve banks with a duty which on occasions may be beyond their power. Whilst agreeing entirely with Governor Strong's view of the matter, it is necessary for us to ascertain the extent of the power of bankers over variations in the volume of their investments and loans, and incidentally over the quantity of credit money.

2 The volume of bankers' investments

It is beyond controversy that the effect of bankers buying securities from the public is to inject credit money into circulation; and that the sale of securities to the public by bankers has the opposite effect.

When bankers are buying securities from the public their balance sheets together show, as regards assets, increases in the quantity of securities held, and, as regards liabilities, increases in deposits in respect of the money due to the public for the securities bought from the latter. Meantime, the resulting rise in the market prices of securities by reason of the injection of bankers' credit money into the market, other things being equal, is usually accompanied by increased final-buying of goods and services on the part of those who are profiting by the rising prices of the securities; and thus more or less additional credit money gets into circulation in industry. Nevertheless, any of the recipients of this new credit money may refuse to keep it in circulation by simply placing it on deposit instead of using it for buying;[17] and investors and stock exchange operators may start profit-taking on securities. In these circumstances, a general fall in both security and commodity prices may take place, causing money losses to bankers and others left with securities and stocks of goods bought at higher prices. The bankers might prevent this, or even cause a rise in prices, by buying in all markets to a sufficient extent, keeping it up until the public, giving up hope of lower prices, or even expecting or fearing progressive inflation, reverses its profit-taking or waiting policy and joins in the buying movement. Such measures, however, even when supported by easy credit conditions and when neutral behaviour on the part of the government can be counted upon, might not force or tempt the public to increase the velocity of final-buying at a time when stocks of goods are increasing—and stocks of goods would be increasing when prices were being maintained by the buying of bankers. At all events, such a policy would be too dangerous and too much for bankers to embark upon.

Vice versa, although bankers, other things being equal, can contract the quantity of credit money by selling securities to the public, they soon must reverse the whole proceeding by buying back the securities before the public starts to pick them up at the lower prices, unless they are prepared to throw their full weight into an extensive deflationary policy, consisting of raising interest rates, restricting credit for development work, and calling in loans on securities, property and stocks of goods. Even then, if the government at once reduced taxation and insisted on obtaining bank credits for the purpose of increased expenditure on the State's services or on development work, they (the bankers) might fail both to contract the quantity of credit money and to recover without loss the securities they had sold.

Thus, whatever the power of bankers as a whole to increase or decrease the quantity of credit money, their policy as regards buying or selling securities cannot be governed, even if it may be influenced, by considerations relating to the desirability of varying the quantity of credit money circulating in industry.

3 The volume of bank loans

The volume of bank loans, standing as it usually does in England in the region of about four times the volume of bankers' investments, six times the volume of money at call and in transit, and six times the volume of reserves, is by far the most predominant element in the quantity of money.

We are about to deal with the suggestion, referred to a few pages back, that the effective demand for loans, together with the volume of bank loans, could be regulated by an arrangement amongst bankers whereby the rate of interest for loans is lowered or raised according to whether it is desired to increase or decrease the quantity of loans outstanding. We shall therefore examine: (i) the causes of variations in interest rates, (ii) the power of bankers over interest rates, and (iii) the power of bankers over the volume of bank loans.

i *The causes of variations in interest rates*

It is more or less axiomatic that variations in interest rates are governed by the supply of loanable money and the effective demand for loans. The conclusions reached in the preceding chapter on the sources of cash supplies and the way in which they determine the lending capacity of bankers, therefore, enable us to enumerate the causes of variations in interest rates, which are as follows:

First, variations in interest rates may be caused by variations in the quantity of gold in the world used as money. Such variations are relatively too small to have any appreciable effect except in the unusual cases when important supplies of gold are coming forward from new sources.

Second, variations in interest rates may be caused by variations in the quantity of fiduciary paper money available. Such variations are also unusual.

Third, variations in interest rates may be caused by variations in the quantity of gold for monetary purposes in a particular country, due either to variations in its foreign trade balance, or to variations in the general yield of money employed abroad.

Fourth, variations in interest rates may be caused by variations in bankers' standard for the proportion of reserves to be held by them in relation to deposits in their books; for when the standard is raised it causes an increase in bankers' cash requirements and a decrease in their lending capacity, and, vice versa, when the standard is lowered it decreases their cash requirements and increases their lending capacity.

Fifth, variations in interest rates may be caused by variations in the effective demand for loans. The effective demand for loans, it will be shown, is the dominant factor determining interest rates, and although it is, itself, in certain respects varied by variations in interest rates, it is governed to a major extent by the state of markets.

ii *The power of bankers over interest rates*

The power of bankers to vary interest rates rests upon their power to vary the standard of the proportion of reserves to be held by them in relation to the deposits in their books. We have seen in the preceding chapter that, where there is a central bank—and there is one in most countries—it normally controls the proportion of the total quantity of actual cash to total deposits of the whole banking system of the country, because, by varying its investments and loans, it varies the reserves of the deposit or clearing banks. Thus, the central bank, by buying or selling securities and by lowering or raising the rate at which it grants loans, *i.e.* the bank rate or rediscount rate, can increase or decrease the lending capacity of the other banks enough to establish interest rates as low or as high as it likes within the following limits:

First, in a country where a gold standard exchange is in operation, interest rates cannot be lowered beyond the point at which a sustained outflow of gold takes place owing to relatively higher interest rates in countries abroad, nor raised higher than the rates at which loans can be freely obtained from abroad. In these circumstances the first concern of the central bank in deciding upon the bank rate is the quantity of gold in the country; and although the policies of central banks in different countries vary in this respect, in all cases there is both a standard for the minimum proportion of gold to be retained in relation to bankers' total deposits and total investments and loans, and some sort of undefined standard for the absolutely minimum quantity of gold to be held. Thus, when the proportion of gold to investments and loans of the central bank, and incidentally of the whole banking system of the country, decreases in a manner that endangers the standard for the minimum proportion of gold, the bank rate is raised, both to attract gold into the country and to reduce bankers' total investments and loans. But even when the proportion of gold is above the minimum required by the standard, the bank rate is raised should, for any reason,[18] gold be going abroad to an extent that endangers the standard for the absolutely minimum quantity to be retained in the country. On the other hand, the bank rate is lowered whenever the proportion of gold to bankers' investments and loans rises too much above the minimum required by the standard, and provided the quantity of gold in the country is sufficiently above the standard for the absolutely minimum quantity. In fact, a central bank raises the bank rate when it requires to cause an inflow or prevent an outflow of gold, more or less irrespective of whether the state of industry and trade may be indicating that bankers' investments and loans should be stimulated by low interest rates; and, vice versa, it usually lowers the bank rate when the quantity of gold in the country rises above standard requirements, doing so sometimes even when it is thought that the state of industry and trade is indicating that bankers' investments and loans should be curbed.

Notice that it is not suggested that the indications of industry and trade are deliberately disregarded by bankers in fixing interest rates. Far from it. But it is not always possible to serve all the requirements of the gold standard and those of industry and trade faithfully at the same time.

Second, where no gold standard exchange is in operation, interest rates can be forced down by the central bank whenever no danger exists of bankers' investments and loans becoming so great that the proportion of cash to deposits falls below legal or conventional requirements, and whenever the assistance of the government in respect of additional supplies of fiduciary paper money is assured or can be obtained. On the other hand, interest rates can only be forced up by a bank handling the entire issue of fiduciary paper money as well as a substantial portion of the reserves of the other banks, and only then to the extent that it is not obliged by government borrowing to abandon any restrictions it may have decided upon in respect of its investments and loans. Subject to these conditions, interest rates can be forced up until the currency reaches and passes its gold parity on the foreign exchange market, and an inflow of gold is induced.[19]

We may conclude, therefore, that the power of bankers over interest rates is limited by the effects of interest rates on inward and outward gold movements where a gold standard exchange is in operation, and by government action in respect of limitations to the issue of fiduciary paper money, and by government borrowing, where there is no gold standard exchange.

Let us now see what effect interest rates have on the effective demand for loans.

iii *The causes of variations in the effective demand for loans*

The causes of variations in the effective demand for loans are: *first*, variations in borrowing by governments; *second*, variations in the condition of markets; and *third*, variations in interest rates.

First, variations in borrowing by governments. Both variations in the expenditure of governments, and variations in the extent to which the expenditure is met by borrowing, are determined by political and economic considerations in which interest rates figure little or not at all.

Second, variations in the condition of markets. The effective demand for loans for financing producers and distributors and for buying stock exchange securities is governed by the conditions in the markets concerned—in which interest rates only play a certain part. The conditions in commodity markets consist of whether markets are "long" or "short", of visible supplies in relation to estimated final-buying at given prices, and of market prices in relation to marginal costs of production—all of which conditions may be, but are not necessarily always, affected by interest rates. The conditions in stock exchange markets consist of whether markets are "long" or "short",[20] whether the prices of securities are relatively low or high as judged by their yields and prospects, whether conditions in commodity markets are such that money is being attracted into, or being turned out of, employment in industry and trade, and whether, because of the monetary requirements of industry and trade or for any other reason, interest rates are high or low. It depends on these conditions whether it is advisable to borrow money to buy stocks of goods, materials or equipment for production, or stock exchange securities, as the case may be. Once an article looks dear, be it any kind of commodity or security, low interest rates will not induce business men to carry any more of it than they can help; and, on the other hand, it is not the difference between 5 per cent. and 10 per cent. per annum that will prevent them from increasing their holdings of goods or securities that look cheap. What influence, for instance, would wide variations in interest rates have had on the effective demand for loans to carry rubber and rubber shares in 1925? It seems certain that higher interest rates would have made the commodity dearer on the upward swing, that at least the same quantity would have been dealt in, and that a greater quantity of credit would have been required to finance it at higher prices.

As a matter of fact, in the case of ordinary shares participating in the current profits and losses of industry and trade, sometimes stock exchange prices and commodity prices move in opposite directions, regardless of whether interest rates are high or low, and sometimes, in spite of high interest rates, they both move upwards, or, in spite of low interest rates, they both move downwards.

It is not always profitable for operators to carry ordinary stock exchange shares on borrowed money whenever conditions in commodity markets affecting the shares in question are good, or whenever it is profitable to carry stocks of goods of the kind concerned on borrowed money. Vice versa, it is not always advisable for operators to sell ordinary shares carried on borrowed money whenever conditions in the commodity markets affecting the shares in question are bad, or whenever it is advisable to sell stocks of goods of the kind concerned carried on borrowed money. For, whereas the reasons for buying or selling ordinary shares at any time are affected by the financial positions of the companies concerned and their average profits and prospects, as well as by the actual state of commodity markets, the reasons for buying or selling commodities at any time—particularly perishable commodities—only stand upon the market conditions of the present or near future. Thus, for instance, sometimes a situation arises in which a shortage of goods due to producers and distributors having allowed stocks of goods to run down too much is accompanied by excessively high stock exchange prices, and when the true position is duly appreciated, stock exchange liquidation may be accompanied by producers and distributors building up stocks of goods and using more or less money released by the stock exchange.

Again, on certain occasions, notably when government expenditure is persistently exceeding revenue, it pays, in spite of high interest rates, to borrow money simultaneously to buy ordinary stock exchange shares and to increase production and stocks of goods. Incidentally, on such occasions rising commodity prices are aggravated by rising stock exchange prices causing increased final-buying of goods by stock exchange operators, and more or less temporary or permanent currency depreciation is the result. On the other hand, sometimes—notably when excessive taxation for reduction of debts is causing the velocity of final-buying to decrease—it pays, regardless of low interest rates, simultaneously to sell ordinary stock exchange shares and to decrease production and stocks of goods, repay loans and hold money on time deposit. Incidentally, in such cases falling commodity prices are aggravated by decreased final-buying of goods by stock exchange operators, and more or less deflation and general trade depression are the result.

Third, variations in interest rates. We know that occasions occur when, in spite of the lowest money rates, the banking system is unable to lend as much credit as the bankers wish. Low money rates in England in 1922–1923 failed to produce an expansion of credit or prevent a contraction in the quantity of currency notes issued; and in the United States in 1924, when the discount rate in New York was standing at 3 per cent for several months and the acceptance rates was down to 2 per cent, the Federal Reserve Bank made a loss through failure to find sufficient employment for loanable credit. We also know that the highest money rates do not always cause a contraction in the effective demand for loans and the cash requirements of the public. In Central Europe, during the latter part of the period of inflation and during the period in which the new gold currencies were instituted, the bank rates for the old currencies were raised, in Budapest to 18 per cent, and in Berlin to 90 per cent, before the desired results were obtained; whilst, as regards the new gold currencies, 10 per cent bank rates, and considerably higher interest rates for commercial and private loans, were barely high enough to hold the effective demand for loans within the desired limits.

So far as day-to-day and season-to-season swings of stock exchange movements are concerned, the data for the period 1872–1914, says Mr. C. O. Hardy,[21] indicate that the rate of interest for call loans[22] is a result, rather than a cause, of the volume of stock exchange transactions. Proceeding to the more important consideration of those longer and wider fluctuations in stock exchange markets which are associated more or less with changes in the activity of business and the profits of corporations, Mr. Hardy says that these major fluctuations have been compared with the history of interest rates, both call-rates[23] and 60- to 90-day paper rates[24] being used in the investigation, and the evidence fails to support the theory that low interest rates cause either increased borrowing for stock exchange purposes or increases in the volume of trade, and that, vice versa, high interest rates cause reduced stock exchange borrowing or decreased business activity. "The most that can be said in confirmation of the theory is that major advances in stock prices are considerably more likely to begin in declining money markets than in advancing money markets."

Messrs. Owens and Hardy, however, concede in their book that their analysis of the behaviour of a selected group of high-grade bonds and preferred shares does give a certain measure of support to the view that the prices of high-grade securities are controlled by money-market movements. In this connection, it may be said here that, whilst market prices of ordinary shares participating in the current profits and losses of industry are highly susceptible to the state of industry at any time, high-grade bonds bearing fixed rates of interest, and shares with a prior claim on current earnings, are less dependent on variations in the state of industry, and their market prices are therefore affected by the quantity of money to be invested and interest rates in a more pronounced manner than are the market prices of ordinary shares. Still, we may agree with Messrs. Owens and Hardy that it seems reasonable to suppose that the declining interest rate of short-time money and the advancing prices of high-grade bonds and preferred shares are both the effects of a common cause—namely, the release of funds from employment in industry and trade.

We may therefore conclude that certain variations in the effective demand for loans are caused by variations in interest rates in the following ways:

(*a*) Variations in the effective demand for loans by producers and distributors are indirectly caused by variations in interest rates, when bankers' deposit rates are varied enough to cause final buyers to place more or less money on time deposit and use less or more money for final-buying, thereby either decreasing or increasing the volume of industry and trade and its monetary requirements.[25]

(*b*) Minor variations in the effective demand for loans by producers and distributors are directly caused by variations in interest rates. Although, usually, high interest rates discourage borrowers and low interest rates encourage them, sometimes an increase in the cost of financing can be added to the prices of the goods concerned without causing decreased final-buying, when more money is thus required to finance the same quantity of goods at the higher prices. Vice versa, low interest rates usually increase, but sometimes reduce, the effective demand for loans.

(*c*) Major variations in the effective demand for loans for buying high-grade bonds and preferred shares, and minor variations for buying ordinary shares, are caused by variations in interest rates, high rates decreasing and low rates increasing such borrowing.

iv *The power of bankers over the volume of bank loans*

Whatever power bankers possess over the volume of bank loans, it rests: first, on their power to refuse to make loans; secondly, on such power as they possess to vary interest rates; and, thirdly, on the effects of interest rates on the effective demand for loans.

As to the first, bankers have absolute power to refuse to make loans to all borrowers other than, perhaps, the government of their country. But there is no reverse to this means of decreasing the volume of bank loans, for they cannot increase their loans by forcing anybody to borrow.

As to the second, we have seen that the power of bankers over interest rates is limited, either by considerations of the effects of interest rates on gold movements, or by government control of the issue of paper money and government borrowing.

As to the third, we have seen that the effective demand for loans by governments is determined by considerations in which interest rates figure little; and that the effective demand for loans for financing producers and distributors and for buying stock exchange securities is governed by the conditions in the markets concerned—in which interest rates only play a certain part.

The power of bankers over the volume of bank loans is therefore limited by their limited power over interest rates, and by the limited effects of interest rates on the extent of government borrowing and on conditions in commodity and stock exchange markets—which together govern the effective demand for loans.

4 Conclusions regarding the quantity of money

Our principal conclusions about the quantity of money at any time may be enumerated as follows:

(i) Apart from variations in the quantity of cash, the total quantity of money varies vastly according to how much of the total quantity of cash is in the banks, and the proportion in which cash is being used as a basis for bankers' investments and loans.

(ii) It is the business of bankers to maintain their investments and loans as large as possible, possibilities in this respect being limited by the question of reserves, by opportunities for making suitable investments and loans, and by considerations regarding currency depreciation.

(iii) The policy of bankers in buying and selling stock exchange securities cannot be governed, even if it may be influenced, by considerations relating to varying the quantity of credit money in industry and trade.

(iv) The volume of bank loans is by far the most predominant element in the quantity of money. But the power of bankers over the volume of bank loans is limited: by their limited power over interest rates; and by the limited effects of interest rates on the extent of government borrowing and on conditions in markets, which together govern the effective demand for loans.

IV Determining factors of the condition of markets and the behaviour of final buyers

1 Determining factors of the condition of markets

Since, as we have seen in the preceding chapter, the volume of bank loans is by far the most predominant element in the quantity of money, and that, apart from government borrowing,[26] the effective demand for loans is mainly governed by the condition of commodity markets and stock exchange markets, we shall now examine the determining factors of the condition of markets.

Again, we have remarked in the preceding chapter that, owing to the fact that the reasons for buying or selling ordinary stock exchange shares are affected by the financial positions of the companies concerned and their average profits and prospects, stock exchange prices and commodity prices often move in opposite directions. Nevertheless, since the financial positions of the companies are dependent upon accumulations of undistributed profits, and since all profits and prospects are dependent upon commodity markets, it is true to say that in the long run the *intrinsic values* of ordinary shares are more or less dependent upon commodity markets. On the other hand, the *market prices* of all stock exchange securities, apart from the ways already considered in which they are affected by interest rates, are governed by their *intrinsic values*, by the money earnings of industry and trade available for investment, and by the extent to which money capital and credit are being attracted into, or expelled from, industry and trade. Our inquiry is, thus, concentrated on the determining factors of the conditions of *commodity* markets.

We have to consider what factors govern the condition of supply and the condition of demand at any time, in commodity markets.

It was stated a few pages back that the conditions in commodity markets consist of whether markets are "long" or "short," of visible supplies in relation to estimated final-buying at given prices, and of market prices in relation to marginal costs of production. In terms of supply and demand this means that supply varies as the velocity of production and the presence of "long" accounts of stocks of goods, and demand varies as the velocity of final-buying, and the presence of "short" accounts or commitments to deliver stocks of goods. Setting aside for the present the important but subsidiary factor of stocks of goods, together with the "long" and "short" accounts relating thereto, we are left with the fact that, fundamentally, supply varies as the velocity of production, and demand as the velocity of final-buying. Thus, it may be said that the primary determining factors of the condition of markets are the velocity of production and the velocity of final-buying.

Since virtually everything that is produced is sooner or later sold to final buyers, the *average* velocities of production and final-buying in a self-contained area must be equal. Further, at a time when stocks of goods are being increased, the *actual* velocity of production must be greater than the *actual* velocity of final-buying, and at a time when stocks of goods are being reduced, the *actual* velocity of production must be less than the *actual* velocity of final-buying. In short, it may be said that the velocities of production and final-buying, acting and reacting on each other and on stocks of goods, fluctuate freely in relation to each other above and below the same average velocity.[27]

However, whereas variations in the velocity of production, other than those warranted by variations in the velocity of final-buying, cause final buyers slowly and with difficulty to alter their behaviour and, incidentally, the velocity of final-buying, producers and distributors are continuously and anxiously seeking to adjust the velocity of production to the velocity of final-buying. Variations in the velocity of production unwarranted by variations in the velocity of final-buying are, therefore, mistakes unwillingly made by producers and distributors, whereas variations in the velocity of final-buying other than those caused by variations in the velocity of production are the result of deliberate changes in the habits and behaviour of final buyers, which changes are limited only by stocks of goods and ready productive capacity. Variations in the velocity of production are therefore dominated by variations in the velocity of final-buying, and deliberate decreases in the velocity of final-buying or insufficient final-buying impede production and the development of productive capacity and efficiency.

As regards the factors governing the velocity of production, in this work we are not concerned with a study of the potential productivity of different kinds of men and different kinds of agricultural, mineral or other developed or undeveloped resources of the earth. We are not seeking to estimate either maximum productive possibilities or maximum ready productive capacity. What we want to know exactly is why ready productive capacity, such as it is at any time, is not always fully engaged. This brings us to the question of incentives and to the velocity of final-buying. It has been said that the number of monetary units used for the final-buying of different kinds of goods are money votes which determine in the most efficient manner possible the quantity and nature of goods to which productive energy is applied. At all events, whilst variations always exist in the manner in which men with different natural or acquired characteristics and with different material resources at their disposal respond to given incentives, incentives to production only build up in the modern economic system through the velocity of final-buying.

Our particular object, therefore, is to examine the factors governing the velocity of final-buying.

2 The purchasing power of final buyers

At this point it may be objected: It is easy to see that the velocity of final-buying can for a time fall below the velocity of production, and it is also easy to see that the velocity of final-buying, by encroaching on stocks of goods in the hands of producers and distributors, can for a time exceed the velocity of production; but it is not so obvious how final buyers as a whole can, even for a time, have enough money to buy goods faster than they are being produced, nor yet how they can always have enough money to buy goods as fast as they have been produced, unless sellers sometimes accept reduced prices.

Let us consider the sources from which final buyers derive their money:

First, the process of production and bringing to market causes producers and distributors to disburse wages, rent, interest, the cost of materials and the amount of their own personal expenses, in money *before* the goods they produce and handle are sold. Thus, enough money is disbursed to final buyers to buy all the goods in question at prices that render their production and bringing to market worth while, regardless of whether they are sold or not, whether producers and distributors are making profits or losses, or whether their outlay or disbursements of money are effected by means of loans from bankers or by means of their own cash or bank balances.

It must be noted that, although bankers can force down prices and cause money losses to final buyers by decreasing the volume of bank loans and causing stocks of goods to be thrown on markets, this does not affect the real purchasing power of final buyers except to the extent that the velocity of production is decreased through market prices being depressed below the cost of production at existing contract prices in respect of wages, rent and materials. In other words, since decreased money income of final buyers as a whole due to a fall in prices is equal to the fall, their money income is always enough to buy the same quantity of goods at the lower prices;—their real purchasing power as a whole can only be decreased to the extent that the velocity of production may be decreased and less real purchasing power is earned by them in wages, rent, interest and materials.

Second, final buyers as a whole always possess large capital resources, both in the form of cash in hand and money on time or demand deposit, and in the form of property, securities and other assets upon which loans from bankers can be readily obtained, which can be used for increased final-buying.

Third, governments can always obtain loans from bankers, and can also create additional cash by the issue of fiduciary paper money.

Fourth, it must be noted that a given quantity of money may be made to negotiate more buying or less buying in a given time. On this point we will content ourselves with the remark that there is a normal velocity of circulation of money, above which the effective demand for loans, the volume of bank loans and deposits, increase, and below which they decrease, until the normal velocity is again reached.

On the other hand, governments can cause a deficiency of money in the hands of final buyers by withdrawing money from them by taxation and using it to repay loans obtained from bankers, whereby, other things being equal,[28] total deposits and credit money are to that extent decreased.

Final buyers can buy more or less to any extent below their money incomes in the past, and to the extent that they together do so the total money income of the population in the area concerned is proportionately reduced, and its real income in goods is reduced to the extent that production is checked or reduced. On the other hand, except when bankers or governments, for the purposes of the gold standard or any other reason, are restricting or decreasing the quantity of money and the velocity of final-buying, final buyers can buy beyond their money incomes in the past, either by employing money savings or by obtaining loans from bankers, and to the extent that they together do so the total money income of the population in the area concerned is proportionately increased, whilst its commodity income is increased or decreased according to whether production is increased or decreased.

3 Distribution of income and the habits of peoples

Broadly speaking, the velocity of final-buying is, within the limits of ready productive capacity, dependent upon distribution of income, and upon the habits of peoples in relation to consumption, utilization of non-productive equipment, and abstinence. The velocity of final-buying is decreased when producers and distributors, in order to obviate excessive accumulation of stocks of goods or for any other reason, decrease the velocity of production, and incidentally disburse less money for services and raw or semi-raw materials to people whose final-buying depends thereon; when producers decrease their final-buying of productive equipment; when governments reduce expenditure on goods and services; and when the belief exists that the currency will appreciate. Vice versa, the velocity of final-buying is increased when producers and distributors for any reason increase the velocity of production, and incidentally disburse more money for services and materials; when producers increase their final-buying of productive equipment; when governments increase expenditure on goods and services; and when the belief or fear exists that the currency will depreciate.

It may be that in some countries the habits and general standard of living of the people are such as to maintain the velocity of final-buying at the maximum that is continuously permitted by ready productive capacity, but this is the exception and not the rule. The reasons for such insufficient final-buying are:

First, the question of unequal distribution of income, to say nothing of foreign debts, which, it is so often urged, limits the income of a vast number of people in a manner that is by no means equitable in relation to their productive output. In fact, the large-scale working of instalment buying in the United States shows that workers borrow part of their own productive output, and that instalment buying and the quantity of goods thereby marketed are limited by the quantity of instalment credit that can be piled up in geometrical progression without excessive risk to financiers. Thus, if the earnings of workers were high enough to enable them to buy right out what they now buy on instalment credit, there would be no question of reducing production merely because too much income has been transferred from willing final buyers to people who refuse to use it for final-buying.

A similar dilemma is introduced into international trade by international investments and international debts; for part of the money disbursed in the debtor countries by the process of production and bringing to market is withdrawn from them and paid to the creditor countries, which by no means always want to buy a corresponding quantity of goods as fast as produced.[29]

Second, in a world where the devil inexorably takes the hindermost, all wise individuals and corporations endeavour to "save," or convert part of their incomes into reserve funds or capital in some form, regardless of whether society as a whole is able and willing to utilize such "savings." This practice, as we shall see, can decrease the velocity of final-buying enough to cause trade depression and unemployment, and commonly does so to a varying extent.

V The nature and effects of saving

1 The different kinds of saving

The expression "saving" is ordinarily used to signify that people are abstaining from spending money income on consumable goods, and disposing of it with a view to adding to their capital or to their incomes or to both. It is necessary to emphasize, however, that any increase of capital or income which, all going well, is thus obtained by the savers, does not represent any increase in the total quantity of commodity capital or commodity income when the money is disposed of or invested in an unproductive manner, as when hoarded or lent to a government to buy perishable goods. It is further necessary to emphasize that the total quantity of commodity capital or commodity income can be increased without recourse to any self-imposed restriction of consumption by anybody. To consider the different kinds of saving, therefore, we must distinguish between (i) the passive part of doing without consumable goods or certain kinds of non-productive equipment, and (ii) the active part of producing commodity capital or ordering it to be produced.

i *The passive part of doing without consumable goods*

In the ordinary sense of the word "saving," the passive part of doing with less goods includes, not only doing with less consumable goods, but also doing with less of certain kinds of non-productive equipment. As we are, here, treating non-productive equipment as commodity capital, there is no more saving in doing with less non-productive equipment than in doing with less productive equipment. There is evidently, however, a saving in doing with less equipment of lower marginal utility for the purpose of increasing the quantity of equipment of greater marginal utility; and the same applies to consumable goods. It would, in fact, be correct to define the passive part of saving as doing with less consumable goods and less equipment of lower marginal utility. We are not, however, going to press this, being content to argue on the basis of consumable goods versus productive equipment. Therefore, on the understanding that, for the present purpose, consumable goods include certain kinds of non-productive equipment, we shall define the passive part of saving as: doing with less consumable goods.

People do with less consumable goods, first, because they want to, or, second, because they must.

As to the first, when they want to do with less consumable goods for any reason we shall call it "abstinence."

As to the second, people may be forced to do with less consumable goods in several ways: Frugality may be imposed on the whole community by an absolute shortage, either through a higher price-level or through a general reduction of money wages and money profits or earnings. Frugality may also be imposed on some sections of the community by other sections, or on some communities by others, by means of unequal distribution of income. In this case, as has been pointed out a few pages back, the velocity of final-buying is decreased below ready productive capacity if the community or section of it imposing frugality on other communities or sections of them is practising abstinence beyond a certain point. Again, when those practising abstinence increase their final-buying of consumable goods—or when those with cash in hand, bank balances or bank loans increase the velocity of final-buying of consumable goods, non-productive or productive equipment—or when producers and distributors increase stocks of goods—other things being equal, a rise in the price-level occurs which automatically forces others to do with less. Frugality imposed automatically in this way we shall call "automatic frugality."[30]

ii *The active part of producing commodity capital or ordering it to be produced*

Those able at a given time to undertake the active part of producing commodity capital or ordering it to be produced may be either producers, or they may be distributors, consumers or governments, but they must possess cash, bank balances or the power to obtain bank loans.

Whether those actually undertaking the active part of producing commodity capital or ordering it to be produced employ money income made available by abstinence, capital in cash or bank balances or loans obtained from bankers, it is this action of producing commodity capital or ordering it to be produced which determines the quantity and nature of commodity capital that is produced.

For people to undertake the active part of producing commodity capital, either they must be producing it directly or indirectly for final buyers, or they must be producing it for their own requirements—in which latter case they are themselves the final buyers of all the goods and services bought for the purpose. Again, for people to undertake the active part of *ordering* the production of commodity capital, either they must be final buyers of non-productive equipment, or they must be producers acting as final buyers of productive equipment, or they must be distributors or others who are renewing or increasing stocks of goods to sell to final buyers. It is, therefore, always the extent of final-buying of commodity capital that, within the limits of ready productive capacity, determines the quantity and nature of commodity capital produced. The question of whether the necessary labour and materials for producing commodity capital are released, on the one hand, by abstinence, or, on the other, by automatic frugality, is a quite different question which affects, directly, only the price-level, monetary stability and incentives to production, but not the quantity of commodity capital. To this question we must now turn.

2   The effect of abstinence on the velocity of final-buying and, incidentally, on the quantity of commodity capital

The objection will surely be made that all money income made available by abstinence is, except in the negligible cases of money hoarded away, and except when it is borrowed for the final-buying of consumable goods, either directly forced, or automatically drawn, into use by those undertaking the active part of producing commodity capital or ordering it to be produced; and that, at all events, unless the money is hoarded away, the velocity of final-buying is not decreased. Let us meet this objection.

The circuit flow of credit money is roughly as follows: Bankers create credit money by making loans and investments. The business men to whom the money is advanced disburse it for wages, rent, interest, materials and personal expenses; and taxation thereon is disbursed in a similar manner by governments. The recipients of the money then use it as final buyers of the goods produced by the activities of the business men, who may then either repay the bankers and thus destroy the credit money, or continue to circulate it by using it to finance production as before. The point is that certain kinds of "saving" withdraw credit money from circulation in industry before it has been returned to the business men who first put it out, and the injection of new credit money into circulation in other ways is not always sufficient to neutralize such withdrawals.

Money made available by abstinence may be used or disposed of in four ways by those who are "saving": (i) Productive equipment and certain kinds of nonproductive equipment may be bought; (ii) stocks of goods may be increased; (iii) stock exchange securities may be bought; and (iv) the money may be held on deposit.

i   *When equipment is bought*

When money income made available by abstinence is used without delay, directly or indirectly, for the final-buying of equipment, the velocity of final-buying is obviously not decreased, and incidentally the production of new equipment is ordered. In the case, however, of equipment bought by borrowers, the velocity of final-buying is decreased if and when the latter either sell the equipment and thereby prevent a similar quantity of new equipment being ordered, or refrain from final-buying with any of their money income in order to repay the lenders.

ii   *When increased stocks of goods are bought*

When money income made available by abstinence is used without delay to finance distributors or others to buy increased stocks of goods, the money is paid by the distributors to the producers who are supplying them, and the producers pay it out again for wages, materials, etc., when most of it will be used for final-buying by the recipients. Thus, new stocks of consumable goods or equipment are ordered and the velocity of final-buying is little or not at all decreased. But whenever distributors or others reduce their stocks of goods, either to repay loans or to increase their cash in hand and bank balances, or simply because they consider themselves over-stocked, any decreased trade-buying from producers so caused decreases the quantity of money paid out for wages, materials, etc., which decreases the velocity of final-buying and causes a further decrease in the velocity of production. A general trade depression may thus be caused, and will last until the velocity of production has been reduced enough below the velocity of final-buying to cause a more or less appreciable decrease in stocks of goods.

iii *When stock exchange securities are bought*

When money income made available by abstinence is used without delay, directly or indirectly, to buy stock exchange securities, and when this influx of money into stock exchange circulation is accompanied by a corresponding amount of new issues of securities for financing the final-buying of goods and services by business enterprise or governments, the velocity of final-buying is obviously not decreased. And when the volume of new issues is not as great as the influx of additional money, stock exchange prices rise, sometimes drawing in additional credit money, but creating profits in the hands of stock exchange operators who usually become final buyers of additional goods and services. In these circumstances the stock exchange acts as a distributor of unused final-buying power resulting from abstinence, and incidentally the production of commodity capital is ordered to the extent that any goods so bought consist of commodity capital.

When excessive abstinence or excessive liquidation of stocks of goods, as indicated by ready productive capacity not being fully engaged, is causing falling commodity prices, reduced monetary requirements of producers and distributors, an influx of money into the stock exchange, rising stock exchange prices and increased final-buying by stock exchange operators, on such occasions the stock exchange tends to neutralize the excessive abstinence or excessive liquidation of stocks of goods. Vice versa, when insufficient abstinence or excessive trade buying is causing rising commodity prices, increased monetary requirements of producers and distributors, the withdrawal of money from the stock exchange, falling stock exchange prices and decreased final-buying of goods by stock exchange operators, the stock exchange tends to neutralize the insufficient abstinence or excessive trade buying.

iv *When the money is held on deposit*

Money income that is not used for final-buying (goods and services), and money capital released by industry and trade, do not reach the stock exchange unless the prospects of ordinary shares are satisfactory or the prices of high-grade bonds and preferred shares sufficiently low. But the prospects of ordinary shares are not likely to be good at a time when the velocity of final-buying is being decreased by abstinence or otherwise, and the prices of high-grade bonds and preferred shares are not usually low during a period when money is being released by industry and trade. Nor yet do stock exchange operators or others selling securities—either at a profit or at a loss—necessarily cause any of the money so realized to be used, directly or indirectly, either for final-buying (goods and services) or for financing industry and trade; for they may neither wish to spend the money nor be able to find safe and profitable employment for it in industry and trade.

The difficulties of the capitalist in the matter of the safe and profitable employment of money in the modern economic system, particularly during certain periods, are well described by the following extract from a leading article of *The Annalist* of July 1926:

> "... this country has an exceedingly ample equipment of manufacturing plant, even when that plant is rated at the efficiency level of three or four years ago. Its efficiency level, in rising decidedly since that time, has for practical purposes increased the proportions of our over-equipment; and it is enabled to continue for the present by the superabundance of capital which seeks incessantly some place in which it may earn a reasonable return for its use. This is the general mechanism by which manufacturing competition has now been sharpened to an unprecedented pitch of severity. The competition must go on, for failure to compete will mean the rapid destruction of capital; necessarily the failure to succeed in the competition will also mean the loss of capital; and loss of this character is certain to occur on a pretty considerable scale because our production is obviously greater than our power to absorb it."

Capitalists in England have, in the past, met the difficulty of keeping both commodity capital and money capital employed by a procedure amounting to lending money to foreigners to buy their goods. But the quantity of goods that can be disposed of by means of making investments and loans abroad is in no way governed by capacity to produce goods in excess of home requirements; and, as a matter of fact, the truth is now being forced upon would-be lending countries that foreigners are either too rich or too poor, too clever or too stupid, some to desire to become borrowers, others to qualify as desirable borrowers, of all that the lenders may wish to "save."[31]

Thus, more or less money income made available by abstinence and not used for final-buying either by the abstainers themselves or by producers or stock exchange operators, and more or less money capital released by industry and trade and not invested on the stock exchange, are held on deposit in the books of bankers whilst awaiting employment.

When money income made available by abstinence is held on deposit, the onus of finding safe and profitable employment for it is left upon bankers. We have just seen that it is not always safe and profitable either to buy stock exchange securities or to employ money in industry and trade, which confirms the conclusions reached in Chapter III, regarding the volume of bankers' investments and the volume of bank loans. We must therefore consider in what conditions the banking system as a whole is able to employ, safely and profitably to itself, money income made available by abstinence and held on deposit.

In the first place, an increase in the quantity of money income made available by abstinence and held on deposit is essential on occasions when ready productive capacity is fully engaged and the effective demand for loans is increasing. For on such occasions decreased velocity of final-buying is necessary, on the one hand, to cause decreased production of certain goods and services and release more or less labour, materials and equipment for the new demands upon them, and, on the other hand, to prevent an increase in the monetary requirements of industry and trade, an increase in the volume of bank loans, and currency depreciation.

In the second place, an increase in the quantity of money income made available by abstinence and held on deposit is essential on occasions when the banking system as a whole absolutely or technically does not possess, or cannot obtain, large enough reserves to act as a basis for increased investments and loans. For increased depositing of cash in the banks by abstainers is necessary to replenish bankers' reserves; and decreased velocity of final-buying of abstainers is necessary to cause a decrease in the production of goods and services, a decrease in the effective demand for loans for the said production, and, possibly, liquidation of ordinary stock exchange shares and the release of money from the stock exchange.

It may be observed "en passant" that, when a monetary shortage occurs but at the same time ready productive capacity is not fully engaged, what really seems requisite is an alteration in monetary technique which renders it possible, on the one hand, to increase bankers' reserves without recourse to increased depositing of cash in the banks by abstainers, and, on the other, to obviate the necessity of liquidation by producers, distributors and stock exchange operators in order to limit or decrease the volume of bank loans.

In the third place, since an increase in the quantity of money income made available by abstinence and held on deposit decreases the final-buying of the abstainers, the production of goods and services for them, and the volume of bank loans required and obtained by the producers and distributors concerned, it follows that the velocity of *aggregate*[32] final-buying, the velocity of *aggregate* production, the *aggregate* volume of bank loans required and obtained, and incidentally total deposits, *other things being equal*, are also decreased. Thus emerges the important and interesting truth that when money income made available by abstinence is held on deposit, *other things being equal*, both the velocity of production and the quantity of money are decreased. But this statement will not be allowed to pass unchallenged either in respect of the quantity of money or in respect of the velocity of production.

It may be objected by some, as regards the quantity of money, that at all events comparisons between, on the one hand, total deposits, and on the other, say, business activity as measured by total cheque payments—which payments constitute some guide for estimating variations in the velocity of final-buying—do not seem to produce any proof that total deposits decrease when business activity decreases. The reply is that the evidence obtained by such comparisons, if properly weighed, does show that total deposits follow the same general trend as business activity.

In the United States, for example, bank debits to individual accounts, which are the true record of all transactions in which payments are made by cheque, amount in any one year to somewhere in the region of thirty times as much as average total deposits during the same period. Thus, if in a given year average total deposits in the books of the banks amount to $25,000 million, total bank debits for the whole year will amount to about $750,000 million; and thus, should business activity as indicated by total bank debits increase or decrease by 10 per cent. in relation to the preceding year, one must not expect to find an increase or a decrease of average total deposits of more than one-third of 1 per cent.

If, therefore, a very substantial difference of 10 per cent. in business activity of two different years is difficult to find reflected in the average total deposits of the respective years, what hope is there of finding therein the reflection of something which is only a part of business activity? For those parts of business activity consisting of the velocities of final-buying and of production may be buried in several ways, such as the following: (1) Decreased bank debits in respect of decreased final-buying or decreased production may be hidden by increased bank debits in respect of increased transactions between distributors or between stock exchange operators. (2) Decreased deposits arising from decreased bank loans to producers or distributors may be hidden by increased deposits arising from increased bank loans to stock exchange operators.[33] (3) A certain quantity of deposits may not be destroyed during a depression, because certain bank loans have become frozen credits. (4) Decreased deposits arising from decreased bank loans may be hidden by increased deposits arising from increased bankers' investments. (5) The converse of all the preceding.

As a matter of fact, the evidence to be obtained from the above-mentioned comparisons between total deposits and business activity is by no means inconsistent with our theory that when money income made available by abstinence is held on deposit, *other things being equal*, both the velocity of production and the quantity of money are reduced. Moreover, although the further objection may be made that frequently the velocity of production increases when money income made available by abstinence and held on deposit is increasing, this objection disappears and the truth of the theory in relation to both the velocity of production and the quantity of money becomes obvious as soon as it is repeated with an amplification of the condition, "*other things being equal.*" We then get:

When money income made available by abstinence is held on deposit—the final-buying of abstainers being to this extent reduced below their incomes—both the velocity of production is reduced in relation to ready productive capacity and the quantity of money in relation to the potential[34] supply, unless the absent final-buying of the abstainers is fully neutralized by the sum of the following kinds of irregular[35] final-buying: (1) final-buying resulting from gold-mining; (2) final-buying by countries abroad from the home country; (3) final-buying by governments; and (4) final-buying resulting from the activities of producers and distributors.

We may therefore conclude that when money income made available by abstinence is held on deposit, should the sum of the different kinds of irregular final-buying be not great enough fully to neutralize the absent final-buying of the abstainers, the velocity of production will decrease in relation to ready productive capacity, and a decrease cannot safely and profitably be prevented in the volume of bankers' investments and loans, and in the quantity of money, in relation to the potential supply of money; and vice versa, should the sum of the velocities of the different kinds of irregular final-buying be greater than any absent final-buying of abstainers, the velocity of production will increase within the limits of ready productive capacity, and the volume of bankers' investments and loans and the quantity of money will increase within the limits of the potential supply of money.

It may likewise be shown that when money capital made available by liquidation of stocks of goods or stock exchange securities is held on deposit, the velocity of production and the quantity of money vary, within the respective limits of ready productive capacity and the potential supply of money, as the extent to which the sum of the different kinds of irregular final-buying are less or greater than any decreased final-buying of producers, workers and stock exchange operators, caused by the liquidation.

In order to complete our inquiry we must examine the causes and nature of variations in the velocities of the above-mentioned irregular kinds of final-buying; meantime the following summary of the present chapter may be given.

3 Conclusions regarding the nature and effects of saving

(i) It is necessary to distinguish between, on the one hand, the passive part of abstinence or automatic frugality, and, on the other, the active part of producing commodity capital or ordering it to be produced.

(ii) In the modern economic system the active part of producing commodity capital or ordering it to be produced is determined by the extent of final-buying of commodity capital.

(iii) In the modern economic system the active part of producing commodity capital or ordering it to be produced is not dependent upon abstinence; for neither abstinence nor automatic frugality is required at a time when ready productive capacity is not fully engaged, and failing enough abstinence at a time when ready productive capacity *is* fully engaged, automatic frugality is imposed.

(iv) When money income made available by abstinence is used without delay, directly or indirectly, for the final-buying of equipment, the velocity of final-buying is not decreased and the production of new equipment is ordered.

(v) When money income made available by abstinence is used without delay, directly or indirectly, for buying increased stocks of goods, the velocity of final-buying is decreased little or not at all, and the production of new stocks of goods is ordered.

(vi) When money income made available by abstinence is used without delay, directly or indirectly, for buying stock exchange securities, the money may be used by the issuers or sellers of the securities for final-buying (goods and services); or it may be used to cause a rise in stock exchange prices, creating more or less profits in the hands of stock exchange operators and others, and enabling them to increase their final-buying (of goods and services). The velocity of final-buying (of goods and services) is therefore decreased little or not at all by money income made available by abstinence being used for buying stock exchange securities, and increased production of more or less commodity capital is usually ordered.

(vii) When money income made available by abstinence, or money capital made available by liquidation of stocks of goods or stock exchange securities, is held on deposit, should the sum of the different kinds of irregular final-buying be not great enough fully to neutralize the absent final-buying of the abstainers and any decreased final-buying caused by liquidation, the velocities of final-buying and production will decrease in relation to ready productive capacity, whilst the quantity of money will decrease in relation to the potential supply; and vice versa, should the sum of the different kinds of irregular final-buying be greater than any absent final-buying of abstainers, and any decreased final-buying resulting from liquidation, the velocities of final-buying and production will increase within the limits of ready productive capacity, and the quantity of money will increase within the limits of the potential supply.

VII   The irregular final-buying by countries abroad from the home country[36]

The final-buying (of goods and services) by foreign countries from—let us say—the home country constitutes the exports of the latter.

The inquiry we are about to make will show that the total money value of the home country's exports in relation to the total money value of its imports only increases—or, in other words, its balance of foreign trade only "improves"—in one or both of the following cases: *first*, when all outward transfers of money income or money capital for use, investment or safe-keeping abroad are increased in relation to all similar inward transfers, the aggregate money value of all visible and invisible exports[37] of goods and services and gold increases in relation to the aggregate money value of all like imports. *Second*, when, other things being equal, the aggregate money value of net imports of gold is increased in relation to the aggregate money value of imports of goods and services,[38] imports of goods and services are decreased in relation to exports of goods and services. In these circumstances it is to be expected that variations in the home country's foreign trade balance must be irregular, and that the velocity of final-buying by countries abroad from the home country must decrease and aggravate, as often as it increases and neutralizes, any inadequate home velocity of final-buying.

For the purpose of this inquiry, we must examine: (1) the effects of variations in price-levels; (2) the effects of foreign payments or transfers of money on price-levels and on rates in the foreign exchange market; (3) the effects of foreign payments or transfers of money on exports and imports; (4) the effects of foreign investments on exports and imports and (5) the relation of the price-level to the foreign exchange value of the currency.

1   The effects of variations in price-levels

The conception of a price-level involves certain difficulties which need not be discussed here. In practice it is calculated by the quantity of some specified combination of necessary kinds of goods and services that can be bought at current prices by a unit of the currency. Needless to say, no combination of different kinds of goods and services fits all requirements of different incomes and different tastes. For the purpose of our examination, however, the expression "price-level" may be treated as an abstraction signifying the quantity of some ideal combination of goods and services that can be bought at current prices by a unit of the currency.

It is the wholesale price-level at which retailers buy, and at which producers, wholesale dealers, exporters and importers buy and sell; and it is their bids for, and offers to sell, goods and services which determine the wholesale price-level at any time. We are therefore concerned with the causes that determine the behaviour of these buyers and sellers on the wholesale markets, and the relation of this behaviour to the wholesale and retail price-levels.

Although the wholesale and retail price-levels are, at all events in the long run, interdependent, it is necessary to observe that the retail price-level, unlike the wholesale price-level, is not subject to continuous fluctuations in response to every shade of real or imaginary variation in supply and demand. This is an important point, because the failure of the retail price-level promptly to adjust itself to a fall in the wholesale price-level is a frequent and important cause of decreased production. Nevertheless, for the sake of simplicity and unless otherwise stated, the fluctuations of the retail price-level will, whenever possible, be regarded as exactly parallel to those of the wholesale price-level, and we shall refer to this concept as the "price-level."

The price-level in a country neither rises nor falls when the sum of the velocities of production and importation equals the sum of the velocities of final-buying and exportation, and provided producers and distributors do not attempt to increase or decrease their stocks of goods. Thus, variations in any of these five factors, or disproportionate variations in all of them, cause variations in the price-level which reacts back upon each of them. Let us therefore note the essential effects of variations in the price-level: (i) on the velocity of production, (ii) on the velocity of final-buying, (iii) on the velocity of importation, (iv) on the velocity of exportation, and (v) on the behaviour of producers and distributors in the matter of increasing and decreasing their stocks of goods.

i *On the velocity of production*

First, a falling price-level. When the price-level is falling as the result of an increase in the velocity of production arising from increased productive efficiency, this increased production is, other things being equal, usually maintained, although producers and distributors may wish to arrange a decrease in the velocity of production in order to arrest the fall in the price-level.

But when a fall in the price-level is due to a decrease in the velocity of final-buying, to goods and services abroad becoming relatively cheaper and causing the home velocity of exportation to decrease in relation to the home velocity of importation, or to producers and distributors reducing stocks of goods, it entails both lower money profits and wages and lower real profits and wages, until all prices are readjusted at a low enough level more or less to normalize demand and supply. In such cases, therefore, a fall in the price-level is resisted both by business men who prefer to decrease the velocity of production rather than suffer losses and by workers who endeavour to prevent unemployment by arranging decreased output—a decrease in the velocity of production being the result. It is important to observe that this is the main resistance, and frequently the only one, to falling prices. It is argued, sometimes, that this resistance is harmful in that it prevents rapid readjustment of cost prices down to market prices. The probability is, however, that without it falling prices might, on occasions, reach the proportions of catastrophe.

Second, a rising price-level. When the price-level is rising for any reason, the rise will cause an increase in the velocity of production, unless ready productive capacity is fully engaged, and unless the rise is so rapid that it renders people indisposed to sell for money and impedes the free exchange of goods and services—as in extreme cases of aggravated currency depreciation.

ii *On the velocity of final-buying*

First, a falling price-level. When a fall in the price-level is due to a decrease in the velocity of final-buying, to goods and services abroad becoming relatively cheaper and causing a decrease in the home velocity of exportation in relation to the home velocity of importation, or to producers and distributors reducing stocks of goods, the fall will be aggravated by lower money profits and money wages and decreased final-buying of the parties affected. But sooner or later the fall will cause an increase in the velocity of final-buying; for the purchasing power of those with fixed money incomes derived from bonds—or any kind of contract for fixed amounts of money—will increase to the extent that the price-level falls, and not only will the rentiers concerned buy more goods without spending more money, but they may even be disposed to spend more money than usual when prices seem to have reached a bargain level.

But when a fall in the price-level is due to an increase in the velocity of production arising from increased productive efficiency, it immediately causes an increase in the velocity of final-buying.

Second, a rising price-level. When a rise in the price-level is due to an increase in the velocity of final-buying, to goods and services abroad becoming relatively dearer and causing an increase in the home velocity of exportation in relation to the home velocity of importation, or to producers and distributors increasing their stocks of goods, the rise will be aggravated by higher money profits and wages, and if an increase is caused in the velocity of production, a further increase in the velocity of final-buying may be caused. But unless the rise is so rapid that currency depreciation is feared and all people are keen buyers with all their cash in hand, bank balances and any bank loans they can obtain, it will sooner or later cause a decrease in the velocity of final-buying; for the purchasing power of those with fixed money incomes will decrease to the extent that the price-level rises, and they and others will be disposed further to reduce their final-buying when prices seem to have reached an unwarrantable level.

But when a rise in the price-level is due to a decrease in the velocity of production, it immediately causes a decrease in the velocity of final-buying.

iii *and* iv *On the velocities of importation and exportation*

When the price-level in the home country falls for any reason, and provided the fall is not neutralized—so far as foreign trade is concerned—by a rise in the value of the home currency on the foreign exchange market,[39] this immediately causes both an increase in the velocity of exportation and a decrease in the velocity of importation. The increase in the velocity of exportation takes place as the prices of increased quantities of home products fall into export parity; and the decrease in the velocity of importation takes places as the prices of increased quantities of foreign (or colonial) products remain above import parity into the home country. Similarly, when the price-level in the home country rises for any reason, and provided the rise is not neutralized by a fall in the value of the home currency on the foreign exchange market, this immediately causes a decrease in the velocity of exportation and an increase in the velocity of importation.

v *On the behaviour of producers and distributors in the matter of increasing and decreasing their stocks of goods*

First of all, it must be observed that the immediate—though not necessarily the ultimate—effects of producers and distributors, as a whole, taking steps either to decrease, or to increase, their stocks of goods is to cause the price-level in the former case to fall, and in the latter to rise. For producers and distributors decrease their stocks of goods either by lowering retail prices until the velocity of final-buying is increased, or by liquidation in wholesale markets and lowering wholesale prices until the velocity of production is decreased—or by lowering both retail and wholesale prices. Vice versa, they increase stocks of goods by raising either the retail prices, or wholesale prices, or both. In fact, other things being equal, more or less intervention of this kind by producers and distributors as a whole causes either more or less deflation, or more or less inflation, to the extent that it causes more or less money profits and wages to be distributed, and incidentally more or less variations in the velocity of final-buying.

However, to come to the effects of variations in the price-level on the behaviour of producers and distributors, whether for any reason the price-level is falling or whether it is rising, they do not intervene either to decrease, or to increase, stocks of goods unless they think such behaviour is justified by the actual or anticipated velocities of production, final-buying, importation and exportation, and by the sizes of stocks of goods. In effect, they will not attempt to increase their stocks of goods unless the velocity of production at home or abroad seems likely to be decreased by failure of harvests, labour troubles or in any other way, or unless the velocity of final-buying at home or abroad seems likely to be increased by government final-buying, new development work, fear of currency depreciation or in any other way, or unless stocks of goods seem relatively small; otherwise they will become over-loaded and sooner or later be forced to liquidate at a loss until the price-level falls to the point at which all supply and demand balance. Vice versa, unless they expect an increase in the velocity of production, or a decrease in the velocity of final-buying, or unless stocks of goods are large, they will not attempt to decrease their stocks of goods; otherwise they will sooner or later have to turn away final-buyers and buy in at prices high enough to cause the required increase in the velocity of production. It is, of course, true that the smaller businesses frequently merely try to adopt the same policy as the big concerns, and it is also true that the latter sometimes behave in a way merely designed to take advantage of, or aggravate, mistakes made by their competitors; but even in such cases it is always the condition of supply and demand which constitutes the background.

The velocities of production, final-buying, importation, exportation and the sizes of stocks of goods, in fact, constitute the standard by which prices are judged high or low from an operator's point of view. It is the business of producers and distributors to know and judge as well as possible the situation at all times in respect of all these factors, for when their judgment is faulty they surely buy too dear and sell too cheap, widening price fluctuations and making losses; whilst, to the extent that their judgment is good, their buying supports prices when unwarrantably low and their selling pulls prices down when unwarrantably high, shortening price fluctuations and making profits.

Summary

Briefly, then, we may conclude that the effects of variations in price-levels are as follows: (i) The velocity of production is decreased by a falling price-level, except when the fall is due to increased productive efficiency; and it is increased by a rising price-level, except when ready productive capacity is fully engaged, and unless the rise is so rapid that it impedes free exchange. (ii) The velocity of final-buying is sooner or later increased by a falling price-level, although sometimes it may be decreased at first; and, except when currency depreciation is feared, the velocity of final-buying is sooner or later decreased by a rising price-level, although sometimes it may be increased at first. (iii) The velocity of importation decreases immediately the price-level falls and increases immediately it rises, provided the said variations in the price-level are not neutralized—so far as foreign trade is concerned—by variations in rates in the foreign exchange market; whilst (iv), with the same proviso, the contrary is true of the velocity of exportation. (v) The behaviour of producers and distributors as regards their stocks of goods is affected by variations in the price-level to the extent that they deem such variations warrantable or otherwise.

We must now consider in what way the effects on velocities of exportation and importation of variations in price-levels may be neutralized by variations of rates in the foreign exchange market.

2 The effects of foreign payments or transfers on price-levels and on rates in the foreign exchange market

Foreign payments or transfers are payments from one country to another in respect of exports or imports of goods and services or gold, and in respect of transfers of money income or money capital (including bank loans) for any reason from one country to another. They are effected by means of the foreign exchange market, which is an international system whereby the currencies of the different countries are exchanged by those who wish to make foreign payments or obtain foreign moneys.

When a country is making a foreign payment, it obtains the required amount of foreign currency in exchange for the equivalent amount of its own currency at the current rate; and when a country is receiving a foreign payment, the amount to be paid in its own currency must be obtained by the paying country in exchange for the equivalent amount of its own currency at the current rate. Thus, whether a country is making, or whether it is receiving, foreign payments, enough of its currency is required and obtained for the purpose.

i *The sources of money with which foreign payments or transfers are made and received*

Money for making and receiving foreign payments or transfers either consists of money obtained from what is circulating in the country, or it consists of additional money thereto.

First, money obtained from what is circulating in the country is derived from the following sources:

> (*a*) Money derived from occupations, from the earnings of productive equipment, or from interest on loans made to governments or individuals for non-productive purposes, and made available by abstinence on the part of those to whom it accrues.
>
> (*b*) Money capital made available by liquidation or sale of stocks of goods or stock exchange securities.

Second, additional money is derived from the following sources:

> (*c*) Money capital made available by the sale of newly imported gold, by encroaching on savings deposits, and by bank loans, in a country at a time when its ready productive capacity is *not* fully engaged.
>
> (*d*) Money capital made available in either of the above ways in a country at a time when its ready productive capacity *is* fully engaged.

The effects of foreign payments being made or received vary, (i) in the home country, (ii) in countries abroad, and (iii) in the foreign exchange market, according to the source from which the home money is derived in the home country, according to how it is used in the home country after it is exchanged for foreign (or colonial) money, according to the source from which the foreign (or colonial) money is derived in countries abroad, and according to the way in which it is used abroad after being exchanged for the home money.

ii *The effects in the home country of foreign payments being made and received*

First, when money obtained from what is circulating[40] in the home country, after being exchanged for foreign (or colonial) money, gets into the hands of recipients who hold it on deposit or use it for repaying loans obtained from bankers, other things being equal, a decrease in the velocity of final-buying and a lower price-level are caused in the home country.

Second, when money obtained from what is circulating in the home country, after being exchanged for foreign (or colonial) money, is used by the recipients for final-buying[41]—necessarily in the home country—other things being equal, the velocity of final-buying and the price-level in the home country remain unchanged.

Third, when additional money[42] in the home country, after being exchanged for foreign (or colonial) money, is held on deposit or used for repaying loans obtained from bankers by the recipients, other things being equal, the velocity of final-buying and the price-level in the home country remain unchanged.

Fourth, when additional money[43] in the home country, after being exchanged for foreign (or colonial) money, is used by the recipients for final-buying—necessarily—in the home country, at a time when its ready productive capacity is *not* fully engaged, other things being equal, an increase in the velocity of final-buying and a higher price-level are caused in the home country.

Fifth, when additional money[44] in the home country, after being exchanged for foreign (or colonial) money, is used by the recipients for final-buying—necessarily—in the home country, at a time when its ready productive capacity is fully engaged, other things being equal, the velocity of final-buying cannot be increased unless, as is unlikely,[45] stocks of goods are allowed to decrease, but the price-level rises rapidly and all the symptoms of aggravated inflation and currency depreciation appear.

Thus, the effects in the home country of foreign payments being made and received depend upon the sources of the home money used and what is done with it in the home country by the recipients who have given foreign (or colonial) money in exchange for it.

iii *The effects in countries abroad of foreign payments being made and received*

In the above manner it may also be shown that the effects in countries abroad of foreign payments being made and received depend upon the source of the foreign (or colonial) money used, and what is done with it abroad by the recipients who have given home money in exchange for it.

    [. . .]

iv *The effects in the foreign exchange market of foreign payments being made and received*

First, when gold standard exchanges are in operation in countries making foreign payments to each other, the foreign payments to be made and received by each one of these countries are exchanged, or set against each other in the foreign exchange market, at their gold parity rates, or at not exceeding a difference from their gold parity rates equal to the cost[46] per currency unit of despatching and delivering gold. Thus, when total foreign payments to be made and to be received by any country do not equal each other at the gold parity rates of the respective currencies to be exchanged, rates of exchange alter enough to cause gold equal to the difference to be despatched and delivered by the country or countries from which the difference is due.

For example, if at any time the payments to be made by England to countries abroad amount to a total of 48.665(x), and payments to be received from countries abroad amount to a total of £10x, both payments exchange, or offset each other in the foreign exchange market, at their gold parity rates—since £1 and $4.8665 both contain the same quantity of fine ounces of gold. In effect, England will be bidding for the 48.665(x), which she requires, and will be disposed to offer £10x, whilst countries abroad will be together bidding for the £10x required by them and will be disposed to offer the 48.665(x) required by England; and thus they will come to terms on this basis. But should foreign payments to be made by England be increased by 4.8665(x) to a total of 53.5315(x), yet foreign payments to be received remain at only £10x, England will either have to settle this difference of 4.8665(x) by shipping £x gold to countries abroad, or she will have to procure the additional dollars by offering additional sterling in the foreign exchange market. Thus, in the foreign exchange market England will have to offer at least £11x in order to procure the required total of 53.5315(x), whilst countries abroad, being only in need of £10x, will not offer more than 48.665(x); and, thus, £11x will only be worth 48.665(x)—namely, the rate of exchange for £1 will have dropped to $4.4223. Somebody, however, will buy the additional £x at, say, $4.84 per £1, and ship it in gold to the United States, where they can exchange it for dollars at its parity rate of $4.8665; and thus the sterling rate of exchange will not fall below $4.84 so long as gold can be shipped from England at this price.

It sometimes happens, that for one reason or another foreign payments to be made by a country are continuously greater, on the basis of gold parity rates, than foreign payments to be received. This, as explained above, involves the continuous export of adequate quantities of gold, which if carried beyond a certain point will deplete the gold supply of the country and force it to abandon the gold standard exchange.

Second, when no gold standard exchange is in operation, total foreign payments to be made by a country at any time are set against the total foreign payments to be received by it at that time, and the rate of exchange of its currency is determined accordingly. If, for example, France has to pay £10x and to receive Frcs. 1240x, then £10x equals Frcs. 1240x in the foreign exchange market, and the rate of exchange for sterling and francs is 124 francs for £1.

Thus, when the quantity of any currency in demand on the foreign exchange market increases in relation to the quantity offered, the foreign exchange value of the currency unit in question rises; and, vice versa, when bidding for it is relatively decreased, its foreign exchange value falls.

3 The effects of foreign payments or transfers on exports and imports

Variations in the quantity of currency of a country in demand on the foreign exchange market in relation to the quantity offered are due to variations in foreign payments to be made or to be received by the country in question in settlement: (i) of any balance between, on the one hand, the money value of its exports, and on the other, the money value of its imports, of goods and services and gold, and (ii) of any balance between its inward and outward transfers of money income and money capital (including bank loans).

i *The effects on a country's exports and imports of foreign payments in settlement of balances between the money value of its exports and imports*

For the sake of simplicity, let us assume that the home money value of the exports of the home country is normally equal to the home money value of its imports. Let us now assume that for some reason[47] the price-level in the home country becomes lower in relation to the general price-level of countries abroad. Then, other things being equal,[48] the velocity of exportation of the home country immediately[49] increases in relation to its velocity of importation. But this may represent little or no gain in money to the home country and it may represent a loss to it in goods and services; for one of the following events will result:

First, if the home price-level falls, other things being equal, countries abroad may buy a larger quantity of goods and services from the home country for the same or less home money, so that, in spite of any decreased imports into the home country, the total home money value of its exports may still be no greater than the total home money value of its imports. Thus, the exports of the home country will increase in relation to its imports as to quantity, but may not increase as to money value, representing a net loss of goods and services to it.

Second, if the price-level in countries abroad rises, other things being equal, they will buy a larger quantity of goods and services from the home country for more home money, but the imports of the home country—even though decreased— may cost so much more at the higher general price-level of countries abroad that the total home money value of its exports will still be no greater than the total home money value of its imports. Thus, the result, as in the preceding case, may be a net loss of goods and services to the home country.

Third, if, as the result of a fall in the home price-level or a rise in the general price-level of countries abroad, the home country does gain foreign money by increasing its exports in relation to its imports, the money will either have to be brought home in gold or it will have to be spent abroad, used abroad or kept abroad. For, in practice, if the money is not used or kept abroad, it will be exchanged in the foreign exchange market; and the rise in the foreign exchange value of the home currency will be enough to make it worth while for the requisite quantity of gold to be brought from abroad. But, if gold cannot be freely brought from abroad, either because it is not freely available or because its import is prohibited, the foreign exchange value of the home currency will rise enough to cause the exports of the home country to decrease in relation to its imports. Thus the foreign exchange value of the home currency will respond to the smallest variations between foreign payments to be made and foreign payments to be received by the home country in such manner as to cause any differences to be settled at once either in gold or in goods and services.

We may therefore conclude that, when the price-level in a country becomes lower in relation to the general price-level abroad and its velocity of exportation increases in relation to its velocity of importation, this may represent a loss in goods without a gain in money to the home country; and if in certain circumstances a money gain is secured, it must either be left abroad, or used for importing gold, or surrendered by increased imports in relation to exports.

ii *The effects on a country's exports and imports of foreign payments in settlement of balances between inward and outward transfers of money income or money capital*

Whereas foreign payments in settlement of foreign trade balances operate upon exports and imports by causing variations in rates in the foreign exchange market, foreign payments in settlement of balances between inward and outward transfers of money income or money capital (including bank loans) may operate upon imports and exports not only in this way through foreign exchange rates, but also by causing variations in the price-levels of the respective countries. Thus, for example, when inward transfers of money income or money capital from abroad to the home country increase in relation to similar outward transfers, either withdrawal of money from circulation abroad causes the general price-level of countries abroad to fall, or injection of additional money into circulation in the home country causes its price-level to rise, or no change is caused in the quantity of money in circulation and in price-levels abroad or at home, but the foreign exchange rate of the home country is caused to rise. Therefore, in one way or another the aggregate money value of all visible and invisible imports[50] of goods and services and gold of the home country is caused to increase in relation to the aggregate money value of all like exports.[51]

iii *The effects on a country's exports and imports of all its foreign payments and transfers taken together*

When a country is receiving a balance of foreign payments in respect of a balance of exports over imports plus a balance of inward transfers of money income and money capital (including bank loans) over similar outward transfers, any such balance of inward foreign payments will cause outward foreign payments of an equal aggregate amount, in one or more of the following ways:

Case 1. An inward balance of foreign payments may all be used for final-buying in the receiving country, which will cause its wholesale price-level to rise and the total money value of its imports to increase in relation to the total money value of its exports to the extent of the inward foreign payments in question. In this case, the marketing of products of the receiving country will not be decreased, for its increased imports or decreased exports are caused by, and correspond with, the increase in the velocity of final-buying in the home markets. Further, increased labour and transport services will be required and employed for handling the increased quantity of goods.

Case 2. An inward balance of foreign payments, even when it causes an inflow of gold into the receiving country, may fail to cause a rise or prevent a fall in its price-level, because the recipients, whether individuals or the government, may hold it or an equal quantity of money on deposit or use it for repaying loans obtained from bankers, instead of using it for final-buying. The effects in this case are malignant both in the paying and in the receiving countries.

(*a*) Withdrawal of money from circulation, in the paying countries, whether due to shrinkage of their gold supplies or not, will cause their general price-levels to fall until either their imports—both as to money value and quantity—from the receiving country are decreased, or until their exports— both as to money value and quantity—are increased, entering the receiving country and displacing its exports to other countries by undercutting the cost of production.

(*b*) In spite of any shrinkage of gold supplies in the paying countries, their general price-level may be kept up by means of the issue of additional supplies of fiduciary paper money and credit money. In this case, the outflow of gold will continue from the paying countries until the money balance against them is settled, or until their gold supplies are exhausted or stopped by government decree. And when the outflow of gold is stopped, the foreign exchange rates of their currencies will be forced down until either their imports—both as to money value and quantity—from the receiving country are decreased, or until their exports—both as to money value and quantity— are increased, entering the receiving country, and displacing its exports to other countries, by under-cutting the cost of production. In other words, the money cost of production in the paying countries will undercut the money cost of production in the receiving country through the fall in the foreign exchange value of the currencies of the paying countries.

(*c*) When an inward balance of foreign payments is not used for final-buying, but placed on deposit or used for repaying loans obtained from bankers, additional supplies of gold are unnecessary to the receiving country. Its government may therefore prohibit the import of gold with a view to stabilizing the general price-levels of the paying countries in the hope that this will protect it against the entry of increased imports, and the displacement of some of its exports, through price-cutting. In this case, the only way of paying money balances to the receiving country is to buy its currency in the foreign exchange market, in case of need at a premium on its gold parity. The currency of the receiving country will thus appreciate in relation to the gold, currencies, goods and services of all other countries until either its exports—both as to money value and quantity—to the paying countries are decreased, or until the exports—both as to money value and quantity—of the paying countries are increased, entering the receiving country or displacing its exports to other countries by under-cutting the cost of production. In other words, the money cost of production in the paying countries will under-cut the cost of production in the receiving country through the rise in the foreign exchange value of its currency.

There is, therefore, no way in which a country can prevent its exports of goods and services[52] decreasing in relation to its imports of goods and services whenever foreign payments being received exceed foreign payments being made, except to the extent that it (the country) may import gold, accumulate inaccessible assets abroad, pay foreign (or colonial) creditors, or make losses—or presents—abroad. On the other hand, a country cannot receive any imports unless they are preceded or accompanied by inward foreign payments to the extent of their money value; or, in other words, the home country cannot obtain foreign currencies to pay for any kind of imports unless it is receiving foreign payments in respect of exports of goods and services or gold, or in respect of net inward transfers of money income or money capital (including bank loans) from abroad.

It is essential to distinguish between *Case* 1, when the receipt of a balance of inward foreign payments from abroad causes the imports of the receiving country to increase in relation to its exports by means of an increase in the velocity of final-buying of its own inhabitants, and *Case* 2, when this balance of inward foreign payments causes the foreign trade balance of the receiving country to undergo the same alteration by means of forced price-cutting. In *Case* 1 no harm can come to the receiving country; whilst the worst that can happen to the paying countries is limited to the imposition of more or less frugality upon them at times when their ready productive capacities are fully engaged, in order to release the required quantity of goods and services for export. But in *Case* 2, the forced price-cutting resulting from the application of economic pressure by the withdrawal of money from circulation in the paying countries, or resulting from the depreciation of the foreign exchange values of their currencies, causes reduced production and losses both in the receiving country and in the paying countries during the period of readjustment, which may be long and difficult.

4 The effects of foreign investments on exports and imports

(i) A country wishing to obtain assets in countries abroad faster than countries abroad are obtaining assets in it, either because it is anxious to extend its position as a creditor country or because it must meet its obligations as a debtor country, can only do so in the following ways: *first*, through people with assets abroad coming to reside in it (the home country); *second*, through money income derived from countries abroad and money capital made available by exports—sales of goods and services in countries abroad—being retained abroad instead of being converted by the home country into additional imports; and *third*, through quantities of the home currency being steadily and continuously sold at a discount in the foreign exchange market, creating net assets for the home country in countries abroad both to the extent that its imports are caused to decrease in relation to its exports and to the extent that the amount of home currency sold to countries abroad depreciates in value.

When the home country obtains such net assets in countries abroad in the *first* way stated above—namely, through people with assets abroad coming to reside in the home country—other things being equal, the world velocities of final-buying and production are not affected. But when the home country, by decreasing its imports in relation to its exports or by selling a depreciating currency, in the above *second* and *third* ways, obtains net assets abroad consisting in whole or in part of money,[53] other things being equal, the velocities of final-buying and production in countries abroad will decrease in relation to their ready productive capacity, causing international price-cutting and general trade depression in the home country as well as in countries abroad. In effect, this is what will happen if such money[54] obtained abroad is held on deposit, instead of being at once used by the home country for making[55] investments and loans in countries abroad in such manner that it is used or caused to be used at once for final-buying there; but it will only happen if the said money is held on deposit (by the home country), and it will not happen if such behaviour on the part of the home country is neutralized by countries abroad increasing their final-buying with additional money made available by encroaching on their savings deposits or by obtaining loans from their banks.

Thus, whatever the advantages to an individual country of obtaining assets in countries abroad faster than they are obtaining assets in it, obviously all countries cannot do so simultaneously; and when some country or countries attempt or manage to do so, the effect is often, if not usually, a decrease in the velocity of final-buying in the other countries, resulting in international price-cutting, and in a decrease in the velocity of production and general trade depression in the former countries as well as in the latter.

(ii) The idea is everywhere prevalent in the creditor countries that on no account should they encroach on any of their foreign capital for current expenditure. But usually the same people are equally convinced that it is a necessity, from the point of view of sound finance, for the debtor countries to reduce their debts to the creditor countries. The facts are that notwithstanding the existence of either trade depression or improvidence in a country, its foreign investments can only be reduced, or its foreign debts increased, by means of (*a*) long-term loans from abroad, (*b*) short-term loans from abroad resulting from interest rates being relatively higher at home than abroad, (*c*) the withdrawal of money from abroad by the actual possessors of the foreign investments, (*d*) the decline in the productivity of the foreign investments, (*e*) the loss or confiscation of money or property abroad, or (*f*) the emigration of capitalists. A country cannot be decreasing its foreign capital when all the above-stated conditions are absent; and, when a country is not decreasing its foreign capital, any efforts on the part of debtor countries to pay off—decrease—any such foreign capital will work against general industrial balance by unduly decreasing the velocity of final-buying both in the paying and in the receiving countries.

(iii) Another important fact which must be emphasized is that, inasmuch as any excess in the money value of a country's imports over the money value of its exports constitutes the delivery of increased purchasing power to it, in any country where continuous "adverse" foreign trade balances constitute equilibrium in respect of its international accounts, the power exists to maintain a higher standard of living or a larger population than would otherwise be the case.

5 The relation of the price-level to the foreign exchange value of the currency

i *Currency appreciation*

To the extent that a fall in the price-level in the home country actually causes increased foreign payments to be made to it in respect of an improved foreign trade balance, *other things being equal*, the foreign exchange value of its currency rises; and thus the internal appreciation of the currency causes its external appreciation. But internal currency appreciation does not *necessarily* cause external currency appreciation; for a fall in the price-level in the home country, *first*, if accompanied by a similar or greater fall in the general price-level of countries abroad, would prevent an improvement in the foreign trade balance of the home country, or, *second*, if accompanied by the transfer of money income or money capital to countries abroad, might create enough or more than enough outward foreign payments to offset any inward foreign payments in respect of an improved foreign trade balance of the home country.

On the other hand, to the extent that a rise in the foreign exchange value of the home currency causes its imports to be cheaper, *other things being equal*, the price-level in the home country falls; and thus the external appreciation of the home currency causes its internal appreciation. But external currency appreciation does not *necessarily* cause internal currency appreciation; for the rise in the foreign exchange value of the home currency may be accompanied by a decrease in the velocity of production or an increase in the velocity of final-buying in the home country, causing the prices of the home-produced goods and services to rise enough and more than enough to neutralize the lower prices of imports.

In general, it may be said that, although sometimes currency appreciation is due to a fall in the price-level caused by increased production, currency appreciation may cause decreased production. For the expectation of a fall in the price-level will decrease or postpone the effective demand for and production of the more durable kinds of equipment; and the expectation of a rise in the foreign exchange value of the currency will attract inward transfers of money from abroad which will decrease its exports in relation to its imports, and displace home production to the extent that such inward transfers may cause money to be withdrawn from circulation and held on deposit or used for repaying loans obtained from bankers.[56]

ii *Currency depreciation*

A rise in the price-level in a country usually causes a fall in the foreign exchange value of its currency, either by causing its imports to increase in relation to its exports,[57] or by creating fear of currency depreciation and causing money to be transferred abroad for safety by capitalists or for profit by currency speculators; and thus the internal depreciation of the home currency causes its external depreciation. But internal currency depreciation does not *necessarily* cause external currency depreciation; for the rise in the price-level in the home country may be accompanied by a rise in the general price-level of countries abroad, or by increased inward transfers of money income or money capital from abroad, enough to prevent a fall in the foreign exchange value of the home currency.

On the other hand, although external currency depreciation is usually followed by internal currency depreciation due to the increased cost of imports raising the home price-level, this may be prevented by an increase in the velocity of production or a decrease in the velocity of final-buying in the home country.

In general, it may be said that, although sometimes currency depreciation is due to a rise in the price-level following on decreased production, after-war experience shows that so long as the depreciation is not too rapid, it stimulates the velocity of final-buying and the production of both equipment and consumable goods. Germany, France and Italy have largely increased and improved their resources in equipment, and even in their foreign investments, as the result of the fact that it was not possible during the periods of currency depreciation to accumulate or maintain capital by buying bonds or holding money on deposit in their own countries. England's equipment and foreign trade suffered during the period 1920–1926—equipment suffering as the result of expectation of lower prices and insufficient final-buying, and foreign trade as the result of inward transfers of money capital seeking safety from countries where currency depreciation was in progress. The United States suffered in the same way during the period 1920–1921; but the period 1922–1924 was one of mild internal and external currency depreciation (*i.e.* rising prices and falling foreign exchange value of the dollar), accompanied by increased final-buying and increased production; whilst, during the period 1925–1926, although internal currency appreciation set in due to increased productive efficiency, the dollar continued to depreciate mildly in relation to the most important currencies, and both final-buying and production increased to record figures.

iii *The standard of living and variations in the foreign exchange value of the currency*

A fall in the foreign exchange value of the home currency does not render necessary a decrease in the velocity of final-buying or a lower standard of living in the home country, unless its ready productive capacity is fully engaged.

Thus, in the case of a debtor country forced to make continuous transfers of money income abroad, the most rational policy would seem to be something on the following lines: *First*, home interest rates to be kept sufficiently low to prevent outward transfers in settlement of debt payments being offset by inward transfers of money capital from countries abroad.[58] *Second*, the home price-level to be kept rigorously in hand, chiefly by regulation of the home velocity of final-buying by means of rational policies in relation to government expenditure and taxes on consumption. *Third*, free dealings in the foreign exchange market on no account to be interfered with, and the foreign exchange value of the home currency not to be prevented from falling except to the extent that rigorous stabilization of the home price-level in the above-stated manner prevents it falling. Thus, the transfer of money to creditors abroad, as well as any outward transfers of money capital due to the low home interest rates, to be allowed to keep the foreign exchange value of the home currency low enough to maintain the ready productive capacity of the country fully engaged without disturbing the price-level. *Fourth*, inward transfers of money from abroad, when not required to finance the purchase of foreign raw materials, to be prevented by taxation of foreign-owned capital. A policy of this kind would, no doubt, involve the abandonment of any gold stand-ard exchange, but, if properly handled by the debtor country, it would exclude imports and force out exports to such an extent that foreign debts would either be quickly paid, or they would impose intolerable economic conditions in the receiving countries.

On the other hand, a rise in the foreign exchange value of the home currency in all cases renders necessary an increase in the velocity of final-buying in the home country, otherwise cheaper foreign products will displace home production. If the rise is due to increased inward foreign payments in relation to outward foreign payments, resulting from increased exports in relation to imports or increased income derived from abroad, such money may be spent as income; but if the rise is due to increased inward transfers of money capital in relation to similar outward transfers, the inflowing foreign money capital must be invested in commodity capital.

6 Conclusions on the prospects of the home country neutralizing excessive abstinence of home final-buyers by improving its foreign trade balance

In the preceding sections (as numbered) of this chapter the following has been demonstrated:

(1) A fall in the price-level of the home country, whether caused by increased production or increased abstinence, immediately causes exports to increase in relation to imports, provided the fall is not neutralized by a similar fall in the general price-level of countries abroad, and provided it is not neutralized by a rise in the foreign exchange value of the home currency.

(2) A fall in the price-level of the home country in relation to the general price-level of countries abroad will be neutralized in the foreign exchange market when the quantity of home currency in demand increases enough in relation to the quantity offered.

(3) The quantity of home currency in demand on the foreign exchange market will increase in relation to the quantity offered when foreign payments to be received increase in relation to foreign payments to be made, which may take place, either (i) because the aggregate money value of exports increases in relation to the aggregate value of imports, and the difference is neither imported in gold nor invested or kept abroad; or (ii) because inward transfers of money income or money capital (including bank loans) increase in relation to similar outward transfers. Thus, whilst increased exports in relation to imports may represent a loss in goods and services without a gain in money, there is no way in which a country can prevent imports being increased or exports being decreased by the receipt of an excess of inward foreign payments over outward foreign payments, except to the extent that it may import gold, accumulate inaccessible assets abroad, make losses abroad or pay foreign (or colonial) creditors. Further, (iii) when the receipt of the inward balance of foreign payments causes the imports of the receiving country to increase in relation to its exports by causing an increase in the velocity of final-buying in the receiving country, no harm can come to the receiving country, whilst the worst that can happen to the paying countries is limited to the imposition of more or less frugality upon them at times when their ready productive capacities are fully engaged, in order to release the required quantity of goods and services for export; but when the receipt of the inward balance of foreign payments causes the foreign trade balance to undergo the said alteration by causing price-cutting in one form or another, losses are caused both to the receiving and to the paying countries, due to reduced production during the period of readjustment, which may be long and difficult.

We may therefore conclude that, since a fall in the price-level of the home country may be neutralized both by a fall in the general price-level of countries abroad and by rates on the foreign exchange market, and since the question of whether it is or is not so neutralized depends entirely upon what is being done by final-buyers in countries abroad, by bankers and governments in the matter of international gold movements, and by capitalists and creditors in the matter of inward and outward transfers of money income and money capital, it is not to be expected that the foreign trade balance of the home country can be improved by any amount of mere abstinence or by any manipulations of foreign trade restrictions or tariffs, but it is to be expected that the velocity of final-buying by countries abroad will decrease and aggravate, as often as it increases and neutralizes, a decrease in the home velocity of final-buying.

Note

The questions of management of currency, problems arising from international debts, and the business of a creditor country, are dealt with in relation to current events in later chapters, which it is hoped will facilitate the understanding of the theory here put forward.

VIII   The irregular final-buying by governments

1 The effects of reduction of government debts, and the effects of government final-buying with money raised by taxation and by borrowing

Final-buying by governments constitutes government expenditure in all departments, excluding the application of money to the service of interest and repayment of government debts. Expenditure on such things as civil administration, public works and national defence, is therefore final-buying by governments.

Our inquiry will show that government final-buying by means of either revenue, loans from the public or bank loans has, hitherto, never been consistently determined by the question of neutralization of harmful variations in the velocity of (general) final-buying and has increased these variations as often as it has decreased them.

The effect on the velocity of final-buying of raising revenue from the public by means of taxation, or of raising funds by means of loans from the public or loans from the banks, depends upon the manner in which money so raised is disposed of, and the manner in which it would have been disposed of had it not been so raised. For the purpose of our inquiry, therefore, we must consider: (i) the effects of reduction of government debts; (ii) the effects of government final-buying when met by taxation and when met by loans from the public; (iii) the effects of government final-buying when met by loans from the banks; and (iv) the effects on foreign trade of variations in the price-level caused in the above ways.

i *The effects of reduction of government debts*

On the velocity of final-buying. When money withdrawn from the public by taxation is applied by a government to the reduction of the national debt of the country, the velocity of final-buying is decreased to the extent that the public abstains from final-buying in order to reserve the money for paying the taxes. When the money remains in the hands of the public, a large portion of it is used for final-buying; whilst when it is taken from the public and is all applied by the government to the repayment of loans from the public and to the repayment of bank loans, none of it is normally used for final-buying. For in the case of the repayment by the government of loans obtained from the public, the public does not use the repaid money—which is money capital—for increased final-buying of consumable goods, and it is unlikely to use it for increased final-buying of equipment and for increasing stocks of goods—except on the rare occasions when, owing to real or technical monetary shortage, the purchase of the said commodity capital is conditional upon the repayment of loans by the government. And, in the case of the repayment by the government of loans obtained from bankers, this does not increase the velocity of final-buying of the public, except on the rare occasions when, owing to the real or technical monetary shortage, an increase in bank loans to the public for increased requirements of industry and trade is conditional upon a reduction of bank loans to governments. Moreover, pronounced reduction of government final-buying for the purpose of applying the money to the reduction of government debts tends to cause a decrease in the effective demand for loans for industry and trade.

On the price-level. As a matter of fact, a process consisting of the application of the proceeds of taxation to repayment of government debts, resulting, as it almost invariably does, in a decrease in the velocity of final-buying of both the government and the public, constitutes the process of deflation as operated by a government. In such cases, there can be no rise in the price-level as a result of new taxation, it being purely a question of whether a fall can be averted by some means or another. The taxation, instead of being passed on to final buyers, is taken out of producers' and distributors' profit-and-loss accounts, wages and—eventually—rents. In the case of a tax on a particular article, if the earnings of the people engaged in the different stages of its production and distribution are too slender for the tax to be borne in whole or in part by them, the tax may be passed on to final buyers to the extent that the latter are willing to buy at a higher price; but, at a time when the process of deflation is being operated by a government, other things being equal, final buyers decrease the velocity of final-buying in all directions to an extent more or less proportionate with any higher price that they may have to pay for a particular article, and this, by depressing profits, wages and rents, tends to lower the price-level. Taxes on imported goods, when the proceeds are applied to the repayment of government debts, operate in a similar manner—namely, final buyers have to decrease their purchases of goods and services in general because they have less money after paying the taxes on the imported goods, and this depresses the price-level—if not the prices of the imported goods.

On the commodity value of the debts. Reduction of government debts when accompanied by deflation does not, in view of the lower price-level, result in any reduction of the commodity value of the debt. The British Chancellor of the Exchequer, in 1926, supplied information showing that, whereas the total interest paid on the National Debt, exclusive of American Debt, had fallen since the Budget year 1920–1921 from £326,000,000 to £274,000,000 for 1925, the burden in terms of commodities at the lower price-level had risen in the same period from £225,000,000 to £274,000,000.[59]

Reduction of the money value of national debts may, therefore, cause a decrease in the velocity of final-buying in relation to the velocity of production, without bringing about a decrease in the commodity value of the debts.

ii *The effects of government final-buying when met by taxation and when met by loans from the public*

On the velocity of final-buying. When money that is either withdrawn from the public by taxation, or borrowed from it, is used for government final-buying or for the service of interest on government debts, the velocity of final-buying is usually increased. For, should the money have remained in the hands of the public, it is unlikely to have all been used for final-buying; but, in the case under considera-tion, it is either all used for final-buying by the government, or it is paid to people as income and mostly or entirely used for final-buying by them.[60] Further, although final buyers may buy less to the extent that their tax payments and, possibly, higher prices affect them, or to the extent that they practise abstinence in order to lend to the government, on the whole they may not reduce the quantity of money that they use for final-buying enough to offset the quantity that they pay or lend to the government for government final-buying.

It is true that, on the rare occasions when the ready productive capacity of a country is fully engaged, an alteration in the kind of goods being bought, arising from government final-buying taking the place of final-buying by the public, may cause a temporary decrease in the velocity of production and a downward adjust-ment in the velocity of final-buying. It is also true that there is a limit to the pro-portion[61] of the income of private enterprise that can be withdrawn by the government without both lowering ready productive capacity by starving labour and equipment, and decreasing incentives to production. But, except in cases of the above kind, the velocity of final-buying cannot be decreased, and is usually increased, as the result of money raised by taxation or by loans from the public being used for government final-buying.

On the price-level. Whether the velocity of final-buying is increased or not as the result of money either withdrawn from the public by taxation, or borrowed from it, being used for government final-buying, a rise in the price-level is not necessarily involved. In the first place, when no increase in the velocity of final-buying is caused, there can be little likelihood of a rise in the price-level being caused; for, when an increase in the velocity of final-buying by the government is accompanied by an equivalent decrease in the velocity of final-buying of the public, it is to be expected that the prices of some articles will fall enough, or almost enough, to neutralize any rise in the prices of others. In the second place, even when the velocity of final-buying is increased, neither a temporary nor a permanent rise in the price-level is necessarily involved. For an increase in the velocity of final-buying may, in certain market conditions, merely prevent a tem-porary fall instead of causing a temporary rise in the price-level; whilst a perma-nent rise in the price-level is not involved except on the rare occasions when the ready productive capacity of the country concerned is fully engaged, or unless the increased home final-buying causes imports to increase in relation to exports, whereby the foreign exchange value of the currency falls.[62] Further, an increase in the velocity of final-buying at a time when ready productive capacity is not fully engaged, whether it averts a fall in the price-level on over-stocked markets or whether it causes a rise in the price-level on under-stocked markets, causes the velocity of production to increase, and the larger turnover may eventually enable producers and distributors to sell at lower prices even when new taxation is added to the cost of production.

iii The effects of government final-buying when met by loans from the banks

On the velocity of final-buying. When additional money created by government borrowing from bankers—with or without resort to any increased issue of fiduciary paper money—is used for government final-buying or for service of interest on government debts, the velocity of final-buying is almost invariably increased. For, except on the rare occasions when increased bank loans to the government are conditional upon decreased bank loans to the public, the increased final-buying of the government with the additional money is unlikely to be neutralized by decreased final-buying of the public.

On the price-level. Inflation is not necessarily involved; for, as we have seen in (ii), an increase in the velocity of final-buying does not necessarily involve either a temporary or a permanent rise in the prive-level, and, by causing the velocity of production to increase, may eventually enable producers and distributors to sell the larger output even at lower prices.

iv The effects on foreign trade of variations in the price-level caused in the above ways

Whether taxation for the purpose of reduction of national debt in the home country causes a fall in its price-level, or whether taxation or government borrowing in the home country for the purpose of government final-buying or service of interest on loans causes a rise in the home price-level, the amount of money corresponding to the *balance* of foreign trade of the home country will not be affected, except to the extent that inward and outward gold movements and inward and outward transfers of money income or money capital (including bank loans) may be affected—which may be little or not at all. For we have seen in the preceding chapter[63] that, whatever the part played by price-levels, the money value of a country's foreign trade balance is determined by the balance of its imports and exports of gold or by the balance of its inward and outward transfers of money income and money capital (excluding payments for goods and services and gold); and that such international gold movements and transfers of money income and money capital are dependent upon the decisions of governments and bankers, capitalists and creditors.

v *The effects on foreign trade of import and export tariffs*

For the same reasons, the amount of money corresponding to a country's foreign trade *balance* is not directly affected even by the imposition of import and export tariffs at home and abroad. If, for instance, a creditor country puts on prohibitive import tariffs, and unless it chooses continuously to import gold or invest or keep money abroad to the extent of its income derived from abroad, the foreign exchange value of its currency will rise so much that not only its exports will be completely stopped, but enough inducement will be created for all its income derived from abroad to be spent abroad by its people travelling or living abroad.

Nevertheless, although—as we have just seen—both taxation operating on price-levels and imports and export tariffs only affect a country's foreign trade *balance* to the extent that they may affect—if at all—international movements of gold, of money income and of money capital, import and export tariffs always closely affect the quantity, nature and the *total* money value of *all* its exports and imports. Hence, in the case of a country where the total quantity of money being received from countries abroad in respect of its exports, plus any net inward transfers of money income or money capital it may be receiving, or minus any similar net outward transfers it may be making, does not exceed the total money value of raw materials that it is receiving from abroad, its population and industry can be increased by the imposition of import tariffs on manufactured goods. For instance, a country that consumes one-quarter of its own agricultural produce, and exports the remaining three-quarters in payment for imported manufactured goods, might, perhaps, double its population by exporting, not the three-quarters, but only half of its agricultural produce, and importing proportionately less manufactured goods. It would then have half, instead of a quarter, of its food production for home consumption—or enough to feed double its previous population—and the substitution of imported raw materials for imported manufactured goods would provide it with the means, both as regards increased raw materials and as regards home markets for manufactured goods, for employing the increased population. Thus, countries like Argentina, Canada, Denmark, Sweden, stand to gain by discriminating tariffs against imported manufactured goods.

In a country, however, where the total quantity of money being received from abroad in respect of the imports, plus any net inward money income or money capital it may be receiving, exceeds the total money value of its requirements of raw materials and foodstuffs from abroad, there is nothing to be gained by import tariffs—so far as industrial activity or increased population is concerned. Whilst the total amount of money corresponding to a country's foreign trade *balance*, as already stated, cannot be affected—except to the extent that international movements of gold, of money income and of money capital may be affected—by import tariffs, alterations in the nature of imports are of no avail when foreign payments to be received from abroad are, for any reason, so great that they entail the receipt of visible and invisible imports in excess of all requirements of imported raw materials and foodstuffs.

2 The question of policy in relation to reduction of government debts, and in relation to government final-buying with money raised by taxation or by borrowing

We have found:

(i) That the withdrawal of money from the public by taxation and its application to the reduction of government debts, other things being equal, causes a decrease in the velocity of final-buying and a fall in the price-level, except on the rare occasions when increased final-buying by the public is conditional upon repayment of government debts to the public, and when increased bank loans to the public in response to increased trade requirements are conditional upon repayment of government debts to banks.

(ii) That the withdrawal of money from the public by taxation or by government borrowing and its application to government final-buying or to the service of interest on government debts may cause an increase, but not a decrease, in the velocity of final-buying; and that whether or not such an increase in the velocity of final-buying is caused, a permanent rise in the price-level is only involved on the rare occasions when the ready productive capacity of the country is fully engaged.

(iii) That the use of additional money created by government borrowing from bankers—with or without resort to any increase in the issue of fiduciary paper money—for government final-buying or for the service of interest on government debts, other things being equal, causes the velocity of final buying to increase; and that inflation is not necessarily involved except at a time when the ready productive capacity of the country is fully engaged.

(iv) That, although the quantity, nature and total money value of a country's exports and imports are always closely affected by import and export tariffs, neither such tariffs nor taxation operating on the price-level affect the amount of money corresponding to the country's foreign trade *balance*, except to the extent that they may affect international movements of gold and transfers of money income and money capital—which may be little or not at all.

These conclusions clarify the question of policy in relation to reduction or increase of government debts.

Reduction of government debts can only be affected by means of (*a*) money withdrawn from the public by taxation, and (*b*) money withheld from the public by decreased government final-buying or by reduction in the rate of interest on government debts. Whether money is withdrawn by taxation or whether it is withheld by government economies, other things being equal, the velocity of final-buying is decreased, and the country suffers to the extent that the velocity of production may be decreased.

When the velocity of final-buying of the public is excessive in relation to the velocity of production, to the balance of imports and exports of gold, and to the balance of inward and outward transfers of money income and money capital, of the country in question, the velocity of final-buying should be decreased to the required extent by taxation or by government economies, and by the application of the money to reduction of government debts. Reduction of government debts should, in fact, take place at times when there is a tendency for the price-level to rise as the result of either any kind of impediment to production, or any excessive increase in the velocity of final-buying.

Whether government debts are reduced by means of increased taxation or by means of reduced government expenditure makes little difference in the long run to the total volume of trade as a whole; but it is important for the welfare of the State that the required decrease in the velocity of final-buying should be effected at the point where final-buying, either by the government or by the public, is least necessary or desirable.

On the other hand, increased government final-buying by means of government borrowing should take place at times when the velocity of final-buying is insufficient in relation to the velocity of production, to the balance of imports and exports of gold, and to the balance of inward and outward transfers of money income and money capital, of the country concerned; and the money should be spent, for preference, on public works of some kind.

There is, to-day, no such thing as an exact orthodox conception of the effects of reduction of government debts, and the effects of government final-buying with money raised by taxation or by borrowing. A hazy idea exists that taxation has the effect of restricting trade, particularly the export trade; that government debts ought to be reduced "gradually," whatever that means; and that the necessary funds should be raised by reduced government final-buying rather than by taxation. At the same time, whilst the public is always pressing for reduced taxation, the different political parties—to say nothing of permanent government officials—are always pressing for something involving increased government expenditure; and, since it is hardly ever possible to satisfy all parties, each gets a turn from time to time in the ebb and flow of its political influence. Thus, ramps occur for such widely different things as: reduction of government debts—capital levies—tariff reform—reduced taxation—state aid for one purpose or another—and eight new battleships. But the question of neutralization of either insufficient or excessive final-buying on the part of the public is never considered at all, and, thus, harmful variations in the velocity of final-buying are increased as often as they are decreased by variations in the extent of taxation and in the extent of final-buying by governments.

IX The irregular final-buying resulting from the activities of producers and distributors

1 The effects of irregular final-buying of productive equipment

Irregular final-buying of productive equipment by producers causes variations in the quantity of money distributed for wages, rent, interest, materials and personal expenses by producers (and shareholders) in industries engaged in the production and distribution of productive equipment.

2 The effects of producers and distributors increasing and decreasing their stocks of goods

Variations in the velocity of final-buying result from variations in the quantity of money distributed by the process of production, through producers and distributors increasing and decreasing their stocks of goods. The effect of producers and distributors increasing their stocks of goods by increased production is to cause an increase in the velocity of production independently of any increase in the velocity of final-buying. This increase in the velocity of production, however, causes an increase in the quantity of money distributed for wages, rent, interest, materials and sometimes personal expenses, and some or all of the additional money is used for increased final-buying. Similarly, the effect of producers and distributors decreasing their stocks of goods by decreased production is to cause a decrease in the velocity of final-buying.

The extent of variations in the velocities of production and final-buying caused by producers and distributors in this way is vast. Minor and major variations in productive activity of particular industries, together with corresponding variations in the extent of final-buying of the people dependent thereon, are caused in this way; whilst minor and major general industrial fluctuations are caused according to the intensity of the fluctuations in each industry, and according to whether they more or less neutralize each other—activity in some being accompanied by slackness in others—or whether the contrary is the case and they more or less aggravate each other.

The larger or major general industrial fluctuations, which are always aggravated when not caused by producers and distributors increasing or decreasing their stocks of goods, are usually referred to as the "trade cycle." The so-called "trade cycle" is to some people a psychological affair, to others a mechanical affair, and there are not lacking those who even regard it as an astronomical affair. The fact seems to escape these people that, if fluctuations are possible—not to say frequent—in the productive activity of every particular industry, it is to be expected that every kind of combination as between conditions in all the industries and trades will occur, and that the general condition of industry and trade as a whole will vary from intensified slackness to intensified activity.

3 Confidence

It is not for fun that producers do not observe regularity in their final-buying of productive equipment, and that distributors increase and decrease their stocks of goods by ordering increased or decreased production, nor yet is it for love of speculation; for the penalty for failure is a capital one. Neither is it a matter of insufficient and defective information about the velocities of production and final-buying of different kinds of goods. In conditions of competitive production, to announce truthfully, for instance, that productive output is small whereas final-buying is going to be large, is to cause a glut the magnitude of which will vary to the extent that the information is acted upon; for when business men know that productive output is too small, they are bound to set about making it too great, unless a "quota" of the required increased output is agreed upon and allocated to each. In fact, more and better information about velocities of production and final-buying cannot help much unless coupled with some perfected system of cartelization, which, however, would entail other and perhaps worse disadvantages.

Moreover, we are not alone concerned with industrial fluctuations. There is also the question of the general low level of the mean productive output as compared with ready—not to say potential—productive capacity. We know that to-day in a well-equipped country even the biggest booms fail to reach the point at which ready productive capacity is fully engaged, unless final-buying is stimulated by a war or by fear of currency depreciation.

Perusal of financial papers and attention to the sayings of "big men" lead us to believe that general trade depressions as well as the general low level of the mean volume of trade are largely a matter of "confidence." Both the production of goods and the supply of adequate quantities of credit are dependent upon the existence of "confidence." But the question is: confidence in what? Confidence that there will be a succession of poor wheat crops in Argentina stimulates wheat-farming in Canada; or confidence that there will be an early imposition of a tax on imported wheat in England stimulates wheat-farming in England. Confidence that a long war is imminent stimulates the production of khaki cloth, guns and munitions—not to say fur coats and pianos; confidence in a lasting peace stimulates nothing in particular—unless it is a desire to make one's allies settle their war debts. Confidence that there will be a shortage stimulates production, and confidence that there will be plenty causes slackness; for the fact of the matter is that productive activity and all interest in it are dependent on the existence of the simple confidence that final buyers will buy, or something is going to happen to make them buy, and productive activity declines as soon as there is any sign that this confidence is not justified by the facts.[64]

Since final-buying by individuals is determined by distribution of income, and by habits with regard to consumption, use of non-productive equipment and abstinence;[65] since final-buying by countries abroad from the home country is determined by a variety of totally different factors at home and abroad;[66] since final-buying by governments is mainly determined by political conditions;[67] and since ready productive capacity is not the governing factor; more or less wide variations in the extent of final-buying resulting from the activities of producers and distributors are inevitable, due to over-cautiousness or over-confidence on their part and on the part of capitalists and financiers at different times, and thus the average velocity of production is correspondingly reduced.

4 A practical view of the mechanism of business activity

The possessors of all the cash, be it gold or paper money, in the last resort are the masters of the supply of credit money in the sense that no credit money can exist without their co-operation. Allowing that they are willing to use this cash for banking operations or to place it at the disposal of bankers, still no credit money can exist unless those who possess capital or wealth in some form are willing to borrow money. But none of them will be willing to borrow unless some of them are willing to buy.

We all want to buy more or less goods and services for our own consumption and use; and those who have got the money not only mean to buy certain things, but they can often be induced to buy more than they intend. Some have extremely expensive tastes; others are ambitious to become very rich; whilst yet others are mild creatures, content to produce and live in any way they can;—and they all desire to be respectable according to their lights. Here we have the qualities or weaknesses which drive people to produce and consume—the primary forces of the economic machine. Those who are ambitious borrow money in order to produce, transport, or hold stocks of goods, on a large scale for the requirements of the rest. Those who produce or increase their stocks of goods at a time when effective demand has reached its lowest point, and sell out when it has reached its highest point, score; and they deserve to score, because, on the one hand, they help to keep production going when such assistance is most required, and, on the other, they create reserves of goods which they bring out when most required. Besides, it is not so easy as it sounds to buy before a shortage and sell before a glut. Not only are variations in harvests, the extent of "saving," stock exchange conditions, banking policy, government policy, and economic and political conditions abroad, to be contended with, but whenever the majority operate on the theory of a prospective glut, a shortage must be the result, and, vice versa, when the majority act on the expectation of a shortage they invariably produce a glut.

Those who score by selling out on buoyant markets at a well-timed moment in advance of the rest may then tuck away all the money proceeds and sit tight until those who find themselves over-stocked, and displaced labour, come round begging for the vanished money. This is the masterly inactivity of the successful operators, and in this policy of laying-in-wait they can count on the assistance of every class and kind of respectable and disreputable buyer. All together, they wait to "slaughter" those who have missed their markets; for they all mean to profit by the situation if they can, and, in any case, to show mercy on such occasions would be risking their own skins. This is what in America is called the "buyers' strike." In the "buyers' strike," apart from a certain number of ne'er-do-well spendthrifts and such-like, "black-legs" are unknown; and the patriotic manner in which a large section of the Press calls loudly and sternly for economy on such occasions is a notable phenomenon of our time. The organized strike of labour is a poor thing, as measured by results, compared with the unorganized "buyers' strike." However, eventually glutted markets are cleared by production being reduced to hand-to-mouth requirements, and by stocks of goods being absorbed, in part by the more or less well-to-do, in part by the unemployed to whom something is given by way of a sort of charity, and in part by the successful operators who acquire the rest of it in exchange for some of the much-needed money which they have got tucked away.[68] This is the turning-point of the slump. The remnant of the once-surplus stocks of goods, having passed into strong hands, is no longer pressed for sale; and some of the erstwhile tucked-away money is out in circulation again.

The successful operators then hold for a rise in prices, and when this is obtained they and others commence to increase production. Trade thus expands again. At first, everybody is very careful; but whilst they are all being careful there is no money in it for any of them. They complain of the general lack of "confidence," so harmful to trade; and, at the beginning of each year, newspapers and "big men" usually make seasonal attempts to manufacture "confidence" by predicting booms. But some operators never again feel sufficiently confident to go full speed ahead and a few may retire rather than do things by halves; others do go ahead and, of these, some take their profits at the right time, and the rest get caught.

In this way, producers and distributors, dependent upon the velocity of final-buying and the way in which it is affected or likely to be affected by interest rates, by the movements of stock exchange prices, by foreign buying and by government buying, increase or decrease the purchasing power of the money in the hands of final buyers by altering the price-level, and increase or decrease the quantity of money in the hands of final buyers by increasing or decreasing the velocity of production. Thus, in their efforts to hold their own or score over each other in the struggle for a variable and usually limited market, they either prevent or cause or aggravate minor or major, particulars or general, fluctuations in industry and trade.

X   The cry for increased consumption

In these wonderful days of high-power machinery, labour-saving devices and organization, a small group of intellectual business men, economists and philosophers are advocating increased consumption as the best economic method of combating general trade depression. They argue that it is under-consumption, itself, which is the cause of poverty, excessive competition and the struggle for existence amongst producers. They urge that a higher standard of living all round would eliminate this struggle for existence in the severe form we know it, and that here lies the only road to the physical, mental and spiritual progress of the human race. Whether they are right or not, it is certain that economic pressure is now forcing man to choose between, on the one hand, some system of general restriction of production, and, on the other hand, consuming and utilizing with freedom and regularity all that can be conveniently produced. The latter alternative has been referred to as the doctrine of "Consumptionism," and to many people appears economically fallacious, basely materialistic and in every way as objectionable as it sounds.

Facts have been told us by many practical business men about consumption being the necessary complement to production; and Mr. Henry Ford, in particular, has developed ideas on the same lines, pointing out that improved standards of living and progress are dependent on high consumption drawn from mass production. All this kind of reasoning, however, is so contrary to daily experience in the poorer countries, and to traditional conception in the richer countries, that considerable opposition to it is only to be expected in a world largely ruled by sentiment. The truth is that such opposition is vast and powerful, and, although it misses the point altogether, it cannot be ignored. It comes, not only from the man in the street, but also from the orthodox economist linked to the Victorian era, and even from the Church. It has fallen to the Church, in fact, to produce an eloquent advocate of the general sentiment; for we find no less a person than Dean Inge writing a long letter to *The Morning Post*, blissfully ignoring the omni-present problems in connection with the necessity of smooth and painless means of adjustment between productive activity and the utilization and consumption of what is produced, and pleading for the precept of St. Paul: "Having food and raiment, let us therefore be content."

The Dean very truly says that we have to balance our account with our environment; that we require to bring what we have, and what we want, into line with each other; and that we may bring them together either by increasing what we have, which is the wisdom of the West, or by diminishing our wants, which is the wisdom of the East. He tells us that the higher interests of life—art, science, philosophy and religion—should be aimed at, and not mere getting and spending; he warns us against developing tendencies that may end in our recklessly using up the natural resources of the planet, as well as defacing its beauty beyond repair; and, finally, he urges that it is desirable and necessary to strike a balance between the ideal of the West and the ideal of the East.

All this is just; but we are not told how the producer is going to earn a living in a world of competing producers equipped with powerful labour-saving machines, if it is to become the fashion amongst consumers to be content with "food and raiment." The question of the determination of market prices—of the basis of the bargaining power of the producer in markets governed by demand and supply—is not mentioned. We are not told how consumers are to determine what constitutes a reasonable balance between the ideal of the West and the ideal of the East. And, assuming that this is successfully accomplished, we still do not know whether producers are to restrict production, and to what extent each one is to do so, or whether they are to resort to dumping abroad regardless of the ideals of foreigners. The point is that without adequate consumptive demand the present system of competitive production breaks down altogether.

In a country where there are many idle factories, many full warehouses and a million unemployed, to propose reduced consumption as the remedy is merely comical. But what is the remedy? A consumer might say:

"Economy in production, reduced costs, lower prices, increased exports." But the producers will reply:

"Why lower prices? In producing the goods, we pay out their gross money cost in wages, rent and interest, as well as the cost of living of all those who take profits or losses in passing them along to market in different stages of production. We reckon that we put into circulation by the process of production the necessary quantity of money to buy all the goods in question without a fall in prices. We cannot produce a greater quantity than you are prepared to buy with the money that our activities put into your hands; and all your economy talk means that you want to force us to sell at a loss. Our reply to you is: Buy all we are able to produce, and you will have a lot and so shall we."

A philosopher, however, might argue that the remedy does not lie either in increased production or increased consumption. "Strike a balance," he might say, "between the ideals of West and East. Reduce the consumption of the rich, and there will be sufficient for the consumption of the poor." To him the producers will reply:

"It is immaterial to us who buys what we produce; but, actually, we are able to produce in excess of effective demand, and it is excessive competition for limited markets that keeps most of us poor. Is it suggested that systematic restriction of production must be resorted to? If so, you must allocate the quantity and kind of work to be done by each of us and give us fixed prices. Only then can we 'be content.'"

When all the producers produce all they can, they are forced to sell at lower prices; when some of them restrict production, they lose business to those who have produced abundantly; and when all of them restrict production, they do make profits, but they are abused by the consumers and the money merchants who wail for lower prices and invoke the aid of the law.

This is well illustrated by recent history in the rubber world. As the result of free production of rubber caused by the big demand and high prices of 1910, a glut began to manifest itself as soon as the after-war consumptive demand for rubber became normal; and the pressure to find a home for all this rubber became so acute that, in many cases, it had to be literally given away in relation to its cost. In these circumstances it was inevitable that rubber estates should be losing money heavily. Things got so bad that, apart from the general check administered to normal activity on new plantation work, the Stevenson scheme was set up in order to regulate the quantity of rubber thrown on the market by British-owned plantations, in a manner compatible with market conditions. This brought relief to the estates, but not soon enough to enable planters, and induce capitalists, to provide for an eventual increase in the consumption of rubber. Meanwhile, in spite of the cheapness of the article, producers and distributors were refusing to carry any stock and would only deal on a "hand-to-mouth" basis. This sort of thing was bound to end in a shortage sooner or later, and 1925 found manufacturers and distributors desperately short. But when the price started going up by leaps and bounds, everybody wanted to stock rubber; and American manufacturers, who did not buy when the market was weak, started crying for State intervention against the wicked Stevenson scheme and the British profiteers.

It is always the same. When the producers restrict production they are anathema; but it is worth nothing that on such occasions, far from any likelihood of a "buyers' strike," there is a general scramble by everybody, consumers or otherwise, to buy all they can, more or less regardless of price, for these are occasions when the wisdom of the West is rampant. But let the producer be caught with a plenitude for market, and there will be a reaction towards the wisdom of the East, visible in the market-place as the "buyers' strike," and no mercy will be shown to the producer.

The truth is that we are all consumers and most of us are producers; and that, under modern conditions, there is normally greater necessity and pressure to sell than to buy. It is certain that, whilst producers or dealers must sell their goods for money, those who have good gold standard money may buy what they like, when they like, or not at all. It is, therefore, quite recognised that buyers with good money have every advantage over the sellers, and that the immediate object of trade is to realise money, in much the same way as the object of a vessel is to bring its cargo into port. Everybody wants to increase his wealth by producing all he dare; but he dare not produce all he can; for often, in spite of the greatest caution, he cannot sell all he produces except at a loss. At the back of the desire to produce and sell there is well-grounded fear as well as ambition. People must produce and sell, and effect an adequate turnover, otherwise they cannot escape the economic millstone that is continuously crushing a certain number of them. On the other hand, for the individual, there is often a real advantage to be obtained by abstaining from consuming or buying. Hence production, under existing conditions, normally overhangs consumption; hence the economic necessity that demand should be stimulated to balance supply; and hence the call for "Consumptionism" in a country with vast resources at home and abroad.

It remains for the philosopher to consider the possible results of the removal of the check on production now exercised by the rich final buyer both abstaining from consuming to the full extent of his income, and waiting for the consumptive demand of others to increase before he undertakes the purchase and operation of new productive equipment.[69] The philosopher might argue that over-production and over-consumption would tend towards the exhaustion of the world's resources, or that over-consumption would bring about the degeneration of the human race; but he would have to remember that degenerates do not shine as producers, and that it is unlikely that they could exhaust anything. On the other hand, he might argue that both the extremes of scarcity and the extremes of plenty have the effect of restricting population and reducing efficiency in production; that, with the removal of all present and future danger of want for the individual, the first orgy arising from any unlimited abundance would rapidly subside as it became more and more realized that to consume often entailed effort and sometimes certain kinds of losses which were by no means always worth while even when the goods and services used could easily be obtained; and that it is only by this route that the mind of man can rise above mere getting and spending, and direct itself to the higher interests of life.

XI What is trade depression?

Supposing that a group[70] of people (which we shall call the Group) were the exclusive holders of all bonds and bills in connection with the entire internal National Debt of Great Britain, and that they, from patriotic or other motives, placed on deposit in their banks £300,000,000[71] annually instead of using it for the final-buying of commodities and services. Would the banks be able to find reliable borrowers willing and able to increase progressively each year their loans to the entent of £300,000,000? and would the production of new commodity capital be increased to this extent beyond the normal increase? What, in fact, would be the economic position after ten years of this—if, indeed, it could be continued for anything like so long? Would there not be a complete stoppage of trade, ending in a revolution? Let us take a rapid glance at the features of such a contingency.

For the purpose of our example, let us assume that almost the whole of the interest on the internal British National Debt is used for final-buying by those who receive it; and that thus, whatever money is withdrawn from business by taxation for the purpose of paying the interest in question is almost all returned without appreciable delay to producers and distributors in exchange for their wares. But, if in any one year a Group, after collecting all the interest on this internal debt, held £300,000,000 of it on deposit instead of using it for buying, the total income of shopkeepers, merchants, manufacturers and others from whom goods and services would have been bought would be reduced that year by the amount in question, and these producers and distributors would be forced to cut down their private expenses to a considerable extent.[72] This would hit more shopkeepers, merchants, manufacturers and others, which again would affect another lot; and so the total loss to business would considerably exceed the £300,000,000 that the Group, in the first instance, merely held on deposit instead of using for buying. There would be a general fall in prices, but it would not be sufficiently rapid, particularly in respect of wages, rents and the cost of production, to prevent heavy reductions in the quantity and money value of sales, loss of employment by workers, and reduced production; and the shrinkage in the quantity and money value of business would necessarily be accompanied by a shrinkage in the effective demand for loans by producers and distributors, in the volume of bank loans, and incidentally in total deposits. Serious as this would be, business might recover the next year under normal conditions. But, supposing the government proceeded, year after year, to drag the usual quantity of money out of the pockets of the people, and the Group, by persistently holding the money on deposit instead of using it for buying, continued to prevent these people earning back the £300,000,000 annually, what then? It may be ventured that before ten years had elapsed and the members of the Group had piled up £3,000,000,000 to their credit in the banks, industry and trade would have shrunk to a shadow, a large proportion of the population would be dependent on emergency government relief financed by loans from bankers, and those capitalist classes dependent on industry and trade would be selling and mortgaging property and securities to the banks in order to raise money to keep going. Thus, the new government securities or promissory notes in respect of the emergency relief loan, all other securities and all property, apart from what belonged to the Group and those similarly placed, would come into the possession of the bankers; but, on the other hand, the bankers would be liable to pay £3,000,000,000 in cash to the Group, which is considerably more than the total quantity of gold coin and bullion in the world, and about eight times as much as the total quantity of gold and fiduciary paper money in the country. Assuming always that the government did not intervene to help the bankers, the Group could then force the bankers to suspend payments, and take them over on their (the Group's) own terms. Probably long before things came to such a pass, the bankers would cease buying securities and granting loans on securities and property. But in this case, the absence or shortage of money in the hands of almost the entire population would enable the Group from time to time to pick up property and stock exchange bargains at panic prices, waiting for the money so paid out to be returned to them via the tax collector; and, in the meantime, the position of the bankers would become desperate, seeing that their investments would become unsaleable except to the Group, whilst their huge liabilities to the Group for deposits would be growing rapidly.

This, of course, is a very inadequate picture of the possibilities involved, but it gives some idea of the uncanny power that can be exercised by a group, equipped with a sufficient quantity of government bonds, merely abstaining from buying.

Let us take another imaginary case. Supposing everybody put one-half their total monthly incomes on deposit in the banks each month instead of using the money for buying, what effect would this have upon industry and trade? It is here urged that very soon all trade would come to a standstill, after shrinking in geometrical progression by upwards of 20 per cent. each month; and that total deposits would shrink until all credits become "frozen"—namely, until the repayment of loans, and consequently the destruction of deposits, became impossible. If the banks, as some people believe, have the power to enforce inflation or prevent deflation, what would they do to save the situation in face of an excessive and persistent wave of "saving" of this sort? Increased final-buying alone would help matters, and failing increased final-buying by the public it would have to be done by the government.

What, by the way, do the advocates of unqualified saving think about the question of middlemen? Does their belief in "saving" force them to press for the abolition of middle-men? It does not seem to occur to people that the continuous multiplication of middlemen is the logical outcome of the continuous tendency of production to be held up by under-consumption, rendering it a more profitable occupation to help the producer to sell than to help him to produce.

The belief is widely held, even amongst economists, that all money not used for the final-buying of consumable goods and non-productive equipment is immediately and necessarily used, directly, through the stock exchange, or through the banking system, for increasing the quantity of commodity capital. But inquiry into the different things that may happen to money income made available by abstinence shows that there is such a thing as excessive abstinence which causes the production of consumable goods, non-productive equipment and productive equipment, alike, to decrease.[73]

When the velocity of final-buying in a country is insufficient in relation to its ready productive capacity, either the velocity of production is to that extent checked, or a stagnant surplus of goods is created—and a stagnant surplus is not even exportable unless, for one reason or another, enough money to buy it is transferred to countries abroad that may be willing but unable to do so.[74]

It is significant that the largest unexportable surpluses occur in the richest countries, and that these are the countries that suffer most from the intensification of the effects of such surpluses. The United States, the richest country in the world, not only wants no foreign goods, but she cannot even deal with her own goods. She frequently resorts to dumping them abroad and sometimes to destroying them. The cry for "protection" against surpluses of other countries has been raised almost everywhere for years past. We find, in countries where there are millions of people in urgent want, manufacturers and workers alike calling for "protection" against the required supplies, lest their occupations become unnecessary and they themselves become victims of the situation. All countries think that salvation lies in reduced imports and increased exports; but they cannot *all* be right. In the creditor countries the fear of receiving anything more than paper payments from the debtor countries causes opinion to be divided between "protection" and cancellation of international debts. The difficulty of selling either at home or abroad is also put down to high prices, particularly by financial interests in the creditor countries, which, seeing increased wealth in lower money prices, have everywhere put the deflationary process into action to a greater or less extent. On the other hand, everybody as a seller wants higher prices, and they all bring much evidence to show that this is a mere necessity in each of their particular cases. Some talk about over-production and even over-consumption; others say that our economic troubles are the result of transit through the depression patch of the trade cycle—a deplorable thing, but more or less inevitable; and historians and politicians, impressed by the *débâcle*, but unastonished, tell us that it is the usual thing after a great war. But in the United States it has been called, both by business men and labour men, what it really is, the "buyers' strike."

It is not generally appreciated that the rich must buy the work of the poor before the poor can buy from the rich, and that lending is only putting off the issue; that, if the creditor countries are unable or unwilling to buy enough from the debtor countries, still less are the debtor countries able or willing to buy enough from the creditor countries; and that inability of the creditor countries to buy more than they do is due to maldistribution of wealth in these countries, whereby the rich are unwilling, and the poor unable, to buy enough. Selling abroad—exporting—by a creditor country is impracticable unless there are people in it able and willing to buy imports in exchange, or unless it is profitable and safe to invest or lend money abroad. Once the rich have bought all they want, selling by them either at home or abroad, except in exchange for more or less distant options to call imports, is impossible. When the rich refuse to buy and the poor cannot buy, all trade stops regardless of political boundaries.

Trade depression in a particular trade may be the result of over-production in that trade in relation to production in other trades; but general trade depression is due to under-consumption arising from maldistribution and false economy which passes in the name of "saving."

Notes on the use of certain terms

All the terms in this volume are used as far as possible in their ordinary sense; but in the case of the terms listed below, which are commonly used by people in a variety of ways, the sense in which each is used for our purpose is indicated to obviate ambiguity.

The terms in question are classified as: GOODS, HUMAN ELEMENTS, INVESTMENTS AND LOANS, MONEY, PRODUCTION, SAVING (PASSIVE), and VELOCITIES. Alphabetical order is observed to this extent, but within the classes the terms are placed in the order of their relation to each other.

GOODS:

Productive equipment: All buildings, machinery and devices for production and distribution. Examples: factories, railways, roads, etc.

Non-productive equipment: Buildings and devices for uses other than production. Examples: churches, museums, dwellings, furniture, objects of art, military equipment, etc.

Consumable goods: Goods for relatively prompt final consumption. Examples: food, clothing, etc.

Services: Services, whether performed with or without the use of any kind of equipment. Examples: ploughing, turning, transporting, domestic services, military service.

Stocks of goods: Productive equipment, non-productive equipment, consumable goods, and raw or semi-raw goods, held for sale by producers or distributors. Examples: tractors on the hands of manufacturers or dealers; buildings for sale on the hands of builders or real estate dealers; wheat on the hands of farmers, merchants or millers.

Commodity capital: Productive equipment and non-productive equipment whether for sale or not, and all stocks of goods. (See respective definitions above.)

Exports: Visible and invisible exports, namely: exported goods, services sold to people residing in countries abroad, and goods and services sold in the home country to travellers from abroad for their own use.

Imports: Visible and invisible imports, namely: imported goods, services bought from people residing in countries abroad, and goods and services bought in countries abroad by travellers from the home country for their own use.

Notice that, unless otherwise stated, "goods" and the terms defined thereunder do not include gold.

HUMAN ELEMENTS:

Workers: Those working for employers by hand or brain for a wage or salary.

Producers: Master producers, such as farmers, fishermen, mine exploiters, manufacturers, builders, or suppliers of any kind of transport service, who are operating for their own account.

Distributors: Master distributors, *i.e.* wholesale dealers, exporters, importers and retailers.

Trade buyers: Producers buying goods for working up or treatment, distributors buying stocks of goods for resale, and producers or distributors buying services for the purposes of their businesses. Examples: motor-car manufacturers buying steel or tyres; farmers buying seed for planting or live stock for fattening; wholesale merchants buying wheat to sell to retailers, millers or other wholesale merchants; retailers buying goods to sell to final buyers; and any of them taking on workmen, clerks or salesmen. Governments are also trade buyers when they are buying as producers or distributors in the above-defined senses.

Trade buying: The act of trade buyers.

Final buyers: Producers buying productive equipment for use in their own businesses; and everybody buying non-productive equipment for their own use, consumable goods for their own consumption, or services for their own comfort, pleasure or safety. Examples: railway companies buying engines or rails; motor-car factories buying lathes or putting up premises; people buying houses to live in, food to eat, theatre tickets, or employing servants; governments buying offices, battleships, etc., or employing fighters, churchmen, gardeners, and clerks or officials for purposes other than State enterprises.

Final-buying: The act of final buyers.

Notice that, whereas producers buying productive equipment for operating themselves are treated as final buyers, when they are buying goods and services to be used in the composition of the goods they produce for sale they are treated as trade buyers. This treatment seems quite called for, because it is certain that final-buying of this kind by producers—like final-buying of non-productive equipment and consumable goods by the general public—is a principal determining factor in the state of trade at any time, whereas all trade buying, as defined above, is more or less the direct reflection of final-buying. This, it is believed, is made clear in the text.

Governments: National, State or municipal authorities.

INVESTMENTS AND LOANS:

Investments: Assets in the form of stock exchange shares or bonds, and property.

Loans: Overdrafts by banks, loans on securities, mortgage loans, and money lent by discounting or re-discounting trade bills, bankers' bills or government bills.

MONEY:

Cash: Gold coin and bullion, and all forms of metallic money and paper money that are legal tender. Notice that money referred to as "deposits" and "balances with banks" may consist of cash in part only.

Fiduciary paper money: Fiduciary issues of banknotes or currency notes, *i.e.*, only those notes issued in excess of a backing of standard metal held by the issuing institution. Example: if a government or bank issues £100,000,000 of notes against a gold backing held of £20,000,000, the fiduciary issue is £80,000,000 and is here called "fiduciary paper money."

Bankers' balances with other banks: Money held on deposit by bankers at central banking institutions and at any other banks.

Reserves: Bankers' cash in hand and balances with other banks.

Deposits: Amounts of money standing to the credit of every class of individual, corporation or government, in the books of the banks.

Notice that deposits constitute liabilities of bankers. Their assets consist of reserves, investments and loans; and their liabilities consist of their capital items, acceptances and deposits. In England it is customary for the banks to retain not less than 10 per cent. of their assets in cash and balances with the Bank of England, but they do not publish what proportion of such reserves consists of cash in hand and what proportion of balances with the Bank of England.

Demand deposits: Deposits on "current account."

Time deposits: Deposits that depositors cannot withdraw without giving an agreed period of notice. Time deposits usually consist of money either being "saved" or awaiting employment by depositors.

The following figures given by the Controller of the Currency in the United States give some idea of the importance of time deposits and their growth in relation to demand deposits.

	Amounts in millions of dollars.		
	1919.	1922.	1926.
Demand deposits . . .	16,337	14,985	18,837
Time deposits . . .	9,748	15,613	24,267
Unclassified deposits . . .	7,090	6,595	5,778

Credit money: Total deposits minus total reserves.

Inflation: An increase in the total quantity of cash and credit money in circulation unaccompanied by a corresponding increase in the total quantity of goods and services being sold, or a decrease in the total quantity of goods and services being sold unaccompanied by a corresponding decrease in the total quantity of cash and credit money in circulation, either of which entails a rise in the price-level. There may be gold inflation as well as fiduciary paper money and credit money inflation.

Deflation: The converse of inflation.

PRODUCTION:

Production: Production and distribution.

Ready productive capacity: The aggregate normal productive capacity of existing producers, distributors and workers operating upon available land, existing equipment and stocks of goods, or as much of them as they can, with normal efficiency.

Notice that ready productive capacity at any time contrasts, on the one hand, with possible productive capacity or the productive capacity of all possible, known, unknown, actual and future resources, and, on the other hand, with actual production at any time. It is certain that possible productive capacity has always, hitherto, been vastly greater than ready productive capacity, which, in its turn, is quite frequently considerably greater than actual production.

Sometimes it may be a debatable matter whether ready productive capacity is fully engaged or not, but sometimes there is evidently and admittedly no doubt one way or another. In the text it is taken as a fact that sometimes ready productive capacity is fully engaged and sometimes it is not, and these alternative conditions are shown to be factors of a primary order.

SAVING (PASSIVE):

Abstinence: Voluntarily doing with less consumable goods and non-productive equipment.

Automatic frugality: Decreased consumption or decreased use of certain kinds of non-productive equipment by some people, who are caused or induced to do with less as the result of the action of others who, by encroaching on their cash in hand or bank balances, or by using newly-created money, increase the velocity of final-buying and raise the price-level.

VELOCITIES:

Velocity: A term for the time-rate of production, final-buying, importation and exportation, of goods and services, irrespective of their money value, for the purpose of making comparisons between quantities being produced or imported, and quantities being finally bought or exported, in a given time. It is, of course, obvious that in a self-contained area the *average* velocity of production and the *average* velocity of final-buying are equal.

Notes to Part II

1 Final buyers: buyers of consumable goods, non-productive equipment and productive equipment who do not intend to resell these goods.

    [See 'Notes on the use of certain termes' at the end of Part II for the meaning of this expression and other terms used in *The Final Buyer*].

2 The difficulties of debtor countries are considered in Chapter VII, 3 (iii), 5 (iii), and in Chapter XV.

3 See "Profits," by Foster and Catchings.

4 Mr. R. McKenna has hinted that in his view the question of monetary shortage does arise in England, and that the adoption of certain reforms is worth considering. Whatever view one takes on the question of monetary shortage, one may well favour the adoption in England of the Federal Reserve System.

5 See the report of the Economic Conference of Geneva, 1927.

6 The remedy advocated by Major Douglas was State subsidies to producers to enable them to sell at lower prices. The same idea was observable in the proposals of Sir Alfred Mond a few years ago for the unemployment dole to be paid to employers of labour—ship-builders being specifically mentioned—to give them assistance against foreign competition, and to enable them to employ men who were being supported by the community without making any return to it.

7 See "Business without a Buyer," by Foster and Catchings.

8 See "The Flaw in the Price System," page 24.

9 Martin's usual expression is "taking goods off the market."

10 See "Profits."

11 It is true that, when lower money prices of goods are obtained by increased productive efficiency or by longer working hours, and provided a proportionately larger quantity of goods is sold, the total money earnings of capital and labour are not reduced by such lower prices. But we are, here, concerned with a fall in money prices of goods caused by limited markets.

12 The substance of some of these essays appeared as articles in the *Economic Review* in 1925.

13 Money differences between exports and imports (visible and invisible).

14 Silver is hereafter disregarded as a monetary standard.

15 The cash ratios of the Bank of England and the Federal Reserve Bank are usually well below maximum, whilst their power to obtain fresh supplies of gold from abroad has never been exhausted by either of them. Therefore, apart from the question of currency depreciation, the said banking systems have practically always possessed wide margins of unused capacity to create credit money.

16 Notice that the meaning of the term "securities" includes only stock exchange shares and bonds. Bills and acceptances drawn by the public or the government and sold to the bankers at a discount for ready money constitute loans from bankers, and when bankers

resell such paper, as they occasionally do, they, the sellers, are borrowers and the buyers are lenders.

17 For the effects of holding money on deposit, see Chapter V, Section 2 (iv).

18 Gold might be going abroad either to settle a debit foreign trade balance, or because money is being transferred abroad for employment, safety or in settlement of debts.

19 In the case of a country where the currency is so far depreciated below its gold parity that there is no question of an inflow of gold resulting from higher interest rates, the bank rate and interest rates in general react upon the quantity of cash in the opposite manner to what they do where a gold standard exchange is in operation. Thus, to the extent that high interest rates fail to cause an inflow of gold, but reduce the volume of bankers' investments and loans, and incidentally both deposits and cash requirements, the quantity of fiduciary paper money is reduced; and thus high interest rates reduce the quantity of cash instead of—as is the case where a gold standard exchange is in operation—increasing it. Vice versa, low interest rates tend to increase the quantity of cash in a country where no gold standard exchange is in operation and fiduciary paper money is concerned, although the contrary is true where a gold standard exchange is in operation and gold is concerned.

20 Operators are said to be "long" when they are carrying goods or securities which they are waiting for a favourable moment to sell; and they are said to be "short" when they have undertaken to deliver goods or securities which they have not got and must buy. The terms are mainly used by speculators. Notice that there cannot be a "short" account, in the ordinary sense of the expression, where such articles as machinery and buildings are concerned. But contractors may be more or less heavily engaged to provide these things to final buyers, which is equivalent to a "short" account.

21 See *The Annalist*, September 25th, 1925; also "Interest Rates and Stock Exchange Speculation," by R. N. Owens and C. O. Hardy, with the aid of the Council and staff of the Institute of Economics. New York, 1925.

22 Day-to-day loans.

23 The rates of interest at which day-to-day loans are made.

24 The rates of interest at which 60- to 90-day bills are discounted.

25 The effects of placing money on deposit instead of using it for final-buying are closely examined in the next three chapters.

26 The question of government borrowing is further examined in Chapter VIII.

27 On occasions when ready productive capacity is fully engaged, not only the velocity of production cannot be increased, but the velocity of final-buying cannot usually be increased, seeing that producers would be usually unwilling to encroach on their stocks of goods by selling faster than they can replace. Only on such occasions or in the absence of stocks of goods—both rare contingencies—is the actual velocity of final-buying limited by the actual velocity of production.

28 For full discussion of this matter see Chapter VIII.

29 The question of international debts and investments is dealt with separately in Chapter VII, 4 and 5, and in Chapter XV.

30 D. H. Robertson's "Lacking which is automatic and lacking which is induced" takes a similar kind of analysis further. See "Banking Policy and the Price Level," page 47, 4.

31 See also Chapter XV.

32 Notice that the expressions "velocity of final-buying, velocity of production, volume of bank loans" in all cases refer to aggregate quantities, and that "aggregate" is inserted in the text, here, to emphasize without modifying this aspect of their meanings.

33 The magnitude of stock exchange loans to all other loans in the United States may be gauged by the following figures given by the reporting member banks on August 10th, 1927.

	New York City.	*All leading cities.*
Loans secured by stocks and bonds	$2,145,864,000	$5,874,639,000
All other loans and discounts.	$2,560,554,000	$8,633,275,000

34 The potential supply of money as determined by existing monetary technique at the time.

35 The next four chapters are devoted to an examination of these different kinds of final-buying and their irregularities.

36 [Chapter VI (not reproduced) examines the irregular final-buying resulting from gold-mining.]

37 Notice that unless otherwise stated the terms "exports" and "imports" always refer to visible and invisible exports and imports of goods and services, but, here, gold is also included.

38 The words "goods and services" are inserted here to obviate any confusion with the imports of gold referred to in the same sentence.

39 It is worth noting here that, as will be shown presently, unless money in sufficient quantity is simultaneously transferred out of a country in which the price-level is falling, or into a country in which it is rising, the tendency for the total money value of its exports and imports to be affected will be neutralized by adequate alterations of rates in the foreign exchange market.

40 This consists of money obtained from sources (*a*) and (*b*).

41 Notice that trade buying for the purpose of increasing stocks of goods, as shown a few pages back, other things being equal, increases the velocity of final-buying and raises the price-level, but when the stocks of goods are decreased an equal and opposite effect occurs.

42 This consists of money obtained from sources (*c*) and (*d*).

43 This consists of money obtained from sources (*c*).

44 This consists of money obtained from sources (*d*).

45 At a time when ready productive capacity is fully engaged, producers and distributors are more disposed to increase stocks of goods than let them decrease.

46 Including profit.

47 The home price-level might become relatively lower as the result of either increased production, decreased final-buying or liquidation of stocks of goods in the home country; or as the result of the general price-level abroad rising.

48 "Other things being equal" refers to transfers of money income and money capital, and the effects thereof in the foreign exchange market.

49 As shown in 1 (iii) and (iv) of this chapter.

50 See footnote 37.

51 Refer 2, (ii) and (iii) of this chapter.

52 The words "goods and services" are here inserted to obviate any confusion with exports or imports of gold, which are mentioned in the same sentences.

53 The sources of money obtained by the home country through selling its goods and services or currency in countries abroad must either be (I) money income made available by people in countries abroad abstaining from the final-buying of goods and services produced in countries abroad, and money capital made available by liquidation of stocks of goods or stock exchange securities in countries abroad (which is money income and money capital made available as in Chapter V, 3 (vii)); or it must be (II) additional money made available by final buyers in countries abroad encroaching on savings deposits or obtaining bank loans. Thus, as in Chapter V, 3 (vii), when, in countries abroad, money income or money capital from sources (I), as above, is held on deposit, the result will be a decrease in the velocities of final-buying and production in countries abroad in relation to their ready productive capacity unless final-buying there is increased in some other way—and, failing increased final-buying in countries abroad by the home country, the only way in which the required increase can be effected is by additional money from sources (II), as above, being used.

54 See footnote above.

55 The home country will not always find it safe and profitable to make investments and loans abroad to the full extent of its capacity to do so—see Chapter V, 2 (iv)—particularly at a time when it is depressing industry and trade abroad by decreasing its imports in relation to its exports.

56 The reader is reminded that money may be withdrawn from circulation in the home country by abstinence or by liquidation for the purpose of exchanging with foreign money, and that the recipients of the home money may hold it on deposit or use it for repaying loans obtained from bankers, see 2 (ii), *First*, this chapter.

57 It is important to note that currency depreciation only causes a country's exports to increase in relation to its imports when its foreign exchange value is falling faster than its price-level is rising, a thing that only occurs when the quantity of foreign payments which it is willingly or otherwise making is excessive in relation to the quantity of foreign payments that it is receiving. But when the price-level of the country is rising faster than the foreign exchange value of its currency is falling, the rising price-level, not being entirely neutralized by the falling foreign exchange value of the currency, must be causing imports to increase in relation to exports—which is the opposite.

58 Low interest rates would tend to cause rising stock exchange prices, profits to stock exchange operators and others, and increased final-buying by them; but this could be handled by taxation.

59 The following table, showing the annual amount of interest actually paid and its commodity value at current prices since 1920–1921, is reprinted from *The Times*.

NATIONAL DEBT INTEREST (DEADWEIGHT DEBT)

Year.	Total interest (exclusive of U.S. debt).	Cost of living index.		Equivalent of interest on basis of present prices.
		Yearly average.	Present.	
1920–1921	£325,785,581	255	176	£224,855,840
1921–1922	298,486,392	206	176	255,017,488
1922–1923	273,133,269	179	176	268,555,584
1923–1924	276,165,826	174	176	279,340,160
1924–1925	278,002,047	175	176	279,590,600
1925–1926	274,047,000*	—	176	274,047,000

* Budget estimate.

60 In the case of foreign payments made in respect of income or capital due to countries abroad, when the money is used for final-buying by the receiving countries, the exports of the paying country can freely expand to the same extent; but, when it is held on deposit, there can be no increased exports from the paying country except by means of forced price-cutting in some form, which is more likely to result in the production as well as the imports of the paying country being decreased than in its exports being increased. See Chapter VII, 3 (iii).

61 This proportion varies with home natural resources, foreign resources, income per head of population, and national and racial traits of the people concerned.

62 The reader is reminded that increased imports in relation to exports will not cause the foreign exchange value of the currency to fall when this increase is accompanied by a proportionate increase of inward transfers of money income or money capital in relation to similar outward transfers. And when increased taxation or government borrowing fails to bring back from abroad, or to retain at home, enough money income or

money capital to prevent a fall in the foreign exchange value of the currency, its exports will increase or its imports will decrease.

63 Refer Chapter VII, 3, 4 and 6.

64 In the case of the value of a currency, its relation to confidence is the same; for a currency rapidly depreciates unless confidence exists that buyers of the said currency will continue to buy it in exchange for goods or services or other currencies.

65 See Chapter IV, 2 and 3.

66 See Chapter VII, 6.

67 See Chapter VIII, 2.

68 The reader is reminded that most, if not all, of this money may be held on deposit whilst awaiting investment or employment in industry, and that, to the extent that it is not being used for final-buying, the volume of bank loans, deposits and the quantity of credit money decreases.

69 That the rich final buyer can, and frequently does, unduly withhold purchasing power from industry in both the above ways is shown in Part I.

70 This group might consist of anything between 500 and 50,000 people.

71 This figure is merely for the purpose of our example. The total interest, less income tax and super-tax, might be considerably less.

72 Some will argue that the £300,000,000 would be used by borrowers for increased development work at home and abroad, and that increased final-buying of equipment and employment of labour in connection therewith would neutralize the decreased final-buying of the Group. It may be argued, however, with greater force that in the long run, if not at once, a decrease and not an increase in the effective demand for loans for development work would be caused by the behaviour of the Group.

73 See Chapter V, 2 and 3.

74 See Chapter VII, 4.

Part III

The Economic Lessons of 1929–1931 (1932)

Bulletin no. 1.

March 7th, 1931.

The beliefs, objects and methods of the Unclaimed Wealth Utilization Committee

The Committee believes that unemployed labour, unemployed capital equipment and unemployed surplus stocks of goods constitute Unclaimed Wealth; that the present world-wide depression of industry and trade, and major fluctuations in industry and trade in general, are by no means due to essentially economic or monetary causes, i.e., to deficiencies in the world's resources in labour, materials and money, or to incapacity of the productive system to expand with regularity, but rather to the general failure of statesmen to understand and act in harmony with the system; and observes that, thus, progress in the arts or methods of production is being nullified or is causing economic chaos.

The objects of the Committee are as follows:—

1. To promote the full and rational utilization of all unemployed labour.
2. To promote the full and rational utilization by labour of as much capital equipment as possible, both to raise the standard of living and to provide the means of useful and profitable investment of an appropriate quantity of savings.
3. To promote the stabilization of the total volume of buying in a manner appropriate to the rate at which producers are willing and able to produce, i.e., to prevent inflation of prices resulting from buyers attempting at any time to buy too much, or to prevent the rate of production being retarded by insufficient buying.

With these objects in view, the Committee proposes:—

1. To endeavour to induce governments and economic institutions in the different countries to estimate or otherwise ascertain what rates of consumption, abstention from consumption and accumulation of capital equipment are appropriate to the incomes and resources of their respective countries.
2. To endeavour, by consistently keeping the press informed and other means, to create a demand by the public for the appointment of a central economic department or institution embracing all countries specially charged:—

(*a*) with the assisting or advising of governments in the estimation of the said rates of consumption, abstention from consumption and accumulation of capital equipment;

(*b*) with the examination of the methods employed by governments or their advisers in the estimation of such rates;

(*c*) with the expression of such estimated rates in terms of a standard common to all countries;

(*d*) with the drawing up of an appropriate international plan correlating the said rates as expressed in the terms of the common standard, in such manner that these rates are, together, appropriate to the world as a whole.

(*e*) with the informing of governments how much total expenditure, how much expenditure on public works, how much reduction of internal and/or external debts, or how much internal and/or external borrowing, by public authorities, and what banking policies, at different times in the different countries, are appropriate to their required rates of consumption, abstention from consumption and accumulation of capital equipment.

3. To recommend the taking of international measures, when necessary, to induce adequate buying of goods and services by the creditor countries from the debtor countries; to prevent excessive buying by the debtor countries from the creditor countries; and to neutralize the effects on the world as a whole of either excessive or insufficient buying of goods and services in one or more countries.

4. To endeavour, by the diffusion of information and other means, to create support in the different countries for the findings and recommendations of the central economic department or institution referred to above.

The Committee—a non-profit making organization—intends at the outset to issue Bulletins from time to time, bringing into prominence the major features of the general economic situation and their probable effect on the course of events. These Bulletins will be sent free of charge to as many people or institutions as possible in all the principal countries. The Committee wishes to present its economic views, not only in their larger application to society as a whole, but also in their application to the daily needs of the business man; and it is, therefore, its aim to make the Bulletin useful to the producer, the merchant, the entrepreneur and the investor, as well as acceptable to the economist. In this connection, readers of the Bulletin are invited to send, whenever possible, unpublished information of general interest and major importance, as well as their views on the outlook in trades in which they specialize; and it is hoped that there will not be lacking people to co-operate in this and other ways. By its efforts to indicate the economic facts of fundamental importance, to interpret them correctly, and to expose economic fallacies, the Committee hopes to formulate an independent and consistent national and international economic viewpoint, and, thus, to create the necessary support for the kind of action it is advocating.

Bulletin no. 2.

March 16th, 1931.

It must be noted that the article below is a slightly expanded version of a memorandum which, after being distributed privately to a number of Delegates at the Assembly of the League of Nations in Geneva in the Autumn of 1930, has since been the subject of attention in important quarters, and is perhaps at the bottom of the revival of the question of revision of Inter-Governmental War Debts.

Insufficient buying and trade depression

In view of the conflicting nature of the statements being made by economists and men of note on the question of whether the present unprecedented extent of unemployment and general trade depression is due to too much or too little buying, it seems advisable that this vital matter should be investigated by the leading economists, that the facts should be ascertained and established beyond controversy, and that national and international policies should be moulded in accordance with these facts.

A widely held opinion, perhaps even the orthodox one, is that the present decreased working of factories and increased unemployment of labour are largely attributable to a shortage of capital due to insufficient saving; and less spending is, therefore, advocated in order to provide the alleged missing capital. This view, however, is not reconcilable with the facts, because the feature of the situation to-day is abundance of capital in relation to the effective demand for it, and not shortage—the quantity of capital equipment, stocks of goods of all kinds and the supply of money at present available being greater than what can actually be employed at the present time. It is true that many manufacturers and other producers are hard up and that it is difficult for them to obtain credit, but this is not due to any general lack of capital. It is due to the fact that they are unable to sell enough. Provide them with the requisite orders, and they will immediately find as much capital as they require. Nor can it be argued in the present case that the trouble is due to the existence of disproportionate quantities of the different kinds of capital equipment and materials in such manner that they are not economically exchangeable with each other, for this implies a shortage of certain kinds of capital equipment or materials, and we know that to-day the common feature in all capital and commodity markets is abundance of supply. Undoubtedly unemployment may be caused by a shortage of capital and undoubtedly the world does sometimes spend too much, but all the evidence shows that, to-day, it is not shortage of capital that is keeping men and factories idle, but too little buying.

That there can be such a thing as too little buying in relation to the general rate at which goods are being produced and brought to market, must be admitted by everybody—even if there are people who, somehow, attribute too little buying to too much spending! But those who realize to what extent debts in one form or another constitute part of the modern economic system, and the way in which the means of making payments open to the debtors are limited by the quantity of goods and services that the creditors are willing to buy from them, will not only admit the possibility of such a thing as too little buying, but will expect it to be the central fact about most general trade depressions.

In spite of the fact that both the war itself and the post-war boom were largely financed with borrowed money, the seriousness of the present position as regards international, internal and commercial debts is little appreciated.

In the international sphere, a great financier recently said that the debtor countries had to make payments amounting to about $2,000,000,000 annually. For these payments to be made and not merely postponed, the creditor countries must allow the value of their imports to exceed the value of their exports by the same amount. But since all the creditor countries are wildly anxious to resist imports, the financier recommended the only alternative to such increased imports, namely, more loans to the debtor countries. Meanwhile, governments cannot lend any more, investors do not want to lend to countries already overloaded with debts, and those debtor countries that meant to pay do not want to borrow any more.

The situation as regards internal and commercial debts is parallel: The debtors (including most of those people who have to make payments in respect of taxes)[1] can only pay with money realized on the sale of goods and services; the creditors (including many of those to whom money collected from taxpayers is paid), having already all the goods and services that they want, refuse to employ more services for the production of more goods, and are afraid to go on lending indefinitely to the debtors for them to produce for each other.

It is true that, in the case of the post-war boom, loans were granted and debts piled up with the utmost freedom, the creditors seemingly being willing to finance the debtors indefinitely. A vast trade was done by selling all kinds of goods— notably motor cars—on the hire-purchase system; a vast amount of money was borrowed and spent on building and construction by public authorities, by business corporations and by private individuals; and a vast amount of money was borrowed by stock exchange operators which, after being recklessly used for bidding up stock-exchange prices and made to yield hundreds and hundreds of millions of dollars of stock-exchange profits, was largely treated as income and spent on goods and services. For instance, the amount of money spent on building and construction in the United States alone rose from about $7,000,000,000 per annum in 1924 to about $9,500,000,000 per annum for the period beginning about the middle of 1925 and ending about the Autumn of 1929. This rise of $2,500,000,000, or 30 per cent, in the amount spent annually on construction may well represent the difference between a depression and a boom. Again, as regards stock-exchange loans—and the profits thereby made and spent—stock-brokers' loans in the United States reached about $7,500,000,000 in the Autumn of 1929 as against about $4,000,000,000 at the beginning of 1928, whilst a writer in "The Annalist" states that total speculative gains in 1928 in the United States were reported to have amounted to about $5,000,000,000 as against about $300,000,000 in 1918.

However, to-day, the instalments of all these international, national and commercial debts are falling due, and the creditors are procrastinating with the dilemma of whether to lend more money or whether to buy more goods and services. Thus, debtors are buying less in order to make payments; creditors are economizing because they cannot get payments; and this decreased buying is aggravating the situation by pulling down prices, wages and profits, increasing the debts in terms of goods and services, and rendering the making of payments in money still more difficult to effect.

Although this enormous amount of borrowing was surely financial madness, this is not to say that the total amount of buying of goods and services effected by this and other means was too great in relation to the supplies that were being produced. The increased buying in the United States, while it lasted, enabled and caused producers to increase their capital equipment and output in the way that only increased buying can, and to this extent it was an important factor in the cause and maintenance of the unprecedented wave of prosperity in that country. Capital and labour alike shared in the prosperity. From the beginning of 1928, to go no farther back, until about the end of September, 1929, the profits of producers showed big increases all along the line, whilst, according to the index figures of "The Annalist," employment rose from 92 to 100, and payrolls from 96 to 110, in the same period. Incidentally, this industrial boom in America may well have been the cause of the increase that occurred in British employment during the first nine months of 1929. Moreover, when the acid tests are applied as to whether or not the amount of buying was excessive, the reactions obtained are completely negative: *First*, the general trend of wholesale commodity prices in the United States, whether reckoned from the beginning of 1925 or only from the middle of 1928, to the end of September, 1929, was clearly downward, which shows that the quantity of goods and services available in the market increased rather more rapidly, even, than the buying. *Second*, not only no encroachment was made on capital, but, quite the contrary, the permanent wealth of the United States in buildings, factories, railways and equipment of every kind was vastly improved and increased; stocks of raw materials and manufactured goods at the end of the boom were larger than ever; and the amount of capital held in the form of net foreign investments had increased substantially.

It is important to observe that the actual deficiency of buying is by no means a question of insufficient gold or insufficient currency. It is true that if the output of new gold could at this moment be increased on a vast scale, whereby a vast amount of additional wages and profits were distributed to miners and mine owners, the additional buying of goods and services so caused would tend to neutralize the actual buying deficiency. It is also true that high interest rates during the major part of 1929 did indicate the possibility of a deficiency of gold—though some people will argue that the high interest rates were due to over-trading. But to-day, when both the buying of goods and services and the effective demand for credit has greatly decreased, the existing supply of gold bullion exceeds the quantity that can actually be employed by the banking system. Nor is the concentration of gold at the present time in certain countries, such as in the United States and in France, at all the cause of our troubles. It is merely one of the effects or manifestations of the debt problem, which, as already indicated, requires that creditors should either lend more money or buy more goods and services—or be content merely to hoard gold in part payment of what is owing to them and let economic and political events take their drastic course.

In this situation there is an important section of opinion in America and in England advocating the necessity of concerted action for the purpose of overcoming the evil of insufficient buying whenever it presents itself. It is urged that the credit of the State should be used to combat the buying deficiency by the employment of labour and materials on extended programmes of public works. But numerous arguments are put forward against such a policy, and althoug most of them are weak, it is a fact that, under existing conditions, the richest countries might not be able to apply it radically, whilst the debtor countries certainly could not afford even to attempt it. The principal difficulty is that increased buying in any one country would tend to cause its imports to increase in relation to its exports. If, for instance, the United States came out with a large enough buying programme to affect the general situation, whilst England and France maintained a tight buying policy and business as usual, the general effect would be to increase business activity all over the world, but to reduce the net foreign investments of the United States and to increase the net foreign investments of the countries that had directly or indirectly increased their exports to the United States without increasing their imports. In other words, some of the debts to the United States would be paid off, but a certain amount of new debts to England and France and other countries would be created. Nevertheless, it is also true that if the matter were dealt with on an international basis, each country doing according to its means, there would be no question in any country of imports being increased in relation to exports, since both imports and exports of all countries would be proportionately increased. History may yet record an international meeting of creditors to decide, not how little cash the creditors must accept, but how much goods and services—and what to do with them.

However, at the moment it is urgently necessary for economists and statesmen to consider the following questions: *First*, is it true that the world sometimes buys too much and sometimes buys too little? *Second*, if so, is it enough to increase output per unit of labour and to try to regulate the production of particular kinds of goods in relation to an often unnaturally curtailed demand? Is not regulation of the total quantity of buying also necessary? *Third*, is it not at all events desirable that steps should be taken to determine the facts in this connection?

A. H. A.

Bulletin no. 7.

August 1st, 1931.

General trade depression in the making

It is evident that the general rate of production cannot for long exceed the general rate at which goods and services are being bought by consumers and investors; that, although excessive abstention from the buying of goods and services with income by some may for a time be neutralized by increased buying of goods and services on the part of those who are able and willing to borrow money for this purpose, there is a limit to the quantity of money that can be lent safely and profitably to finance either consumption or production; and that when this limit is reached the buying of borrowers and debtors must be decreased, causing lower prices, trade depression, financial losses all round, decreased buying by the creditors and aggravation of the buying deficiency. Thus, to the extent that the general rate of buying is inadequate, the general rate of production is retarded; and to the extent that the amount of buying by those using loans intermittently decreases and fails to neutralize the absence of adequate buying by those using their own money, the general rate of buying and the general rate of production are intermittently retarded. Hence, the intermittent presence of acute trade depression.

We propose to show: (1) that the amount of money furnished to willing buyers by means of international loans has been excessive in relation to the growth of the imports of the creditor countries; (2) that the amount of money furnished to willing buyers by means of stock exchange loans (i.e., the amount of money lent to stock exchange operators, converted into stock exchange profits by them and used for the buying of goods and services), has been excessive in relation to the long term profits of industry; (3) that the amount of money furnished to willing buyers by means of loans on the hire-purchase system has been excessive in relation to the growth of wages in the creditor countries; (4) that in spite of all this buying with borrowed money, the total amount of buying has not been excessive; (5) that the end of the excessive financing of buyers with loans has disclosed a deficiency of buying of goods and services by the lenders or by creditor countries and creditors in general; (6)[2] that this deficiency of buying of goods and services by the creditor countries has been partly due to excessive withdrawals of money by taxation from the public in these countries for the purpose of over-rapid reduction of their national debts; (7) that the conflict between, on the one hand, honourable debtors to repay their debts, and on the other, creditors or investors to increase their bondholdings, has been the main cause of insufficient buying and trade depression; (8) that the declining birth rates in the creditor countries has increased the difficulties of an economic system in which the necessary amount of markcting is only maintained by the excessive piling up of debts; (9) that the unstable nature of this economic and financial structure has been demonstrated by the effect of the breach made in it by the impending collapse in wholesale prices; and (10) that, in effect, less should have been lent and more should have been bought by the creditors.

We, therefore, conclude that there is a minimum as well as a maximum to the quantity of net money income that should be received by willing buyers, and that when this minimum is not reached—and it will not be reached when potential buyers are unwilling to buy adequately and to maintain adequately the profits and wages of producers and workers—it must be attained by the intervention of governments with appropriate measures.

1 The financing of buyers by means of international loans

The following observations on problems arising from international debts, written in 1926, appear in *The Final Buyer* (Chapter XV):—

"Although, normally, there should be neither difficulty in maintaining a gold standard currency, nor any tendency for a properly "managed" currency to depreciate, the question of the transfer of huge amounts of money in respect of indemnities or international debts introduces a special feature of such a serious kind that it is difficult to estimate what will be its outcome if such international payments are persisted in. It is a question of the economic effects of the debtor countries endeavouring to make money payments to the creditor countries at a time when the latter are unwilling to receive quantities of goods and services of adequate total money value from the former . . .

"If the creditor countries increase sufficiently their buying of foreign goods and services without reducing their buying of home-produced goods and services, then, other things being equal, their exports will not diminish, and home production and employment will not suffer as the result of increased imports of foreign goods. Nor will the standard of living of producers abroad be forced down in this case; for . . . increased production in the debtor countries may be expected to be great enough to enable them to deliver the necessary quantity of goods and services to the creditor countries without reducing their own standards of living. In view, however, of the general effort of individuals to accumulate wealth by means of abstinence, and the backward state of economic science as regards the proper correctives to this tendency, it is hardly likely that the velocity of buying will be sufficiently increased by the recipients of money payments in respect of debt instalments. . . .

"For the creditor countries to demand real net money payments from the debtor countries whilst seeking to abstain from doing the requisite amount of buying . . . must result in prices, profits and wages in the debtor countries being subjected to a continuous process of squeezing, or in the foreign exchange values of their currencies falling, and in international price-cutting in general. Nobody can say where the gentle art of price-cutting may lead, but it is certain that any harm done to producers and workers in the debtor countries by the ruthless application of economic pressure, will react continuously upon prices, profits and wages in the creditor countries—whose producers and workers will be starved by the continuous fall in the prices of foreign products with which they have to compete—or, if the creditor countries put on tariffs to impede or prevent the import of foreign goods, they will thereby impede or prevent both their own exports to the world in general and the receipt of real net payments from the debtor countries. Re-investment in the debtor countries of money paid or due by them will help matters, but the prospects of investment of this kind must deteriorate to the extent that incomes of buyers in the debtor countries are reduced by taxation and shrinking markets—and in any case the debts can only be piled up in this way. . . ."[3]

The position to-day is that, in fact, payments obtained by the creditor countries in respect of their exports, of their profits earned abroad, and of interest and capital due to them from the debtor countries, have not been used adequately by the recipients for the buying of goods and services from the debtor countries; and that, in fact, the debtor countries have met these foreign payments by means of loans obtained from the creditor countries and by shipping gold to them.

In effect, from the best though somewhat scanty statistical evidence available, the total net foreign investments[4] of the creditor countries—England, the United States, France, Holland, Switzerland, Belgium and Sweden—appear to have risen from about $27,000,000,000 at the end of 1920 to about $45,000,000,000 at the end of 1930, or an increase of over 60 per cent in ten years, and[5] an increase of over 230 per cent in their commodity value. The total amount of interest and earnings on these foreign investments appear to have increased from about $1,500,000,000 in 1920 to about $2,500,000,000 in 1930, and when the average annual Reparations instalments at $485,000,000 are added, total net payments in respect of the said interest, earnings and Reparations to be made annually by the debtor countries now amounts to about $2,985,000,000, or about 50 per cent greater than the amount for 1920 in respect of similar items, and about three times as great in terms of commodities.

In effect, also, nearly three-quarters of the world's monetary gold is now concentrated in the United States of America and in France.

In the days when England had practically a monopoly as banker in this game of progressive international loans, it was perhaps a drawing-room game, but since one or two other countries have entered on the scene as bankers, it has become modernized and now surpasses in fierceness the unlimited poker of gangsters. As for Reparations, considering that the cry of the leading Allied statesmen before Germany asked for the Armistice was for "no indemnities," it may well be supposed that at the Peace Conference the desire of these patriots to obtain justice for their countries exceeded their desire to do justice to themselves. At all events, their behaviour in this respect brought about the collapse of the old Mark, the subsequent over-borrowing by Germany, and the present impasse in respect of the transfer of huge payments to countries that are declining to buy enough goods and services. And *à propos*, we have not yet seen any very satisfactory explanation as to why certain governments obtained cash by the unloading of Young Plan bonds on the public at a price yielding 6½ per cent when these governments were able to obtain the same cash—if it was cash they wanted—at 4 to 4½ per cent on their own signatures.

Evidently, such huge international payments in respect of interest and earnings on foreign investments and in respect of Reparations cannot be trebled, doubled or even increased by 50 per cent every ten years. And when it comes to the question of amortization of repayment of capital in respect of these foreign investments, that is out of the question, since, amongst other reasons, the creditors do not want their foreign investments to be reduced. Meantime, unless we are mistaken, debts to foreigners and foreign claims on property can be legally cancelled by declaration of war,[6] when the dispossessed creditors must go and fetch what was theirs. What are we to think of those statesmen, economists and bankers who have put us into this?

2 The financing of buyers indirectly by means of stock exchange loans

In a communication sent by Sir Arthur Salter to the recent Congress of the International Chamber of Commerce at Washington, he lays special emphasis on the American "speculative boom" of 1929 as being one of the main causes of the present general trade depression. But however speculative this boom may have been and however disastrous its reaction, it cannot be treated as a main cause of the depression, since as a matter of fact it was rather an effect than a cause—the effect of the injection of tens of thousands of millions of dollars of borrowed money into circulation by means of abundant quantities of loans to governments, to builders and to buyers in general, and the effect of industrial profits outrunning wages.

At the time, Mr. Snowden described the stock exchange speculation in question as an "orgy," and in this connection we give the following extract from a letter sent by the writer of this article to *The Times* of London on the 10th October, 1929—about a week before the crash:—

> "This speculation is, no doubt, an 'orgy' in the sense that it has taken New York stockbrokers' loans from about $3,800,000,000 at the beginning of 1928 . . . to the present figure of about $6,500,000,000. This fabulous increase may well indicate that a proportionately large sum of money has been withdrawn from the market by investors and other operators, and that sooner or later there will be dark days of tribulation for quite a lot of people, unless these investors and other operators come back with their money and take

securities off the hands of speculators who are carrying too much on borrowed money. But operators withdrawing from the market in such circumstances do not usually entertain the idea of coming back to help those on whom they have unloaded. Quite the contrary, a policy frequently adopted by them is to employ the money by lending it to the speculators in the market at short notice, pending the arrival of the time when the 'bulls' are 'slaughtered' for the benefit of bargain hunters. The instability and viciousness of the financial aspect of the matter is therefore evident.

"When, however, we turn to the effects upon industry of this same stock-exchange speculation; we find a much brighter picture ... the New York Stock Exchange has yielded thousands of millions of dollars of profits, which money has largely gone into the buying of industrial products. This increased buying of goods and services has enabled and caused producers to increase their output in a way that only increased buying can, and to this extent it has been an important factor in the cause and maintenance of the unprecedented wave of prosperity now in progress in the United States. Capital and labour alike have shared in the prosperity ... Moreover, there has been no inflation of commodity prices ... Neither can it be argued that the country has been encroaching on its capital ...

"Thus, we see one side of speculation as financial madness, and the other as economic progress ..."

The situation a year later is well described in another letter by the same writer, sent to Mr. R. C. Fletcher (Stockbroker), London, on the 8th October, 1930:—

"... I think we must be prepared for heavy liquidation accompanied by big failures, perhaps this side of Christmas, ... the debtor countries are all more heavily in debt than ever before, and their difficulties are aggravated by the disastrous fall in commodity prices, whilst ... Germany is forced to undercut the cost of manufacturing everywhere in order to meet Reparations payments, and Russia must resort to wholesale dumping in order to obtain the means of importing essential goods that she cannot produce herself ...

"The question is, what are bargain prices? How long is this slump going to last, and what will it bring in its train? ... There may be some very drastic times to go through. Then why not stick to bonds? Even that is not safe, because the gold standard ... is a god that now distinctly rocks, and thus our rulers may try to escape their difficulties by means of inflation ...

"I am afraid that there may be heavy forced selling in conditions of panic. The prices of many stocks are still higher than is justified by dividends ... Reasonable readjustment is still due, and if it takes place it will surely bring out unreasonable liquidation. Study the behaviour, not only of business men, but also of great soldiers, great statesmen and solemn learned judges, and the absence of reason in their actions from time to time emphasizes the fact that all men are born of women. Thus, the unreasonable is often to be expected, and thus one must try and buy at unreasonably low prices in order, when the whole story is told, not to find that one has bought at unreasonably high prices."

However, it is certain that large amounts of industrial profits have been placed to reserve, whereby shareholders or partners in the concerns in question have not bought goods and services adequately with such profits as earned; that the shares of all prosperous businesses have attracted stock exchange operators who have used borrowed money to bid up the stock exchange prices concerned, whereby stock exchange profits were created and largely treated as income; that, thus, both the making and the withholding of large industrial profits have resulted in the obtaining of stock exchange loans, in the transformation of these loans into stock exchange profits, and in the spending of the stock exchange profits thus built up on credit or debt—instead of in the spending of unentailed industrial profits.

3 The financing of buyers by means of loans on the hire-purchase system

In the period 1924–1928, the total amount of money invested in building and construction in the United States amounted to the colossal sum of $45,000,000,000. This investment was not spread evenly over the period, but rose from about $7,305,000,000 in 1924 to about $9,936,000,000 in 1928. Expenditure on building since then has declined heavily and continuously, and the annual amount of such expenditure is now about $3,000,000,000 less than in 1928. Most of this money was obtained by borrowing in one way or another, and as about half of it went into residential building which is largely financed by means of mortgage loans and instalment credit, the amount of this kind of financing must have been enormous. In addition, huge sums were advanced on the hire-purchase system for the buying of furniture, motor cars, radio sets etc.; and the evidence, such as it is, appears to indicate that the annual amounts of such loans rose from 1924 to 1928–1929, and fell thereafter, in a manner more or less in sympathy with the rise and fall of loans for building. Some idea may thus be formed of the magnitude of the amount of money furnished to buyers in all countries by means of mortgage loans and instalment credit, and the part played by such loans in the making of the boom.

It is now obvious, perhaps even more to those who have granted instalment credit than to those who have obtained it, that the amount of such financing was excessive. But this is not to say that the quantity of goods and services so bought, or even the total quantity of buying by this and other means, during the boom was too great in relation to productive capacity at the time—and we shall show, in fact, that the total amount of buying was not too great. It must therefore be urged, so far as workers are concerned, not that the amount of goods and services bought was excessive, but that the buying of all these goods and services ought to have been effected by the raising of wages instead of by means of excessive instalment credit.

According to estimates of the United States Commissioner of Labour, the average yearly earnings of workers employed in the manufacturing industries in that country had increased, in comparison with 1909, by 55.2 per cent in 1921 and by 77.6 per cent in 1929; but the value of the output per worker had increased, over that of 1909, by 101 per cent in 1921 and by 156.2 per cent in 1929. From this and other evidence it may be said that real wages have not advanced as much as progress in the arts or methods of production.

In effect, had profits been smaller and wages greater during the boom—had the charges of labour on profits been greater—the same amount of goods and services could have been bought by workers with less recourse to instalment credit, and, incidentally, the excessive stock exchange speculation and unstable rise in stock exchange prices induced by the abnormal rise in industrial profits would have been averted.

Thus, it is evident that increased effectiveness of labour has not been accompanied by a corresponding increase in the return to workers; that a necessary increase in sales to workers has been obtained, not by increased wages, but by means of the hire-purchase system; and that the mortgaging of future wages for the paying of instalments entails a reduction of the purchasing power of workers, which can only be overcome by means of adequate advances in wages in the creditor countries where increased buying is desirable.

4 The total amount of buying has not been excessive

Although this enormous amount of borrowing by governments, by stock exchange operators and by consumers in general was surely financial madness, the total amount of buying of goods and services effected by this and other means has not been too great—perhaps not even great enough—in relation to the rate at which producers were able and willing to produce at current prices. As stated in our Bulletin No. 2, when the acid tests are applied as to whether or not the buying was excessive, the reactions obtained are completely negative: *First*, the general trend of commodity prices has been definitely downward since 1920, showing that the quantity of goods and services for sale tended to increase even more rapidly than the buying. *Secondly*, not only no encroachment has been made on capital, but quite the contrary, permanent wealth in buildings, factories, railways and equipment of every kind have been vastly improved and increased, whilst stocks of raw materials and manufactured goods at the end of the boom were larger than ever.

5 The end of buying by borrowers and the disclosure of a deficiency of buying by the creditors

When the furnishing of buyers with loans had reached its limit and debtors were forced to buy less in order to make payments to the creditors, commodity prices declined as the result of the reduced buying, and the steady concentration of cash in the hands of creditors and of gold in the creditor countries took place. In effect, the fall in prices would not have occurred had the creditors bought enough goods and services with the payments being made to them by the debtors, instead of receiving too great a proportion of such payments in cash and gold. Thus, the cessation of the unsound buying of goods and services with borrowed money by the debtors disclosed a deficiency of buying by the creditor countries and creditors in general.

6 The deficiency of buying by the creditor countries, and excessive taxation and over-deflation by their governments

The United States of America has reduced its national debt from $25,482,000,000 to $16,185,000,000, or by over $9,000,000,000 in the ten years 1920–1930. The British national debt has been reduced by nearly $2,000,000,000 in the same period. France has reduced its national debt by over $1,208,000,000 in the three years 1927–1930. This has been done mainly by means of money taken from taxpayers. But, in the ten pre-war years 1903–1913, the American national debt was *increased* by about $34,000,000, the French national debt was *increased* by about $500,000,000, whilst the British national debt was reduced by less than $400,000,000.

We have, here, some explanation of the concentration and sterilization of gold in the United States and in France in recent years. Without attempting to discuss this matter at length, the following may be said:—

It is generally agreed that a budget deficit, i.e., an excess of expenditure over revenue that increases the public debt, tends to inflate the quantity of circulating money, and to cause a rise in prices or currency depreciation. It may therefore be suggested that a budget surplus, i.e., an excess of revenue over expenditure that reduces the public debt, tends to deflate the quantity of circulating money, and to cause a fall in prices or currency appreciation.

In effect, the withdrawal of income from the taxpayer and its transference as liquid capital to the investor against the surrender and extinction of government securities held by him, reduces the buying of goods and services by the taxpayer without necessarily causing increased buying of goods and services—increased investment in new capital goods and/or increased consumption—by the investor or those he may directly or indirectly finance. Further, whether or not the recipients of the money use it for increased investment and/or increased consumption, the result is almost sure to be deflationary. For: (i) when there is no increased buying by the recipients of the money, the quantity of circulating money is reduced and prices are depressed; (ii) when increased investment in new productive equipment or in new stocks of goods takes place, the increased productive capacity or increased production so caused, combined with the decreased buying of the taxpayers from whom the money was taken, will tend to depress prices and reduce the quantity of money in circulation; and (iii) when the financing of new non-productive equipment or of new consumption takes place, debts are created that sooner or later tend to reduce the buying of the debtors and the quantity of circulating money, and to depress prices.

Again, so far as the banks are concerned, the effective demand for loans by the public will not, other things being equal, increase as the result of the transfer of money from taxpayers to financiers and rentiers. And, if the effective demand for loans does not increase, the retirement and extinction of government securities held by the banks, i.e., the reduction of bank loans to the government, will not be offset by increased bank loans to the public. Thus, the withdrawal of money from the public by taxation for extinction of government securities, will tend to cause the investments and loans of the banks to decline, the deflation of credit, and the decline of cash and bank deposits at the disposal of buyers.

It may, therefore, be said that excessive taxation for the purpose of over-rapid reduction of national debts in the creditor countries has partly, if not largely, prevented taxpayers in these countries from buying enough goods and services from their home producers and foreign debtors, has driven many financiers and investors into unsound investments at home and abroad or into stock exchange speculation, and has thus largely helped to bring about the collapse of markets, the severe deflation of credit and the actual hoarding of money in the hearth and the virtual hoarding of money in the banks.

7 *The conflict between honourable debtors and creditors or investors*

Although large government debts and debts in general may be undesirable, it must be urged that any attempt by debtors to reduce debts as a whole at a time when creditors or investors are not disposed to reduce their savings or to convert their bondholdings into new capital goods, must result in falling prices, deflation and trade depression.

The repayment of interest and principal on international, internal and commercial debts is dependent on the debtors producing surplus goods and services, selling them to the creditors, and using the money so obtained for the payment of debts—either directly or through the tax collector. But since the creditors cannot be forced to buy more goods and services than they like, they have at least as much say as the debtors in the matter of whether such debts are to be reduced or to be increased. However much the debtors produce and however much they economize—however great the surplus of goods and services that they make available for the creditors—their efforts will bring them no more money than the creditors are willing to pay; and, in fact, when such a surplus of goods and services exceeds the quantity that the creditors are willing to buy, it fetches less money instead of more, and debts are increased instead of reduced, because lower prices, trade depression and loans to relieve distress are the result.

In effect, as the result of the fall in prices, which as urged above was due in no small measure to the deflationary policies of the governments of the creditor countries, the reduction of national debts in terms of money has been accompanied by an increase in the debts in terms of commodities. Even the valiant behaviour of the United States Government in reducing its public debt from $25,482,000,000 to $16,101,000,000 in ten years, has so far proved abortive in terms of commodities—and who can say that such valiance on the part of the creditor governments is not one of the main causes of the present difficulties of debtors in general? Honourable and sound finance ministers in the creditor countries are well aware of the difficulties to be overcome in the provision of sinking funds for the reduction of public debts, but they do not seem to be aware that difficulties in connection with the real reduction of such debts only begin, and do not end, with the withdrawal of money from the public by taxation and the withholding of money from the public by decreased government expenditure.

The truth is that—apart from a few ne'er-do-well spendthrifts—creditors and investors are not at all disposed to reduce, but determined to increase, their holdings of home and foreign bonds, and the results of their endeavours in this respect during the last half-century have been gratifying to the point of the miraculous, for, in spite of ever-increasing taxation, confiscatory death duties, acute trade depressions, the collapse of certain currencies, devastating wars, the attacks of poor relations, the exertions of honourable borrowers to repay quickly, and the efforts of dishonourable borrowers not to repay at all, the holding of interest-paying bonds now reach astronomical figures which at once dazzle the statistician, delight the mathematician and defy the imagination.

Thus, honourable debtors have economized in order to pay their debts, whilst creditors and investors have economized in order to increase their bondholdings; and these economies with opposite aims have been a major cause of insufficient buying and trade depression.

8 The declining birth rates in the creditor countries

The wonderful rise of bondholders during the last few generations has been largely assisted by the rapid increase of populations, whereby the limits imposed by considerations of maximum debt per head of the population have been largely extended. The fact is that the birth and upbringing of these additional people has served as a developer and stabilizer of markets, of industry and of investment in a way that altogether surpasses the effects of the popularization of such things as motor cars, radio sets and silk stockings. For babies are not obtained on the hire-purchase system; the cost of their maintenance is constant and progressive; and eventually they release both "hoarded savings" and the bonds of debtors in substantial quantities—the poor new generations do so by establishing higher consumption standards that are more compatible with the increase of surplus productive capacity everywhere on offer; the rich new generations do so by extravagance and even by dissipation. The recent tendency for birth rates to decline in the creditor countries is, therefore, tending to expose the top-heavy nature of the present structure of national and international debts.

9 The breach made by the impendent collapse in wholesale prices

In recent years there has been an attempt to combat under-consumption by curtailment of production. Great and small optimists have used all the secrets of science and organization to increase the effectiveness of labour and to reduce the cost of production, and at the same time have hoped to maintain wholesale prices by regulation of supplies. We have seen cartels, pools and even governments handling steel, rubber, coffee, wheat, etc., with this end in view. But the efforts of all these organizations—undermined continuously by surging masses of eager and hungry outside producers pressing for a place in the sun, undermined continuously by the withdrawal and "hoarding" of profits by businesses and savers, and undermined continuously by the deflationary action of the governments of the creditor countries—were only sustained, and could only be sustained for a time, by the super-feeding of loans to buyers; and when this piling-up of debts in geometrical progression had reached its limit, prices in all markets began to give, and the whole abnormal structure rocked and collapsed with a crash, leaving vast quantities of debris in the form of colossal debts magnified and multiplied by the drastic fall in prices.

10 The creditors should have lent less and bought more

Briefly, then, the extent of the debts contracted, their rapid rate of increase and the unwillingness of the creditors to receive adequate quantities of goods and services in payment, show that less should have been lent. Whilst, on the other hand, the efforts of producers to maintain prices by artificial means show that the extensive additional buying of goods and services effected with borrowed money has by no means always been sufficient to maintain prices since the break in prices of 1920.

11 General conclusion

Evidently, whilst it is true that there is a maximum to the quantity of net money income that can be received by willing buyers if monetary depreciation is to be avoided, it is also true that there is a minimum to the quantity of net money income that must be received by willing buyers—and received without charge on their future income—if the general rate of buying is to be adequately and healthily maintained in relation to the general rate at which producers are able and willing to produce. In other words, there is a minimum as well as a maximum to the proportion of income that the creditor countries and their inhabitants must be willing to use for the buying of goods and services from the debtor countries and from workers in general. Our general conclusion, therefore, is that when this minimum is not reached by the voluntary behaviour of potential buyers, it must be attained by the intervention of governments with national and international arrangements to provide work for, and to distribute adequate wages and salaries to, the unemployed and workers in general in the creditor countries.

Bulletin no. 8.

August 17th, 1931.

Budgetary policy in the present situation

Resolution

The following Resolution was adopted by our Committee at a meeting held to-day:—

The Unclaimed Wealth Utilization Committee

(*a*) *Believing* that upward readjustment of prices to the average price-level for the period 1926–1929 is highly desirable, and that further downward readjustment of prices and wages would be disastrous—

(*b*) *Believing* that a further fall in the prices of commodities would increase the quantity of non-liquidable international debts, internal debts and private debts, cause more forced selling of securities and more big failures, intensify trade depression and unemployment, and aggravate an already dangerous political situation;

(*c*) *Believing* that further curtailment of the total amount of buying in the world would entail a further fall in the prices of commodities;

(*d*) *Believing* that a simultaneous attempt of all governments to balance their budgets *at the present time* would reduce the total amount of buying of goods and services by governments and/or taxpayers by about $2,500,000,000[7] per annum, that this decreased injection of money into circulation might reduce the total turn-over of world trade by a vastly greater amount, and that further declines in revenues would thus be caused that would again unbalance budgets;

(*e*) *Believing* that it is highly desirable that the debtor countries should, immediately, both balance their budgets and increase the total money value of their exports in relation to the total money value of their imports, and that this cannot be done unless the creditor countries increase the quantity of their imports from the debtor countries in relation to their exports to them and/or pay higher prices for their imports from the debtor countries;

(*f*) *Believing* that it is urgently necessary that the creditor countries should expand the total quantity of money in circulation, increase the total amount of buying and raise the price-level;

(*g*) *And, believing* that the actual buying deficiency by creditors is partly due to excessive confidence in the rising value of gold or in the rising values of the currencies of the creditor countries;

Recommends that the creditor countries, i.e., Great Britain, the United States of America, France, Holland, Switzerland, Belgium and Sweden, should agree amongst themselves and undertake to put the following emergency measures forthwith into effect for a period of twelve months:—

(1) *Taxation to be reduced* immediately in such manner that the total revenues of the said creditor countries be reduced by 30 per cent, and the people so affected to be invited to buy goods and services with the money so left in their hands.
(2) *Total Government expenditure not to be reduced* in all the said countries.
(3) *Total Government expenditure to be increased* in the United States of America and also in France by the immediate raising of salaries and wages of all government employees, and the said employees to be invited to buy goods and services with the money so placed in their hands.
(4) *Budgetary deficits* in each of the above countries to be met by the governments in question arranging with their respective central banks to open the necessary credits at a total charge of half of one per cent per annum.

Resolves that the necessary steps be taken for the said recommendation to receive due consideration at the coming Assembly of the League of Nations.

It was further urged at this meeting of the Committee: (i) that the expansion of the quantity of money in circulation in the creditor countries in the manner recommended would promote investment and thereby promote the circulation of the present immobile stocks of gold in certain countries, facilitate the inflow of money into the debtor countries, and tend to overcome the foreign exchange difficulties of the debtor countries in the obtaining of currencies of creditor countries for the purpose of making necessary payments to them; (ii) that the putting into effect of the measures in question by all the creditor countries *simultaneously* would reduce to manageable proportions any question of excessive loss of gold by one or more of the creditor countries, which would arise in the case of excessive expansion of credit in one or more creditor countries in relation to the expansion of credit in the others; (iii) that the raising of the price-level to the 1926–1929 average level would revive industry and trade as well as reduce the commodity value of debts enough to render them liquidable; and (iv) that, at all events, it would be better business for the creditor countries to extend credit and purchasing power to their own solvent people, than for them to extend, willingly or unwillingly, long or short term credits to debtor countries whose solvency—so far as international payments to the creditor countries were concerned—was questionable at the existing price-level.

Note

Since the adoption of this Resolution on August 17th, 1931, the suspension of gold payments by England—which the prompt adoption of the measures advocated above would have prevented—occurred on September 21st, 1931. In these circumstances the terms of the Resolution became obsolete. The Committee, therefore, decided to recommend that the creditor countries remaining *on the gold standard* should reduce taxation, increase government expenditure and meet budgetary deficits by special central bank credits until the internal and external values of their respective currencies were reduced to the level of sterling; and that the same policy should be continued by these creditor countries, and by any other creditor countries thus automatically brought on to the gold standard, until the wholesale price-level in gold reached the average level of 1926–1929.

In this connection, the Committee has recently issued Bulletins Nos. 12 and 13 (copies sent on application) on the case for a "moratorium" for taxpayers in the over-deflated creditor countries. Here is a proposal for the United States of America where the Authorities—now more or less converted to the idea of the necessity of an extraordinary expansion of credit in their country—are lending newly created money to banking institutions, producers and exporters, instead of using it to enable the American people to absorb more goods and services from their producers at home and their debators abroad. It is also to be hoped that this proposal will interest the voter in France, where so far the Authorities do not want to hear of anti-deflationary measures.

The Search for Confidence
in 1932 (1933)

Bulletin no. 12.

January 1, 1932.

The case for a "moratorium" for taxpayers in the over-deflated, gold-logged countries

We are about to urge that the present business crisis is largely due to excessive deflation in the gold-logged creditor countries, and that anti-deflationary measures are necessary in these countries. Budget deficits are the natural cure as well as the best antidote to excessive deflation, and suspension of taxation for a suitable period in these countries would bring about general prosperity.

In the period 1920–1930, the United States of America reduced its national debt, mainly by means of money taken from the taxpayer, from $25,482,000,000 to $16,185,000,000, namely, by over $9,000,000,000 in ten years, and at the rate of about $900,000,000 a year. But in the ten pre-war years, 1903–1913, the American national debt was not reduced, but was *increased* by about $34,000,000.

In the three years 1928–1930, France reduced its national debt, mainly by means of money taken from the taxpayer; by over $1,208,000,000, that is, at the rate of about $400,000,000 a year. This was due to the vast amount of new taxation that was imposed to arrest the fall in the franc in 1926, which drastic deflation was not discontinued when its object had been attained. Nevertheless, in the ten pre-war years, 1903–1913, the French national debt was not reduced, but was *increased* by nearly $500,000,000.

Americans and Frenchmen who wish to know why so much gold has been dragged to earth in their countries in recent years have, here, something to think about.

In the period 1920–1930, the British taxpayer has been forced to surrender enough money to reduce the British national debt by nearly $2,000,000,000, namely, at the rate of about $200,000,000 a year. Yet at the end of 1913 the whole of the British national debt only stood at about $3,150,000,000; and it had been reduced by less than $400,000,000 in the ten years, 1903–1913, or at the rate of under $40,000,000 a year.

Some will object that pre-war national finance was unsound. But surely everybody ought to see that the expression "sound finance" is grossly abused when in its name the three great creditor countries, England, France and the United States, proceed to squeeze over $12,000,000,000 of purchasing power out of their wretched taxpayers, and to deflate the quantity of government securities by this amount, in the brief space of ten years. To give an idea of the kind of results that may, in certain circumstances, be involved in such drastic deflation, it may be said that had the $12,000,000,000 remained in the hands of the taxpayers and had they turned this amount over in 1930 no more than three times in the buying of goods and services, the total amount of buying in that year would have been increased by $36,000,000,000—or by enough to prevent the depression.[8]

Sound or unsound, such an idea as the deflation of national debt by $9,000,000,000, or even by $2,000,000,000 within a period of ten years was quite unknown in pre-war days. From the man in the street to the inmates of the great institutions for the insane, it had occurred to nobody; and there is no evidence that it had so much as begun to germinate even in the great institutions of the intelligentsia. The notion, it may be supposed, was the creation of post-war geniuses, and of heroes whose nervous systems had been irreparably shattered whilst defending the home fronts in the perilous moments of air-raids.

Again, the inter-governmental debt question—another phase of post-war mentality—would never have become acute had it not been for excessive taxation and deflation in the creditor countries. The fact is that, had gold been allowed to perform its normal function, it would have raised prices in the countries it entered until the imports of these countries increased in relation to their exports enough to cause inter-governmental money payments to be transformed into payments in goods and services. This is really very simple; and the day will surely dawn when school children, merely bored when the duffer of the class suggests that two and two make five, will shriek with laughter when he announces that annual payments of, say, $400,000,000 collected by a great country from (taxpayers) abroad, should be applied to the reduction of its national debt—used in a deflationary manner in the receiving country—at a time of falling prices, and thus be sterilized, instead of being re-injected into circulation by being used for increased buying of goods and services.

Post-war directors of national finance in the creditor countries, mad with inflation-fright, have indulged in an orgy of deflation.

Statesmen have yet to learn that there is an appropriate rate, varying with circumstances, at which national debts should be reduced; and that if the docile taxpayer can be driven to death, he cannot be driven to by-gone pre-war positions.

The truth is that deflation, like inflation, may become ruinous; and that if inflation must be arrested at all costs by budget surpluses, it is equally important to arrest deflation by budget deficits. Budget deficits are, in fact, the natural cure of deflation. We know that when deflation passes a certain point, it either forces debtors to suspend gold payments, or it brings out budget deficits. Either way, additional money is directly or indirectly furnished to debtors, and the result is of an order that tends to bring about the reversal of the downward course of prices.

Thus, whilst it is certain that, at the present time, balanced budgets are essential in countries that have been forced to suspend gold payments by excessive deflation in the gold-logged creditor countries, it is equally certain that a large temporary remission of taxation, involving budget deficits in these over-deflated countries, is the only sound policy for them to-day.

In effect, a suspension of taxation for a suitable period, corresponding budget deficits and corresponding increases in government securities in, say, the United States and France:—

(i) Would enable taxpayers in these countries to absorb an equivalent quantity of goods and services made available for them by their producers at home and their debtors abroad.

(ii) Would raise the gold prices of commodities, restore the values of securities and property, and raise the foreign-exchange values of sterling and other currencies off the gold standard.

(iii) Would enable large and small debtors to make payments, liquidate a generally "frozen" internal and international position, and be an excellent solution for the inter-governmental debt *impasse*.

The granting of a moratorium to their debtors abroad may seem a necessary evil for the gold-logged creditor countries, but a moratorium to their own taxpayers may be a boon that enables these countries to *collect* their debts from abroad.

In advocating this suspension of taxation, we are able to state that we are doing so after consultation with nearly a dozen of the leading authorities on these questions, and that our facts and arguments have been admitted as correct by at least one eminent lord, by at least two eminent millionaries, by at least three eminent baronets, and by at least six of the leading economists.

These gentlemen, however, declined to make a public statement on the matter, and most of them gave the reasons for their reticence. Some said that it was useless to agitate because the French mentality on such matters was too rigid—or because the Americans would think the proposal was an English ramp. Others, on the contrary, were afraid that the idea would take on too well and that the public might, afterwards, refuse to pay taxes again. And the rest excused themselves, saying: the first, that he would not like to lose his job (wise man!); the second, that he would not take the responsibility (prudent man!), and a third, that he would take a wife (imprudent man—but bless his heart!). Happily there were not lacking City Editors of daily and weekly papers with courage enough to voice the truth, and they, like the sergeant-major, carried on—whilst the general staff took cover.

However, we fear that it will be impossible to convert Old Mother Hoobbard and all the worthy folk with bare-cupboard and poor-dog complexes, who cannot realize the significance of an economy of plenty.

We assert that the purchasing power of the taxpayer on the one hand, and government securities held by the banking systems on the other, in the gold-logged creditor countries have been unduly deflated by excessive taxation and sinking funds in these countries. In the absence of adequate recognition of this fact by the Governments concerned, it is for the worker, the producer, the taxpayer and public opinion the world over to call for the necessary anti-deflationary remission of taxation in the over-deflated countries in question. The golden idol of balanced budgets must not be allowed to stand in the way of rectification of past errors.

Years ago Bryan, the famous American statesman, asked: "Shall man be crucified on a cross of gold?" To-day it is different, but the same.

Bulletin no. 13.

January 15, 1932.

Statement on the case for a "moratorium" for taxpayers in the over-deflated countries

We, the undersigned, consider:

(i) That the fall in gold prices of commodities, securities and property has been too great in relation to existing undertakings of debtors to make gold payments.

(ii) That the concentration of gold in the United States of America and in France has been largely due to the receipt by these countries in gold of too great a proportion of the payments due to them from abroad—and not enough in goods and services.

(iii) That both the excessive fall in gold prices of commodities and securities, and the concentration of gold in the United States and in France, have been largely due to insufficient buying of goods and services by these countries from their producers at home and from their debtors abroad.

(iv) That this deficiency of buying of goods and services by these creditor countries (partly concealed for a time by loans to debtors)[9] has been largely due to excessive withdrawals of money by taxation from their respective publics for the purpose of rapid reduction of national debts. In other words, excessive taxation has largely prevented taxpayers in these countries from buying enough goods and services from home producers and foreign debtors; whilst the drastic retirement of the obligations of their governments has, on the one hand, deflated their money markets, and has, on the other hand, driven investors into unsound investments at home and abroad, into stock exchange speculation, and into the actual hoarding of money in the hearth or the virtual hoarding of money in the banks.[10]

(v) That in the present circumstances it is highly desirable that the debtor countries, the creditor countries that have suspended gold payments, and the creditor countries where there has been no deflation in post-war years of the kind described above, should both balance their budgets and increase the money value of their exports in relation to the money value of their imports; and that this cannot be done unless the United States of America and France adopt reflationary measures to increase the total amount of buying of goods and services by them and to raise the gold prices of commodities and securities.

(vi) That a suspension of taxation for a suitable period, with corresponding budget deficits, in the United States and in France is a reflationary measure capable of immediate application, which (*a*) would enable the people in these countries to absorb the goods and services made available for them by their producers at home and by their debtors abroad, (*b*) would raise the gold prices of commodities and securities as well as restore the values of unduly depreciated currencies on the foreign exchange market, and (*c*) would enable home and foreign debtors to make internal and international payments.

(vii) That a "moratorium" to their own solvent taxpayers is better business for America and France than a moratorium to foreigners whose solvency at the present gold prices of commodities is questionable.

Readers can assist us by letting us have their views on the preceding Statement.

Communications sent in confidence should be marked "CONFIDENTIAL."

Bulletin no. 14.

February 20, 1932.

The economic crisis and the disarmament conference

One of the things decided at the first meeting of the Bureau of the Disarmament Conference was that "*in view of the existing world-wide crisis, the absolute suppression of fêtes and receptions be recommended to the Conference.*" (Our translation.)

The Bureau of the Disarmament Conference has thus—no doubt quite innocently—taken a position on a controversial economic question of the most fundamental order. It has raised the question, *To buy or not to buy?* and it has recommended people *not to buy* as the appropriate economic course in the present crisis.

Potential buyers in Geneva, and incidentally in the world in general, have been advised not to buy by a body comprising some of the world's leading statesmen, and since this advice will surely be largely followed, we cannot let it pass unchallenged. We therefore beg to point out:—

(i) That the prices of goods, securities and property have fallen to ruinous levels as the result of insufficient buying.

(ii) That millions of workers are to-day unemployed because of the ruinous fall in prices resulting from insufficient buying.

(iii) That thousands of capitalists are to-day insolvent because of the ruinous fall in prices resulting from insufficient buying.

(iv) That this insufficient buying is being aggravated by the reduced earnings of producers and workers and the losses of capitalists, and by the fact that debtors are buying less in order to make payments, creditors are buying less because they cannot get payments, and entrepreneurs are buying less new capital equipment because of the decreased buying and decreased production of consumable goods.

(v) That in fact it is generally agreed that the present crisis is, by all indications, mainly a crisis of insufficient buying by potential buyers.

(vi) That in these circumstances potential buyers should buy as much as they can afford, and that *the suppression of fêtes and receptions by such people only tends to intensify the crisis.*

No doubt the eminent gentlemen of the Bureau of the Disarmament Conference would readily admit that marketing—selling—is an integral and necessary part of the economic system, but it is not clear that they feel the same about buying. Yet any tradesman in Geneva can tell them that every sale is a purchase, and every purchase is a sale.

The undefined attitude of statesmen in the creditor countries on the simple truism that *every sale is a purchase* has intensified and prolonged the crisis. Taxation has been increased, and wages and salaries in governments' services have been cut down—purchases have been curtailed when increased sales were desired.

Some of these statesmen would have us believe that reduced expenditure on armaments will improve trade. Others assure us that such reduced expenditure will not make trade any worse. M. Jouhoux, secretary of the C.G.T., recently said[11] that disarmament would not cause unemployment, because the money saved "would be utilized otherwise." But surely this is merely the voice of optimism, for if M. Jouhoux can definitely state that any money saved by means of disarmament will be used for increased buying in other trades, and if he knows something definite about the manner in which the said increased buying will take effect, he ought not to withhold this information from producers and workers in the armament trades—nor yet from the multitudes of producers and workers in the trades that supply them with food, clothing, shelter, etc.—whose jobs are in jeopardy.

What, for instance, would happen to these producers and workers, and to industry and finance in general, if (i) the annual injection into circulation of, say, $5,000,000,000 via the armament professions and trades were to cease, (ii) the money were used to repay government debts to investors and financiers, and (iii) the financiers and investors could not invest it safely and profitably, and did not attempt to do so, because of this cessation of the flow of purchasing power into the hands of consumers dependent on armaments?[12]

Loose statements are being made by embarrassed finance ministers and by eager humanitarians about the favourable, or not unfavourable, economic effects of disarmaments. This will not do.

If armament factories are to be shut, producers and workers in the armament trades, and producers and workers in general, should be told exactly what is going to be done with the money saved in this way. For the truth is that expenditure on armaments, to-day, constitutes a major factor in the maintenance of markets; that any reduction of the importance of this factor needs to be neutralized by the raising of the standard of living; and that this transition from armaments to a higher standard of living cannot be left to chance.

In these circumstances, voters should obtain adequate guarantees from governments that any money saved as the result of reduced buying in connection with armaments shall—pending the expansion of other markets—be used in full for the extension of public works and, until such work can be put in hand, for the reduction of taxation.

Economic Readjustment in 1933 (1934)

Bulletin no. 26.

June 1, 1933.

Gentlemen prefer gold

II A midsummer night's dream of 1928

As stated in our last Bulletin, *A Midsummer Night's Dream of* 1928 is, so far as we are concerned, the prologue to *Some Facts of* 1929–1932 *and After*. We are giving it last instead of first for the following reasons:—

In the first place, we wanted to put forward certain facts as soon as possible in order to give our readers the opportunity of picking up some good gold-mining shares before prices rose any farther. In effect, the suspension of gold payments by the United States of America, coming as it did whilst the Bulletin in question[13] was being multigraphed, showed that there was no time to lose and amply justified our "visions of the dollar . . . going to a discount in relation to gold." We may add that more than one of our readers, acting on that Bulletin, and taking advantage of the sharp recession in the prices of gold-mining shares resulting from the temporary scare caused by America going "off" gold, invested substantial amounts in the best Rand mines.

Secondly, in moving over the border of recognized economic territory into the realm of dreams, we knew that we should incur the scorn, if not the wrath, of quite a number of people. In fact, we felt that action of this kind was bound to be regarded as an unwarrantable adventure by some, and as an illegitimate incursion by others. Neither were we at all sure that Bunyan, the dreamer of *Pilgrim's Progress*, or even Dante, the dreamer of *The Divine Comedy*, would approve our behaviour. In these circumstances, we thought that *A Midsummer Night's Dream of* 1928 would be more acceptable, as well as easier to relate in a dreamy style, to people who already had before them our presentation of certain relevant facts that had occurred in subsequent years—which facts, we believe, suggest that "the rise in the value of gold since 1929 may not have been altogether a normal economic development."[14]

To the scornful, and to those who deny *everything* about dreams, we wish to point out that this dream should *at least* be instructive to theorists and others who pin their faith to such widely different things as free trade, protection, emergency currencies, state ownership of the banks, balanced budgets . . . We confess that, for obvious reasons, we have deliberately coloured the dream, and that for the same reasons the characters are as fictitious as we can make them. We certainly hope no *gentleman* will feel that any reference is being made to him.

One midsummer night in 1928, a week or two before the strange and dramatic end of a famous international financier, somebody dreamed a dream. It was about a conference of multi-millionaires, a score or so of them, that took place somewhere, possibly in the City, or in the Champs Elysées—or even *through the ether!*

1 The characters

Old Göbbelstein, fat and red, presided. He was known in Berlin as Der Grübler, and in London as Old Gobbler. In truth, he was almost always ruminating, either with his mind or with his mouth, or with both; and some asserted that, for this reason, he had almost lost the power of speech. But if he was no speaker, he was said to be worth $550,000,000.[15]

There was James Raid, the great gold-mining magnate, bullion broker and general financier. His grandfather had been an Armenian opium merchant in Constantinople; his father, who was educated at Eton and Oxford and who had married a Mackintosh, had changed his name from Radian to Raid; and nobody will be surprised if, following on any eventual downfall of the golden god, his grandson changes the name to Radium. He was supposed to be worth some $450,000,000, and his assets largely consisted of gold, cash and very liquidable securities. His ability and skill as a "raider" were unequalled, as was shown by the brilliant manner in which he had taken possession of several fair-sized banks with good connections in America and elsewhere. Apparently he had managed to flood these banks with demand deposits for a number of years until a substantial proportion of the money had got tied up in long-term credits such as three-year mortgages, and then, suddenly calling in all these deposits, he had forced the banks to suspend payments. Rumour even had it that he had made a nice pile by pulling a debtor country off the gold standard.

There was Richard Devoschère—known as Dick in London, Devonshire Cream in New York and Le Diable in Paris—with his Amsterdam correspondent, Hans Rotterdam. The former was reputed to be worth $300,000,000; and as the king of moneylenders, he looked upon all other branches of finance, such as company promoting and the like, with a certain amount of suspicion if not contempt. Latterly his speciality had been lending money to governments and placing the bonds with the public. There were usually some excellent lines in his shop window marked 7 per cent at 92½, which price covered his commission of 2½ per cent. The secret of his success was his extraordinary aptitude for persuading governments to borrow when their countries were not really in need of public loans. He certainly much preferred to lend to governments that could just as easily have lent to him, for his motto was "Safety First;" but, at a time when the public with which he placed his new issues was "confident," he would sometimes lend to governments that badly wanted such accommodation. He still did "a fair business" at around 120 per cent with the heirs of rich noblemen and of the "nouveau riche."

There was George G. Boomer, the great Wall Street operator. What he was worth varied considerably and rapidly. There had been times when his financial position had balanced—somehow and wonderfully—at much less than nothing. But in the summer of 1928, after five years of very successful trading as a "bull," and with the prices of securities standing at "record highs for all time," he was worth $400,000,000 if he was worth a cent.

Perhaps the most interesting person in the conference was the smart and polished Parisian, Frank le Boilin. His was the master mind that had conceived and carried out the idea of revaluing the unsaleable surplus war stores and war materials of a Western country and the worthless bonds of an Eastern country by negotiating the war materials for the bonds, whereby the Eastern country was able to get Georgianople, Marianople—and financial pull. Even George G. Boomer admitted that "Frank Lee Boiling" was "pretty hot stuff." He, at all events, was the only one in the conference who cultivated the art of oratory.

These men and others were there, and if the fortunes of some did not run to nine figures in dollars, altogether they amounted to at least $2,500,000,000.

A wireless message sent by Ol Cocke from Palm Beach was read. It stated that the sender regretted he could not join the conference as he was entertaining a president (?), but that the conference could rely on his doing anybody (on being repeated, "anybody" came back as "anything") if there was money in it.

It must here be stated that we have been unable to ascertain in what language this wireless message was sent and read, or in what language the address by Frank le Boilin that followed was delivered. Italian, French, English and American were all indicated, but without guarantee. Indeed, this matter of the terms in which the thoughts in question were transmitted remains too vague for words. But apparently the address, if not the wireless message, was delivered very distinctly; everybody at the conference got it clearly, and it penetrated so effectively into the mind of our dreamer that he found no great difficulty in reproducing it.

2 *The address of Frank le Boilin*

(i) *The Inverted Pyramid.* The wealth of the world, said Frank le Boilin, can be compared with an inverted pyramid resting on an apex of gold. The volume of the golden apex may, for our present purpose, be taken as equal to half of 1 per cent of that of the whole pyramid. Anybody who can take away enough of the golden apex can bring down the whole pyramid in any direction he likes. All the gold in the apex—the total quantity of monetary gold—at the present time amounts to about $11,000,000,000, and of this we, between us, can take away $2,500,000,000, or enough to fell the pyramid, so to speak, into our zone.

The situation is entirely favourable for such a proposition, for the pyramid as it stands to-day is very unstable.

You know the position in commodity markets. As the result of progress in mechanization, the output of the labour unit is constantly increasing. In spite of a tendency for wages to advance, the advance nowhere corresponds with increased output. Production is everywhere overhanging consumption, and the frantic efforts of the kind now being made by trusts, cartels and even governments are barely enough—and will not be enough—to hold up the price structure. You well know, for instance, the position in steel, copper, oil, rubber and wheat. It would not take much to pull large sections of these trades on to markets and sell them up, bag and baggage, at distress prices.

You know the position on the stock exchanges. In America the Member Banks of the Federal Reserve system, alone, have out some $7,000,000,000 in loans on securities, and most of these securities are much over-valued even on the basis of actual prosperity earnings. It would not take much to bring the "bulls" to the slaughter-house—in fact, as soon as commodity prices break, they will themselves proceed to the slaughter-house.

You know the position as regards international debts. You know that, quite apart from the inter-governmental debt question, and notwithstanding the great excess of exports over imports of the debtor countries, there is still a "gap" of about $2,000,000,000 in the annual balance of payments as between debtor and creditor countries—a "gap" which is being bridged, and, under existing conditions, can only be bridged, by the transfer of capital in the form of new loans and investments from the creditor countries to the debtor countries. You know that international loans are constantly being made or refunded at 6 per cent, 7 per cent and even 8 per cent. Some of you know that the net foreign investments of the creditor countries (excluding inter-governmental debts) have risen since 1920 from about $27,000,000,000 to the present figure of about $40,000,000,000. This sort of thing cannot go on. As soon as new loans are not forthcoming the debtors must begin to default; their bonds and their assets—like the bonds and the assets of most producers, merchants and "bull" operators—will be marked for liquidation; and in those days the gold merchant will be dictator and the cash buyer will be king.

In truth, Gentlemen, the position is that unless we take the offensive abroad, we shall soon have to defend ourselves singly and precariously on our own ground. I have, therefore, been asked to put forward a defensive and offensive programme. It takes the form of three campaigns.

(ii) *The First Campaign.*   The objectives of the first campaign will be, on the one hand, to equip ourselves with some $2,500,000,000 in ready cash in order to put ourselves in a position to remove, when the time comes, that much in gold from the apex of the pyramid; and on the other hand, to undermine the apex thoroughly without moving it. In other words, we shall have to realize this enormous amount of cash by unloading vast quantities of securities and property on markets, which means that we shall have to do so without destroying the confidence of buyers until the required amount of selling by us has been effected.

We shall commence with a full twelve months of orderly profit-taking, and of quiet conversion of our assets into cash, bank deposits, short loans and first-class self-liquidating commercial loans. Whenever buyers show any signs of fatigue and depression during this period, we shall suspend all liquidation and, in case of need, revive confidence and markets by a few weeks' treatment of the highly developed "bull" technique of George Boomer and the lavish but selective financing employed so effectively by James Raid.

At the end of the twelve months, say this time next year, having saturated buyers, including the less speculative ones, we shall retain the initiative by means of a big "bear" attack on the more speculative elements. With this end in view, we shall proceed to give markets three months' treatment—the maximum does—of the Boomer-Raid mixture. Then in the autumn, when the confidence of optimists with something to lose has been restored and they are again ready at top prices, we shall sell them all they will take. Having delivered this frontal attack on the "bulls," we shall then surprise their rear by withdrawing our deposits and calling in our loans from the banks and financial houses that are financing them. Forced liquidation and heavy selling will ensue; we shall comfortably "slaughter" both the tame and the wild "bulls," and make a huge cash profit by covering our short sales.

Thus, by the end of 1929 our first campaign will have been completed. On the one hand, we shall have converted our investments into liquid assets and realized some $2,500,000,000, which we shall take care to hold only in cash, first-class bank deposits and adequately secured short loans. On the other hand, the values of commodities, securities and property will be considerably lower, consumption and buying will be substantially reduced by losses and unemployment, and the menace of the debt question in all its national and international aspects will begin to make itself felt.

(iii) *The Second Campaign.* The second campaign will be one of masterly inactivity. In other words we shall hoist the flag of Devoschère—"Safety First"— and call for music about drastic economy and lower costs. We shall repose thus comfortably all through 1930, whilst the pressure of commodities, securities and property coming on to markets—intensified by reduced consumption, forced liquidation and scrambling for safety—continues to pull down prices. We shall repose, thus, peacefully until the debt question is battering down the door.

(iv) *The Third Campaign.* The objectives of the third and last campaign, which will commence in 1931 and take about three years, will be: first, to get into gold; secondly, to divorce the gold currencies from gold and create, *de facto*, a gold premium; thirdly, to establish this gold premium *de jure* by the devaluation of the currencies; and fourthly, by a collateral movement, to acquire first-class securities and property at distress prices with paper money, and to obtain this paper money at a discount for gold.

Whilst all loans are being "frozen" by the continuous fall in the values of commodities, securities and property, and as we develop appropriate operations at different points, our batteries will fill the air and plaster their objectives with such projectiles as: the gold shortage; the debt question; and the necessity for balanced budgets, for drastic economy, for healthy liquidation, for raising the price-level, and for general devaluation.

We shall easily persuade the financial purists to persist with the drastic economy and the healthy liquidation; and we shall turn to the currency cranks and the socialists for an attack on the general principle of the gold standard.

Devoschère and myself will feel around for countries susceptible to panicky propaganda. We might even lubricate a few communist scares—and no doubt the offices of Ol Cocke would be invaluable here. A little street fighting, advertised as necessary to prevent a country lapsing into Bolshevism—or even into a Monarchy—is a potent means of formenting a flight from its currency.[16]

Our main operations, of course, will consist in converting our $2,500,000,000 into gold, and manoeuvring with currencies and with gold over and around the country or countries on which our treatment is concentrated. Having carefully nourished some of the principal banks in these countries with deposits and short term credits, we shall start "runs" on these banks and induce flights from the currencies in question. This argument, presented with the superb and unequalled skill of James Raid, will be *formidable*.

The storm will break in all its violence when one or two large banks are forced to suspend payments; and if this is followed—and we shall see that it is followed—by the suspension of gold payments by a leading creditor country, world-wide panic will reign supreme. Frantic liquidation and savage scrambling for gold will ensue; the central banks will be the first to remove their gold into the safety of their own vaults; and one by one they will suspend gold payments to prevent all this gold being taken out and hoarded by their depositors.

In effect, these operations will be based on the simple principle that, under existing conditions, the removal by us of our $2,500,000,000 of gold from the apex of the pyramid will bring about the removal from it of the remainder of the gold.

It is unfortunately true that once our money is converted into gold it will yield no income—and we shall certainly find it painful if not ruinous to forgo interest on our money. On the other hand, it must be remembered that, in the absence of any income, we shall not be liable for income tax and surtax; so that in the case of, say, James Raid, who is normally liable for over thirteen shillings in the pound and who, of course, pays it religiously, the British Government will bear most of the loss.

When the movement into gold and the divorcing of gold from gold currencies are in full swing, it will not be difficult to create and establish a gold premium. A country the currency of which has fallen to a discount in relation to gold, and which is thus getting some relief from the effects of excessive deflation, will be anxious to maintain the discount. It may maintain this discount, amongst other ways, by buying gold at a premium. In effect, we may expect it to buy gold at a premium, partly to neutralize the effects of falling values of goods and property in relation to gold, partly to assist its exports by lowering their gold prices, partly because it does not like the alternatives of buying goods, securities, property or foreign currencies, and, generally, because *gentlemen prefer gold*. We may expect countries even to outbid each other with these ends in view; we may, thus, expect the gold premium to increase, and we may expect general devaluation of currencies at fixed ratios to put an end to this chronic exchange instability.

Meantime—probably in 1932—we shall introduce the collateral movement. When gangsters, "banksters," and finance ministers are zealously putting the finishing touches to our carefully designed economic paradise of *virtuous* economy and *healthy* liquidation, we shall quietly commence to buy first-class securities and property—mostly with borrowed money—at one-tenth, one-twentieth and even one-fiftieth of the prices at which we sold in our first campaign. We shall buy back Union Pacifics at 29 that we had sold at 290; United States Steel that we had sold at 250 we shall certainly buy back at 25; Anaconda Coppers sold at 130 will return to our portfolios at, perhaps, 3. And we shall produce the grand finale with an artistic flourish when we pay back the paper money that we had borrowed to buy these securities; for we shall secure the required paper currencies by selling gold at a premium of 30 per cent, 50 per cent or more.

In effect, this collateral movement will be based on the simple principle that, if an adequate portion of the golden apex of the inverted pyramid be removed, the whole structure will fall on the side on which the gold is removed.

Having felled the pyramid and earmarked the best lumps, we shall reverse the whole process—but that is another story!

(v) *Budget Deficits are the only Danger to the Proposals.* There is, I think, only one thing that could prevent all the events of our programme from following, one after the other, as naturally and surely as day follows night. I mean the possibility of the creditor countries resorting in concert to the principles of war finance. If, for instance, they increased their expenditure, met budget deficits by selling treasury bills, and passed this sort of finance off in a halo of glory as patriotism, the injection of additional money into circulation by these means would reverse the process of deflation, cause prices to rise, and remove the object of devaluation. But I think we may take it as certain that nothing, apart from a big war, would induce these governments to do anything of the sort early enough to prevent the attainment of all our objectives.

To guard against this possibility—and in general to assure the march of events without diversion, we shall freely resort to conferences. Orators will not make war on anybody who will listen to them making speeches. At conferences, then, politicians shall obtain the attention and applause so dear to their hearts, by singing our favourite operas. They shall not know that, in playing their different games, they are all playing the same game for us.

The *libretti* will suggest that the economic system is a sort of drawing-room game in which you just establish confidence and all make money. They will announce that there are villains in the room. From different quarters will be arraigned such widely different culprits as "dumping," "import restrictions," "the capitalist system," "socialism," "Russia," "prevention of the proper functioning of the gold standard," "the gold standard itself," "unbalanced budgets" ... Well-worn and worn-out villains will be placed conveniently at every cross road, so that there will be villains for all—and even the most fastidious villain-hunter will not lack quarry.

We ourselves shall say that confidence cannot be established whilst these villains, especially "unbalanced budgets," are at large; and Göbbelstein will use his influence with central bank directors, finance ministers, presidents and kings to obtain the strict balancing of budgets. Thus, we shall get everybody off on a different scent; and we shall tie the governments of the creditor countries down to balanced budgets as an article of faith, when they will easily perform the miracle of drowning themselves in a teacup.

(vi) *The Proposals are by no Means Directed against Labour.*   In case any of you claim to be—in theory, if not in practice—socialists, I will not omit to assure you that the proposals I have outlined are by no means directed against labour. We have much to lose and nothing to gain by a conflict with labour. In effect, labour has little or nothing for us to cut at. It is the rich and juicy that we are after, from big financiers and rentiers down to thrifty little business men and shopkeepers. Naturally labour will feel the draught whilst our operations are in progress; but when these operations are successfully completed—when we have secured vast interests in every branch of industry and trade, and the time has come to restore and establish prosperity by the development and stabilization of markets—I shall certainly insist on shorter hours and higher wages as an essential part of any pro- gramme for overcoming the buying deficiency. Far from being directed against labour, these operations are exclusively intended to squeeze the juice out of capi- talists and the bourgeoisie.

(vii) *No Centralization.*   Gentlemen! the general line of action is simple and clear; and although its details and their execution must necessarily vary with cir- cumstances, this will present no difficulties to men who can interpret the news, read markets and act quickly. As already pointed out, the inverted pyramid is very unstable and threatens to fall on our heads. I am not arguing with you, I am telling you; and you can do as you like—I know what I am going to do! Whatever you decide, there will be no centralization, no correspondence and not necessarily any talk. We shall play our hands separately, reading each other's games from afar as we have done in the past, guided by that innate *flair* which has made us the money masters that we are, and guided by the golden rule: *gentlemen prefer gold.*

3 The general discussion

To call the talk that followed a discussion is, we admit, an exaggeration; but, although this talk was brief even for business men who had no use for speeches, the remarks of the few who spoke and the silence of the rest were heavy with meaning.

James Raid said "Great Scott!" with considerable emphasis. George G. Boomer exclaimed "Gee!" what at least as much emphasis and a touch of enthusiasm. Richard Devoschère, being half French and naturally more loquacious than the others, said more. He said, "Nom d'un chien!" which old Göbbelstein, the chair- man, regarded as an unnecessarily long speech. The latter concluded the proceed- ings with a very enlightening "Ach!"

No resolution was proposed, but a most effective resolution was passed silently and, probably, unanimously; after which the gentlemen dispersed to dine, to sleep the sleep of the rich, and to get much richer.

Bulletin no. 27.

July 25, 1933.

America takes the lead

THE HEMAN AND THE SHEMEN

I The Heman

On the accession of President Roosevelt, although liquidation and deflation had been pushed to the bitter end and a reaction was due, and although considerable mental readjustment had occurred everywhere, positive economic readjustment amounted to little more than the arresting of liquidation and deflation in the countries that had suspended gold payments. The position in the United States of America remained catastrophic. Within two months the Roosevelt Administration has completely transformed the situation, not only in the United States, but also in the world as a whole. Moreover, the President inspires confidence everywhere in his determination and ability to continue his big advance. The United States of America has taken the lead in the fight against the crisis; the leadership is good; and President Roosevelt is a he-man.

1 The position on the accession of President Roosevelt

(i) On March 4, 1933, the *New York Times* index of business activity in the United States stood at the record low point of 61.4, as against 70.7 on January 7, 1933.

(ii) In February, 1933, building contracts awarded in the United States dropped to $53,000,000,[17] or the lowest figure for many years past. The figures for February and December, 1932, were $89,000,000 and $81,000,000 respectively.

(iii) On February 28, 1933, the *Annalist* index of wholesale commodity prices stood at 79.8, the lowest in the post-war period, having dropped steadily from 96 in September, 1932.

(iv) On February 28, 1933, most of the prices of industrial shares in the United States were nearly back to the record low points touched in June/July, 1932.

(v) On March 4, 1933, the banking system of the United States collapsed. The banking position, like the economic position in general, was, in fact, catastrophic.

(vi) In the rest of the world, particularly in countries still on the gold standard, a similar deflationary trend with similar symptoms of crisis was to be observed—though in a less acute form—at that time.

(vii) On the other hand, the rapid growth of stocks of commodities everywhere, which commenced towards the end of 1929, and which was one of the main features of the crisis, had definitely slowed down.

As regards this decline in the growth of stocks of commodites, the financial purists tell us to-day that, thanks to "healthy" liquidation and such-like "natural" processes, readjustment had been completed, and would have been completed much sooner had these "natural" processes been allowed to do their work without the interference of governments.

To this we may reply as follows: Although certain Goverments—notably the Hoover Administration—made some feeble and inept attempts to arrest liquidation and deflation, these "natural" processes were, in fact, much intensified and prolonged by mistimed false economy and new taxation imposed by governments. The economic situation, in fact, continued to get worse in all countries where liquidation and deflation were in progress, a change for the better only occurring when and where this liquidation and deflation had arrested its own progress by bringing about the suspension of gold payments. And the small measure of economic readjustment attained in the world as a whole was due, in fact, not to liquidation and deflation, but to reduced production on the one hand and increased buying on the other, brought about for the most part by other causes.

No doubt the reduced production was partly the result of liquidation, that is, to the putting out of business of marginal producers; but it was mainly due to more or less voluntary curtailment of production. The increased buying, however, was entirely due: (*a*) to the growth of population, which, excluding China, had probably increased by about 4 per cent, or by about 60,000,000 people, since 1929; (*b*) to the end of liquidation and deflation in countries off the gold standard; and (*c*) to the growing reaction against curtailment of government expenditure on unemployment relief and on new public works.

The truth is that, although liquidation and deflation had everywhere been pushed by gangsters, "banksters" and finance ministers to the bitter end—that is to say as far as the credulity and patience of the public would permit—and although for this and other reasons a reaction was due, there was no sign of any such reaction in the United States at the time of the exit of President Hoover. A reaction for the better, in fact, might have been delayed indefinitely by an incompetent Administration.

Briefly, then, the position on the accession of President Roosevelt was as follows: Everywhere producers had had enough of vainly trying to undersell each other; the public had had enough of drastic economy, of sacrifices and of the financial purists; and politicians—always anxious to please—had begun to abandon their old tune, without, however, knowing how to play another tune or exactly what other tune to play. This mental readjustment was being followed by economic readjustment wherever liquidation and deflation had been more or less arrested by the suspension of gold payments. The United States of America was still in the hands of the financial purists and still being swept unmercifully by drastic economy, liquidation and deflation, but mental readjustment was so far advanced as to bring a man like the new President to the fore to effect the required economic readjustment.

2 *The position to-day*

Within two months President Roosevelt has completely transformed the situation. From chaos and catastrophe he is rapidly leading the United States to prosperity, and this is reviving the rest of the world which, as already indicated, was muddling along with a sub-normal temperature.

(i) *Banking Measures.*   On his accession President Roosevelt had to face an unprecedented run on the banks, which threatened even the big and highly liquid banks of New York City. He met the situation: (*a*) by the declaration of a banking holiday, (*b*) by the prohibition of hoarding, of the melting down of currency, and of the export of gold without special permission, (*c*) by measures for the withdrawal of all gold and gold certificates from the public and the commercial banks, (*d*) by the pledging of Federal credit for the reorganization of certain impaired banks, and (*e*) by the authorization of an issue of new currency to the Reserve Banks against government and certain other securities.

By the prompt employment of these simple and effective measures, he stopped liquidation, drove hoarders into markets, and obtained results that entitle him to say—so far as the banking crisis is concerned: "I came, I saw, I conquered."

(ii) *Deflationary Measures.*   Then followed a series of measures that must be regarded as deflationary.

First, the President turned his attention to the budget, which was showing a deficit of $1,786,000,000. Here he introduced an Economy Bill whereby $500,000,000 was to be saved by reductions of pay to Federal Employees and reduced compensation to war veterans.

Secondly, according to reports, he proposed to liquidate some 3,000 insolvent banks alleged to be "unworthy."

Thirdly, at first he seemed anxious to maintain the gold standard, and to make his public works programme dependent on—and consequently limited by—the amount of money that could be borrowed for this purpose from the general public.

The announcement of these measures—intended, no doubt, to restore "confidence"—gave rise to the feeling that there would be no active measures to raise the price-level. The confidence of hoarders was restored; selling was induced and buying discouraged; and prices of commodities and securities, which had advanced under the influence of the suspension of gold payments in early March, fell back.

Subsequently, however, the Economy Bill was cut down by about $100,000,000, and no attempt was made to fill the gap by further taxation; we have heard no more about the liquidation of the 3,000 "unworthy" banks; and the gold standard has not been maintained.

(iii) *Inflationary Measures.   First*, the Federal Reserve System has been ordered to buy large quantities of Government securities; and in effect, the System is to be used to create a demand for Government bonds that will make possible enormous Treasury borrowings at low interest rates.

Secondly, the gold standard was officially suspended on April 17, 1933; and on May 26, 1933, a bill was introduced in Congress formally annulling the "gold clause," that is, a clause in contracts providing for payment in gold dollars of specific weight and fineness.

The annulment of the "gold clause," if regarded as a move towards devaluation of the dollar—that is, towards the return of the dollar to gold with a lower gold content—is a step in the policy of the devaluationists, or those who want the value of gold to rise and think this is the best remedy for the crisis. In fact, as suggested in Bulletin No. 25, the gold interests may well be at the back of the suspension of the gold standard in the United States.

We have all along urged—and it is now generally agreed—that the raising of prices to a higher level is an equitable and expedient way of liquefying, or restoring, the positions of large and small debtors, the money value of whose assets has been drastically reduced by the fall in prices. Moreover, it is certain that rising prices usually stimulate increased buying by trade buyers, investors and those whose earnings are being increased by the rising prices. On the other hand, once prices have been raised to the desired level and devaluation is effected, rising prices and currency depreciation cease to operate as a stimulus to increased buying; whereupon, in the absence of a new factor to maintain the volume of buying, profit-taking, if not forced selling, ensues and prices decline. No doubt such an eventual fall in prices can again be neutralized by further devaluation, and no doubt the devaluationists would again say that this was the obvious solution; but we do not like this game of currency debasement, and we fear that it would infect the West with that fell disease of the East—the hoarding of precious metals in preference to investment in useful equipment.

But, besides the gold interests which want devaluation, there is another quite different camp devoted to the final and absolute demonetization of gold. The demonetizationists want gold demonetized, partly because they look upon it as something in the nature of an instrument of Satan, the baneful influence of which must be removed before the human race can emerge into its rightful heritage of liberty, equality and fraternity, and partly because they do not think that the price-level can be stabilized where a currency based on gold is in use. Mr. Steagall, chairman of the Banking and Currency Committee and sponsor of the bill to annul the "gold clause," seems to belong to this camp; for he described the bill as "a final, definite and determinate step," the enactment of which would mean that "the United States has declared by statute the abandonment of any obligation to maintain the gold standard as a permanent law of this country."

We do not pretend to be qualified to discuss such questions as the relationship between Satan and gold; but we venture to assert that, given concerted international action, it is easier to stabilize the price-level where currency is based on precious metal than where currency has no such basis. It is well known that the gold prices of commodities can be made to rise by means of controlled inflation "within gold," and that such prices can be made to fall by means of deflation. But in the case of a purely paper currency, we fear that it would often be necessary to resort to drastic restriction of credit, involving very high interest rates and heavy taxation, to prevent an over-rapid rise in prices. We certainly fear that, whatever the official currency, gold would remain the real standard of value, and we fear— what we fear about devaluation—that a premium would be placed on the hoarding of precious metals in preference to investment.

However, it seems that the suspension of the gold standard by the United States has been chosen as the site for a battle between the devaluationists or those who want the value of gold to rise, and the demonetizationists or those who want the value of gold to fall. As for the prospects of the battle, the devaluationists possess, and the demonetizationists lack, all the sinews of war, namely, energy, experience, organization and funds. Only President Roosevelt can prevent a sweeping victory[18] for the devaluationists, but he does not declare his position in the matter—he is lying low.

Meantime, in Bulletin No. 10, dated October 19, 1931,[19] we wrote:—

". . . should the United States meet the eventuality by simply suspending gold payments, she would undoubtedly join in a revival with England and the other countries off the gold standard . . ."

For

". . . those who had hitherto sought relief and safety in the acquisition and hoarding of gold standard money by the reckless selling of goods and investments and by valiant thrift, would turn for relief and safety to the dishoarding of money that had become non-convertible into gold and to the reckless buying of goods and investments."

This, in effect, is what has been happening in the United States. It has its disadvantages as well as its merits—its chief disadvantages being that, whilst stimulating production, it causes producers and distributors to be more anxious to increase their stocks of goods than to dispose of the goods quickly to final buyers.

We consider that it would have been better to have increased business activity by the distribution of additional purchasing power to final buyers, and at the same time to have maintained the gold value of the currency.[20] Of course, this would have required the application of much skill, but surely it was possible.

Thirdly, as integral parts of President Roosevelt's economic programme, measures have been proposed to subsidize farming, to reduce farm acreage, and to compel all businesses to secure Federal licences. Some will regard these measures as Americanized Bolshevism. We ourselves do not look upon this sort of thing as very effective, and we fear that, if persisted in, it will lead its sponsors into trouble.[21]

Fourthly, the Industrial Recovery Act has been passed, which, according to the President, "represents a supreme effort to stabilize for all time the many factors which make for the prosperity of the nation and the preservation of American standards."

The fundamental purpose of the Act is to fix maximum hours and minimum wages for industrial employees, which measure is badly needed to adjust the purchasing power of willing buyers in relation to production.

The great measure of this Act is the Government's $3,300,000,000 construction programme. Already President Roosevelt has allotted $400,000,000 to States for the purposes of highway construction, and $238,000,000 to the Navy Department for construction under the new naval programme. Although we find that the total amount is not large enough, especially as it will be spread over several years, the measure constitutes a solid and positive means of providing work for the unemployed, of increasing the effective demand for goods and services, of raising prices, and of increasing the real wealth of the State. Undoubtedly it is something that constitutes a real and valuable nourishment for the economic system where currency debasement can only be a temporary stimulant.[22] Its effect on the situation is shown by the following extract from the weekly report of the New York correspondent of *The Times*.[23]

"When . . . it was prematurely reported that 'stabilization' or 'equalization' of the pound and the dollar had been arrived at, the assumption was common that this must end for a time the hopes for a reckless inflation of currency here. The mere suggestion precipitated a sharp fall in security prices and in some commodity prices likewise . . . At the end of the week there was a fair recovery, partly automatic, *partly due to the discounting of the Government's forthcoming heavy expenditure for public buildings and naval construction.*" (The italics are ours).

(iv) *The Results Obtained.*   The *Annalist* index of wholesale commodity prices in the United States has risen from 79 at the beginning of March, 1933, to 98 at the end of June, or by 24 per cent; whilst the *Annalist* index of 43 American stocks has risen from 18 to 40 during the same period, or by 122 per cent; and these rises have only been partly offset by a simultaneous fall of 21 per cent in the gold value of the dollar. In the same period the prices expressed in gold in the international markets of six principal staple commodities have risen to the extent of something around 20 per cent.

Higher prices, of course, do not necessarily indicate increased prosperity; but in the present case they indicate the liquefication of enormous quantities of frozen assets, a vast increase of purchasing power in the hands of all debtors and most primary producers, and increased buying in general.

Industrial production in the United States, according to the Federal Reserve Board index, has risen sharply from 60 in March, 1933, to 76 in May; and employment has advanced from 58 to 61 during the same period. These increases have since been extended. In the United States steel industry, production has been increased from 15 per cent of capacity in March, 1933 to 53 per cent at the end of June. In the rest of the world, particularly in countries off the gold standard, the improvement in the United States had been closely followed by a marked, though less impressive, movement in the same direction.

In Bulletin No. 5, dated May 25, 1931, we wrote:[24]

> "To the practical business man the course of the depression is indicated by the quantity of buying, and he will only see the turning point with the end of decreased buying by those whose purchasing power is determined by the amount of money the crops will fetch, and with the end of decreased buying in general by individuals and public bodies."

We are now able to state that the action of President Roosevelt has resulted, and is resulting, in increased buying by those whose purchasing power has been increased by the rise in the value of the crops, and in increased buying in general by individuals and public bodies.

3 The prospects

As these words are being written, a heavy recession in prices of commodities and securities is in progress. This recession, however, was to be expected for the following reasons:—

In the *first* place, the spontaneous readjustments that have been made by way of curtailment of production, increase of population and growth of popular resentment against false economy and excessive taxation, provide no adequate grounds for a substantial rise in prices.

Secondly, the enormous advance in prices that occurred in the United States between early March and the middle of July this year was, in any case, bound to end in more or less heavy profit-taking and selling in general.

Thirdly, heavy buying of dollars may commence at any moment, partly by foreign buyers of the autumn exports of American crops, such as cotton; partly by Americans anxious to repatriate their capital before, or in case, the foreign exchange value of the dollar rises; and partly by Americans and others wishing to transfer money to America because they fear a fall in the gold values of certain gold currencies.

Thus, a substantial rise in the foreign exchange value of the dollar—unless prevented by action of the United States Government—will occur. Such a rise would probably induce a sympathetic rise in the internal value of the dollar, that is, cause a fall in the domestic prices of commodities and securities in the United States. It would certainly cause a fall in the dollar prices of American goods for export.

In this situation, and in the absence of exact information as to the intentions of President Roosevelt regarding the gold value or the commodity value of the dollar, business men are selling freely after the advance in prices whilst awaiting the next moves of the President.[25]

Everything, then, depends on the action taken by President Roosevelt:—

(*a*) If he raises or arrests the fall in domestic prices by devaluation of the dollar—that is, by returning to the gold standard with a debased dollar—he may only succeed in raising or maintaining prices for a time.

(*b*) If he raises or arrests the fall in domestic prices by the operation of an Exchange Equalization Fund whereby the foreign exchange value of the dollar is depressed by being sold at a discount for gold, he will surely eat into the gold reserves of the "gold countries" and perhaps soon force at least some of them to suspend gold payments. Increased buying would then be induced—or, at all events, fears of further deflation would be definitely removed—in these countries, and the situation there and elsewhere would to that extent be improved. Such an improvement, at this stage, might well constitute the final factor for something in the nature of a general revival—though in the absence of active support by way of heavy expenditure on public works, such a revival would surely be slow and unstable.

In this case, the gold premium would probably rise, and gold-mining shares, like all first-class industrial shares, would be good buying.

(*c*) If he raises or arrests the fall in domestic prices by acceleration of his $3,300,000,000 construction programme, the *gold* prices of commodities and securities will rise everywhere; a solid advance will be made on the road to prosperity in the United States; and a general world revival will be the result. Although it may not be possible to accelerate this construction programme, its effects will not fail to make themselves felt as it comes into full operation.

The rapid application of this construction programme would render all first-class industrial shares, other than gold-mining shares, good buying. It would reduce the profits of the gold-mining industry to the extent that it raised the gold prices of commodities.

President Roosevelt has shown that he grasps the fundamental elements of the trouble, and knows the kind of remedies to apply. Above all he has shown that he is a man who talks little and gets things done. If he is moving through new country and does not altogether know the way, and if he has made a few false movements, he inspires confidence everywhere in his determination and ability to push the American advance to the point of prosperity. We may, therefore, expect a permanent increase in the amount of buying by consumers and investors both in the United States and in the world in general; and we may hope that the Sterling Area, followed by most other countries, will soon join in the great American advance.

We certainly think that, in one way or another,[26] the President will not allow the present recession in prices to go far; and, at the lower prices, we venture to advise the business man and the investor to take their seats for the Roosevelt boom.

4 General conclusion

Our general conclusion is that President Roosevelt has done what a World Economic Conference should have done long ago. He has decided upon a programme to restore prosperity by raising wholesale prices, by shorter hours and higher wages, and by appropriate expenditure on construction. A big movement towards prosperity has, in fact, been initiated in the United States; the leadership is good, and the American President is a he-man.

Note

February, 1934. In some quarters the summer and autumn relapse was attributed to speculative over-production of consumable goods, due to distributors increasing their stocks of goods in expectation or fear of currency depreciation. This so-called speculative over-production, however, was only part of the story, for there would have been no relapse but for the failure of demand on the part of final buyers. The real trouble was that the Government was not getting along fast enough with its emergency expenditure. Inevitable delays were occurring in the making of contracts for new public works. Even by November relatively little money had been actually received by contractors, and the additional purchasing power passed into the hands of the public was, thus, insufficient to support markets.

On October 22, 1933, the Roosevelt Administration commenced buying all newly mined American gold at a premium, which premium it increased at short intervals. On October 28, the President announced that gold would also be purchased abroad. This, together with his assurance that, by one means or another, prices would be raised, arrested liquidation and caused a certain amount of buying. The position was thus held until the effects of Government expenditure began to make themselves felt.

The gold-buying policy did not raise commodity prices, much to the gratification of those who held that the price-level could not be raised by the reduction of the gold value of the currency. But perhaps it was not intended to do more than arrest the recession in prices. It was certainly not carried nearly far enough for its effects to be tested, for purchases abroad of gold were so small that the market price of gold in London remained much below the London equivalent of the American price. The test would only have come if all gold on offer had been bought by the American Government until the dollar was at a discount of, say, 45 or 50 per cent below its former gold value, until the British Government was induced to bring sterling also to a discount of, say, 45 or 50 per cent, and until the *gold bloc* countries had lost so much gold that they were forced to suspend the gold standard. Then we should have seen what currency debasement everywhere, plus huge gold-mining profits, would have done for commodity prices.

Clearly the real gold-buying game is not a drawing-room game. Perhaps President Roosevelt came to the same conclusion, and perhaps this was why he suddenly called the game off and turned to devaluation. At all events, on January 31, 1934, he fixed the gold content of the dollar at 59.06 of its former weight—but reserved the right to reduce it later to not less than half of that former weight.

The effects of this devaluation or provisional stabilization were, *first*, to create a profit for the American Government estimated at about $2,793,000,000 on the gold holdings of the Federal Reserve Banks; *secondly*, to tie the gold prices of commodities in the world's markets to the dollar prices of commodities; and, *thirdly*, to cause heavy gold-running into the United States from the *gold bloc* countries—the currencies of which were, and are still, not considered as strong as the new gold dollar. The provisional stabilization is also said to have created "confidence," and no doubt it has done so—chiefly in those who were anxious to liquidate goods or securities, and to take profits, but were afraid to realize in inconvertible paper dollars.

Thus, if *reflation* in America results, as desired, in the raising of the dollar prices of commodities, it will also result in the raising of the gold prices of commodities everywhere. And if the *gold bloc* countries—which consist of relatively rich populations amounting to a total of over 100,000,000 people—are forced to suspend gold payments, and are thus converted from deflationary to inflationary countries, the successful raising of commodity prices by *reflation* in America would be assured.

But the British Authorities—wedded to the old obsession that it is better to undersell competitors than to convert them into buyers—are, it is said, out to support the efforts of the *gold bloc* countries to remain on the gold standard, and it is even asserted that the American Authorities are to use their new Stabilization Fund for the same purpose. If, in fact, the large and important populations of the *gold bloc* countries are to be kept on the gold standard, deflationary tendencies in these countries will tend to handicap *reflation* in the United States. In the first place, these deflationary tendencies and the restriction of buying resulting therefrom in the *gold bloc* countries will tend to depress the gold prices of commodities everywhere to a greater or less extent. In the second place, the risk—no matter how small—of this *reflation* eventually resulting in another gold-run from the United States to the *gold bloc* countries cannot be ignored; and, at all events, relatively higher prices in America than elsewhere, whether brought about by *reflation* or in any other way, would certainly result, sooner or later, in heavy liquidation for the purpose of realizing profits, if not for the acquisition of foreign gold coin. It is true that, at this stage, such possibilities are not likely to develop enough to prevent the return of prosperity, but they may easily delay it.

Thus, if the devaluation or provisional stabilization of the dollar is to force the *gold bloc* countries to suspend gold payments, it will assist *reflation* in the United States. But if the *gold bloc* countries are to remain on the gold standard, this provisional stabilization of the doller should, we think, have been delayed until American business activity had been fully restored by the emergency expenditure. Meanwhile, it must be observed that, had the *gold bloc* countries been forced off gold without any return to gold of the dollar, a worldwide *reflationary* movement might have been initiated that would have raised commodity prices enough for a general return to the gold standard at former parities—which would have been in every way preferable to general devaluation.

However, from the above considerations two major difficulties emerge in connection with *reflation* by means of loan-expenditure: *First*, delays in the planning of public works that prevent the required amount of loan-expenditure being effective quickly enough. *Secondly*, unwillingness on the part of other creditor countries to do their share of loan-expenditure.

But these two difficulties are surely not insuperable. In case of need, governments could undertake big land reclamation schemes, or, when convenient, the making of artificial lakes, capable of being proceeded with on any scale or at any speed compatible with the amount of Unclaimed Wealth awaiting utilization. As for the conversion, when required, of a deflationary creditor country into an inflationary one, effective treatments are: the moratorium for taxpayers, running out gold reserves, and, in certain cases, economic isolation.

Notes to Part III

1 It is necessary to classify and include as debtors all those whose payments in respect of taxes exceed any payments received by them in respect of public loans of which they are bondholders, because it is they who pay and are the real debtors to the bondholders.
2 (5) and (6) as above, and the expositions on pp. 55–57 in connection therewith, were not in the original Bulletin.
3 See also *The Unclaimed Wealth* (1924), p. 143, "When it comes to international debts that are too large to be lost in the ordinary trade balances, the same problem presents itself in a manner openly to flog and mock mankind. France and Italy prefer the mocking to the flogging; and they lie low when confronted with their international debts, or they change the subject to Reparations. The British cannot pay the debt to the United States, and have funded it for repayment; but it remains to be seen whether, thereby, England or America escape both the mocking and the flogging."
4 Excluding inter-governmental War Debts and Reparations.
5 Reckoning the fall in the price-level at 50 per cent.
6 At all events enemy property was confiscated during the last War.
7 Subsequent events have shown that this figure was too low by at least $1,000,000,000.
8 "In effect, the withdrawal of income from the taxpayer and its transference as liquid capital to the investor against the surrender and extinction of government securities held by him, reduces the buying of goods and services by the taxpayer without necessarily causing increased buying of goods and services—increased investment in new capital goods and/or increased consumption—by the investor or those he may directly or indirectly finance. Further, whether or not the recipients of the money use it for increased investment and/or increased consumption, the result is almost sure to be deflationary. For: (i) when there is no increased buying by the recipients of the money, the quantity of circulating money is reduced and prices are depressed; (ii) when increased investment in new productive equipment or in new stocks of goods takes place, the increased productive capacity or increased production so caused, combined with the decreased buying of the taxpayers from whom the money was taken, will tend to depress prices and reduce the quantity of money in circulation; and (iii) when the financing of new non-productive equipment or of new consumption takes place, debts are created that sooner or later tend to reduce the buying of the debtors and the quantity of circulating money, and to depress prices.

"Again, so far as the banks are concerned, the effective demand for loans by the public will not, other things being equal, increase as the result of the transfer of money from taxpayers to financiers and rentiers. And, if the effective demand for loans does not increase, the retirement and extinction of government securities held by the banks, i.e., the reduction of bank loans to the Government, will not be offset by increased bank loans to the public. Thus, the withdrawal of money from the public by taxation for extinction of government securities, will tend to cause the investments and loans of the banks to decline, the deflation of credit, and the decline of cash and bank deposits at the disposal of buyers." (See *The Economic Lessons of 1929–1931*, pp. 56–57.)

9 See *The Economic Lessons of 1929–1931*, p. 5.

10 As stated in Bulletin No. 12, "the United States has deflated in this way by over $9,000,000,000 in the ten years 1920–1930, and France by over $1,208,000,000 in the three years 1927–1930, as against increases in the national debts of these countries of about $34,000,000 and $500,000,000, respectively, in the ten pre-war years 1903–1913."

11 Speech Nantes, 15th February, 1932.

12 Shortly after this Bulletin was issued, an enquiry into this matter was commenced at the London School of Economics under the Chairmanship of Lord Sankey. The result of this enquiry—if it had a result—did not reach us.

13 No. 25, dated April 15, 1933.

14 See p. 20 [Bulletin No. 25].

15 All dollars in this Bulletin are the old dollars with full gold content not the devalued dollars of 1934.

16 We remind the reader, without prejudice, that street fighting occurred in Geneva during the heavy run on the Swiss gold reserves of the Autumn of 1932, and that street fighting in Paris coincided with the great run on the French gold reserves in February, 1934.

17 All dollars in this Bulletin are the old dollars with full gold content, not the devalued dollars of 1934.

18 *February*, 1934. In effect the recent devaluation of the dollar at 59.06 per cent gives the victory to the devaluationists.

19 See *The Economic Lessons of 1929–1931*, pp. 79–80.

20 *February*, 1934. Perhaps the recent return to gold in America signifies that President Roosevelt now takes the above view.

21 *February*, 1934. It has, in fact, led to a good deal of trouble of one kind or another.

22 *February*, 1934. In his budget message of January 4, 1934. President Roosevelt disclosed the latest position. For the year ending June 30, 1934, the total amount of "emergency" expenditure will be $6,357,486,700, which includes $1,677,190,800 for Public Works Administration, and $3,969,740,300 for the Reconstruction Finance Corporation. The excess of expenditures over receipts in that year will amount to $7,000,000,000. For the year ending June 30, 1935, "emergency" expenditure already decided upon will amount to $1,213,723,100, of which $1,089,883,100 will go to the Public Works Administration; and the budget deficit is given at $2,000,000,000. Thus, for the two years, expenditures will exceed receipts by $9,000,000,000, and as most of this will presumably be financed by newly created credit, it represents the measure of President Roosevelt's *reflation* programme. A recent addition to this programme is the creation of a Stabilization Fund of $2,000,000,000 for buying gold or foreign currencies or Government Securities. *The Annalist* of New York estimates (February 2, 1934) that by means of this fund and $950,000,000 excess member bank reserves now in existence, the member banks may be permitted "to expand their loans and investments by the astronomical sum of $29,500,000,000." (Above dollars are, of course, the devalued dollars of 1934.)

    Not the least fruitful of President Roosevelt's measures was the withdrawal of Professor Sprague from the Bank of England for *sterilization* in America. But the good Professor will never believe that it was his *sterilization* and not his advice that the world most needed.

23 London, June 19, 1933.

24 See *The Economic Lessons of 1929–1931*, p. 29.

25 *February*, 1934. These moves are described in the later Note at the end of this Bulletin.

26 *February*, 1934. As a matter of fact the following October, President Roosevelt gave a definite assurance to the same effect.

Part IV

National debt and taxation

To the Editor of *The Economic Review*,
5 December 1924

Sir,—The main feature about the evidence given before Lord Colwyn's Committee on National Debt and Taxation is its emphasis and agreement on the following points:—

That heavy taxation has the effect of restricting trade.

That provision ought to be made for gradual reduction of the National Debt.

That reduction of National Debt should be effected by reduction of Government expenditure, accompanied, if possible, with reduction of taxation.

This is all clear as far as it goes; but it is superficial and, consequently, rather misleading.

First of all, let us be quite clear as to why heavy taxation has the effect of restricting trade. The reasons given before Lord Colwyn's Committee are, briefly, to the effect that such taxation increases the cost of production, and that, at the higher prices, there is a more restricted market both at home and abroad. This explanation, however, does not stand inspection. There cannot be a rise in the general price level unless an expansion in the total supply of money takes place in relation to the total quantity of commodities and services for sale; and, when such inflation of money does take place, a proportionate depreciation in the monetary unit compensates, in markets both at home and abroad, for the higher price level. Thus, when there is no inflation there can be no rise in prices to restrict trade, and when there is inflation it is compensated for, as regards trade, by depreciation in the monetary unit.

The truth is that taxation only restricts the total volume of trade when it causes *deflation*, or a reduction in the supply of money in relation to the total quantity of commodities and services for sale; for, in this case, manufacturers and merchants, when suddenly faced with the necessity of selling their stock at lower prices, are unable or unwilling to continue trading to the same extent. It is deflation, therefore, that restricts trade; and, although one of the principal causes of deflation is the withdrawal of money from the people by means of taxation, whether it is caused in this way or in any other is rather immaterial as regards the effects on the total volume of trade.

As regards the question of reduction of National Debt, gradually or otherwise, this can only be effected by means of the application of (*a*) money withdrawn from the people by taxation, and (*b*) money withheld from the public by the reduction of Government expenditure. Nevertheless, be the money withdrawn or be it withheld, the application of such money to reduction of National Debt, other things being equal, causes more or less deflation with restriction of trade.

Further, reduction of National Debt accompanied by deflation does not necessarily, in view of the lower prices that are the essential feature of deflation, result in any reduction of the commodity value of the debt.

Reduction of National Debt, therefore, can only be harmful in the circumstances described, regardless of whether it be effected by means of taxation or by means of reduction of Government expenditure.

In circumstances, however, when the supply of money is being increased by the people independently of the Government, the required amount of money for reduction of National Debt can be either withdrawn from them by taxation, or withheld from them by reduction of Government expenditure, and still leave sufficient money in their possession to obviate deflation and its restricting effect upon trade. This might mean that reduction of National Debt should be commensurate with increased production of commodities, increased production of money, or increased prosperity; but whatever it means, it is much too vague. We must be precise about the matter.

In order to consider the question clearly, it is necessary to appreciate the fact that the total supply of money does not vary as the total production of commodities and services for sale, the curves of each being quite different. Thus, earning and saving in respect of money, and in respect of commodities, are two different things with totally different effects as a rule. The manner in which they affect each other cannot be pursued here; but what is mainly involved in the question of reduction of National Debt is the principle that every loan from a banker creates a deposit and every repayment of a loan to a banker destroys a deposit of money.

The National Debt is an obligation to pay money, not commodities, and, therefore, an increase in the quantity of money in relation to the quantity of commodities and services for sale is required, whereby the excess of money can be (*a*) withdrawn from the people by taxation, or (*b*) withheld from the public by reduction of Government expenditure, and applied to the reduction of the Debt.

Reduction of National Debt, therefore, should only take place at times when there is a tendency for inflation to take place as the result of (1) reduced production of commodities, or (2) increased supplies of money arising from the people obtaining larger quantities of credit from bankers. At such times, reduction of National Debt should, imperatively, take place in order to counteract the inflation, by a reduction of expenditure by the people and the Government; because, in this way, (1) reduced production of commodities would be met by reduced consumption, or (2) an increase in the supply of money arising from an increase in the people's loans from bankers could be accompanied by a corresponding reduction of the National Debt.

Whether reduction of National Debt be achieved by means of increased taxation or by means of reduced Government expenditure makes little difference to the total volume of trade as a whole; but it is important for the welfare of the State that the required economy be effected at the point where expenditure is least necessary or desirable, be it Government expenditure or certain classes of expenditure by the people. This last point, however, is a large subject of another kind.

Yours faithfully,

H. ABBATI.

Hotel Londra, Sanremo, Italy.

What is saved?

The Economic Review,
18 December 1925

"Less fresh capital is annually saved to-day for investment abroad than before the war, and it is to be feared that many would-be borrowers will be disappointed when the embargo is removed. Our capacity to lend will depend upon the growth of prosperity, out of which alone additional savings can be made."

This was the impressive pronouncement of the City Editor of *The Times* on October 21, 1925. It sounds more like schoolroom economics than high finance; but does it mean anything of practical interest, or is it a mere platitude capable only of application to some hypothetical case? The expressions "capital" and "prosperity" must refer to one or more of the following: capital goods (buildings, machinery, etc., and stocks of consumable goods), money, and man-power equipped with some sort of capability; and the object of our enquiry is to determine whether saving is at all times consistent with increases in the quantity and total value of any or all of these things, either for use at home or for export.

Saving may be divided into the following five classifications: (1) Investing money in new capital goods, either by buying them personally or by subscribing to the capital of a company which is buying them. (2) Lending money to others who are investing in new capital goods. (3) Lending money for any other purpose on good security. (4) Buying existing stocks and shares from other holders. (5) Leaving money "on deposit." In any of these ways money may be saved or reserved for the use of the saver at a later date; but the question is, Does saving money, in all these ways, at all times increase the total quantity and value of capital goods, money or man-power? Let us consider the effects on the quantity and value of capital goods of each of these five ways of saving, leaving the questions of money and man-power for separate treatment. This will give us the economic effects of every kind of saving and answer the question, What is saved?

(1) Investing money in new capital goods, directly or indirectly, by an individual or by a company, does increase the quantity of capital goods. When new capital goods consist of buildings, machinery, etc., money invested in this way instead of being spent on final consumption of goods and services causes productive energy to be diverted from consumable goods to such capital goods. On the other hand, when new capital goods consist of consumable goods in course of production, in transit, or in stock, money invested in this way instead of being spent on final consumption of goods and services causes consumption to be

restricted without restricting the production of such consumable goods. In both cases, therefore, something is added to the stock of capital goods. It may be noted that investing money in old or second-hand capital goods is frequently equivalent to investing in new capital goods, inasmuch as it frequently causes the seller to replace the old capital goods sold by new ones.

(2) Lending money to others who are investing in new capital goods similarly adds something to the stock of capital goods; but (3) lending money for any other purpose on good security does not add anything to the stock of capital goods unless it indirectly causes an investment in new capital goods.

(4) Buying existing stocks and shares from other holders does not, in itself, add anything to the stock of capital goods, being merely a reciprocal transfer of ownership. But something is added if, after one or many of such transfers of ownership, the money gets into the possession of someone who invests it, or causes it to be invested, in new capital goods. It is most important, however, to observe that, so long as the money is circulating in such stocks and shares, it is withdrawn from circulation in industry and, other things being equal, causes an equivalent stoppage in new production.

(5) Leaving money "on deposit" in banks does not, in itself, add anything to the stock of capital goods; it merely leaves the onus upon the banker of lending it to someone who will invest it, or cause it to be invested, in new capital goods. But the success of the banker in being able to do so is by no means assured, and his difficulties in this direction are enhanced to the extent in which money is being confined to deposit accounts or otherwise withheld from the purchase of goods and services; for, in such circumstances, the accommodation required by industry and commerce is proportionately reduced. It is true that, when prices of securities are low, a certain quantity of the surplus money can be profitably absorbed by the purchase of securities, either by the banks themselves or by borrowers. On these occasions the money, by causing a rise in market prices of securities and creating profits, is sometimes returned to industry and commerce through increased buying of goods and services on the part of those who have made the profits; but little or none of it will be used for buying new capital goods at a time when the bankers themselves cannot find sufficient borrowers wishing to invest in new capital goods. Thus, productive energy, by being turned away from consumable goods, may be stopped altogether without being diverted into capital goods. It is only when the rate of consumption is great enough to draw the rate of production out to its full capacity that holding money "on deposit" instead of spending it increases the quantity of capital goods, for only in these circumstances does money invested in this way divert productive energy from consumable goods into capital goods, and not merely hold up production.

Normally, in the creditor countries capital equipment is not fully utilised. In England and America, since about the beginning of 1921, the average use of capital equipment has not exceeded 70 per cent, of its actual capacity. In these circumstances, if the savers do not buy consumable goods, and if, instead of buying new capital goods, they prefer to hold the money "on deposit" or buy securities, what hope is there of anybody with anything to lose seeking loans in order to increase the quantity of buildings, machinery, etc., or the stock of consumable goods? At all events, our traders do not think they have anything to gain from this sort of saving, judging from their advertisements. Buyers are what they want, not capital goods.

Briefly, then, money that is said to be saved is not necessarily used to increase the quantity of capital goods; and, even when it is so used, the increased total quantity of these capital goods is not worth any more unless a corresponding increase takes place in their use. That is to say, there must be an increase in the consumption of these goods for the provision of which new buildings, machinery, etc., have been set up, or an increase in the consumption of those goods the quantity in stock of which has been increased, otherwise there can be no increase in either their total utilisation or total market value.

Let us now consider saving in relation to the quantity of money. Money exists in three different forms in England: gold, paper money, and what is known as bankers' "deposits." The world supply of gold is obviously not greatly affected by saving and spending; but the quantity in England would, other things being equal, increase as the result of exporting more goods or importing less goods. We know, however, that an influx of gold, whatever its cause, must soon be reversed in face of persistent reduced consumption and reduced trade activity at home; for, if the gold cannot be employed more profitably abroad, its accumulation at home would tend to raise prices, reduce exports of goods and increase imports of goods, which, other things being equal, would cause an outflow of gold. Reduced consumption, therefore, cannot for long increase the quantity of gold in the country.

It is perhaps convenient to observe, here, that in the past we have maintained a considerable volume of our export trade by lending foreigners the money with which to buy our goods; and in this way, without inflating our gold supply, we have disposed of great quantities of goods which, otherwise, we would have had to have either abstained from producing or utilised and consumed at home. But the quantity of savings that can be disposed of in this way is by no means governed by our capacity to produce goods in excess of our home requirements; and, as a matter of fact, the truth is now being more and more forced upon would be lending countries that foreigners are either too rich or too poor, too clever or too stupid, some to desire to become borrowers, others to qualify as desirable borrowers, of all that the lenders may wish to save.

As regards money which takes the form of bankers' deposits, it arises from loans from bankers. It is an axiom that every loan from a banker creates a deposit and every repayment of a loan to a banker destroys a deposit. The loans are paid away to landlords and workers and suppliers of materials, and eventually appear in the banks as deposits; and, in the case of the repayment of a loan, the money leaves the deposits in the banks of buyers of goods and services and is used to cancel the loan. Loans are obtained from bankers to finance production and distribution to an extent proportionate with the actual or anticipated demand of buyers. Thus, both loans and deposits vary as the volume of buying; and, therefore, in spite of additions made to deposits by those who are saving in this way, the total deposits are reduced to the extent in which the total volume of buying at the same or lower prices is reduced. The quantity of paper money is governed by the quantity of deposits; for more or less paper money is required as cash reserves by the banks to the extent in which deposits, and the cash demands of the public upon them, are more or less great.

We may, therefore, conclude that the total quantity of gold, paper money, and deposits in a country vary as the total volume of buying, regardless of the nature of the goods, services or securities bought; and when saving causes a reduction in the volume of buying it causes a proportionate reduction in the quantity of money.

When it comes to man-power, it may be questioned whether the City Editor of *The Times*, any more than the average "pater familias," looks upon the money spent upon the upbringing of a family as saved. One may even doubt whether he would endorse the view of the writer that "purchasing power can only be truly saved when it is fully utilised by being all spent without delay on those things that maintain human life in its highest form, not merely bare necessities but luxuries, art and education; and by being so spent it creates automatically that quantity of labour-saving machinery and plant that is required for the purpose."* However if it is allowed that man-power constitutes capital, the City Editor of *The Times* surely cannot maintain that would-be borrowers would have cause for disappointment in face of our existing reserve of 1,200,000 unemployed.

In conclusion, then, the truth is that, at all events in England, saving can be of two kinds, namely, positive and negative. The positive sort consists of spending income without delay on those things that maintain human life in its highest form; but, although this sort of saving could immensely increase the quantity and value of all forms of capital, it would not necessarily increase our exportable surplus with which to back loans to foreign countries. It would be neither practicable nor desirable to lend abroad a part of any improved and increased quantity of buildings, transport systems, and industrial mineral and agricultural equipment; and, as for consumable goods, productive capacity would be so fully engaged in supplying the home market that the disadvantages would generally outweigh the advantages of sending goods abroad except to balance our international accounts. The negative sort of saving, on the other hand, consisting as it does of holding our capital and men insufficiently employed and restricting production, whilst it reduces the capacity of home or foreign borrowers to employ loans profitably, it does increase our potential surplus for export and, to this extent, it increases our capacity to lend abroad. However, in face of the vast extent in which our industrial equipment is idle and our men unemployed, there seems no justification for the fear of the City Editor of *The Times* that insufficient is being saved to-day in this way and that foreign borrowers have been at all disappointed with our capacity to lend.

Note

* *The Unclaimed Wealth*, p. 120.

Lord Keynes' Central Thesis and the Concept of Unclaimed Wealth (1947)

1 The thesis

In a leading article of *The Times* of London (April 22, 1946) highly praising Lord Keynes, the following passage appeared:—

"The late Lord Keynes' central thesis was that there is no mechanism in *laissez-faire* capitalism to ensure adequate total demand for the products of labour, and more especially that the productive resources left unused in consequence of 'saving' are not automatically put to use by the business community through 'investments' in the creation of productive capital. His argument led to the conclusion 'that in contemporary conditions the growth of wealth, so far from being dependent on the abstinence of the rich as is commonly supposed, is more likely to be impeded by it. One of the chief justifications of great inequality of wealth is, therefore, removed.' Lord Keynes became convinced 'that a somewhat comprehensive socialization of investment will prove the only means of securing an approximation to full employment'."

"The Keynesian approach offered a bridge between the academic economists on the one side and 'the brave army of heretics'—Mandeville, Malthus, Gesell, and Hobson (to name only a few)—on the other. This may yet prove to have been Lord Keynes' most valuable achievement."

Without being in agreement, or acquainted, with all the views expressed by Lord Keynes, I am prepared to allow that perhaps the above gives the principal line of thought voiced by him since 1930, notably in *A Treatise on Money*, which appeared in that year, and in *The General Theory of Employment, Interest, and Money*, published in 1935. But to say that Lord Keynes was advocating this thesis is one thing; to attribute its origin to him, or even to say that he had mastered all its implications, is quite another.

For the purpose of examination, the passage may be split up into five parts and numbered, as below:—

1. "The late Lord Keynes' central thesis was that there is no mechanism in *laissez-faire* capitalism to ensure adequate total demand for the products of labour."

2. "and more especially, that the productive resources left unused in consequence of 'saving' are not automatically put to use by the business community through 'investments' in the creation of productive capital."

3. "His argument led to the conclusion 'that in contemporary conditions the growth of wealth, so far from being dependent on the abstinence of the rich as is commonly supposed, is more likely to be impeded by it. One of the chief justifications of great inequality of wealth is, therefore, removed'."

4. "Lord Keynes became convinced 'that a somewhat comprehensive socialization of investment will prove the only means of securing an approximation to full employment'."

5. "The Keynesian approach offered a bridge between the academic economists on the one side and 'the brave army of heretics'—Mandeville, Malthus, Gesell, and Hobson (to name only a few)—on the other. This may yet prove to have been Lord Keynes' most valuable achievement."

Nevertheless, as we shall see, already in 1924 the following had been contended in *The Unclaimed Wealth*:—

1. "*Laissez-faire* is an imperfect system" which does not "ensure" that income is "fully utilised." (Page 184.)

2. Abstention from consumption or "saving" does not necessarily cause, and may even prevent, an increase in the quantity of capital goods and equipment. (Chapters IX and X, notably pp. 110–111; also *The Final Buyer* (1928), chapter V.)

3. "Utilisation of material, therefore, takes place in proportion to the justness of the distribution of the power to utilise *consumers' surplus*; and wealth is, therefore, greatest when distribution is most just." (Page 6.)

4. It is necessary for the State to nationalize the monopolies, "to distribute justly the *consumers' surplus* arising therefrom," and to "ensure" that it is "*fully utilised*" by being "converted into permanent public wealth." (Pages 184 and 185.)

5. And Mr. J. A. Hobson, in an introduction to the book, wrote (page 13): "I plead for a fair consideration of the substance of" Mr. Abbati's "argument, which seems to me an important and original contribution to the solution of the darkest and most urgent economic problem of our time."

Reference to *The Unclaimed Wealth* will show that these contentions, as here briefly expressed, are, as far as conveniently possible, based on the wording in the original texts, which will be quoted later.

Again, the following observations, which appeared in the same article of *The Times*, are worth noting:—

A. ". . . . the publication of his (Lord Keynes') *General Theory of Employment, Interest, and Money* has been described as the beginning of a new era—the 'Keynesian era.' . . . . With the available resources and technique, he believed the Western World, at last, was capable of reducing the Economic Problem, which now absorbes our moral and material energies, to a position of secondary importance. . . ."

B. ". . . . Once it had become clear to him that the classical theory was unable to explain, or to prescribe remedies for, the outstanding economic malady of mass-unemployment, his honesty drove him to challenge orthodoxy with ever-increasing severity. . . ."

And here is what we find in *The Unclaimed Wealth* on these matters:—

A. "Things, nevertheless, have totally altered" in relation to what they were "before the Coal Age . . . . Today, if we understand our world aright, increased consumption and utilisation of commodities and services, as a whole, would go hand in hand with increased profits of entrepreneurs and increased wages of workers; and lordly mansions could grow up freely whilst garden villas take the place of slums." (Page 27.)

B. ". . . . Once this is clear," (namely that the classical theory as regards saving is incorrect) "there can no longer be any room for doubt that both the production of consumable goods and the production of capital goods are strictly determined by the positive or anticipated *effective demand* for them." (Page 110.)

Furthermore, *The Times Literary Supplement* (April 27, 1946), commenting on my work, writes: "Doubtless it is galling for a writer to find his intuitions adopted and developed into a logical system by other writers."

I have drawn the attention of *The Times* to these matters, and I think I need make no apology for putting the facts of the case, as known to me, on record.

Before proceeding, however, it is perhaps worth remarking that *A Treatise on Money* is in two volumes, comprising over 750 pages, that *The General Theory of Employment, Interest, and Money* is in one volume, comprising over 400 pages, and that a wide range of questions are considered, which gives the work the character of a comprehensive—rather than systematic—dissertation on economics and economists.

It may further be observed that Unclaimed Wealth is defined in my Geneva Bulletin No. 1 (March, 1931) as "a surplus of goods and services made available by saving and by taxation which, for one reason or another, is not utilized for investment nor employed for public services." And hence, "unemployed labour, unemployed capital equipment, and unemployed surplus stocks of goods constitute Unclaimed Wealth." (Title page and page 1.)

2 The Hobsonian theory

As a close observer of events after the first World War, and especially the great deflation of 1920–21, I learnt that effective demand in wholesale markets usually vanishes with the prospect of abundance and falling prices. Thus I came to the conclusion that trade depression and unemployment of both labour and capital were due to excessive saving and the withholding of purchasing power, that is, to a general buying deficiency, and I decided to write a book advancing this theory.

Accordingly, in 1921, I wrote a synopsis of the proposed book and sent it to Sidney Webb, afterwards Lord Passfield. His reaction was that it was not possible for purchasing power to be withheld. Purchasing power, he wrote and explained at length, was equal to production; and he argued that whatever was saved, that is, not spent on consumption, was invested in the production of new capital goods. He quite saw, he added, that over-saving might result in over-production of capital goods in relation to the rate of consumption, that is, it might result in over-investment and in the losses arising therefrom; but this, he wrote, was J. A. Hobson's over-saving theory, and was quite different to my thesis that over-saving stopped the production of capital goods as well as the production of consumable goods.

Sidney Webb's version of Hobson's over-saving theory seems to be supported by the following quotation from *The Physiology of Industry*, published in 1889, by J. A. Hobson and A. F. Mummery (page v):—

"Now saving, while it increases the existing aggregate of capital, simultaneously reduces the quantity of utilities and conveniences consumed; and undue exercise of this habit must, therefore, cause an accumulation of capital in excess of that which is required for use, and this excess will exist in the form of general over-production."

Commenting on this in 1935, Lord Keynes writes in *The General Theory of Employment, Interest, and Money* (page 367): "In . . . this passage there appears to be the root of Hobson's mistake, namely, his supposing that it is a case of excessive saving causing the actual accumulation of capital in excess of what is required . . ." Lord Keynes further writes (page 370): "Mr. Hobson laid too much emphasis (especially in his later books) on under-consumption leading to over-investment, in the sense of unprofitable investment, instead of explaining that a relatively weak propensity to consume helps to cause unemployment by requiring, but *not* receiving, the accompaniment of a compensating volume of new investment. . . ."

Lord Keynes notes earlier in the same book (page 19) that in *The Physiology of Industry* (page 102) Hobson had quoted Marshall's statement, "But though men have the power to purchase, they may not choose to use it," and that he (Hobson) had justly made the point that Marshall "fails to grasp the critical importance of this fact."

However, in view of what Sidney Webb wrote about the Hobsonian theory, all of which was quite new to me at that time, I sent my synopsis to Mr. Hobson and shortly after went to see him. I gathered that he found my thesis new, but that he thought there was no vital difference between his position and mine.

He said that the great difficulty was that in the modern economic system people did not hoard their unspent money but put it in the banks; that apparently the banks could not pay interest on deposits unless they employed or invested the money in one way or another; and that this resulted in the orthodox conclusion that saving involved the production of new capital goods, whence he drew the conclusion that over-saving resulted in the over-production of capital goods. He asked me to explain exactly what happened to excessive savings that were deposited in the banks; and, at that time I was unable to do so. I could only urge that, in fact, the banking system did not, and could not, increase the production of new capital goods as a result of the effect on their deposits of over-saving.

In the end Mr. Hobson said that he accepted my thesis. But he added that he was too old to alter what was known as his over-saving theory, which had been identified with his name for over forty years; and he encouraged me to carry on with my book. The result was that I wrote *The Unclaimed Wealth*, which contended amongst other things that bank deposits in certain circumstances were *hoarded* savings, and which thus removed the great difficulty indicated by Hobson.

3 The distinction between saving and investment

The job of elucidating the underlying monetary facts in connection with what was afterwards called "the distinction between saving and investment" proved too much for me at first, (which is not surprising seeing that it had baffled Hobson and all the other economists), and I failed to make any progress for a year; but, after giving up business in 1923, I was free to make the necessary effort, and the book was finished and published in 1924.

Chapter IX on "Saving," and Chapter X on "Saving and the Utilisation of Purchasing Power," show in what manner savings may be *hoarded* and in what manner they may be *truly saved.* The expressions *hoarding* and *hoarded,* which I think I was the first to introduce in connection with savings deposits, appear repeatedly; whilst the savings that materialize in the form of new capital goods are expressed in a number of ways, including the words *truly saved* (page 120).

The basic idea is that abstention from consumption does not necessarily cause, and may even prevent, an increase in the quantity of capital goods and equipment; and this distinction between the passive part of saving and the active part of production of new capital goods is brought out and emphasized, as is shown by the following quotations from the book:—

" 'Spending' is the term commonly used as equivalent to *effective demand* for consumable goods, and 'saving' is commonly used as equivalent to *effective demand* for non-consumable goods; but, as is shown, money may be withheld from either of these uses by certain forms of *hoarding*." (Page 101.)

"Today . . . . the usual position is that the *effective demand* for commodities and services is never as great as the supply for sale; . . . . In such circumstances, keeping money in banks instead of spending it not only saves nothing, but wastes things that are actually produced and ready for use, and prevents the further production of similar things." (Pages 110 and 111.)

"Once this is clear . . . . there can no longer be any room for doubt that the production of consumable goods and the production of capital goods are strictly determined by the positive or anticipated *effective demand* for them . . . . It may be that there is a tendency for the idle surplus of the rich to be pressed towards over-production of capital goods in relation to the production of consumable goods; but it is certain that any unwarrantable check on the *effective demand* for consumable goods freezes the whole system of production . . . ." (Pages 110 and 111.)

"Before the Steam Age . . . . the difference between true saving and *hoarding* was unmistakable." (Page 117.)

"As modern wealth is *hoarded* it disappears." (Page 119.)

"Purchasing power . . . . can only be truly saved when it is fully utilized by being *all spent* without delay on those things that maintain life in its highest form . . . . and only in this way is anything truly saved." (Page 120.)

"*Laissez-faire* is an imperfect system unless the supplies of all factors of production are capable of the same expansion . . . It is therefore necessary to make all such factors of production common property, and justly to distribute the *consumers' surplus* arising therefrom. It then remains for the State to ensure that this justly distributed *consumers' surplus*, as well as all monetary purchasing power, are not *hoarded* but *fully utilized.*" (Page 184.)

"Surpluses arising from the nationalised monopolies, instead of being *hoarded* and lost for ever, would be converted into permanent public wealth . . . . in the form of buildings, roads, railways, harbours, forests, parks, and all such works which directly enrich a country as a whole, but cannot be undertaken extensively by private enterprise." (Page 185.)

The distinction between saving and investment is also fully analysed by me in an article in *The Economic Review* (December 18, 1925). The article begins as follows:—

"Saving may be divided into the following classifications: investing money in new capital goods, lending money, buying existing stocks and shares, and holding money on deposit. In any of these ways money may be saved or reserved for the use of the saver at a later date; but the question is, does saving money in all these ways at all times increase the total quantity of capital goods, money, and man-power?"

The article goes on to examine these different ways of saving, and to show that abstention from consumption is a very different thing to making an investment in new capital equipment.

This method is developed in my second book, *The Final Buyer*, published in 1928, which contends: that the passive part of saving makes materials and labour available; that the active part of investment in new capital equipment employs materials and labour; and that the saved materials and labour are not employed for investment in new capital goods unless somebody decides to "undertake the active part" of making the investment. (Chapter V.)

The monetary aspects of the matter are also examined at length. Here *The Unclaimed Wealth* finds that "the total supply of cash and credit money expands and contracts as the *effective demand* for goods and services and not as their production." (Page 99.) And, furthermore, from the analysis in *The Final Buyer* of bankers' deposits, investments, and loans, "emerges the important and interesting truth" that withholding purchasing power and saving it in a bank tends to cause a decline, and not an increase, both in productive activity and in the *quantity of money* as measured by bankers' deposits.

4 The concept of hoarding, the effective demand, and the virtue of thrift

As regards the concept of *hoarding*, it may be said that in *Banking Policy and the Price Level*, published in 1926, Mr. D. H. Robertson (like myself) adopted the expression *hoarding* in connection with uninvested savings; and, since then, the word has been commonly used in this sense.

For instance, Lord Keynes writes in *The General Theory of Employment, Interest, and Money* (1935): "The concept of *Hoarding* may be regarded as a first approximation to the concept of *Liquidity-preference*. Indeed if we were to substitute 'propensity to hoard' for 'hoarding,' it would come to substantially the same thing." (Page 174.)

It may also be noted in connection with the term "liquidity-preference" used by Lord Keynes in 1935 that the same idea was very fully exposed by me in Bulletins Nos. 25 and 26, which were issued in Geneva in April and June, 1933. These Bulletins were entitled. "Gentlemen Prefer Gold," and gave the facts and also a story about the "severe liquidation" that commenced in 1929. (See *Economic Readjustment in* 1933, notably pages 19 and 20.) In effect, the idea of "liquidation" resulting from "gold-preference" may be regarded as substantially the same thing as the idea of "liquidation" resulting from "liquidity-preference."

Further, as regards this question of choice between spending and hoarding money, *The Unclaimed Wealth* makes the following point: "The amount continuously earned will be admittedly equal to the amount continuously spent, regardless of the rapidity with which transactions are taking place and the money changing hands between buyers and sellers. This rapidity will be determined by how soon after each transaction the sellers who have received the money decide to spend it again: for, evidently, those who have parted with the money in exchange for commodities and services cannot bring about any new transactions until those who have got the money wish to do so. As a matter of fact, those who have got the money normally control the situation. They can take their own time as regards new transactions; and the pace at which they spend money will, in like manner, adjust the pace of money again being earned." (Pages 102 and 103.)

In *A Treatise on Money*, I think Lord Keynes writes something to the same effect; and I understand that he said in the House of Lords in 1944 that "employment and the creation of new income out of new production can be maintained only through expenditure on goods, services, and capital equipment of the income previously earned."

The concept of Unclaimed Wealth also brings to the fore the fundamental importance of *effective demand*, which is active and positive where *hoarding* is passive and negative; and the expression *effective demand* (underlined) is constantly used in *The Unclaimed Wealth*.

Here it is interesting to note that although the expression "effective demand" is used little or not at all by Lord Keynes in 1930 in *A Treatise on Money* (and I have not found it mentioned even once by him in that book), it is used extensively by him in his later work, *The General Theory of Employment, Interest, and Money* (1935). In the latter book he writes:—

"The idea that we can safely neglect the aggregate demand function is fundamental to the Ricardian economics, which underlie what we have been taught for more than a century . . . . Not only was his theory accepted by the City, by statesmen and by the academic world. But controversy ceased; . . . . The great puzzle of Effective Demand with which Malthus had wrestled vanished from economic literature. You will not find it mentioned even once in the works of Marshall, Edgeworth, and Professor Pigou, from whose hands the classical theory has received its most mature embodiment. It could only live furtively, below the surface, in the underworlds of Karl Marx, Silvio Gesell, or Major Douglas."

"The Completeness of the Ricardian victory is something of a curiosity and a mystery . . . ." (Page 32.)

"But although the doctrine itself remained unquestioned by orthodox economists up to date, its signal failure for purposes of scientific prediction has greatly impaired, in the course of time, the prestige of its practitioners." (Page 33.)

This brings us to the question of the *virtue of thrift*. Since *hoarding* is negative and the creation of new capital goods is dependent upon positive *effective demand*, the *virtue of thrift* becomes suspect. Here is what we find about it in *The Unclaimed Wealth* (page 119):—

"We hear a good deal about the virtue of economy and thrift, but when it consists of abstaining from the consumption of things that exist . . . . then it is no virtue but pure and simple waste. On the other hand, virtue or no virtue, one cannot use or consume things that do not exist or . . . . are beyond one's reach."

"This does not mean that there is no virtue in abstaining from the use of one thing in order to be able to use more of another. . . ."

And this is what Lord Keynes writes about the virtue of thrift in *A Treatise on Money* six years later (page 177):—

"This is splendid, or it seems so. The Thrift Campaign will not only have increased saving; it will have reduced the cost of living. The public will have saved money without denying themselves anything. They will be consuming just as much as before, and virtue will be sumptuously rewarded."

"But the end is not yet reached . . . . the entrepreneurs will suffer an abnormal loss . . . . The continuance of this will cause entrepreneurs to seek to protect themselves by throwing their employees out of work or reducing their wages . . . . they will continue to make losses so long as the community continues to save in excess of new investment."

5 How the concept of unclaimed wealth was received

If all this had already been said, or was being said, there would have been no reason for me to have gone to the extreme trouble of working it all out myself. In fact, it never would have occurred to me to do so. We have, however, plenty of direct evidence, both from Mr. Hobson's introductory chapter in *The Unclaimed Wealth* and from press reviews that appeared at the time, that the concept of Unclaimed Wealth was new, clear, and well defined.

Here are some extracts from Mr. Hobson's introduction:—

"It is in this situation that Mr. Abbati presents a new and rigorous investigation." (Page 10.)

"The originality of his contribution consists partly in his examination of the actual process by which production is checked and retarded, partly in his doctrine of consumers' surplus, and lastly in the boldness of his public policy for remedial measures." (Page 11.)

"Now the common assumption that everyone will and must spend all his money in one or other of these two ways, and without delay, is controverted by Mr. Abbati, who shows that under certain conditions money which might 'work' in stimulating production does, in point of fact, lie idle in banks or strong-boxes, or operates slowly as purchasing power." (Page 11.)

"His distinction between Consumers' and Producers' Surplus will be found to be an interesting attempt to reconcile socialist with individualistic doctrine in the distribution of the product." (Page 12.)

The book was extensively reviewed in Britain, Canada, America, South Africa, Australia, New Zealand, Germany, and Japan, and short extracts from some of these reviews are given in the appendix at the end of this memorandum. Four of these extracts, however, are given below in order to hold the continuity of the evidence that is being given under this heading.

The Times writes (September 11, 1924): "The element of truth . . . . is that the recipients of wages, salaries, and profits may withhold their purchasing power from the market by allowing it to accumulate in the form of bank deposits . . . . It is this element that Mr. Abbati has grasped and elucidated with great acuteness . . . . He has a mind that is at once systematic and penetrating, and he uses it to follow out all the complexities of the relation of credit to production and consumption."

The Spectator writes (December 20, 1924): "And this is the importance of Mr. Abbati's book, to which we wish to draw attention; one of the most significant books on the theme in recent years. . . ."

The Daily Times, Otago, New Zealand (November 29, 1924), writes: "Now the common assumption that everybody will and must spend all of his money in one or other of these two ways, is controverted by Mr. Abbati. . . ."

The Japan Chronicle, Kobe (May 14, 1925), writes: "Mr. Abbati, who is exploring in the right direction in a very important matter, springs this upon us. . . ."

A short extract from a review of *The Final Buyer*, which appeared in *The Economic Journal* (December, 1934), may also be reproduced at this stage: "Some years ago, in a book called *The Final Buyer*, Mr. Abbati gave an analysis of the relation between savings and investment which was, in many respects, in advance of anything else of its kind at that time existing in the English language."

As a matter of fact, *The Final Buyer* in no way altered or modified the concept of Unclaimed Wealth. But it analysed the monetary system and the principal aspects of national and international business activity in relation to the new concept, and set out the whole thing in a systematic manner.

6 A Treatise on Money

Exactly when Lord Keynes took a position in the matter is not for me to say; but I, for one, did not know that he had adopted ideas of a kind similar to mine until his book, *A Treatise on Money*, appeared in 1930. Up to that time, judging by the writings of his that I had seen, I thought that he was mainly concerned with the theory of bank rate and open market operations as the regulators of business activity—which I associated chiefly with the name of Mr. R. G. Hawtrey. The only leading economists known to me who were interested in the new idea of hoarded savings at that time were Mr. J. A. Hobson, Dr. T. E. Gregory (now Sir Theodore Gregory), and, in 1926, Mr. D. H. Robertson.

I was then living on the Continent, but at different times in 1925 and 1926 I saw and had discussions with Mr. Hobson and Dr. Gregory; and Lord Keynes had not, to my knowledge, altered his position at that time. Later, in 1932, Dr. Gregory wrote in his introduction to *The Economic Lessons of* 1929–1931 (page vii): "I would like to call attention to Bulletin No. 3 on the Distinction between Saving and Investment, and the pioneer work done by Mr. Abbati in this important field."

I met Mr. Robertson in London in 1927, and he gave no hint that he was aware of any change in the position of Lord Keynes at that time, but he told me that my name had been before him for some years.

However, writing in *A Treatise on Money* (pages v–vi), Lord Keynes himself says: "As I read through the proofs of this book, I am acutely conscious of its defects. It has occupied me for several years, not free of other occupations, during which my ideas have been developing and changing, with the result that its parts are not all entirely harmonious with one another. The ideas with which I have finished up are widely different from those with which I began."

Lord Keynes was sent a copy of *The Final Buyer* towards the end of 1929, and the book is mentioned by him in *A Treatise on Money*. Here is the passage (I, pages 171–172):—

"The notion of the distinction which I have made between Savings and Investment has been creeping into economic literature in quite recent years. The first author to introduce it was, according to the German authorities, Ludwig Mises in his *Theorie des Geldes und der Umlaufsmittel* . . . . Later on the idea was adopted in a more explicit form by Schumpeter, and 'Forced Saving' . . . . has become almost a familiar feature of the very newest German writings on money. But, so far as I am concerned—and I think the same is true of most other economists of the English-speaking world—my indebtedness for clues which have set my mind working in the right direction is to Mr. D. H. Robertson's *Banking Policy and the Price Level* published in 1926. More recently, Mr. Abbati's *The Final Buyer* (1928) has reached—independently I think—substantially similar results. Mr. Abbati has probably failed to make his thought fully intelligible to those who have not already found the same clue themselves. But the essence of the distinction between saving and investment is to be found in his Chapter V. Moreover, by the aggregate of 'Final-buying,' Mr. Abbati means expenditure on consumption *plus* investment, and he attributes depressions to a failure of this aggregate to reach the aggregate of money-incomes."

In this connection, however, two things must be noted:—

First, the theories of Ludwig Mises and Schumpeter are not concerned with *hoarded* savings (which arise as a result of excessive voluntary saving), but with "forced saving" (which takes place as a result of insufficient voluntary saving). The *hoarding* of voluntary savings and the notion of "forced saving" involve two totally different ideas, and the idea of "forced saving" certainly affords no clue to the concept of *hoarding*.

Secondly, it is perhaps true that *Banking Policy and the Price Level* (1926) is largely, if not mainly, dependent on the concept of *hoarding*, which is the central thesis of *The Final Buyer* (1928) as well as of *The Unclaimed Wealth* (1924). But I do not think that this similarity justifies any suggestion that Mr. Robertson's book and mine are similar in other respects. As a matter of fact both my books are largely concerned with describing and establishing the concept of *hoarding*, as well as with its implications, whereas, unless I am mistaken, Mr. Robertson's book takes the concept of *hoarding* as established.

Thus, in this passage Lord Keynes is at least confusing, and he makes no attempt to show whether or not he thinks there is any difference between his thesis and the concept of Unclaimed Wealth. At the same time, and in the same book, however, he makes his position perfectly clear in relation to the Hobsonian theory. Here is what he says (page 179):—

"In so far . . . . as these theories maintain that the existing distribution of wealth tends to a large volume of saving, which leads in turn to over-investment, which leads to a large production of consumption goods, they are occupying an entirely different *terrain* from my theory; inasmuch as, on my theory, it is a large volume of saving which does not lead to a correspondingly large volume of investment (not one which does) which is the root of the trouble."

But this is only another way of saying that abstention from consumption does not necessarily cause, and may even prevent, an increase in the quantity of capital goods and equipment, which, as we have seen, is the essence of the concept of Unclaimed Wealth.

And whilst we are on this question of the results reached by me in *The Final Buyer*, I may perhaps mention *en passant* the following point dealt with in that book, which point, although only one of monetary theory not directly connected with my present subject matter, excited some controversy at that time.

In 1926, or thereabouts, a discussion was going on in one of the banking journals as to how bank deposits were created. I do not remember that the matter was satisfactorily settled at the time, but I wrote in *The Final Buyer*: ". . . . an ordinary deposit or clearing bank cannot make investments and loans relatively more freely than the other competing banks, for if it attempts to do so its reserves start draining out into the other banks. It is inevitable that, whatever the total volume of bankers' investments and loans being made in relation to total bankers' reserves at that time, all the competing banks must adhere to about the same proportion, for only on this condition are the reserves paid away by each bank replaced in each bank." (Page 25.)

In *A Treatise on Money* (1930), Lord Keynes takes the same view. He writes: "Every move forward by an individual bank weakens it, but every move forward by one of its neighbour banks strengthens it; so that if all move forward together, no one is weakened on balance." (Page 26.) Also (page 30): "I have endeavoured to say enough to show that the familiar controversy as to how and by whom bank-deposits are 'created' is a somewhat unreal one . . . . the rate at which an individual bank creates deposits on its own initiative is subject to certain rules and limitations: it must keep step with the other banks and cannot raise its own deposits relatively to the total deposits out of proportion to its quota of the banking business of the country."

7 After 1930

However, after 1930, and especially between then and 1933 (during which time my Geneva Bulletins* were appearing), the new ideas made rapid progress; and in 1944 we find Sir William Beveridge (now Lord Beveridge) writing in *Full Employment in a Free Society* (Summary, page 8):—

"First, to prevent unemployment, it is not sufficient that the demand for labour should be stable. It must also be high enough. This means that consumption and investment together must add up to a total of expenditure sufficient to set up a demand for the whole of the available labour. At one time it was supposed that, apart from current cyclical depressions of trade, this would happen automatically. Whatever people saved, i.e. did not spend on consumption, would be invested, i.e. spent on means of production; if people were trying to save more than could be invested, the rate of interest would fall, discouraging saving and encouraging investment, and so bringing them into line again. According to the new economic theories associated with the name of J. M. Keynes, now Lord Keynes, and accepted substantially by all people qualified to judge, this does not happen. Decisions to save and decisions to invest are made by different people at different times for different reasons. They do not start with any initial tendency to march in step, and there is no automatic painless way of keeping them in step or bringing them together if they fall out; the rate of interest, which was supposed to serve this purpose, fails to do so. There is thus the possibility of chronic deficiency of demand for the products of industry, leading to chronic underemployment both of labour and of other productive resources."

Here we must note several things:—

First, we have it from Lord Keynes himself in the passage already quoted from *A Treatise on Money* (I, page 171), that "by the aggregate of 'Final-buying,' Mr. Abbati means expenditure on consumption *plus* investment, and he attributes depressions to a failure of this aggregate to reach the aggregate of money-incomes."

Secondly, we find in *The Unclaimed Wealth* (page 33): ". . . . it is erroneously believed that the total amount of money continuously earned is all used, in one form or another, to demand effectively all the commodities and services produced." And again (page 101): "Our present object is to cut away the belief that the total amount of money spent, or the *effective demand*, is equal to production."

Thirdly, in *The Final Buyer* (Chapters IV, V, VI, VII, VIII, and IX), it is shown in detail that, given the number and varieties of individuals, institutions, and governments involved, and the way in which their decisions are affected by different and changing conditions, it is not to be expected that, normally, total expenditure on consumption and outlay on investment will often coincide with the ready productive capacity of industry. In effect, it is found (page 107) that "since ready productive capacity is not the governing factor, more or less wide variations in the extent of final-buying . . . . are inevitable at different times, and thus the average velocity of production is reduced." And it is found in the introductory chapter (page 15) that everything turns "on how the multitude of large and small final buyers settle the question: *to buy or not to buy*."

To this Lord Keynes assented in *A Treatise on Money*, where he writes (I, page 279): "Not only are the decisions made by different sets of persons; they must also, in many cases, be made at different times."

Fourthly, as regards the "chronic deficiency of demand," the following appears in *The Unclaimed Wealth* (page 110): "Today . . . . the usual position is that the *effective demand* for commodities and services is never as great as the supply for sale; . . . ." And in *The Final Buyer* (page 106), we find:

"Moreover, we are not alone concerned with industrial fluctuations. There is also the question of the general low level of the mean productive output as compared with ready . . . . productive capacity."

It is thus clear that if Lord Beveridge's paragraph correctly describes "the new economic theories associated with the name of J. M. Keynes" it also correctly describes the concept of Unclaimed Wealth as put forward in not altogether different language in 1924 and 1928.

It is true that Lord Keynes himself never mentioned Unclaimed Wealth, but in an article in *The Times* (September 13, 1938) he wrote: "We are still allowing a great volume of potential wealth to evaporate unrealized." But he would have said the same thing in fewer words had he written: "A great volume of Unclaimed Wealth is vanishing." And, at all events, the principle of the thing is enunciated in *The Unclaimed Wealth* (page 119): "As modern wealth is hoarded it disappears."

In his preface to *The General Theory of Employment, Interest, and Money* (page viii), Lord Keynes writes: "The ideas which are here expressed so laboriously are extremely simple, and should be obvious. The difficulty lies not in the new ideas but in escaping from the old ones, which ramify, for those brought up as most of us have been, into every corner of our minds."

In my case, however, the difficulty was very different. Not being a member of what Lord Keynes calls "the faculty of economists" (see *The General Theory of Employment, Interest, and Money*, page 339), my mind was not possessed by the old ideas. And again, unlike him, I was at a disadvantage in the matter of helpful clues; because, as we have seen, he says that he was indebted to *Banking Policy and the Price Level* (1926) for clues that set his mind working in the right direction, whereas I, writing in 1922–24, had to manage without any such clues.

For me, therefore, it was not a question of escaping, but of creating and setting up something new without adequate materials and in face of every kind of obstacle. In effect, at that time the new concept lacked a documentary basis in that it was contrary to economic teachings as well as apparently contrary to some obvious facts of individual experience; and its initial formulation was thus an arduous and solitary job, effected without recourse to reference books, and without even the existence of an adequate terminology.

Coming to the end of *The General Theory of Employment, Interest, and Money*, and to the question of those who played a part in originating the new economic theories, Lord Keynes writes (page 371):—

"Major Douglas is entitled to claim, as against some of his orthodox adversaries, that he at least has not been wholly oblivious of the outstanding problem of our economic system. Yet he has scarcely established an equal claim to rank—a private, perhaps, but not a major in the brave army of heretics—with Mandeville, Malthus, Gesell, and Hobson, who, following their intuitions, have preferred to see the truth obscurely and imperfectly rather than to maintain error,. . . ."

But Wicksell, who is said to have a position in the matter, and to whose writings, at all events, Lord Keynes gave a large measure of attention five years earlier in *A Treatise on Money*, is not given a place—though there are a few lines about the Wicksellian *natural rate* of interest. (Pages 183 and 242.)

As for myself, after the publication of *A Treatise on Money* (1930), in which appeared the passage about me already quoted and discussed, I met Lord Keynes (then Mr. Keynes) a number of times between that time and 1934, and had some talks with him. But in *The General Theory of Employment, Interest, and Money* (1935) in which, as we have just seen, he gives places of one kind or another to orthodox and heterodox economists, not to say "brave heretics," he makes no reference at all to the concept of Unclaimed Wealth, which, I think I am right in saying, put the matter on a new, rational and permanent basis, and to which little or nothing has since been added.

Lampeter, June, 1947.

Note

* *The Economic Lessons of 1929–1931; The Search for Confidence in 1932;* and *Economic Readjustments in 1933.*

APPENDIX

Extracts from some press reviews of "The Unclaimed Wealth"

All the reviews that appeared cannot be here reproduced in full, but the following short extracts from some of them are given, which is enough for our present purpose.

The Economist (August 30, 1924), showing that the concept of Unclaimed Wealth was new:

"The author of this book owes a considerable debt of gratitude to Mr. J. A. Hobson, the writer of his introduction. Mr. Hobson assures us that the book contributes something to his own doctrine of under-consumption, and that it is in itself a work of real distinction and value. Without such an apologia the ordinary reader might find himself intimidated on the very threshold by the obscurity of the author's reasoning. . . ."

The Times (September 11, 1924), showing that the new concept was presented systematically:
"The element of truth . . . . is that the recipients of wages, salaries, and profits may withhold their purchasing power from the market by allowing it to accumulate in the form of bank deposits, which are not loaned out again by the bank. This does result in a temporary, but recurrent, disequilibrium of production and consumption that compels a fall in prices. As such it is an element, and an important element, in the causation of trade fluctuations. It is this element that Mr. Abbati has grasped and elucidated with great acuteness . . . . He has a mind that is at once systematic and penetrating, and he uses it to follow out all the complexities of the relation of credit to production and consumption."

The Star, Auckland, NewZealand (October 18, 1924), showing that the concept of *hoarded* savings deposits was new:
"It seems to us, however, that his idea of money being locked up in banks is not altogether in accordance with fact, because the banker uses money as stock in trade, and dislikes 'dead' stock as much as any retail trader, and keeps his money moving."

The Economic Review (October 3, 1924), defining the new concept:
"The trouble, in the author's view, is that the effective demand, in anticipation of which, production takes place, always disappoints expectations; if it kept pace with production there would be no trade depression. By a penetrating analysis he shows that it is the effective demand for commodities, and not their production, which controls both rapidity of circulation of money and the expansion and contraction of the total supply of cash and credit money. If, therefore, those in possession of money refuse to expend it on commodities and services they force down the total supply of cash and credit money in relation to the quantity of commodities and services for sale, and thus bring about the fall in prices which is a familiar accompaniment of depressions. And that is just what happens; instead of spending their money as they ought, they allow it to lie fallow in the form of bank deposits. On the virtues of spending, Mr. Abbati is rhapsodical: 'Purchasing power, whether it is derived from any sort of wages, rent, interest, or profit, can only be truly saved when it is fully utilised by being all spent without delay on those things that maintain human life in its highest form. . . .'."

The Spectator (December 20, 1924), showing that the concept of Unclaimed Wealth was new:
"And this is the importance of Mr. Abbati's book, to which we wish again to draw attention; one of the most significant books on its theme of recent years . . . . It is a question of the money being always available at the right time and place. And his distinctive work is to have revealed certain new facts concerning the

existing monetary system which go to show at just what point it seems susceptible of the change which would let this readjustment take place. We can only say here what we think it most important that people should realize; that is, that at once our greatest hope and biggest risk is in work of this kind. . . ."

The Daily Times, Otago, New Zealand (November 29, 1924), showing that the concept of unclaimed wealth was new:
"If everybody 'spent' all the money he received, either in buying consumable goods or in buying capital goods (plant, materials, etc.), there could be no failure of effective demand, apart from minor errors and miscalculations. Now the common assumption that everybody will and must spend all his money in one or other of these two ways is controverted by Mr. Abbati, who shows that under certain conditions money which might 'work' in stimulating production does, in point of fact, lie idle in banks or strong-boxes, or penetrates more slowly than usual as purchasing power. . . ."

The Spectator (December, 1925), suggesting that the concept of Unclaimed Wealth was an advance on the work of Mr. J.A. Hobson and Mr. Keynes:
"We must settle for ourselves which group of economists mark the last point reached in the advance of economic science. The one particular in which the present volume (*Revolution by Reason*, by John Strachey) strains our confidence is its appearance of having accepted the work of eminent thinkers like Mr. J. M. Keynes and Mr. J. A. Hobson without considering it necessary to inquire whether the limit of their advance really still marks the 'farthest north.' That in an important matter it has been definitely passed by the work of Mr. Henry Abbati is a conviction which the present writer for one has found it increasingly difficult to resist. The matter in question is the economic incidence of money placed on deposit in banks. If it were true, as Mr. Abbati holds, that money placed on deposit is simply money withheld from circulation, then a great many things might follow. . . ."

The Weekly Westminster (September 5, 1925), indicating the difference between the concept of Unclaimed Wealth and the Hobsonian theory:
"Mr. Abbati is a bold man. In a little book which he calls *The Unclaimed Wealth* he has ventured to put forth a new and original theory as to the cause of poverty and unemployment. This book is hard reading; but then there is a good deal of hard thinking in it. Briefly, his theory may be set forth as follows: 'If all wealth that is produced were immediately used for buying goods either for immediate consumption or for "capital" use, the demand for goods would be so great that there would be no unemployment, ... and the amount of wealth produced would go on increasing . . . . Unemployment and poverty are due to the fact that a large part of the wealth we produce is not quickly enough spent.'
"Why does this happen? Partly because the majority of possible purchasers do not get a big enough share of the wealth produced to be able to spend on a large enough scale; that is because purchasing power is badly distributed. So far Mr. Abbati is in agreement with Mr. J. A. Hobson that under-consumption is a main cause of economic ill-fare.

"But he goes on to urge that the unequal distribution of wealth would not seriously matter if those who received it spent it promptly either for immediate use or by investing it in new productive activities. It would not matter, because if all the wealth was expended upon new goods there would be such a demand for workers to produce these goods that they would be able to earn higher wages, and thus themselves take part in spending.

"What happens to the wealth that is not spent, the unclaimed wealth which is not performing its proper function in enriching the community? Much of it, says Mr. Abbati, is lying in deposit accounts in banks, either because its owners *can't* spend all they receive, or because, owing to the notion that it is virtuous not to spend, they *won't* spend it. And he has an elaborate discussion on banking, credit, and money (which occupies the major part of his book) to prove that these funds lying in the banks are, in fact, idle and unproductive . . . . and so demand for commodities, which ought to produce abundant employment and prosperity, is not forthcoming."

The New Clarion (November 19, 1932), article by Mr. (now Lord) Pethick-Lawrence, bringing in Lord Keynes:

"Saving is of no value . . . . it may even prove harmful to the community unless the money so saved is used in promoting capital development.

"This is new teaching. It used to be assumed that every pound saved automatically found its way into investment, but the latest investigations of Maynard Keynes, Abbati, and others have shown that this hypothesis is not always true. We now know that there are times of depression when money lies idle in the banks unwanted, and when the credit which could be built on it is unused; . . . ."

The Economic Journal (December, 1932), from an article by Mr. D. H. Robertson:

"Mr. Abbati is an eclectic writer of shrewd and independent judgement; and no son of London has written more trenchantly on the follies of uncontrolled inflation, miscellaneous state trading, commodity-boosting schemes, and instalment buying, or more soberly on the limitations of the power of the banking system to control the volume of active money and the level of prices. His inflationist sympathisers will find a good deal that is unpalatable, his deflationist opponents a good deal that is sympathetic, in his work.

"It is true, however, that Mr. Abbati's chief concern is to hammer into the public mind the disastrous effects of 'wasted savings' which, failing to find embodiment in new concrete capital, result in real wealth remaining 'unclaimed' because in large measure it remains unproduced. . . ."

The New Economic Theories and the Great Depression of 1930–1933 (1955)

To start with it must be observed that the inter-war period which I am about to cover is so rich in major economic events and incidents that, even after cutting out a good deal of interesting material, I can only give here a few sentences, or at the most a few paragraphs, to each of the items under review.

In the second place, I would like to point out that the inter-war period was dominated by deflation and its ill effects. But if *de*flation appears as the villain in the inter-war period, this is not to say that *in*flation is never a villain and has not been a villain in the post-war period. The thing to be remembered in this matter is that enough – and not more than enough – additional money should be injected into circulation to utilize a surplus of goods and services that may be made available by excessive saving.

It was in the post-war boom conditions of 1919 that I first began to think that trade depression was usually attributable to a buying-deficiency.

Before the First World War it was never an easy matter to find employment. Anybody looking for a job, whether he was an ordinary individual just content to live, or whether he was capable, energetic and ambitious, might spend weeks and months hearing that trade was slack and that employers were over-equipped and over-staffed. And anybody, whether dependent upon employment or whether the owner of a business, might come to the conclusion that, although both the resources of the earth and the possibilities arising from the use of productive equipment were far from fully developed, and although too often there were large quantities of food, materials and productive equipment awaiting consumption and utilization – immobilized by the absence of buyers – vast potentialities in men and women were continuously being stifled by lack of opportunity. To those who, before the First World War, vaguely suspected that there must be something arti-ficial rather than inevitable about these conditions, the magnitude of wartime pro-duction, and the wonderful manner in which young and old quickly rose to the occasion, came as practical confirmation (*Final Buyer*, p. 12).

Then came the post-war boom with business activity, employment and earn-ings at a high level. It continued, I think, in full swing until the latter part of 1920 and was fomented by inflationary finance in most countries. In the summer months of 1920, however, inflation in Britain showed signs of coming to an end; and it may be urged that, under an appropriate financial policy, the inflationary boom might have subsided in an orderly manner into conditions of stable prosperity. But the appropriate financial policy does not seem to have been forthcoming. It is true that on this occasion the British authorities did not go in for inflationism as they did after the Second World War. But they went to the opposite extreme and before the autumn of 1920 they came down heavily for deflation. The Bank rate was raised to 7 per cent; and from then until the end of 1921, in spite of increasing supplies of labour and materials pressing on markets, the cry was for lower prices, lower wages and drastic economy. Indeed, the anxious calls for economy to be heard on all sides sounded strange whilst the wartime performance of women, children and men unfit for military service was still fresh in the memory, and whilst the mind was still in wonder at the vast quantity of goods that were consumed by civilians and soldiers, destroyed in the battlefields and lost at sea. However, under this deflationary activity of 1920–1 business declined sharply and unemployment was rife. On the other hand, in France, Germany and Italy, where the cry for lower prices, lower wages and drastic economy was drowned by noises of another kind, and where inflation was present and in some cases ran amuck, there was at all events no trade depression (*Final Buyer*, p. 13).

Observing these things, I came to the conclusion that man had not yet learnt to utilize properly the great productive powers that had only recently come into his hands. For thousands of years he had been forced to wrestle with nature for subsistence, and this long contact with an economy of scarcity had led him to believe that what was one man's gain was necessarily another man's loss. No doubt before the coal age this idea was very near the truth, and no doubt it had been hammered in so deeply that man could hardly be brought to believe that things had altered. But it seemed to me that in modern times, in an economy of plenty, increased consumption and utilization of goods and services could go hand in hand with increased earnings for both employers and workers and that lordly mansions could grow up freely whilst garden villas took the place of slums (*Unclaimed Wealth*, pp. 26–7).

I came to the conclusion that trade depression was usually a matter of a buying-deficiency due to the withholding of purchasing power, and that by way of remedy national finance should aim at equating supply and demand. And I decided to read up what had been said on the subject and to write a book if I found that what I had to say had not already been said.

I found that Haney's *History of Economic Thought* (recommended to me by the London School of Economics) reported that Lauderdale (James Maitland, eighth Earl of Lauderdale, 1759–1830) had inveighed against abstinence and hoarding. I found that Karl Marx had argued that trade depression was caused by maldistribution of capital and income, but his loquacity was more than I saw fit to try and disentangle. I noted the Malthusian theory that population tended to outrun subsistence, but I did not come across what Keynes fifteen years later referred to as 'the great puzzle of effective demand with which Malthus had wrestled', and which Keynes said 'had vanished from economic literature' (*General Theory*, p. 32). I gathered that the possibility of delay in the exercising of purchasing power was not denied in economic circles, but that such delay was attributed to 'friction' or perhaps a 'breakdown' in the economic system. It seemed to me, in fact, that in the minds of the economists the problem centred around the prevention of 'friction' and 'breakdown'. This was all I found at that time which seemed to me to be relevant to what I had in mind.

With the aid of this slender knowledge of economic literature I slowly and with difficulty, after office hours, wrote a synopsis of my proposed book and, being a member of the Fabian Society, I sent it to Sidney Webb (later Lord Passfield), the founder of this Society, for his comments. A few days later I met Mr F. W. Galton, the well-known Secretary of the Fabian Society. He said: 'Mr Sidney Webb is not of your opinion *at all*', adding 'We don't want any more books'. Nevertheless, later on his scepticism wore off and now I have a large file of correspondence exchanged with him.

However, soon after, I received a letter from Sidney Webb. It was in his own handwriting and covered both sides of two or three sheets of notepaper. His reaction to my synopsis was that it was wrong to suppose that purchasing power was withheld in the way I thought. He argued at length that purchasing power was equal to production and that, although individuals could abstain from spending and could save the money, practically all such savings were deposited in the banks, where the savings were automatically invested and soon appeared as outlay on new capital goods. He quite saw that over-saving might result in over-production of capital goods in relation to the rate of consumption or, in other words, that it might result in over-investment and in losses arising therefrom. But this, he wrote, was J. A. Hobson's over-saving theory, and was quite different to my thesis which was that over-saving stopped the production of capital goods as well as the production of consumable goods.

Sidney Webb's version of the Hobsonian theory, in fact, was what was generally understood to be the essence of Hobson's over-saving theory. And Hobson himself had written something to the same effect in *The Physiology of Industry*, published in 1889 (Hobson and Mummery 1889: v).

In view of what Sidney Webb wrote about the Hobsonian theory, all of which was new to me at that time, I sent my synopsis to Mr Hobson and shortly after went to see him. I gathered that he found my thesis new, but that he thought that there was no great difference between his position and mine.

Hobson said that the great difficulty was that in the modern economic system people did not hoard their unspent money, but put it in the banks; that presumably the banks could not pay interest on deposits unless they employed or invested the money in one way or another; and that this investment of savings by the banks resulted in the orthodox conclusion that saving automatically involved the production of new capital goods, whence he drew the conclusion that over-saving may result in over-production of capital goods.

He did not tell me that he himself in the *Physiology of Industry* had quoted Marshall's statement: 'though men have the power to purchase, they may not choose to use it'; and that he (Hobson) had made the point that Marshall 'fails to grasp the critical importance of this fact' (Hobson and Mummery, 1889:102).

Indeed, I only learnt fifteen years later that Marshall had made that statement and that Hobson had noted its vital importance.

However, Hobson failed to refute the argument that the banks automatically invested all savings deposited with them; he failed to clear up the question of whether or not purchasing power could be withheld; and thus he was unable to contend that over-saving *stopped* investment. It is certainly clear that he had *not* been able to find the answer to the 'great difficulty' which he had described to me and which had stood in his way. He asked me to explain exactly what happened to excessive savings that were deposited in the banks. I, being unable to do so at that time, could only urge that the banking system did not, and could not, invest bank deposits of excessive savings in the production of new capital goods.[1]

In the end Hobson said that he accepted my thesis. He added that he was too old to alter what was known as his over-saving theory and had been identified with his name for over forty years. He encouraged me to carry on with my book and later he wrote an introduction to it.

The difficulty of elucidating the underlying monetary facts in connection with the distinction between saving and investment proved too much for me at first – which is not surprising seeing that this question of 'hoarded' bank deposits had baffled Hobson and other economists. In fact I was unable to get on until, after giving up business in 1923, I was free to make the necessary effort. Thus my book, *The Unclaimed Wealth*, was not finished and published until 1924. Before summarizing my results, however, I will give a brief account of what I found, at that time and in later years, other men were saying in the early 1920s about the economics of trade depression.

First of all, since Keynes in his *General Theory* (p. 32) has mentioned 'the underworlds of Karl Marx, Silvio Gesell and Major Douglas', I think I may say a few words about the work of these men.

I am not competent to define the message of Karl Marx, but I have written in *The Unclaimed Wealth*: 'When the Haves refuse to buy and the Have-nots cannot buy, all trade stops'. And no doubt Marx would endorse that.

Silvio Gesell advocated a gradually depreciating currency, which would naturally prevent people from withholding, or delaying in using, monetary purchasing power. He, however, did not attempt to show how money could be 'hoarded' where a banking system is in operation, nor did he meet the inherent troubles arising from consistent, if gradual, currency debasement.

As for Major Douglas, who I think was writing freely in the early 1920s, he rightly saw that there was often a buying-deficiency. But he and his followers said that it was due to something in the price system, whereby the process of production did not distribute enough money to the public to enable them to buy the product without a fall in prices. This was where they fell down, yet their name was legion.

Mr R. G. Hawtrey and J. M. Keynes were most in the news at that time. Hawtrey, I think, was mainly concerned with urging that the bank rate and open market operations could and should be used as regulators of business activity. It was a question of *banking* policy – a question of the banking system regulating the quantity of money in active circulation by means of the monetary instrument, in order to iron out booms and depressions. I think Keynes adopted a similar line in his *Tract on Monetary Reform*, which appeared in 1923.

Mr Hawtrey seems to have stuck to this attitude ever since. No doubt he now recognizes the distinction between saving and investment on which the new economic theories are based. But I am not sure that he fully assents to the notion of over-saving resulting in the '*hoarding*' of bank deposits. At all events, when I saw him a few years ago he said that *all* the necessary machinery existed for the investment of all savings; by the necessary machinery, I take it, he meant: the Bank rate, open market operations, the Stock Exchange and bankers or financiers of one kind or another. But I do not know what he thought happened to excessive savings, if and when for any reason this investment machinery failed to operate. Perhaps he thought it *never* failed to operate. Keynes, however, as we shall see, changed his position in his *Treatise on Money* published in 1930 and in his *General Theory* published in 1936.

It is, perhaps, of more importance to record that Professor Pigou, in his *Industrial Fluctuations* published in 1920 wrote: 'By accumulating unused purchasing power people have not automatically accumulated also unused savings of real things' (Pigou, 1929: 812), and he goes on to imply that this process accentuates depression. He, however, argues – I think *not* quite correctly – as both Mr D. H. Robertson (now Sir Dennis Robertson) and Keynes did some years later (see Keynes, 1930, vol. I: 174) that saving *un*accompanied by a corresponding volume of investment causes prices to fall, which enables and causes the general body of consumers to buy the 'saved' goods, as well as their usual purchases, and thus it causes 'a transference of consumption from savers to the general body of consumers'. But I think that the existence of such a 'transference' at all times is difficult to sustain. As I wrote in my *Economic Lessons* (pp. 15–16).

> a fall in prices caused by over-saving will start with a fall in wholesale prices, which will decrease the rate of production, together with the total income of consumers, long before they are able to buy at lower prices from retailers; and thus the savings are *lost* by decreased production before they can be transferred to other consumers.[2]

Lavington's *Trade Cycle* published in 1922 moved things forward in the same direction as Pigou's *Industrial Fluctuations*. It is true that the scope of this book was limited, being mainly concerned with the so-called 'cyclical' changes in business activity – that is with alternating booms and slumps – resulting from business men, for one reason or another, alternately increasing and decreasing their stocks of goods and/or the rate of investment in new capital equipment. But the book raised the vital question of saving and of 'idle' bank balances and 'hoarding'. 'In the typical case', writes Lavington, 'those who save, will accumulate idle balances at their bankers . . . a larger part than usual of their deposits is idle . . . and the volume of currency in active circulation is still further reduced' (Lavington, 1922: 83).[3]

This was the critical point at which Hobson's difficulty arose and where his progress and that of other economists was stopped. Lavington's *Trade Cycle* appeared *after* my talks with Hobson on the question of excessive savings that were deposited in the banks; the important point made by Lavington on this question was only brought to my notice by Mr D. J. Coppock's article in *The Manchester School of Economic and Social Studies* of January, 1954. However, Lavington's idea of the 'hoarding' of 'idle' bank deposits was not the same as *my* idea of 'hoarding'. *His* 'hoarding' arose from a distinction being made between deposit accounts, which he regarded as deposits of 'idle' money, and current accounts, which he regarded as deposits of active money. But *my* 'hoarding' implies that excessive savings deposited in the banks cause a decline in bankers' loans and investments and a corresponding *decline* in bank deposits. This was the idea I put forward in *The Unclaimed Wealth*.

I made it my business to show that 'hoarding' in connection with the banking system is possible; that *excessive* savings are not always invested by the banking system; that bank deposits vary as the *effective demand* for goods and services and *not* as production (*Unclaimed Wealth*, p. 88); that over-saving not only saves nothing, but stops production and prevents investment (*Unclaimed Wealth*, pp. 110–11); that 'as modern wealth is "hoarded" it disappears' (*Unclaimed Wealth*, p. 119); that sometimes investment exceeds voluntary saving, when forced saving 'automatically' occurs (*Unclaimed Wealth*, p. 107); and that it remains for the government to ensure that 'all monetary purchasing power is not "hoarded", but fully utilized' (*Unclaimed Wealth*, p. 184).

To put this sort of thing over at that time was no easy matter and my book certainly got plenty of criticism and comment of one kind or other. For instance, whilst *The Times* said the book was 'systematic and penetrating', *The Economist* called it 'economic confusion'. Again, *The Star* of Auckland, New Zealand, thought that the idea of money being hoarded in banks 'is not altogether in accordance with fact . . . because the banker keeps his money moving'.

As for the Fabians, when *The Unclaimed Wealth* appeared Mr Galton was not unfavourably impressed. Harold Laski seemed to like it, because he jumped up when I entered the Fabian Society's common room and shook me warmly by the hand. But with Sidney Webb I made little or no progress.

I had never spoken to Sidney Webb or to his wife, but I went to a reception given by them to the Fabians at their house in Chelsea in 1925. I do not remember seeking out, or being introduced to, either of them, but somehow I found myself sitting on the stairs with Mrs Webb, just as in earlier days I had sat on the stairs at dances with nice young girls. She was about sixty, fully twenty-five years older than I. She was small, refined, dignified and rather ascetic and, as I learnt from her published dairy many years later, the early collapse of capitalist civilization was a matter of concern for her. Her attitude was very friendly and sympathetic, even sisterly and motherly. She listened to what I had to say about the buying-deficiency and about government action to utilize the 'unclaimed wealth'. When I talked of public works, she did not tell me – what I found out seven years later – that she herself, in the Minority Report of the Poor Law Commission of 1909, had proposed public works as the remedy for unemployment. On the contrary, she gravely passed on to me the sort of arguments that had no doubt been handed out to her fifteen years back. It was the sort of stuff that had smothered these promising ideas. The economists, she said, did *not* accept the notion of a buying-deficiency and then, she said, there were difficulties about employing labour on public works. She talked about the *im*mobility of labour, of the need for realism and so forth. I, being youngish and impatient, thought that it was hopeless to bother any more with the Webbs. But there, perhaps, I was wrong. Indeed, I learnt many years later that Bernard Shaw had said that the cleverest thing he had ever done in his life was to make a point of becoming a close friend of the Webbs.

In 1926 Mr D. H. Robertson's *Banking Policy and the Price Level* appeared. For some years back Robertson had been familiar with the idea that investment is not dependent on voluntary saving and that, in the absence of enough voluntary saving, saving could be imposed or forced by an inflationary rise in the price level. In his *Banking Policy* I think he called it 'automatic lacking'. But now he came out with 'hoarding', which completed his notion of the distinction between saving and investment. He fully analyzed this question. Indeed, in some respects he over-analyzed it – going as far as 'short lacking' and 'long lacking'! But this distinction between saving and investment was the crux of the whole question, and I liked his method of handling it. Also, it is worth noting that Keynes did not begin working on the same idea until several years later.

However, Robertson's idea of 'hoarding' was more like Lavington's than like mine. *For them* it was more a matter of 'idle' deposits on deposit accounts (time deposits as they are called in the United States), whereas *for me*, as already indicated, it was the evaporation of bank deposits. It must also be noted that with Robertson, as with Hawtrey and Keynes, it was still a matter of banking policy.

How bank deposits evaporate as a result of excessive savings being deposited in the banks is a complex question. I gave six pages to it in *The Final Buyer* (pp. 54–60), but it requires more complete treatment than it has yet received; I think it would be well for it to be described in detail by a competent banking official who has had personal experience in dealing with the placing of banking funds and allied matters at the Bank of England or in a leading clearing bank. However, for the benefit of those who find it difficult to believe in this evaporation of bank deposits, the following may be said here.

In the first place, we know that the central bank can either increase or decrease the reserves of the clearing banks that are held on deposit by it. In other words the central bank can increase or decrease the credit base. It can do so by open market operations and by increasing or decreasing its total loans and investments of one kind or another. By making loans and investments of any kind the central bank can inject money into circulation, most of which will be deposited in the clearing banks and re-deposited in the central bank; thus the central bank's balance sheet will show increased assets in loans and investments accompanied by increased liabilities in bankers' deposits – which increased bankers' deposits constitute an increase in the credit base on which the loans and investments of the clearing banks are made. Vice versa, by reducing its loans and investments the central bank can withdraw money from circulation, reduce the bankers' deposits in its books and thus reduce the credit base.

Secondly, the clearing banks can inject money into circulation by making loans and investments of one kind or another, causing their balance sheets to show increased assets in loans and investments accompanied by increased liabilities in the bank deposits standing to the credit of the public. Vice versa, the clearing banks can withdraw money from circulation by reducing their loans and investments, which will cause a decline in their deposit liabilities standing to the credit of the public. The clearing banks, however, have little or no control over the size of the credit base, since this mainly depends on the quantity of loans and investments made by the central bank itself. Moreover, the total amount of loans and investments that can be made by the clearing banks is at all times limited by the size of the credit base, that is by their reserves deposited by them at the central bank. It is also limited by the quantity of loans and investments that can be made safely and profitably. Most of these loans and investments must *not* be permanent or long term and all of them must be safe. It is not always possible for the clearing banks to employ their loanable credit up to the hilt and in fact money market reports sometimes record that the banks are left with some loanable credit on hand.

In order to consider the principles involved in the effects on bank deposits of spending and saving, the matter can be simplified by taking the central bank and the clearing banks together, that is, the banking system as a whole.

When the total expenditure by the government and the people (the velocity of final-buying) is excessive in relation to production and total income,[4] there will be a big demand for credit and finance. Entrepreneurs will want finance for new capital equipment, business men will want loans for trading and financing stocks of goods and a plentiful supply of commercial bills will be constantly on sale for the banks to buy. Such conditions are usually, if not always, present when government expenditure exceeds revenue. Indeed, excessive government expenditure is often, if not usually, the cause of such conditions. And when government expenditure is excessive, the government will require loans of one kind or another, and treasury bills – and sometimes also short and/or long term government bonds – will be on sale. In these conditions we shall find the clearing banks making loans and investments and buying commercial and treasury bills – and sometimes government short and/or long term bonds – up to the maximum permitted by their reserves, that is, up to the maximum permitted by the credit base. We shall also find the central bank buying treasury bills – if not making other loans and investments – which will increase the reserves of bankers' deposits in its books and enlarge the credit base; this will enable the clearing banks further to increase their loans and investments. With the general increase in loans and investments made by the banks, there will be a corresponding increase in bank deposits (since every loan or investment made by a bank creates a deposit). Finally, the increase in bank deposits will call for increased supplies of cash for circulation in the hands of the public and increased supplies of paper money will be printed and supplied to the banks for this purpose. It is thus clear that excessive expenditure (resulting from insufficient voluntary saving) causes an increase in the quantity of money as measured by bank deposits and paper money.

Let us now take the reverse case, namely when the total amount saved by the government and the people is excessive in relation to production and total income.[5] In this case the velocity of final-buying and business activity will be retarded. Entrepreneurs will want less finance for new capital equipment, business men will want smaller loans for trading and financing stocks of goods and the supply of commercial bills available for the banks to buy will be smaller. Interest rates will be low, but however low they may be, their lowness will have little effect in increasing the effective demand for loans and credit. Such conditions are likely to be present at a time when government expenditure is being reduced. And when government expenditure is low enough to be fully covered (or more than covered) by revenue, the government will not require to borrow, there will be no new government bonds on sale and the supply of treasury bills available for the banks to buy will be at a minimum. In these conditions the making of loans and investments safely and profitably by the clearing banks will be more difficult and sometimes they will be left with loanable credit on hand, which will be accompanied by a decline in their deposits on their books (bank deposits). The central bank, also, will be experiencing the same difficulty. Absence of adequate supplies of treasury bills and of other suitable investment opportunities will cause the central bank's holdings of such securities, and its total loans and investments, to decline. This will reduce the deposits and reserves of the clearing banks (bankers' deposits) on its books. With the reserves of the clearing banks and their credit base thus reduced, a contraction of the total loans and investments of the clearing banks will occur, together with a corresponding decline in the deposits of the people on their books. Less cash will also be required for circulation in the hands of the public and a proportionate decline will occur in the issue of paper money. It is therefore evident that excessive saving by the government and the people causes a decline in the quantity of money as measured by bank deposits and paper money.

It must be noted that excessive saving by the people can be neutralized by reflationary measures on the part of the government. An integral part of such reflationary measures would be increased government expenditure, for instance on public works, which would be financed, not by increased taxation, but by central bank credit. This would at once inject additional money into circulation, provide treasury bills of the central bank to buy and thus enlarge the credit base of the clearing banks.

In view of the comment and criticism that had been engendered by *The Unclaimed Wealth*, I felt impelled in 1926 to begin writing *The Final Buyer*, which was published in 1928 and in which I put forward the same ideas in a different way. Here are the main points of my theory.

The 'unclaimed wealth' is 'a surplus of goods and services made available by saving and taxation, which, for one reason or another, is not utilized for investment nor employed for public services' (*Geneva Bulletins*, 1931–3).

Saving is 'the passive part of doing without consumable goods', which *make available* labour and materials (*Final Buyer*, p. 49). Investment is 'the active part of producing' capital goods and equipment, which *employs* labour and materials (*Final Buyer*, p. 51). As a result of this distinction we find: (i) that saving does not necessarily cause, and may even prevent, investment; and (ii) that investment is not dependent on voluntary saving (*Economic Lessons*, p. 12).

Excessive saving reduces the demand for new investment and, also, as we have seen, it causes a *decline* in the quantity of money as measured by bank deposits (*Final Buyer*, p. 57). Thus, when saving exceeds investment, unemployment and deflation are caused. On the other hand, insufficient voluntary saving – which is almost always due to inflationary finance – results in a rise in the price level whereby 'automatic frugality' is imposed (*Final Buyer*, p. 50). Thus, when investment exceeds voluntary saving currency depreciation and forced saving are caused.[6]

Decisions to save and decisions to invest are very often made by quite different people. In effect, given the number and varieties of individuals, institutions and governments involved, and the way in which their decisions are affected by different and changing conditions, it is not to be expected that investment will usually be equal to saving (*Final Buyer*, pp. 63–103). The rate of interest is only a minor factor in determining these decisions to save and to invest.

Minor and major fluctuations in industry and trade turn on the manner in which the multitude of large and small final buyers settle the question 'to buy or not to buy'. 'If general trade depression is to be prevented, intelligent regulation of the velocity of final-buying is indispensable' (*Final Buyer*, p. 15). Governments, being the biggest final buyers, should therefore aim at equating total demand with total supply.

In 1930, when Keynes' *Treatise on Money* appeared, it was clear that a radical change had taken place in his ideas. Exactly when this change occurred I do not know, but I can say that in 1927 I met Mr Robertson in London and that he did not seem to be aware of any change in Keynes' position at that time.

In his *Treatise* Keynes acknowledged his indebtedness to Mr Robertson's *Banking Policy* 'for clues which have set my mind working in the right direction' (Keynes, 1930a, vol. I: 172). His position then was the following: he endorsed the distinction between saving and investment; he seemed less concerned with banking policy; and he had moved to the question of over-saving, in which he took the position that over-saving stopped investment. This was similar to what I had defined as my own position in *The Final Buyer* (p.10, 4b). He writes: 'on my theory, it is a large volume of saving which does not lead to a correspondingly large volume of investment (not one which does) which is the root of the trouble' (Keynes, 1930a, vol I: 179).

He acknowledged my *Final Buyer* (Keynes, 1930a, vol. I: 172). His last book, the *General Theory*, published in 1936, like my *Unclaimed Wealth* (1924) is full of the term 'effective demand', but I have not found it (effective demand) mentioned even once in his *Treatise*. When I asked him in 1932 what was the difference between his theory and mine, he replied: 'we are working on parallel lines'.[7] I think he was reluctant to shed his ideas about the rate of interest. He suggested that I should read Hayek's latest book and expose its fallacy, but I thought that

Time would expose Hayek's fallacy without any help from anybody. Besides, reading Hayek is no picnic.

In my first *Geneva Bulletin*, which was issued in 1931, I proposed that an international organization should be instituted (*Economic Lessons*, pp. 2–3). Its business would be to foster maximum employment at stable price levels in the different countries according to their resources and to promote orderly regulation of international accounts. To this end the international organization would endeavour to ascertain and recommend appropriate financial and monetary policies – whether reflationary or deflationary – for each and every country. A reflationary policy would be indicated in a country at a time when its international accounts were in surplus, when the internal purchasing power of its currency was high (i.e. when its price level was low) and when its productive activity was retarded by a buying-deficiency. Vice versa, a deflationary policy would be indicated in a country when the reverse conditions were present. By these means an attempt would be made to establish appropriate velocities of final-buying in each country, both for the purpose of maximizing business activity in each country, and for the purpose of correlating the international trade of each country with that of other countries.

So much for the change in economic theories that occurred between the wars, and especially in the 1920s. We now come back to the economic events of the same period, which engendered and established the new theories, and to the economic situation where we left it at the end of 1921.

By 1924 the post-war deflationary policy initiated during 1920 had subsided. Business men who had been holding more than adequate stocks of goods having been punished, had become too cautious to expose themselves in this way again. In fact there was little hope of getting prices lower without a previous decline in rents and wages, and wages could only be forced down slowly by means of drastic economic pressure. Business activity was sluggish and much unemployment was in evidence. In the debtor countries inflation was coming to an end. In Germany, for instance, after all phases of inflation had been experienced, beginning with intensified productive activity and ending with disorganization, the new gold mark was eventually instituted with much rigour.

The great decline and complete collapse of the old German mark may be linked with the question of reparations. At the Treaty of Versailles the French wanted at least £6,000 million. Keynes wrote in *The Economic Consequences of the Peace* (1919) that Germany's capacity to pay could be put at about £2,000 million – though, as we shall see, he failed to envisage the problem from quite the right angle.

Hugo Stinnes, the great German financier, said, I think at the Spa Conference in 1922, that France and her allies were suffering from a surfeit of victory, for which they would have to pay. He, in fact, anticipated the fall in the German mark and he put all he had into its collapse. It is said that he bought property, hotels, newspapers and other businesses in Germany and it seems that he sold marks freely all over the world. From Amsterdam to London, from Paris to New York, from Hong Kong to Buenos Aires and to Valparaiso, everybody, from foreign exchange operators down to waiters, bought German marks. The occupation of the Ruhr by the French in 1922–3 did not worry him. In truth, he may have had a hand in engineering it, for it caused the German people to put pressure on the German government to send aid to their 'brothers in the Ruhr', and great quantities of marks were printed and dropped in bundles on the Ruhr by aeroplane. This was the end of the old mark – on which Hugo Stinnes and others had banked.

Thus, at this time, the attention of politicians and business men was being focused on the settlement of reparations and war debts. Britain and America, being well supplied with unemployed labour, with unemployed capital equipment and with unemployed surplus stocks of goods – being full of unclaimed wealth – did not want any payments in goods and services. On the contrary, they wanted 'protection' from imported goods, that is, protection from the only way in which they could receive large payments from abroad. Britain was willing to cancel old foreign debts, and even to grant further loans to debtors abroad, rather than receive anything more than book payments for money already owed. The capacity of Germany to pay reparations depended, not *only* on her capacity to produce, but *also* on the capacity of her creditors abroad to import and utilize German goods in addition to their own home products. This is what Keynes should have said, instead of giving an arbitrary figure of £2,000 million. However, under the Dawes Plan reparations were fixed at some such figure. This was accompanied by the Dawes loan to Germany and was followed by a series of municipal and other loans made by America to Germany on a large scale, whereby during the next five years Germany borrowed abroad considerably more new money than she paid back in reparations. By 1929, in fact, the Dawes Plan had run into difficulties and it was agreed in official circles that reparation payments needed to be 'commercialized'. This was done under the Young Plan which also, in due course, went into default. Conscious of the unsatisfactory nature of the Dawes settlement and of the way in which these matters were being handled at that time, I wrote in *The Unclaimed Wealth* (p. 143):

> When it comes to international debts that are too large to be lost in the ordinary international trade balances, the same problem presents itself in a manner large enough openly to flog and mock mankind. France and Italy prefer the mocking to the flogging, and they lie low when confronted with their international debts, or they change the subject to 'reparations'. The British cannot pay the debt to the United States and they have funded it for deferred payment; but it remains to be seen whether England and America escape both the mocking and the flogging.

In 1925, with much unemployment still in evidence, Keynes wrote a booklet entitled *The Economic Consequences of Mr Churchill*. It attacked Churchill, who was then Chancellor of the Exchequer, for restricting credit in order both to bring down prices and to restore sterling exchange to its pre-war parity with gold and the dollar. Keynes alleged, *not only* that the restriction of credit in Britain had been harmful to British trade, but *also* that the rise in the foreign exchange value of sterling (i) had encouraged imports of foreign goods by making them cheaper in sterling and (ii) had handicapped British exports by making them dearer in foreign money.

Perhaps these arguments were inspired by political as well as economic considerations. They certainly had a profound effect on Mr Bevin, on labour men and on many other people, who remembered them even in the inflationary conditions ruling after the second World War. Personally I found these arguments unconvincing. No doubt the restriction of credit at a time when trade was depressed was indefensible; and the rise in the foreign exchange value of sterling certainly caused imports to be cheaper in sterling money. But I am not sure that British exports were caused to be dearer to buyers abroad. For, since the restriction of credit was intended to lower the sterling prices of British goods, any such drop in sterling prices may well have neutralized the rise in sterling exchange. However, I wrote an article at the time (in *The Economic Review*) suggesting that, with full utilization of 'unclaimed wealth', British resources were strong enough both to support a policy of full employment and to restore sterling to its gold parity, without the introduction of any such obnoxious measures as devaluation or ill-timed deflation.

Keynes showed no aversion to devaluation, either at that time or in 1931 when sterling was devalued. Perhaps he was influenced by Sir Henry Strakosch, the great gold-mining magnate and former President of a leading German bank. Anyway, we are told by Mr R. F. Harrod (in his *Life of Keynes*) that Strakosch contacted Keynes in 1923 or thereabouts.[8] Sir Henry Strakosch wanted the foreign exchange value of sterling low in order that the price of gold should be high. He consistently advocated something like devaluation at League of Nations meetings in Geneva, and elsewhere, particularly during the great depression of 1930-3, when he argued that the price level needed to be raised and that devaluation was the 'obvious solution' to the economic troubles of that time.

From 1925 or thereabouts until the crash on Wall Street of October, 1929, business activity increased, especially in the United States, and superficially, at least, the economic position seemed to be improving. But buying for consumption and investment, both in the debtor countries and in the creditor countries, was being financed by loans or credit of one kind or another on an enormous scale, which was creating and building up debt to a vast extent.

In the international field, loans or finance in one form or another were freely furnished to the debtor countries, generally at 7 per cent, particularly by the United States. In effect, between 1920 and 1930 the total net foreign investments of all the creditor countries together seem to have risen from about £5,500 million to about £9,000 million (*Economic Lessons*, p. 48), whereby the debtor countries had been able to buy more goods from the creditor countries and to sell less goods to them. Observing this phenomenon in 1926, I wrote in *The Final Buyer* (p. 176):

> For the creditor countries to demand real net money payments from the debtor countries whilst seeking to abstain from doing the requisite amount of buying ... must result in prices, profits and wages in the debtor countries

being subjected to a continuous process of squeezing, or in the foreign exchange values of their currency falling, and in international price-cutting in general . . . Re-investment *in* the debtor countries of money paid, or due, by them to the creditor countries will help matters for a time, but the prospects of investment of this kind must deteriorate . . . and in any case debts can only be piled up in this way.

As for internal loans, in the United States tens of thousands of millions of dollars of borrowed money was injected into circulation by means of loans freely made to builders and buyers in general. Stockbrokers' loans rose from $3,800 million at the beginning of 1928 to $6,500 million in October 1929; at that time Mr Snowden, then Chancellor of the Exchequer, called the speculation going on in Wall Street an 'orgy'. I myself a week before the crash wrote to *The Times*: 'This fabulous increase in stockbrokers' loans may well indicate . . . that sooner or later there will be dark days of tribulation for quite a lot of people . . . when the bulls are "slaughtered" for the benefit of bargain hunters' (*Economic Lessons*, pp. 50–1).

The financing of buyers for *other* purposes by means of loans was also on an enormous scale. In the United States expenditure on building and construction – which is always a major factor in business activity – rose from $7,300 million in 1924 to $10,000 million in 1928 and most of this money was obtained by borrowing in one way or another. In addition vast sums were advanced on the hire-purchase system for buying furniture, motor-cars, radio sets, etc. (*Economic Lessons*, pp. 52–3).

However, since prices in America and in Britain certainly did *not* rise during this time, it is evident that the total amount of buying for consumption and investment was not excessive in relation to productive capacity and to the actual rate of production (*Economic Lessons*, p. 54).

When the furnishing of buyers with loans reached its limit, and debtors were forced to buy less in order to make payments to the creditors, commodity prices declined as a result of the reduced buying and the steady concentration of cash in the hands of creditors, and of gold in the creditor countries, took place. Thus the curtailment of unsound buying of goods and services with borrowed money by the debtors disclosed a buying-deficiency of the creditor countries and of creditors in general (*Economic Lessons*, p. 55).

A major cause of the buying-deficiency of creditors was excessive taxation by their governments. Between 1920 and 1930 the amount of money withdrawn from the British public by taxation was enough to reduce the national debt by £400 million. In America, during the same period, the amount withdrawn from the public by taxation and used to reduce the national debt was over $10,000 million. France reduced its national debt by £240 million between 1927 and 1930. We have here some explanation of the concentration and sterilization of gold in the United States and in France which occurred at that time (*Economic Lessons*, p. 55).

The wonderful rise of bondholders during the Victorian and Edwardian eras was largely assisted by the rapid increase of population during that time, whereby the limits imposed by considerations of maximum debt per head of population were largely extended. The tendency for birth rates to decline after the First World War therefore tended to expose the top-heavy structure of national and international debts.

Before the great depression of 1930–3 many attempts were made to combat buying-deficiencies by means of curtailment of production. On the one hand all the secrets of science and organization were used to increase the effectiveness of labour. On the other hand we have seen cartels, pools and even governments handling steel, rubber, coffee, wheat, etc., in order to maintain wholesale prices by means of regulation of supplies. But the efforts of all these cartels and pools, continuously undermined by masses of eager and hungry producers pressing for a place in the sun, were only sustained for a time by the super-feeding of loans to buyers. And when this piling up of debts in geometrical progression had reached its limit, prices in all markets began to give and the whole abnormal structure rocked and collapsed, leaving quantities of debris in the form of colossal debts magnified and multiplied by the drastic fall in prices (*Economic Lessons*, p. 60).

By 1931 it was clear enough that a vast world buying-deficiency had developed. This buying-deficiency I estimated at the time, on annual basis, at $15,000 million (*Economic Lessons*, Bulletin no. 4); and I urged that, had expenditure by the world's creditor countries and by creditors in general been greater, there would have been no trouble.

But most people even in well-informed quarters thought quite differently. Some of them, without settling the question 'to buy or not to buy', talked about lack of confidence. Others talked about a shortage of capital resulting from insufficient saving and many thought that the trouble was due to a 'breakdown'. Lloyd George, looking at the *débâcle* in 1921, said that it was the sort of thing that always happened after a great war (*Unclaimed Wealth*, p. 134). Ten years later President Hoover attributed the *débâcle* in 1931 to the same great war and saw the remedy in disarmament. Then there was the perpetual tariff question in many people's minds as the cause and cure of all our economic worries.

There was also a lot of talk about over-production; but people were far from unanimous as to the remedy. Some of them advocated curtailment of production, others demanded curtailment of consumption as well. In fact most people wanted drastic economy, for, as I wrote at the time (*Geneva Bulletin* no. 5), '*sauve qui peut*' was the order of the day – in which saving one's money and saving oneself were at once the general aim. The Monthly Letter of the National City Bank of New York (January, 1931) said: 'Hopes for 1931 continue to be based on drastic curtailment of output . . .'. But the New York correspondent of the London *Times* (March 30, 1931) asserted: 'the best that is expected now is that good harvests will bring a real upturn in the autumn' (*Economic Lessons*, p. 26). 'Good harvests!' I wrote at the time,

> Quite right, provided somebody buys them at fair prices. But why good harvests when they provoke a ruinous fall in wholesale prices, destroy the purchase power of producers and debtors and end in a buyers flight? . . . As things are, the business man will keep his powder dry and if he prays for good

harvests he will make it clear that he is only referring to his own sowings . . .
good harvests this year may do good in a way that is a little too subtle and
painful to be quite to the liking of most of us, and in a way that may not be at
all to the liking of those who could only ask for economy and resignation,
whilst the golden moments for doing something slipped away.

(Economic Lessons, pp. 29–30)

In these conditions of drastic economy, the quantity of money as measured by
bank deposits declined, confirming the theory put forward by me in my first and
second books. I have not seen the figures for some years, but I think I am right in
saying that in the United States *total* bank deposits, both on deposit account and
on current account, declined by about 40 per cent between the end of 1929 and
early 1933. In Britain also a decline occurred, but it was of a smaller magnitude.
I think it ended in 1931, when Britain suspended gold payments and when the
authorities began to increase the quantity of bank money by buying gold, and in
other ways.

However, in 1931, with *sauve qui peut* as the order of the day, and two months
before Britain suspended gold payments, I proposed that the situation should be
met by the seven creditor countries agreeing, first, to reduce the taxation by 30 per
cent; second, to refrain from reducing government expenditure; and third, to meet
budget deficits by means of new central bank credit (*Geneva Bulletin* no. 8).

No notice was taken of these proposals at that time by any government. But, as
I had written four years earlier in *The Final Buyer* (p. 167), 'A government, before
risking political instability, will usually relax taxation, introduce relief measures
for unemployment, raid sinking funds or borrow from banks to meet budget deficits, and thus abandon a policy of economic pressure'. As we shall see, something
like this was done by the United States government and by many other governments in the end.

Meantime, Sir Henry Strakosch and others went on saying, rightly, that it was
necessary to raise the price level and, *not* rightly, that devaluation was the 'obvious
solution'. The press began to decry British resources, saying that Britain was
over-spending and that there was a deficit in the balance of trade of £180 million
for the first six months of 1931. Yet this deficit was less than the one in the corresponding period of the previous year. The May Committee, which was appointed
in March 1931, and which dished up its first-of-April report in July, pretended that
there was a budget deficit of nearly £120 million – and nasty things of that sort.
But £50 million for the budget deficit was, I think, nearer the truth.

It was the sudden and combined action of these factors in July 1931, which
then and there brought about a universal panic in which the economic structure of
the world was tried to the utmost. The flight of gold from Britain began and soon
the major part of British gold reserves, plus about £125 million hastily borrowed
abroad, had left the country; on the 21 September Britain suspended gold
payments (*Search for Confidence*, pp. 29–31).

Contrary to what one would have supposed, the fall of sterling was received
with satisfaction in many quarters. It pleased Conservative candidates whom it

provided with votes. It pleased 'bull' operators in commodity markets, who wanted commodity prices to rise. It pleased the currency cranks who did not like the gold standard. Most of all it pleased those who wanted the price of gold to rise. It caused the price of gold in Britain, and later in South Africa, to rise from about 85 shillings an ounce to about 120 shillings; and it caused the working profits of the South African gold mines, according to market calculations, to increase by anything from 70 per cent to 600 per cent, the low grade mines being the ones that benefited most. And thus it provided some people – gold-mining people, as well as foreign exchange operators – with a safe and easy way to get rich quickly (*Economic Readjustment*, pp. 22–7).

The Beaverbrook press took the line that the fall of sterling 'didn't much matter'. A new catchy ditty was in the air in which sterling was linked to the standard, 'another little drop won't do us any harm', which to some people is a golden rule if not a gold standard. In 1932 the Exchange Equalization Account was instituted, ostensibly to iron out fluctuations in the rate of exchange, but really to prevent sterling exchange from rising and returning to its old gold parity, as it certainly would have done had not the British authorities met the strong demand for sterling, that prevailed on the foreign exchange market, by consistently buying gold at the new price of 120 shillings an ounce. In effect, the oversea demand for sterling was so consistently strong from then until the war commenced in 1939 that, during this period, Britain was able to buy enough gold to increase her gold reserves by about $3,000 million, or £600 million.

In November that year, 1932, the German government introduced a new economic programme, whereby large Reichsbank credits were provided for new public works, for employment premiums and for relief for the taxpayer (*Search for Confidence*, pp. 75–9). The year 1932, in fact, marked a definite drift towards economic rationalism. The need was generally admitted for a rise in the price level, for budget deficits, for increased private and public expenditure and for expenditure on new public works. Support for these things was voiced in all directions by reports of committees, such as the Monetary Committee of the Ottawa Conference; by letters to the press from economists, such as Professor Gustav Cassel, Professor Pigou, Professor J. R. Bellerby, Mr Guillebaud, Mr J. E. Meade and many others; and by politicians, such as Winston Churchill (*Search for Confidence*, Bulletin no. 23). More important still, a good deal of new money was injected into circulation, and deflation in Britain began to subside.

But in the United States it was different. The first effect of the devaluation of sterling was to hit the American export trade; and deflation continued with increased violence. By early 1933 the *New York Times* index of business activity stood at a record low level, whilst the prices of commodities and industrial shares were also at extremely low levels. For instance, Union Pacific Railway shares, which had stood at 300 in 1929, had been as low as 25 and Anaconda Copper which in 1929 had stood at 150, touched 3 in 1932. Bank deposits, as already stated, had shrunk by I think about 40 per cent and the banking system was in a state of collapse. Numerous banks were forced to close their doors and even the big banks of New York City were threatened.

But on the accession of President Roosevelt in March, 1933, the position soon began to improve. The new President met the situation by a number of measures, the principal of which were: the declaration of a banking holiday; the pledging of Federal credit for the reorganization of certain impaired banks; the authorization of an issue of new currency to the Reserve Banks; the creation of large quantities of new bank money through the buying of government securities by the Federal Reserve System; the fixing of maximum hours and minimum wages; a $3,300 million public works programme; and, some weeks later (on April 17), the suspension of the gold standard. The most effective of these measures, I think, was the public works programme. It is true that it was not large enough and that delays occurred in its planning and execution. But it directly provided work for the unemployed, it increased the demand for goods and it tended to raise the price level. It thus provided real and valuable nourishment for the economic system, where devaluation could only operate as a temporary stimulant.

But the President did not stop at these *re*flationary measures. He showed a predilection for driving with one foot on the accelerator and the other on the brake and he did not refrain from attempting a number of *de*flationary measures. He introduced an Economy Bill, whereby $500 million were to be saved by reductions of pay to Federal employees and by reduced compensation to war veterans. He proposed to liquidate some 3,000 insolvent banks alleged to be 'unworthy' and he proposed to compel all businesses to obtain Federal licenses. He wanted to make his public works programme dependent, not on new Federal Reserve finance, but on loans from the public. At first, also, and no doubt rightly, he seemed disposed to adhere to the gold standard.

Subsequently, we heard little more about these deflationary measures. The gold standard, as already stated, was suspended in April, the authorities started buying gold at premium in October that year and in January, 1934, the dollar was devalued, bringing its foreign exchange value back to its old parity with sterling. We must not forget to observe that the devaluation of the dollar, like the devaluation of sterling, provided some people with a safe and easy way to get rich quickly (*Economic readjustment*, Bulletin no. 27).

As a result of Roosevelt's intervention, deflation was arrested and the American economy was reflated. Recovery was slow and hesitant, but the level of business activity was gradually raised during the next few years. This assisted recovery in the sterling area and elsewhere; and a substantial measure of world economic readjustment was thus effected.

In 1937 the British authorities got the idea, with little or no foundation, that danger of inflation had arisen. The idea was mooted that Britain should stop buying gold and soon the papers and low grade minds were full of it. 'Why should we tax ourselves in order to buy gold?' asked a leading banker. In an article in the *Financial Times* (May 13, 1937) I pointed out that there were no signs of inflation, that if Britain stopped buying gold, sterling exchange would shoot up and stop the export of British goods, and that if *both* America *and* Britain stopped buying gold, all the gold mines in South Africa and elsewhere would probably have to shut down, with disastrous repercussions everywhere. Then Sir Henry Strakosch gave about a quarter of a million pounds to an important charitable institution and thereafter little more was heard about Britain ceasing to buy gold.

With the assistance of growing expenditure on rearmament in most countries, business activity remained on a fairly even keel – though below the full employment level – until the commencement of the war in 1939, when a period of inflation began which I fear is with us still.

Notes

1 It seems to me that Hobson, as a result of my interview with him at this time, may well have discussed my contention – that excessive saving resulted in the 'hoarding' of bank deposits – with other economists. Something he wrote at the time makes me think so. Anyway Lavington, soon after, in his *Trade Cycle*, published in 1922, raised the vital question of saving and of 'idle' bank balances and 'hoarding' (see later on).
2 [See W. Hessling, *The Distinction between Saving and Investment*, Appendix.]
3 See note 1.
4 [In another version of this passage Abbati wrote 'in relation to production and ready productive capacity'.]
5 [See note 4.]
6 [When ready productive capacity is fully employed.]
7 [See Keynes' letters to Abbati, Appendix.]
8 [Harrod also tells us that 'At this time he [Keynes] entered deeply into certain plans of Mr Henry Strakosch for setting up a new company to sell South African gold. He and Strakosch were to be managers' and that 'there was meeting with the Rothschilds and consultation with the South African Government' (Harrod 1951 [1952]: 288).]

Appendix

Letters from J.M. Keynes to H.A. Abbati[1]

From Keynes *to* Abbati, 30 June 1932

46, Gordon Square,
Bloomsbury.

H. Abbati Esq.,
5 Square Montchoisy,
Geneva.

Dear Mr. Abbati,
I have regularly read your bulletins with the greatest interest and a very large measure of sympathy and agreement. Though we may differ in details on this matter, we are together on the same side of the frontier. I will certainly do what I can to see that the reprint of the bulletins is well reviewed[2].
                    Yours sincerely,
                         J.M. Keynes

From Keynes *to* Abbati, 10 January 1933

46, Gordon Square,
Bloomsbury.

H. Abbati Esq.,
5 Square Montchoisy,
Geneva, Switzerland.

Dear Mr. Abbati,
I appreciate your letter of December 20. If you will get me appointed International Economic Coercer, I shall be delighted! I should thoroughly enjoy the job. But the first task is to persuade the world, and when the world is persuaded, the existing jacks in office will be only too delighted to carry out the popular will.

As for the necessary propaganda, each of us is, I think, doing what we can in our own way. Our ideas and objects are substantially the same, and the difference is of secondary importance. I shall be very glad to help your side of the work, if at any time what seems to me to be a suitable opportunity for me to do so turns up.

But, as I said before, I am very doubtful indeed both of the wisdom and utility of writing prefaces to other people's books. I am quite sure that it would not have the effect on the circulation which you hope and believe it would[3].

Things may appear on the surface to move slowly, but really, in my judgement they are moving at a remarkable rate. The wind of popular favour is changing its direction. But it is an enormous job to undo in a few years the influences of economists and moralists and all virtuous and scientific persons over the great tract of time separating us from the Battle of Waterloo.

Yours sincerely,
J.M. Keynes

From Keynes *to* Abbati, 9 June 1933

46, Gordon Square,
Bloomsbury.

H. Abbati Esq.,
Unclaimed Wealth Utilization Committee,
5 Square Montchoisy,
Geneva.

Dear Mr. Abbati,
Thanks very much for sending me a copy of the new collection of Bulletins. You are still keeping up a fine combination of amusement and sound doctrine.

Yours sincerely,
J.M. Keynes

Correspondence between H.A. Abbati and D.H. Robertson[4]

From Abbati *to* Robertson, 20 July 1948

Dear Robertson,

Thank you for your letter of the 9th July, together with enclosures, which I have read with the greatest interest. As you see I am still in this country, and since I am likely to remain so, I should be very pleased if you would send me on loan the article in the Economic Journal of America [*The American Economic Review*] mentioned by you.

I return herewith the Preface of the reprint of your 1915 book [*A Study of Industrial Fluctuation*], which gives me some idea of what the book is about. It also makes it quite clear that you are well in the forefront in the questions of over-saving and shortage of saving, and no doubt also of the distinction between saving and investment, having given them much consideration thirty-five years ago. I shall read the book as soon as it appears.

Meantime I may say that the information that you give me in your letter is practically all new to me. I consider that you are fully justified in having 'an abiding sense of grievance in the way in which this whole order of ideas is now associated throughout the world with Keynes' name and his alone'. I must say also that I think you have acted with the utmost restraint and generosity throughout, and I admire you for it. But I, as primarily a business man who has been accustomed to dealing with people who give no more change than the right amount, only feel called upon to be strictly truthful.

In writing the booklet on Lord Keynes' central thesis and my concept of Unclaimed Wealth I was anxious that my presentation should be purely objective and I decided that, apart from what I had to say about Sidney Webb and Hobson, I would not put in any more material than what was already available in the published literature. But since you have a personal stake in the matter and I presume you are desirous of knowing all I have to say about it, I am going to give you for your own guidance the information that follows. It takes up more space on paper than it does in my mind, but I think you will find that it is all relevant. If you think that I have fallen into any errors I hope that you will be good enough to put me right.

First of all, however, as regards my project to going to America which you mention, I may as well say that I have more or less given it up.

[. . .]

You say that you have been trying to remember whether my *Unclaimed Wealth* was known to you when you were writing your *Banking Policy*. You also say that you do not feel confident that you would have felt called upon to mention it even if you *did* know of it. I agree that your attitude is justified, which is clear from what follows.

Your book is still with my furniture in Geneva and I have not seen it for fifteen years, but when I read it in 1926 I made a mental note of a number of points: (i) The book was a very elaborate analysis of the distinction between saving and investment. (ii) Banking policy was, I thought, treated as the main if not the only determining factor of both. (But I am not quite clear on this point). (iii) Your use of the word Hoarding seemed to be similar though not necessarily the same as mine. And your Automatic Lacking amounted to the same thing as what I had in mind when I explained in *The Unclaimed Wealth* (p. 107) that, at a time when productive capacity was unable to cope adequately with new equipment plus consumption, the respective quantities of each 'for which the *effective demand* is strongest' were 'automatically' secured by the highest bidders. (iv) Your book did not cover the same ground as mine even on the question of Hoarding, because you seemed to take the possibility of Hoarding as established; whereas I, as a result of the views expressed by Sidney Webb and Hobson, was mainly concerned with showing that Hoarding was possible through the banking system, that at that time it was taking place on a large scale, and it was at the root of all national and international marketing problems and debt problems of those days.

I wondered whether you had seen *The Unclaimed Wealth*, or my article in the *Economic Review* (since defunct) of December 18, 1925; and later, when I met you at the house of Norman Wylde in the summer of 1927, you said to me: 'Your name has been before me for some years'. I can almost hear your words as I write them down.

I did not know until 1947, when I was writing my booklet on Lord Keynes' central thesis, and when I had occasion to look more closely into Keynes' *General Theory* than I had done before, that Marshall had written: 'Though men have the power to purchase, they may not choose to use it'. Neither had I any idea that you had written on the subject as far back as 1915, until I received your letter a few days ago.

Sidney Webb had definitely rejected the idea that money deposited in a bank could in any circumstances be Hoarded. He stated also that no such thesis had ever been advanced to his knowledge, and that it did not even form any part of Hobson's over-saving theory. He wrote to me quite clearly and with supporting arguments that, with a modern banking system in operation, all savings were automatically invested; and I supposed that this was the teaching of the London School of Economics. As for Keynes, at that time I thought he was mainly concerned with the theory of bank rate and open market operations as the regulators of business activity – which I associated with Hawtrey. In short, I thought he was barking up the wrong tree! I have since learned from his *General Theory* that the doctrine that savings were automatically invested (by the banks) had become accepted as beyond discussion, in that he wrote: 'The idea that we can safely neglect the aggregate demand function is fundamental to the Ricardian economics, which underlie what we have been taught for more than a century'.

The idea that aggregate effective demand remained unaffected by saving had certainly blocked the way for Hobson, since he had been constrained to argue, not that over-saving stopped investment, but that it resulted in over-investment and losses arising therefrom. Hobson had, therefore, shown the greatest interest in what I had to say, being troubled only about the fundamental question of what exactly happened to money deposited in the banks. He wanted to know exactly how the banking system hoarded excessive savings. I gathered that this question had not been asked before and the answer was certainly not easy to find at that time. I made it my business to deal with this question in *The Unclaimed Wealth*. I think I did so satisfactorily in that book, and I did so again on more comprehensive lines in *The Final Buyer*. But I wonder how many people know the answer even today?

Had I known that the authority of Marshall was available in support of the concept of Hoarding, and that you also had a position in the matter, my task would have been much easier. I might even have kept out of it altogether, and I dare say that it would have been much better for me if I had just kept out.

I learnt in 1932 from your review in the *Economic Journal* (and your letter now confirms) that you were not in agreement with me on all points, especially on the question of Hoarding money in banks. It is not clear to me exactly how we are at variance on this Hoarding question, but I wish to urge for your special considera-tion that the whole of the concept of Hoarding in modern economic and monetary conditions rests on the validity of the thesis that *excessive* savings held on deposit in banks are inevitably Hoarded by the banking system, without which the old orthodox view must be accepted that every saving deposited in a bank automati-cally results in a corresponding investment, and diverts without reducing the aggregate effective demand.

I think Keynes assented to this, though for all I know he, like others, may have by-passed the monetary details involved without bothering to look into them. At all events, had you got me correctly on this Hoarding question, I do not think he would have been able to soar away into the sky with what *The Times* calls *his* central thesis, as he did, leaving everybody else, so to speak (I think in Keynesian language), 'twittering in the bush'.

Perhaps, also, in your eyes I had got tarred with the same brush as the inflation-ist men of faith. If so, this was partly my own fault because, thinking that these people could do no harm at that time, I did not bother to show where I thought they were wrong. This was in line with my policy not to report and criticize what others say, but to deliver my own message.

My concept of Unclaimed Wealth and theory of Final Buying are not intended as refutations of other economic theories, any more that they are intended to incor-porate other economic theories. All I claim is that I have shown how the decisions of men, taking form as *effective demand* and operating through the monetary system, can result in the failure of aggregate demand to equate at all times with aggregate supply, and how deflationary, inflationary and other effects may result in this way. You may, perhaps, object that I have not given 'sufficient attention to underlying structural maladjustments' and perhaps you are right; but I see from your Preface to your reprint that you have made the same charge against Marshall, so I am in good company. My aim has been to extract a major concept from a vast maze of economic complexities, and to isolate it and present it systematically for inspection. I am also under the impression that I am the only one to have suspected that excessive savings were Hoarded by the banking system and, later, to have shown in theory that this was so. And in Bulletin nos. 25 and 26 on Gentlemen Prefer Gold, I gave at least one detailed demonstration of the cumulative effects of excessive saving, severe liquidation and Hoarding on a world-wide scale.

Unfortunately, so far as this country is concerned, the Unclaimed Wealth has been lost; and I am afraid that misconceptions in this matter together with the process of government by trial and error that we have witnessed, are going to operate against the new economic truths, which may be called inflationary fallacies. But there is nothing inflationary about the concept of Unclaimed Wealth, which is rational and exact, and reliable if properly handled.

I am sorry to learn that you have not got a copy of *The Unclaimed Wealth*. Numbers of people I know who had copies cannot find them. Even the copy that was in the Fabian library disappeared. The only spare copies I know of are two or three that I have stored with my furniture in Geneva. The book is still of interest. It covers the required ground adequately and clearly. It even contains some important material that I had forgotten I had ever written. Some of it is very crude, as is to be expected in the circumstances; but there is nothing in it that does not completely square with everything I have since written. And if some of it is like 'the innocent prattle of a child', we are told that this is 'at times, truly prophetic'.

Twenty-five years ago I gave up business – perhaps very stupidly – and took to writing *The Unclaimed Wealth* and, although since then I have done a lot of work, and the labourer is supposed to be worthy of his hire, I have got nothing in return. Leading economists have thought my work good enough for them to read and, in general, competent people are very willing to read what I write; but I have much difficulty in getting anything published. In fact, for me, the amount of work involved in writing anything is small compared with the amount of work involved in getting it published. I make no bones about admitting this, since even men like H.G. Wells have found it so until they became well known.

No doubt there are more than one reasons for this state of affairs, but one thing is certain, namely that in these days when publishing is largely done on the reputation of the author and on any 'news value' that his name may carry, it is very vital for a writer on scientific subjects to get due acknowledgement from anybody who makes even the smallest use of his work. Without this, his difficulties begin with the publishers' readers, whoever they may be, and he is entirely at their mercy. But what is worse is that there is always a tendency for everybody to quote well-known writers even when the latter are admittedly using the work of lesser men.

[. . .]

At all events, I am strongly of opinion that the utmost importance should always be attached to conscientious acknowledgement of all work done by individual writers on scientific questions. What the newspaper men do in such matters may be beneath consideration. But academic men should see to it punctiliously that every man, particularly the unknown man, should get his due; because only in this way can the best men be brought to the fore quickly and be given the necessary prestige and other means by which to carry on their work, and only in this way can the advance of knowledge be removed from the mercy of newspaper men feverishly in search of headline personalities and names that carry a 'news value'.

Between 1924 and 1934 I did a good deal in order to interest the leading economists and politicians in the concept of Unclaimed Wealth. The Bulletins that I issued from Geneva during the period 1931–3 became well known and were largely quoted by the press in England, America and elsewhere. The one about Roosevelt (No. 27, The Heman) was reprinted in full both by the *Daily Herald* in England and the *National Sphere* in America. They were also something of a feature in Geneva. I got to know Professor Cannan through these Bulletins and he wrote me suggesting that I should send them to Harrod, R.L. Hall, L.M. Fraser and a fourth – perhaps J.E. Meade. I do not remember to what extent I followed out this suggestion, but I do remember that my mailing list was already larger than I could afford. As you know, I was sending copies free of charge to all applicants and inviting voluntary subscriptions to cover the cost of multigraphing, paper and postage. You were good enough to send me a subscription regularly, but you were one of the few economists who did so; and the absence of enough subscriptions, combined with a 40 per cent reduction of my income in Swiss francs resulting from the debasement of the gold value of sterling and the dollar, prevented me from carrying on as I would have liked, and eventually put a stop to my activities.

The Economic Section of the League of Nations was costing, I think, about £20,000 a year. Moreover in this section more than one member of the secretariat of quite mediocre ability were recommended for notice by the Rockefeller Foundation and were awarded grants of about £1,000 each. With a little influential support (which Keynes could have given at no cost to himself), and at an extremely low cost compared with the stately salaries received by the members of the secretariat, I would have given a first class service with a view to obtaining important practical results.

Of course I gave special attention to Keynes, and I saw to it that it was sent a copy of every one of my books and Bulletins as soon as they were published. In October 1924 (when I was at San Remo) I received a card from him. It was written entirely in his own handwriting, and referred to a review of *The Unclaimed Wealth* that appeared in *The Nation* of September 27 of that year. It also invited me to become a subscriber to the journal. This card, and two or three letters that I subsequently received from him when I lived in Geneva, are with the furniture and effects that I put into warehouse in that town when I left, and I hope to be able to produce this correspondence in due course. In one of these letters he wrote: 'I regularly read your Bulletins with much sympathy and a large measure of agreement' [30 June 1932]. But he never gave me any support by word or deed.

Here is an extract from the review in question: 'The choking of the investment market through the money "saved" (either directly or through the agency of the banks) tends, according to Mr Abbati, to check production, and in that way to reduce the volume of money distributed as income, either as profit or wages. His remedy involves the handing over of all industries, tending to monopoly production, to the State, which must ensure, by a system of minimum wage-rates, that the effective demand for goods is always in line with the industry's productive capacity'.

This extract may be compared with the passage in *The Times* purporting to describe 'Lord Keynes' central thesis', which is quoted in the booklet sent to you. It is also interesting to note the use of the words: 'The choking of the investment market through the money "saved"', because this line of thought indicates that the writer of the review was influenced by the Hobsonian theory, which suffers from the absence of the concept of Unclaimed Wealth introduced by me. In effect, according to the concept of Unclaimed Wealth the investment market is not choked by the money saved, but by the money saved that is Hoarded.

I am well aware that Keynes was generous in his acknowledgements to young people and to his juniors in general. He was certainly much admired by large numbers of them and I think some of them almost worshipped him. I imagine also that some of them did a lot of work for him; and Kahn, whose 'multiplier' he acknowledged, was no doubt one of these. Incidentally, I do not think there was anything much, or new, in the idea of a multiplier. I, for one, mentioned it long before Kahn and that was *en passant*, without bothering to give it a name, in my article in the *Economic Review* already referred to. Cannan told me that Keynes once remarked to him ironically, 'I don't know these new economics!'. I wondered at the time if this applied to or included economic equations; and I have since wondered if Keynes looked upon these equations as anything more than good ammunition with which to make a display of intellectual force. He certainly knew how to use them effectively. My guess is that Harrod did them for him, but of course I may be entirely wrong.

I visited Keynes at his house in Gordon Square twice. On the second occasion, which was in December 1931, he said of a Cambridge colleague who was working on the new economic ideas: 'His temperament is warring with his intellect!'. Keynes also mentioned Hayek. We both thought that Hayek's position was in conflict with the concept of Hoarding, but I said that I had not read Hayek and was therefore unable to put my finger on the fallacy which, in my view, existed in his argument. Keynes, though he had read Hayek, seemed to be also at a loss in the matter of the fallacy, and he suggested that I should look into it. He told me which one of Hayek's books I should read and I took a note of it. But, although I was still to some extent under the influence of Keynes' glamour, I did not bother to pursue the matter. He had said of me to the person who had sent him a copy of *The Final Buyer* in 1929 that I was 'very promising'; and, whilst appreciating this tribute, it did not give me enough confidence to suppose that I, or anyone else, had a chance of finding out something of importance that he did not already know.

When I read Keynes' footnote mentioning *The Final Buyer* in his *Treatise* I was not impressed. And my wife, who has no knowledge on such matters, said that it was 'a rather back-handed sort of compliment!'. Indeed, it may have done me more harm than good; for, after all, who was going to bother about Abbati's unintelligible stuff – and who was Abbati anyhow? – when Keynes, himself, was telling them all about it?

No doubt much of the phrasing of my book was not as clear as it might have been. In fact, at the time I was writing it I was suffering from a painful malady which I afterwards discovered was chronic appendicitis, and all the energy and patience I could muster were taken up with working the matter out and putting it down in good order. But it certainly seems strange that Keynes, after talking about the forced saving of Schumpeter, the 'clues' he had got from you, and the distinction between saving and investment to be found in my book, should thereafter proceed to write: '. . . *on my theory* (italics mine), it is a large volume of saving which does not lead to a correspondingly large volume of investment (and not one which does) which is the root of the trouble'.

What did he mean by *his* theory? Why *his* theory, when I had written two books and spent four years on exactly that? And if it was *his* theory and he thought it differed from mine, why was it not your theory as well as his? What did he mean by his statement that he was indebted to you for clues? Was it not clear from his own footnote that he had discussed these matters frequently and fully with you, so that – as you yourself put it in your *Banking Policy* – neither of you knew in the end how much of the ideas contained in your Chapters V and VI were his and how much yours? Besides, a number of passages in his *Treatise*, and especially the way they were worded, suggested to me that when writing them he had had before him both *The Unclaimed Wealth* and *The Final Buyer*. Indeed, I wrote fully about this matter at the time to Allen & Unwin, the publishers of *The Unclaimed Wealth*.

Mr Hessling (a Geneva friend) and myself felt that it was possible that Keynes had got considerably more than clues from you, that it was not excluded that you had put the whole position before him, and that it was not unlikely that he had found my *Unclaimed Wealth* clear enough – even though he thought that *The Final Buyer* was not sufficiently intelligible. It seemed possible to us that his talk about your clues and my failure to be intelligible might be the Keynesian way of politely side-tracking us both.

I did not understand why you appeared to acquiesce in playing the part of provider of clues that he seemed to have given you, particularly as I thought that he and you were in full agreement about the concept of Hoarding. I was rather puzzled. But I now see that there was some divergence between his views and yours which gave him the means of saying, as he did later on to me in December 1931: 'We must all sail under our own flags'. Those were his very words. I did not know exactly what his flag was like, though I knew it was of an embracing kind and that it probably had frills and trimmings that mine lacked. But all he said on the subject was: 'We are working on parallel lines'. Again I am reporting him *verbatim*.

However, in face of these uncertainties Hessling and I were not disposed to indulge in any hasty conclusions, but he advised me to form my Geneva Committee and to give it a name that made our position quite clear. He also insisted on putting the facts as we knew them on record objectively and unaggressively, and Bulletin no. 3 was designed for this purpose.

I have not been a very diligent reader of Keynes' *Treatise* and I have only got what I wanted out of his G*eneral Theory* by using the index; but, so far as I can gather, the second book does not take the concept of Hoarding any further than the first, and neither of them take the matter any further than, or deal with as fully as, my *Unclaimed Wealth*. The *General Theory* comes in heavily on *effective demand*, as does *The Unclaimed Wealth*; but in the *Treatise* little or no mention is made of *effective demand*. Indeed, *I have not found it mentioned even once*, just as Keynes tells us that 'you will not find it mentioned even once in the works of Marshall, Edgeworth and Professor Pigou, from whose hands the classical theory has received its most mature embodiment'. Perhaps before Keynes finished the *Treatise* he would have liked to incorporate *effective demand* in it, but this would have meant recasting both his own ideas and the whole book; so he contented himself with writing in the Preface: 'The ideas with which I have finished up are widely different from those with which I begun'.

I find it hard to believe, as you suggest, that it was a pure oversight that he did not report in his *General Theory* that I had a position in the matter. He did not make mistakes like that. He did not do so because he had his reasons for not doing so. When I saw that he had left me out I did not even write to him about it, though a business friend of mine in an important position advised me to do so. I just decided to leave him alone in future. I knew that it was worse than useless to quarrel with him about anything so elusive and little understood as the concept of Hoarding. I myself never knew exactly what the so-called Keynesian analysis was and until *The Times* told us what his central thesis was, I did not know that he had one. I would never have been able to do anything about it had not *The Times*, in giving him the lion's share of the credit for the new economic theories, given me something short, sweet and concrete to deal with.

I should certainly be most interested to learn who wrote the passages in *The Times* and in Beveridge's book, quoted in my booklet on the subject.

Thank you for sending the booklet to E.A.G. Robinson for review in the *Economic Journal*. The *Economist* said they were going to review it, but have not done so. Could you not write them a line offering to do so?

Well! I am afraid that this letter has extended itself out of all bounds. I thought that a couple of pages would have been quite enough for my purpose. However, now you know the truth. It is not the sort of stuff that I want to put around, so please keep it for your personal use and the use of any *special* friends of yours who would be interested. I am of course keeping your letter personal and private as requested. With kind regards,

                    Yours sincerely
                    Henry Abbati

From Robertson *to* Abbati, 15 August 1948[5]

Trinity College,
Cambridge

Dear Abbati,

Thanks for return of the A. E. Review [*The American Economic Review*, March 1945, with an article by L.A. Hahn 'Compensating reactions to compensatory spending'], and for your supplementary letter. And I have now re-read carefully your long letter of July 20.

I don't know that I have anything helpful to add, but here are some rather random remarks.

(1) The current (June) Economic Journal list your pamphlet [Lord Keynes' Central Thesis and the Concept of Unclaimed Wealth, 1947] among 'New Books' and adds the following remarks.

'Mr Abbati claims in this pamphlet [Lord Keynes'] that *The Times*, in a leading article written at the time of Lord Keynes's death, was wrong if it meant to attribute to the latter the origin of the thesis that "there is no mechanism in laissez-faire capitalism to ensure adequate total demand for the products of labour". He draws attention to his own claims as author of *The Unclaimed Wealth* (1924) and *The Final Buyer* (1928), and discusses his ideas and those of Hobson in relation to those of Keynes'.

I imagine [E.A.G.] Robinson wrote this himself. Such a notice customarily indicates that there will be no further review.

The well-known American economist, J. M. Clark, in a new work called 'Alternative to Serfdom' has a chapter called 'Revolution in Economics: after Keynes What?' in which he talks about the 'long line of heretics' who 'failed to dislodge the "orthodox doctrine" . . . that what is saved is spent as surely as what is consumed' and adds this footnote: 'Keynes pays his respects to them in is *General Theory*, ch. XXIII, his honor roll in including Mandeville, Malthus, Gesell and John A. Hobson. Other names (some of which Keynes mentions) include the Earl of Lauderdale (1804), Rodbertus (1850) and socialist writers following him, Uriel Croker (1884), John M. Robertson (1892) (DHR's marginal comment: 'No relation! DHR'), N. Johannsen (1908), C.H. Douglas (1920), H. Abbati (1924), P.W. Martin (1924) and Foster and Catchings (chiefly 1923–8)'.

(2) I agree that Hahn's (DHR's note: 'Note Keynes *does* mention him, – though only just, – Treatise I, 171, note') work (my knowledge of which I must confess to be second hand, – derived from an admirable work called 'German Monetary Theory', by H.S. Ellis – Harward Press, 1934) seems to be mainly in a different part of the terrain from yours (DHR's note: 'Though I see he claims the propositions "that unemployment originates in consumption deposits" and that the saving-investment then is frequently interrupted'), and I only mentioned him as another person who had some right to feel associated at the world's exclusive association with Keynes of this whole order of ideas.

(3) So far as I can make out, the true Keynesian distinguishes pretty sharply

between K.'s recognition of the importance of what you and I call 'hoarding' (for further remarks on this word see (5) below) – the stage which he had reached in the *Treatise* – and his final systematic formulation of his theory in the *General Theory*. In the former they would admit he had predecessors; it is the latter – with its interweaving of the hoarding concept, the multiplier technique, and his own development of the theory of the rate of interest – which they claim to be the great constructive achievements setting the whole bag of tricks on a firm intellectual basis, and casting everybody else's contribution completely into the shade. It is there, of course, that I personally part company, for I think this final formulation is full of holes. But in considering this question of acknowledgement, I think we must bear in mind that in his own view this final formulation represented a great advance, and that at this stage he naturally confined his 'mentions' to those who he felt had helped him with it, and did not feel it necessary to go back over old ground.

I think that by then it had become psychologically necessary to him greatly to over-stress the differences between himself and other people, dead and living, especially as regards the rate of interest (I won't bother you with [. . .] this); but as regards his treatment of myself I ought to have called your attention to a passage in which, in controversy with me and others, in the Economic Journal in 1937 (June number, p.242), he wrote: 'I regard Mr Hawtrey as my grandparent and Mr Robertson as my parent in the paths of errancy and I have been greatly influenced by them'. As regards yourself, obviously the treatment of the 'free lances' in ch. XXIII isn't meant to be exhaustive, and I think we can see how, having spread himself over Mendeville and Mummery, and possibly remembering that he had already admitted you to his gallery in the *Treatise*, he may have felt entitled to leave it at that.

(5) [*sic*] This lends me to venture another word on the general, and very difficult, subject of acknowledgment. I am sure academic persons in established positions ought to bear in mind very vividly what you say about this on page 5 of your letter (I am assuming you have kept a copy). And I'm sure, as I said before, that Keynes was both scrupulous and generous in intention about this, especially where 'free-lances' were concerned, even if you feel that in your case the tribute was inadequate. But (as in the case of tipping!) it *is* very difficult to got it just right, – one is apt to oscillate between excess and defect. Economics – and I suspect the some is true of philosophy – is an odd subject in this respect – in a way there is nothing really new – the history of ideas goes round in circles. One may be conscious that somebody A has said a thing, and yet rightly feel that one has not in fact been particularly influenced by his having said it, – it may have been somebody quite different B who has set one's own thought moving, though what one ends by thinking is much nearer what A said them what B said. E.g. you may be quite right in thinking I had seen *The Unclaimed Wealth* before writing *BP and Price Level*, – I am pretty certain I had seen Johannson. But since I wasn't attempting to give a bibliography of the whole subject, my selection of those to be mentioned in my preface may well have been the right and reasonable one to give. I think if Keynes were alive he might be able to persuade you that while he had been *interested* by

your work, the development of his own line of thought didn't really *owe* anything to it.

(6) Footnote on 'hoarding'. It is a curious fact that Keynes himself and his intimate disciples took a great dislike to this word, – see the article by Mrs Robinson entitled 'The Concept[6] of Hoarding' in E.J. June 1938 (<u>DHR's note</u>: 'She uses the phrase "the fallacy of hoarding" in the "Introduction to the Theory of Employment"'). So you will not impress the stricter Keynesians by claiming to have discovered 'hoarding'! For my view on this terminological point, see p.212 of the enclosed book [Money][7] – of which I have pleasure in asking your acceptance, – I think you will find ch. XI fairly congenial.

(7) Footnote on the passage in my 1932 review criticizing your handling of the hoarding concept. The point is simply this. I am under the impression, though you may be able to prove me wrong, that the picture which you painted was that of people carrying legal tender money – notes or coin – into the banks, and the banks keeping it in their vaults instead of lending it out again or investing it in securities. Now in a country where most business is done with notes, that may be the predominant way in which hoarding takes place. But for England or the USA it is an unrealistic picture. In such countries hoarding takes place predominantly simply by people *not drawing cheques against their existing bank deposits*. And that is a much more insidious thing; for the quantity of 'money', in the broad sense, in the hands of the public will not decline; and if, as in England, the banks are working to a fixed proportion of cash reserves to total deposits, that proportion will not increase, and the banks therefore will feel no impulse (as they would in the process which you picture) to look round for new outlets for loans and investments. I think that the account given on pag. 53 of *Banking Policy and P.L.*, which makes the simplifying assumption that all 'money' consists of bank deposits, gives a better picture of the essence of the 'hoarding' process then does the picture which (if I am right) you painted.

With all good wishes for the success of your decision – which sounds to me a wise one – to stay in England, yours sincerely

Dennis Robertson

From Abbati *to* Robertson, 19 August 1948

Dear Robertson,
Thank you for your letter of the 15th inst. and for the information it contains. Thank you also for sending me a copy of your *Money*. I am very glad to have this book, particularly as I think it makes your position quite clear, and enables me to see where I stand in relation to you. I have not had time to read all of it, but it seems to be a very clear statement with which I am in general agreement. But I have some observations to make on bankers' investments and loans, bankers' deposits, and Hoarding, which have perhaps escaped your attention and to which

I think you will assent. I will, however, reply to the remarks in your letter first, as numbered by you.

(1) Thank you for giving me the quotation from the June Economic Journal. The thesis that 'there is no mechanism in laissez-faire capitalism to ensure adequate demand for the products of labour' is, of course, only part of the story. I attach most importance to the concept of Hoarding; and I claim that the passage in my booklet quoted from *The Times* is an accurate description of the concept of Unclaimed Wealth as put forward in *The Unclaimed Wealth*; whilst the passage quoted from Beveridge's book is also an accurate description of the concept of Unclaimed Wealth as put forward in *The Final Buyer*.

I am inserting a quarter page advertisement of the booklet in the September number of the Economic Journal, and I think I had better quote some of the notice about the booklet that appeared in the June number.

I note what J.M. Clark has to say about the 'long line of heretics who failed to dislodge the orthodox doctrine that what is saved is spent as surely as what is consumed'.

In the first place, some of these heretics, such as Douglas, P.W. Martin, Foster and Catchings, alleged that the money earned was not enough to pay for the goods produced. Which is a very different proposition. Others, such as J.A. Hobson, alleged that what is saved is invested, therefore over-saving resulted in over-investment. Then there were those who said that what was saved was not necessarily invested.

These three theories are as different to each other as chalk is to cheese, so why lump them all together and confuse them unnecessarily? Neither do any of them allege that what is saved is *not* spent. Incidentally, I observe that you are not listed among the long line of heretics! People who attempt to display erudition in that way make me suspect that they have not read, or perhaps even seen, some of the books that they list in that rough way. Still, the publicity they give is always worth something, and we must be thankful for small mercies.

In the second place, Marshall wrote: 'though men have the power to purchase, they may not choose to use it'. So it looks as if he, also, ought to be included in the long list of heretics!

In the third place, it can be demonstrated with certainty that *excessive* savings are Hoarded by the banking system. This means that the actual goods corresponding to the money Hoarded will be consumed or invested, but new production is stopped until they are consumed or invested. (See later).

Finally, I imagine the J.M. Clark's trouble will be the same as that of Sidney Webb and Hobson when I first contacted them on the saving question in 1921. They intimated, as I imagine he will intimate, that, where a modern banking system is in operation, all savings are automatically invested, and that consequently the aggregate effective demand – the total amount of buying for consumption and investment – remained constant, whatever the proportion of saving to spending. In other words, I think Clark will insist that the banks lend or invest in one way or another all the money that is being saved, or otherwise not being used, by their customers on deposit and/or current account. But if he (Clark) had read *The Unclaimed Wealth* or *The Final Buyer*, he would know the answer to this objection. I think you will agree that the answer to this objection is of fundamental importance. In any case, it is here that my main contribution comes in. I shall revert to this matter again when I deal with the question of Hoarding.

(2) I note that Hahn is mentioned in the *Treatise*, I, 171, footnote (in the same place as myself). But like myself, he his not mentioned at all in the *General Theory*. (Actually my copy of the *Treatise* is still with my books in Geneva, so I cannot at the moment look up the note).

(3) I am glad to have the information and observations contained in this paragraph. Whatever the true Keynesians think, or whatever Keynes himself thought, I do not consider that the *General Theory* takes economic theory a bit further than the *Treatise*. Neither of them are in good order and both of them are patchwork, but no doubt the *General Theory* is an improvement in these respects on the *Treatise*. The *General Theory*, also, comes in heavily on Effective Demand, which the *Treatise* fails to mention. It also comes in heavily on Laissez Faire, which I cannot remember that the *Treatise* has anything to say about. That is all the advance I can see – perhaps because Effective Demand and Laissez Faire are two fundamental points of my *Unclaimed Wealth*. I do not think there is much in the 'multiplier' question. If the multiplier is what I have in mind, it is a variable multiplier that does not always multiply! As for Keynes' development of the rate of interest, I cannot see that there was, or is, anything to develop in this matter; and I should certainly be glad to know what new light, if any, Keynes has thrown on it. You are not the only one who considers that the 'final formulation is full of holes'. I have no authority to mention any names, but I can tell you that the leading professional economist of a country on the sterling area recently told me that he thought these two books of Keynes were 'very badly written' and that he had not had the patience to wade through them. I have also a letter from the president of a leading research institution in Washington, D.C., and he also does not think highly of the intellectual standard attained in these books.

I do not know who you mean by the true Keynesians, but I dare say Kahn, Mrs Robinson, Hawtrey and Harrod (who are mentioned in the Preface of the *General Theory*) are among them, especially Kahn and Mrs Robinson. Hawtrey is a more independent figure, though an obstinate one, whilst Harrod, though not so conspicuously independent as Hawtrey, is shrewd – and perhaps has mental reservations that he has not so far seen fit to declare. At any rate, in this show, Keynes performs the double part of the Walrus and the Carpenter, whilst the others (who only take a walking part) are the Oysters. They are not eaten, of course, but they amount to little more than the *claque*! However, they get valuable publicity, so everybody should be satisfied.

I suppose that very large numbers of the *Treatise* and the *General Theory* were sold; but the number of people who have read right through them and understood everything in them is quite another matter. Many people have these books in their bookshelves, or have had them on their tables and desks, who are quite incapable of making heads or tails of them. But their friends come in and observe that they have the books, and think what 'brainy' fellows they must be . . . to read Keynes: 'So and so reads Keynes. My hat! Some brains!'.

I appreciate your wish to be generous with K. But rightly or wrongly I do not take the same view as you. The reference in the *General Theory* (p. 371) to Douglas, Mandeville, Malthus, Gesell and Hobson do not in the least cover the omission to mention my work as well. On the contrary, in my view the omission is aggravated in this way. K knew well enough, none better than he, that the concept of Hoarding was quite a different proposition to anything these men had touched. K never mentioned *The Unclaimed Wealth* at all; and, in my view, his footnote on *The Final Buyer* was more of a repudiation than an acknowledgement. Incidentally *The Final Buyer* was sent to him by Mrs S.L. Courtauld. The Courtaulds, like himself, were interested in modern art and they met on that level. Mrs S.L. Courtauld is a cousin of mine. I do not suppose, however, that these facts are relevant to the point at issue. And whilst we are on the subject of art, in which respect I am not unlike even Picasso, who said to the director of the Welsh Gallery here: 'Moi, je deteste ces modernes' (he, Picasso, having been the prime mover in making them fashionable!).

But coming back to Keynes, I have not attempted to make a case against him, nor do I wish to do so. I am certainly not the right man to judge him. I think that Harrod is better able to assess Keynes than either of us. He knew him very well and I dare say he is unbiased. I cannot say that I know much about either Keynes or Harrod, but when I have read Harrod's book on Keynes I shall know all about Harrod, as well as all that Harrod is able to say about Keynes.

(6) and (7) Whether or not I impress the stricter Keynesians on the Hoarding question is immaterial to me. I have nothing to retract on what I have said on this question and I do not wish to retract anything I have said. But it now seems that you, for one, have not got me right in this matter.

I do not know what could have given you the impression that my idea of Hoarding consisted of 'people carrying legal tender money – notes or coin – (I call it *cash*) into the banks, and the banks keeping it in their vaults instead of lending it out again or investing it in securities'. Nothing has ever been further from my thoughts. I agree that the question begins with people 'not drawing cheques against their existing bank deposits' – which is what you write in your letter. I also agree with the statement in your book *Money* (p. 213): 'Anybody is hoarding who does something "calculated", as the police would say, to cause a hitch up in the flow of income money . . .'. But I think I take the matter a good deal further than that.

My proposition in *The Unclaimed Wealth* (p. 99) was: 'The total supply of cash and credit money expands and contracts as the effective demand for commodities and services and not as their production'. By *cash* I mean paper money or coins and by *credit money* I mean what you called *chequeries*.

Again, my proposition in the *Final Buyer* (p. 57) is: 'Thus emerges the important and interesting truth that when money income made available by abstinence is held on deposit, other things being equal, both the velocity of production and the quantity of money are decreased'. Here, by the *quantity of money* I mean total bankers' deposits, which are mentioned in the previous sentence, and which, again, are what you call *chequeries*.

I have, and am, repeatedly using the proviso 'where a modern banking system is in operation' whenever I am dealing with the Hoarding question. I therefore stipulate, like you in *Banking Policy*, 'money consists of bank deposits'. Where we seem to differ is at another point:

You write in your letter: 'for the quantity of money, in the broad sense, in the hands of the public will not decline; and if, in England, the banks are working to a fixed proportion of cash reserves to total deposits, that proportion will not increase, and the banks therefore will feel no impulse (as they would in the process which you picture) to look round for new outlets for loans and investments'.

My contention is that *excessive* savings, that is to say, anything in excess of the appropriate amount of saving, will result in a decline in bankers' deposits. In other words, the quantity of money in the hands of the public will decline. And furthermore, the ratio of cash and reserves to deposits will increase.

I assumed that you and Keynes saw this; otherwise you were up against the objection made by Sidney Webb and Hobson, and 'fundamental to the Ricardian economics', namely that, where a banking system is in operation, all savings are automatically invested by the banks, and that consequently the aggregate effective demand is not reduced by saving. (See also pag. 2, paragraph 4, of this letter). If the banking system does not Hoard the money as well as the people who refrain from 'drawing cheques against their existing bank deposits', the word Hoarding does not fill the bill, and that would explain why the Keynesian people dislike the word.

I have taken a lot of trouble over this matter. The way I dealt with it in *The Unclaimed Wealth* did not satisfy me and I therefore went more fully into the banking system in the *Final Buyer*. In writing Part I of that book my object was certainly not to try and provide a text book. Still less did I wish to produce a book for people to leave about on their bookshelves and tables as evidence of their intellectual pursuits!

If you will refer to Chapters II and III in *The Final Buyer*, you will observe that I make a distinction between 'The Potential Supply of Money' and 'The Quantity of Money'. I think Keynes read these chapters carefully, and I find substantial traces of them in the *Treatise*. However, to put the matter briefly, Chapter II reaches the conclusion (on the *potential supply*) (p. 26): 'Taking into consideration possibilities in connection with the issue of fiduciary paper money, and the fact that government policy and action in this respect are largely determined by banking influence, the capacity of a whole banking system to create credit money is at all times more or less vast, and is, subject to government co-operation, in the last resort only limited by the question of currency depreciation'.

Chapter III reaches four 'principal conclusions' regarding the *quantity* of money. The fourth one reads as follows (p. 41): '(iv) The volume of bank loans is by far the most predominant element in the quantity of money. But the power of bankers over the volume of bank loans is limited: by their limited power over interest rates; and by the limited effects of interest rates on the extent of government borrowing and on conditions in markets, which together govern the effective demand for loans'.

So far, I think, we are broadly speaking in general agreement. But now we come to Chapter IV on 'Determining Factors of the Condition of Markets and the Behaviour of Final Buyers'. It is vital and fundamental, because this is what determines the effective demand for bank loans, which 'is by far the most predominant element in the quantity of money'. Then we come to Chapter V on 'The Nature and Effects of Saving'. This introduces the crux of the Hoarding question. On page 56 the following paragraph appears: 'When money income made available by abstinence is held on deposit, the onus of finding safe and profitable employment for it is left upon the bankers. We have just seen that it is not always safe and profitable either to by stock exchange securities or to employ in industry and trade, which confirms the conclusions reached in Chapter III, regarding the volume of bankers' investments and the volume of bank loans. We must therefore consider in what conditions the banking system as a whole is able to employ, safely and profitably to itself, money income made available by abstinence and held on deposit'. And on page 61 I give my seventh conclusion regarding the nature and effects of saving. The phrasing is not as good as it might be, but if you give it your best attention for not more than five minutes, you will see that the meaning is quite clear. Here it is: '(vii) When money income made available by abstinence, or money capital made available by liquidation of stocks of goods or stock exchange securities, is held on deposit, should the sum of the different kinds of irregular final-buying be not great enough fully to neutralize the absent final-buying of the abstainers and any decreased final-buying caused by liquidation, then the velocities of final-buying and production will decrease in relation to ready productive capacity, whilst the quantity of money will decrease in relation to the potential supply; and vice versa . . .'

Actually, every time a depositor uses income in order to repay a bank loan, bankers' deposit (the quantity of money) decline. And the decline will be permanent unless the same, or another, bank makes a new loan or investment. This is clear enough. But will the same or another bank be able to make a new loan or investment? The answer is: all depends on the velocity of final-buying – on the amount of expenditure on consumption and outlay on investment that is going on. If the velocity of final-buying is being retarded by saving, i.e. the withholding of income, the banks will not be able to make new loans and investments safely and profitably. And the more the velocity of final-buying is retarded, the more bankers' investment and loans will decline, and to that extent bankers' deposits and the quantity of money will decrease. The reserve ratio of the clearing banks may remain unchanged, but their discounts at the central bank, and the loans and investments of the central bank will decline; and the reserve ratio of the central bank will to that extent increase.

The conclusions implicit in these considerations are: (i) When saving is excessive, the savings will be Hoarded, production to that extent will be reduced, and the quantity of money will to that extent be reduced. The people who save, as well as the banking system that holds the savings, will both be Hoarding. (ii) When the amount of saving is appropriate to the requirements of the effective demand for new investment, no Hoarding will take place, and the economic system will be in equilibrium. (iii) When the amount of saving is insufficient for the requirements of the effective demand for new investment, forced saving will take place, that is to say, there will be currency depreciation.

I thought had made all this quite clear in *The Final Buyer*. But I now think that perhaps even Keynes did not get the whole of my story. He knew that I knew what I was talking about; and he unconsciously paid me more of a compliment than he imagined, if he gave my work the O.K. without checking it in detail. Had he given me the right kind of acknowledgement, my work would have got serious attention from others, who would not have failed to get the whole story.

I have now read the last two chapters in your *Money* (though not all the other chapters). These are good chapters and I have noted a number of points about them. However, this letter is already much too long, so I shall only mention two of this points:

As regards the 'Club movement' mentioned at the end of Chapter IX, I find the following in *The Search for Confidence* (Bulletin 20, p. 70), which, although it does not altogether fit the case, is to some extent relevant:

> 'there are many "wild-cat" schemes for raising' (and I may now add, stabilizing) 'the price-level. One of the oldest is the reduction of the gold content of the monetary unit, whilst the latest is the creation of international "common funds" for juggling in wholesale commodity markets and foreign exchange markets. But we suggest that in budgetary policy lies the scientific means of controlling at once the gold value and the commodity value of the monetary unit of a well-managed currency'.

The second point concerns your statement at the end of Chapter X, that all these things may turn out much better than you have ventured to predict. Personally, I do not think they will turn out a bit better, and we shall be lucky if they do not turn out a good deal worse, than you predict. For the last three years I have been troubled about a major point in the situation that so far does not seem to have been noticed by anybody else. I have not said anything about it, and perhaps I shall not do so; but I can say that I do not like the look of things at all.

I am sorry to trouble you with another long letter; and I must apologise for the numerous corrections, which are due to the fact that this letter is a first draft.

With kind regards, yours sincerely

Henry Abbati

Review of *The Economic Lessons of 1929–31*

The Economic Journal, December 1932[8]

D.H. Robertson

Mr. Abbati is a skilful writer, with a trenchant and impish pen: he runs an organisation with the sensational title set out above: he advocates deliberate budgetary deficits, financed by central bank credits, in all creditor countries, with a view to restoring wholesale prices to the 1926–9 level; and he is capable of writing that "had there been two men in the world of state-craft equivalent to an Edison, a Ford or a Selfridge, they could have ended the depression any time this year [1931]: had there been three such statesmen, they could have prevented it altogether." Here is enough to make many people throw this book into the waste-paper basket as just one more of the pieces of crude inflationary propaganda with which the world has been flooded in recent years. Yet, as readers of his previous work *The Final Buyer* will know, and as Prof. Gregory warns us in his wise little introduction to the present volume, to treat Mr. Abbati in this way would be a great mistake. He is an eclectic writer of shrewd and independent judgment; and no son of London or Vienna has written more trenchantly on the follies of uncontrolled inflation, miscellaneous state trading, commodity-boosting schemes and instalment buying, or more soberly on the limitations of the power of the banking system to control the volume of active money and the level of prices. His inflationist sympathisers will find a good deal that is unpalatable, his deflationist opponents a good deal that is sympathetic, in his work.

It is true, however, that Mr. Abbati's chief concern is to hammer into the public mind the disastrous effects of the "wasted savings" which, failing to find embodiment in new concrete capital, result in real wealth remaining "unclaimed" because in large measure it remains unproduced. I am glad of the opportunity to endorse the tribute already paid by Mr. J. M. Keynes in his *Treatise on Money* to the vigour and independence of Mr. Abbati's pioneer work in this field (though I think he has run the risk of obscuring the essentials of his theory by a tendency to identify hoarding in the form of bank deposits with a carriage of actual cash into the banks). Further, it is clear that Mr. Abbati considers this danger to have been in some sense chronic in the post-war world—at all events more persistent than its opposite, the danger of excessive buying with its corollary of "forced abstinence," or whatever we like to call it. With one of his reasons for this judgment there will be general sympathy nowadays even in the most "orthodox" quarters—namely, the reluctance of creditor countries to buy the goods and services in which their debtors try to pay them. But Mr. Abbati also seems to believe (1) that a similar reluctance exists in creditor *individuals* as a class, so that the whole process of interest payment has a chronically deflationary tendency; and hence (2) that the reluctance of creditor countries to buy is not due mainly to tariffs or other manifestations of economic nationalism but to a maldistribution of wealth,—the rich do not wish to buy and the poor cannot. Thus he is at times led very close to that Hobsonian variant of the under-consumption theory which on other occasions he has criticised.

I do not feel at all sure that his mind is wrong to be moving in this direction; but once readiness to spend, rather than capacity to earn, is to be taken as the test of fitness to receive an income, it is difficult to see where, short of World Communism, Mr. Abbati or any of us can logically end up. I do not think Mr. Abbati squarely faces the fact that the reason why since 1929 (and indeed before) manygroups of producers lost buying-power is that, on the ordinary criteria of individualism, they were not fit to receive it, and that the plenty amidst which the survival of poverty is such a paradox has been partly a sham plenty due to the natural determination of high cost producers not to surrender the positions to which they had, through no fault of their own, lost their title. The I. L. O. Report of 1931 was right in recording "the difficulties in the way of adjusting movements of population to the possibilities of exploiting the resources of the world" and the speed of technical improvement and rationalisation as causes of depression, and Mr. Abbati is wrong in saying that they are not causes but "the *effects* of forcing under-consumption on millions of people." But his peculiar doctrines, and especially his doctrine that the expenditure of money earned is better because more stable than the expenditure of money borrowed, are, I think, of real service towards forming a judgment both on the historical question of what really happened in America in 1922–9 and on certain problems of present and future policy. As to the past, he is, I think, in error in taking the approximate stability of the American price-level, in those years of rapidly increasing productivity, as evidence of the absence of inflation; but is there not much to be said for his thesis that it would have been better if the new money had got about in the form of increased wages instead of in the form of "bad" loans abroad and of mortgages on buildings and instalment credit at home? Has he not reached by a different route the same conclusions as the neo-Wicksellians, with their over-lengthening of the period of production through the depression of the rate of interest below its natural level? And as to the future, in these days when so much is heard about the necessity for a revival of foreign investment by the creditor countries, is there not much force in Mr. Abbati's constant reminders that it is better to enable people to earn an honest living by buying their goods than to bankrupt them by tariffs and other means in order to chivvy them into new borrowings which they know they cannot afford?

Readers who wish to do justice to Mr. Abbati's position will do well to pay most heed to the weighty Bulletin No. 7—passing rather lightly over No. 4, in which he attempts to evaluate the "unclaimed wealth" by a weird farrago of methods, and the shrewd but somewhat ephemeral Nos. 9–10 on the position of sterling (it is brave of him to reprint his contention that there was nothing wrong with the British balance of payments in 1931). But throughout this short book they will find much to amuse, stimulate and provoke them; and will doubtless desire to receive the further bulletins of the enterprising Committee with the preposterous name.

D. H. ROBERTSON

The distinction between saving and investment

W. Hessling

BULLETIN NO. 3.

April, 1931.

The distinction between saving and investment

> "Saving may be divided into the following classifications: investing money in new capital goods, lending money, buying existing stocks and shares, and holding money on deposit. In any of these ways money may be saved or reserved for the use of the saver at a later date; but the question is, Does saving money in all these ways at all times increase the total quantity and value of capital goods, money and man-power?"

The above is an extract from an article by Mr. Abbati which appeared in the *Economic Review* (Dec. 18th, 1925), and which suggests that a distinction must be made between saving money and the act of increasing the quantity and value of capital and wealth. For the purpose of observing this distinction in the present essay, we will define "Saving" as the passive part of abstaining from spending income on consumable goods, which *makes available* labour and materials, and we will define "Investment" as the active part of converting income into new capital equipment and increased stocks of goods, which *employs* labour and materials. Thus, unless Saving and Investment are always equal to each other and always go hand in hand, it is evident that there is a very real distinction between the one and the other, which may involve very real economic disequilibrium.

To recognize that Saving carried beyond a certain point operates to prevent and not to increase the production of capital equipment and stocks of goods, is to recognize that the cause of trade depression and poverty is often to be found where previously it was considered absurd even to look; whilst to recognize that Investment often takes place most at a time when voluntary Saving is least, is to recognize that the utility, if not the virtue, of voluntary Saving can be over-rated. To fail to recognize these things is to fail at the crucial point of economics.

This, then, is the Thing we are about to consider. By definition alone it is an interesting Thing. But the interest it engenders does not end with its appearance, for, whilst the unenlightened deny its very existence, the question of the identity of its progenitor is not as clear as all respectable people feel such questions ought to be. We propose, first of all, to cite Authority for the benefit of those inclined to dismiss the Thing as a myth, and then to discuss its characteristics together with the several culprits who may be responsible for its having been brought into the world of light, leaving it to the readers to draw their own conclusions. The quantity and kind of un-invested Savings—the dimensions of the Thing—will be left to the Committee to deal with in later Bulletins.

The existence of a distinction between Saving and Investment is now recognized, not only by several leading economists (see Mr. J. M. Keynes' *A Treatise on Money*, Mr. D. H. Robertson's *Banking Policy and the Price Level*, and Professor T. E. Gregory in *The Economic Journal* of Dec., 1930), but also by one of the greatest bankers, for the Rt. Hon. R. McKenna, Chairman of the Midland Bank, speaking at the General Meeting on January 31st, 1931, said:—

> "The non-use of money . . . may be at times the consequence of excessive Saving . . . Whatever blessings thrift may confer on the individual, there are times when, judged by the interests of general economic welfare, it may be carried to excess . . . the point of maximum advantage . . . may be roughly defined as the amount of Saving necessary to meet all demands for capital which can be profitably employed."

From our preliminary definitions, it will be observed that the Thing has two characteristics: (i) that Saving does not necessarily cause, and may even prevent, Investment, and (ii) that Investment is not dependent on voluntary Saving.

(i) *As regards Saving* (*as defined*).   In the past, the negative nature of "abstinence" and the economic disequilibrium caused by under-consumption have been urged from time to time by widely different men. There is the great arraignment of "abstinence" by Lauderdale (James Maitland, eighth Earl of Lauderdale; 1759–1839). Then, Carl Marx has declaimed against under-consumption as the cause of trade crises, though he saw the trouble in maldistribution of income rather than in "abstinence." In effect, buried in the voluminous writings of Marx is to be found the important argument—generally unknown to both his friends and his foes—that the rich, by taking part of the share of the poor and by failing to consume it all as fast as it accrues to them, cause under-consumption, which reduces the rate of production, the amount of employment and wages. For the last fifty years Mr. J. A. Hobson has been pointing to the losses arising from under-consumption and the over-production of capital goods that he attributed to it, and recently Messrs. Foster and Catchings have been propagating a similar line of thought with great energy and considerable success (see *Profits*, published 1925, and subsequent books by the same authors). Again, Mr. N. Johannsen in *A Neglected Point in Connection with Crises*, published in 1908, brought out his doctrine of "Impair Savings," i.e., Saving unaccompanied by a corresponding amount of Investment; and Mr. Abbati in *The Unclaimed Wealth*, published in 1924, called attention to surpluses of goods and services made available by saving which were frequently not wanted for the production of new capital equipment and new stocks of goods, and which, when thus unclaimed by consumers, entrepreneurs and merchants, were the cause of trade depression and unemployment.

These two latter theories appear to be in line with the theory of Mr. Keynes, who writes: ". . . it is a large volume of Saving which does *not* lead to a correspondingly large volume of Investment (not one which *does*) which is the root of the trouble" (see *A Treatise on Money*, published in 1930, Vol. I, p. 179). The point is that it has been assumed, and is still assumed, in many important quarters that the only effect of Saving is to *divert* productive activity from the production of consumable goods to the production of capital equipment and capital goods, and that, thus, Over-Saving can only cause Over-Investment and any losses connected therewith. But according to the theory of *Unclaimed Wealth*, it is the absolute reduction of productive activity that is to be feared as the result of Over-Saving, and not the *diversion* of productive activity. However, when in 1921 a synopsis of *The Unclaimed Wealth* was shown to Mr. Hobson—whose name is generally associated with the theory indicating that over-production of capital goods results from Over-Saving—he assented to the proposition that the production of capital goods, like the production of consumable goods, could be reduced by Over-Saving; but he pointed out that this involved the suggestion that on such occasions the banks could not be employing all the savings deposits on which they were paying interest, and that this difficulty would have to be cleared up. Thus, at the suggestion of Mr. Hobson the solution of this apparent difficulty became a feature of *The Unclaimed Wealth*, which explains: (*a*) that, if it be true that the failure to buy enough consumable goods with money income tends to decrease the production of both capital equipment and consumable goods, it follows that Over-Saving tends to reduce the volume of bankers' investments and loans—and thereby to reduce bank deposits; (*b*) that the placing or the holding of money on deposit tends to transfer cash from the hands of the public to the reserves of the banks; and (*c*) that, thus, the result of Over-Saving, so far as the banking system is concerned, is to reduce deposits and to increase reserves (see Chapters IX, X and p. 86. It may also be noted here that, to-day, although the quantity of monetary gold in the banks is greater than ever, total deposits in the books of the banks have recently declined considerably). The book, however, does not state in so many words that, since the actual quantity of cash in gold and banknotes in the banks is always very much less than the total of bankers' investments and loans, there is no question of savings deposits remaining absolutely unemployed. In a word, the depositing, in certain circumstances, of money in banks is represented— probably for the first time—as a form of "hoarding" (see note on the cover of the book to this effect, also the statement on page 119: "parsimony is negative and creates nothing" and "as modern wealth is *boarded* it disappears").

This treatment seems to be in accord with the later use of the word "Hoarding" by Mr. D. H. Robertson in *Banking Policy and the Price Level*, published in 1926 (see pages 45–46); but Mr. Robertson apparently makes no mention of the difficulty raised by Mr. Hobson regarding the paying of interest by the banks on "hoardings" deposited with them. In 1928 *The Monthly Review of the Midland Bank*, and in 1930, Mr. Keynes in *A Treatise on Money*, presented the idea of the "hoarding" of money in banks by making a distinction between deposit accounts (money that may be regarded as being Saved) and current accounts (money regarded as being spent on consumable goods or as being used to trade capital goods). This treatment certainly appears to show that, other things being equal, production tends to decrease as deposit accounts increase in relation to current accounts, and that, thus, it is not the Saving of money, but the circulation of money, that induces productive activity.

Another point worth mentioning is that Mr. Keynes and Mr. Robertson explain that Saving unaccompanied by a corresponding amount of Investment causes prices to fall, which enables and causes the general body of consumers to buy the "saved" goods as well as their usual purchases, i.e., it causes "a transference of consumption from the Savers to the general body of consumers" (see *A Treatise on Money*, Vol. I, p. 174). But one may well have doubts about the existence of any such *transference*. According to Mr. Abbati, a fall in prices caused by Over-Saving will start with a fall in wholesale prices, which will decrease the rate of production together with the total income of consumers long before they are able to buy at lower prices from retailers, and, thus, the Savings are *lost* by decreased production before they can be transferred to other consumers.

(ii) *As regards Investment (as defined).   The Unclaimed Wealth* explains that the respective quantities of labour and materials secured by the producers of the different kinds of consumable goods and capital equipment are "automatically" determined by the quantities for which these producers bid and the prices they are able and willing to pay; and that when consumers do not Save enough, producers of capital equipment appropriate the proportions of labour and materials they require by outbidding consumers with the help of credit directly or indirectly obtained from the banks, whereby consumers are "automatically" forced to do with smaller quantities. (See p. 107 and footnote—which was written at the special instance of Mr. Hobson—pp. 110–111, also last paragraph, p. 120). Hence, Investment is represented as occurring "automatically," as the result of increased effective demand for capital goods, independently of voluntary Saving; since, when necessary, consumers are "automatically" forced to reduce consumption. Later, Mr. Robertson adopted the expression "Automatic Lacking" for that part of the process whereby consumption is "automatically" reduced by Investment (see *Banking Policy and the Price Level*, pp. 47–48). But the same idea, apparently, was brought out by Ludwig Mises in 1912 in his *Theorie des Geldes und der Umlaufsmittel* (1st edition, pp. 227 ff. and 411 ff.), and by Schumpeter in his *Theorie der wirtschaftlichen Entwicklung* (2nd edition, p. 156), published in 1926, whose "Forced Saving" has (according to Mr. Keynes) since become a familiar feature of German monetary literature.

Thus, it has been shown that Saving does not necessarily cause Investment, and that Investment is not dependent on voluntary Saving.

W. HESSLING.

Introduction to *The Unclaimed Wealth. How Money Stops Production*

J.A. Hobson

Recurring periods of trade depression, holding up the general course of industrial activity, and causing great unemployment and distress, have long presented an open challenge to economists and statesmen. One of the main by-products of the Great War has been an accentuation of this economic problem, complicated by new heavy disturbances of monetary apparatus and trade channels, with industrial dislocations and social upheavals. Many diagnoses of the disease and many remedies have been offered. The validity of most of them has been impaired by over-stressing the exceptional character of the existing situation. For the war and post-war phenomena are only significant so far as they bring out in strong relief the normal nature of the economic disease.

But even among those who have adopted this saner attitude, little agreement has been reached about causes and remedies of periodic trade depressions. Indeed, the whole notion of periodicity may plausibly be challenged. For there is very little regularity either in the intervals or the general shape of trade curves. Every few years the ordinary machinery of industry has to be slowed down, through inability to find markets at remunerative prices for the goods which could continue to be produced. But there is no generally accepted view of why this stoppage occurs. Learned doctors have once more brought out their theories of "sunspots" and failing harvests, rhythms of confidence and mistrust in the business mind, defects in the banking policy, or errors of investment.

But confused as the discussion has been, I think there has emerged a common acceptance of the view that the direct and immediate source of a depression is to be found in the failure to apply enough money in effective demand. Goods are being produced faster than they can get sold. It would seem that someone must possess the purchasing power to buy everything that is, or can be, made. Yet it is evident that, when a trade boom has run a certain course, a congestion of the markets takes place, implying the unwillingness of purchasers to buy fast enough. There is evidently a failure to apply purchasing power as freely and as fast as it might be applied.

It is to this situation that Mr. Abbati presents a new and rigorous investigation. He places himself in general accord with the upholders of what is known as the under-consumption theory of depressions, a theory which finds in the normal and habitual failure of consumption to keep pace with the rising volume of production the core of the trouble. For we now know that the waste of productive power, through unemployment, under-employment, and misemployment, is far greater than is represented by any accepted trade figures. With a full and constant stimulus of effective demand the volume of production, and therefore of consumption, could be enormously enhanced. Not merely in times of admitted depression, but normally, full productive power is withheld, because the business world is well aware that its application would bring nearer that congestion of markets which is the beginning of depression.

Mr. Abbati is also in agreement with most members of the "underconsumption" school in tracing that failure of effective demand to a maldistribution of income, which deprives the workers of a large portion of the spending powers which they would like to exercise, and which are their rightful share of the social heritage of skill and knowledge in the arts of production.

The originality of his contribution consists partly in his examination of the actual process by which production is checked and retarded, partly in his doctrine of consumers' surplus, and lastly in the boldness of his public policy for remedial measures.

If everybody "spent" all the money he received, either in buying consumable goods or in buying capital goods (plant, materials, etc.), there could be no failure of effective demand, and therefore no unemployment, apart from minor errors or miscalculations. Now the common assumption that everyone will and must spend all his money in one or other of these two ways, and without delay, is controverted by Mr. Abbati, who shows that under certain conditions money which might "work" in stimulating production does in point of fact lie idle in banks or strong boxes, or operates more slowly than usual as purchasing power. In any given condition of the industrial arts there must exist a right relation between expenditure upon final commodities and upon productive goods and machinery. If the distribution of income is such as to impel some classes of the recipients to endeavour to "invest" too large a part of their income, they will soon discover that the investment market is choked and that their money must wait some time in idleness. Mr. Abbati shows by a close analysis of our financial machinery that this operates so as to check production and so to reduce the volume of money distributed in income. His insistence upon effective demand as the true controller of the cash and credit system is of crucial importance to his analysis, and readers who find these chapters difficult will have their perseverance well rewarded by the powerful grasp of the monetary system which they will obtain.

His distinction between Consumers' and Producers' Surplus will be found to be an interesting attempt to reconcile socialist with individualist doctrine in the distribution of the product. In a concluding chapter, "The Remedy," he assigns a large place to the State, as charged with the responsibility for distributing consumers' surplus so as to ensure that the effective demand of the community keeps full pace with the powers of production. Though Mr. Abbati's discussion of this public policy is too brief to enable him to deal with the many objections which will be raised against some of the proposals here outlined, he has exercised a wise discretion in the brevity of the application of his theory. For the freshness and originality of his diagnosis give the real distinction and value to his book. These qualities come from his direct contact with the business world, and the slenderness of his acquaintance with economic literature. He thus obtains a direct unspoiled vision of the actual phenomena, and of the order of their appearance, which commonly escapes the academic student of economic science. This vision enables him to expose in a most convincing way the folly of those who regard periods of depression as necessary incidents in the normal healthy life of a modern industrial community, or who find in some simple nostrum of wage-adjustment, profit-sharing, bank control, a sufficient cure for the wasting malady of unemployment. One word of warning I would give to economic students. Mr. Abbati's disregard for the conventional meaning of some portions of the accepted economic terminology is likely to cause misconception, and certain of his *obiter dicta* to evoke dissent which may or may not be justified. I plead for a fair consideration of the substance of his argument, which seems to me an important and an original contribution to the solution of the darkest and most urgent economic problem of our time.

J. A. HOBSON.

May 23, 1924.

Introduction to *The Economic Lessons of 1929–1931*

T.E. Gregory

When a professional economist is asked to write an Introduction, his task is, I take it, to vouch for the *bona fides* of the author and to offer an assurance that the author has something to say that ought to be considered. Like the Chairman at a public meeting, his function is to appeal for a hearing for the speaker and not to speak overmuch himself. I have known Mr. Abbati for many years, but if this little book were merely another appeal for immediate and ill-considered inflation, I should have left it to others to commend it to the public. It belongs, fortunately, to another class of literature. The point of Mr. Abbati's argument is, I suppose, that modern Capitalistic society cannot function unless the goods and services it produces are effectively bought and consumed; there must be, to use his own terminology, a Final Buyer. The proces of finding the Final Buyer, i.e. the attainment of Economic Equilibrium, is liable to be delayed and interrupted by different circumstances: by ill-considered monetary policy, by "hoarding" on the part of the recipient of money income, and by the substitution of loans to producers in place of the effective purchase and consumption of his goods. Mr. Abbati, in effect, is one of those who are engaged in the task of working out the new and exciting ideas which in the last ten years have made monetary theory something very different to what it was at the outbreak of the War. The War Inflation, the Post-War Recovery and the World Depression have all stimulated thought in the field of monetary theory to an altogether unprecedented extent: events have changed very rapidly, and ideas have changed as well. Such a state of affairs has its own disadvantages. The first consists in an exaggeration of the differences between the old state of theory and the new. I do not think for instance, that by their insistence upon "Abstinence" the older economists meant that production could go on without consumption; what they did mean was that the creation of capital goods was only possible on condition that not all the available labour power was utilized for the production of consumption goods. How much of the labour available should be utilized in the creation of capital goods, they thought could be left to the rate of interest to determine; and all our modern discussions really turn round the question of to what extent this is true. A further danger lies in the difficulty of distinguishing, at a time of rapid change, cause from effects. I believe that "hoarding" at the moment is one of the causes which perpetuate the depression; but as the crisis proceeds, the factors which loom large at any given moment are not necessarily the factors which played the largest quantitative rôle at a previous moment, or which may play the largest rôle in the future.

Now this has important consequences. The first is that remedies which may be appropriate at one stage of a crisis become *in*appropriate at another stage. Cheap money, financing budgetary deficits through Central Bank Credit, a policy of public works may all be appropriate at one stage; but any or all these measures may become highly dangerous poisons at a later stage. And the second consequence of the varying quantitative importance of different factors at different times is that the degree of difference of opinion among economists seemingly become greater as the situation develops. Yet that is not because economists do not recognise that many factors are operative in a situation, but because they assess the importance of different factors differently.

Above all, the complexity of the facts and the constantly changing nature of the situation ought to warn writers and readers alike against a premature closing of the mind to new arguments and counter-arguments. It is not because I am in full agreement with Mr. Abbati that I am writing the Introduction; on the contrary, it is because I think that the problem is so vast that much further detailed discussion is called for that I am acting as a critical but friendly sponsor on this occasion.

I would like to call attention to Bulletin No. 3 by Mr. Hessling on the distinction between Saving and Investment and the pioneer work done by Mr. Abbati in this important field.

Finally, I may say that the dates at which the Bulletins were issued, when considered in relation to the contents of these Bulletins and subsequents events, show that so far the Unclaimed Wealth Utilization Committee has been fulfilling its intentions to provide independent and penetrating comment on current economic events for business men, economists and statesmen. I think the reader will agree that it has been doing so in an entertaining and vigorous manner.

T. E. GREGORY.

April 12th, 1932.

Introduction to *The Search for Confidence in 1932*

B.P. Blacket

It is related that Sir Rabindranath Tagore, when visiting New York, was travelling up Town by the Subway in company with two eminent Americans. As the train entered Grand Central Station his companions observed a local train which would take them to their destination about to start from the opposite track. Having hustled and jostled their distinguished guest into this train just in the nick of time, they explained to him with unquestioning satisfaction that the special exertion was well worth while as it had saved at least three minutes. "And what do you propose to do with them?" was his comment.

If Hindu speculative thought could help Western civilization to find the right answer to that question, India would render as great a service to the world as when she gave the Occident through the Arabs the device of the cypher which has made possible modern mathematics and mechanics. The Unclaimed Wealth of which this book treats arises from that same ignorance of ours how to employ the time and energy which applied science continually renders surplus to man's immediately effective demands. This surplus energy appears in many forms—as unemployed men and women, as enforced leisure, as hoarded money savings, as misdirected production, even as wasteful consumption.

The republication of these essays in a single volume entitled *The Search for Confidence in 1932* is timely. The World Monetary and Economic Conference is about to meet in London. All those who are to take part in the Conference and all who wish to take an intelligent interest in its proceedings will be well advised to study these lively and unorthodox pages. Written in 1932 they are fully relevant now, and all the more instructive for those who note their original dates and perceive that many, if perhaps not all, of the fears and hopes expressed have been fulfilled, and that suggestions which appeared at the time startlingly novel have since secured general acceptance. Sadly too the thoughtful reader cannot but reflect that some of the remedies proposed would have been admirably effective a year ago, but are now useless owing to the increasing gravity of the world's ills.

At the moment at which this introduction is being penned, the British public is anxiously awaiting the Budget for 1933–34. It is being increasingly realized that the decisions to be taken in this Budget are fateful for the future not of Britain only, not of the British Empire only, but of Western Civilization. Will the powers that be rise to their opportunity and give the world that lead for which it is longing towards revived activity, increased employment, and a recovery in prices and in demand? The writer of the two articles on "The Strength of Sterling" was wise enough to see the truth as long ago as June, 1932. "Reduced Government expenditure and increased taxation are the appropriate measures in the case of an inflationary rise in prices resulting from a shortage of goods in relation to effective demand. But at a time when deflation is running riot as the result of the glutting of commodity markets, reduced Government expenditure and increased taxation—when applied by creditor countries with claims on debtor countries—can only aggravate the trouble. . . . Let us be realists; let us not say that the balancing of the budget, in the circumstances of to-day, is a good thing when we know that it is only doing harm." The time has indeed come for "a moratorium for taxpayers."

There are many advocates to-day of the idea, itself not new, of new public works as a remedy for unemployment. On this subject a word of caution may not be inappropriate. It would be well to give a chance first, before embarking on costly governmental schemes, to the unfortunate taxpayer. If by a reduction of taxation he can be encouraged himself to give expression to his spirit of enterprise, the resulting recovery will be swifter and better balanced and far more widely spread. There is a tendency on the part of those not intimately connected with particular classes of work to think that on funds being sanctioned work can forthwith proceed and labour be at once absorbed. This is not so.

In normal times consulting engineers are carrying out works and at the same time developing schemes and plans for further works. There is a continuous flow of employment in the trades concerned in the execution of works and their equipment. To-day works are mainly in the condition of being near completion, while few plans and schemes for new development are in hand. The wise spending of money on schemes requires a period of many months of planning before work can proceed and labour be employed. The present is a very suitable time for putting in hand the necessary scheming and planning, as with idle staffs engineering firms can give greater attention to details than in times of high pressure. Government Departments and others might wisely proceed at once with preparations for schemes they have in mind. The cost would be trifling even if the schemes do not mature. At best a very long interval must elapse before the schemes can reach the stage at which a serious inroad on the volume of unemployment can be effectively made.

The title of this book *The Search for Confidence in 1932* is happily chosen. Confidence and leadership are the two greatest needs of the world in 1933. To English readers the two bulletins entitled "The Strength of Sterling" will have a special appeal. The world has learnt the enormous strength of sterling, and looks to England for a lead. Why does England still refuse to share the world's Confidence in her and to accept the Leadership?

BASIL P. BLACKETT.

Editor's notes

1 These letters belong in a group of 8 letters and notes, unpublished, written by Keynes to Abbati between 9 December 1930 and 3 November 1933. Private archive. I would like to thank the Provost and Scholars of King's College, Cambridge, for permission to publish these letters.

2 The reprint of the first series of Bulletins (1932a) was reviewed by D.H. Robertson (1932).

3 A previous letter from Keynes to W. Hessling, Secretary of UWUC, dated 16 December 1932 evinces that Abbati asked Keynes to write the introduction to the second series of Bulletins (1933a). Keynes declined, and the introduction was written by B.P. Blacket.

4 These letters belong in a group of 15 letters (1932–58), ten of them from Abbati (Abbati's copies), and five from Robertson. These letters are unpublished and conserved in a private archive. Five among these letters (from Abbati: 4/11/1932, 20/7/1948, 9/8/1948, 19/8/1948, 5/11/1948) are also contained in *Robertson Papers*, Wren Library, Trinity College, Cambridge (see Mizen, Moggridge and Presley 1997). I am indebted to Don Moggridge for making the letters of the Wren Library available for me before I found them in Abbati's papers.

I would like to thank Mrs Judith Brown for permission to publish Robertson's letter.

5 I thank Don Moggridge for revising my transcription of this letter (Robertson's handwriting is sometimes problematic). This version, however, is my responsibility alone.

6 Robertson had written 'Fallacy' instead of 'Concept' but then cancelled it.

7 Presumably the new edition of 1948 with two new chapters: IX and X.

8 Reproduced with the permission of Blackwell Publishing Ltd. Copyright 2010 Wiley–Blackwell.

I thank Mrs Judith Brown for permission to publish this review.

List of Press Reviews of Abbati's writings

L = Letter
o.m. = only mentioned

The Unclaimed Wealth. How Money Stops Production (UW)

'UW', *Aberdeen Press and Journal*, 7 August 1924.
'Money matters', *The Journal of Commerce*, 18 August 1924.
'UW', *The Scotsman*, 21 August 1924.
'UW', *The Sheffield Daily Telegraph*, 21 August 1924.
'Economic confusion', *The Economist*, 30 August 1924: 351–2.
'Credit and other panaceas', *The Times Literary Supplement*, 11 September 1924.
'UW', *The Manchester Guardian*, 16 September 1924.
'UW', *The Nation and the Athenaeum*, 27 September 1924.
'Is victory worth while?', *The Star*, Johannesburg, 30 September 1924.
'The evils of under-consumption', J.C.J., *The Economic Review*, 2 October 1924.
'UW', *The Star*, Auckland, N.Z., 18 October 1924.
(o.m.), *The Spectator*, 29 November 1924.
'Wealth and unemployment. Two pressing problems', Constant Reader, *Daily Times*, Otago, N.Z., 29 November 1924.
'The way out', J.W. Scott, *The Spectator*, 20 December 1924.
'The monetary system and the food supply', (L), J.W. Scott, *The Economic Review*, 26 December 1924: 567–8.
'UW', J.M. Clark, *The Journal of Political Economy*, 1925: 476–7.
'Production and consumption', F.W.I.S., *The System*, January 1925.
'The golden calf: are we fools to worship it?', *Daily Herald*, 4 February 1925.
'Is money the cause of unemployment?', R.B. Suthers, *The Clarion*, 20 February 1925.
'A repulsive vocabulary', *The Japan Chronicle*, 14 May 1925.
'UW', Harold L. Reed, *The American Economic Review*, XV, 3, September 1925: 505–6.
'The new theory of poverty', J.K.S.T., *The Weekly Westminster*, 5 September 1925.
(o. m.), *Evening Transcript*, 1 December 1925.
'Revolution by reason', J.W. Scott, *The Spectator*, 19 December 1925.
'UW', *Weltwirtschaftliches Archiv*, Bd. XXIII/I, 1926.
'UW', Werner Spohr, *Wirtfchafts und Sozialwiffenfchaften*, 1926.
'UW', *Evening Transcript*, 20 February 1926.

The Final Buyer (FB)

'FB', *The Economist*, 22 September 1928.
'FB', *Evening Transcript*, 6 October 1928.
'FB', *Publishers' Circular*, 27 October 1928.
'FB', *Business*, November 1928.
(o. m.), *The New York Times*, 11 November 1928.
'FB', *The Anglo-American Trade Journal*, December 1928.
'Industrial depression', *The Times*, 6 December 1928.
'An economic theory', *The Star*, 21 December 1928.
'FB', *Manchester Guardian Commercial*, 21 February 1929.
'FB', *Labour Magazine*, April 1929.
'FB', *Evening Transcript*, 25 May 1929.
'FB', *Commerce & Finance*, New York City, 26 June 1929.

Bulletins 1931–3 (BU)

'Higher wages asked for creditor nations', *Christian Science Monitor*, Boston, 8 July 1931.
'For general wage increases', *St Louis Mo.*, 8 July 1931.
'Urge worldwide pay boosts', *News*, Chicago, 8 July 1931.
'Money and employment', W. Foster, W. Catchings, *Newark*, N.J., 26 July 1931.
'Unclaimed wealth', W. Foster, W. Catchings, *Times Star*, Cincinnati, 27 July 1931.
'The week in the city', Toreador, *The Statesman and Nation*, 12 December 1931.
'BU', *Daily Herald*, 12 December 1931.
'Enter the world's dictator', A. Emil Davies, *The Clarion*, January 1932.
'Income tax payers down tools', A. Emil Davies, *The Clarion*, February 1932.
'BU', *New Statesman and Nation*, 13 February 1932.
'The week in the city', Toreador, *New Statesman and Nation,* 20 February 1932.
'BU', *La Tribune*, Geneva, 25 February 1932.
'BU', *New Statesman and Nation*, 16 April 1932.
'BU', A. Emil Davies, *The Week-end Review*, 4 June 1932: 718.
'Are attempts to balance budget doing harm?', Francis Williams, *Daily Herald*, 16 June 1932.
'Real significance of United States Relief Bill', Francis Williams, *Daily Herald*, 15 August 1932.
'Here are the facts. Unorthodox but wise', *The New Clarion*, 10 September 1932.
'World conference agenda', Francis Williams, *Daily Herald*, 22 October 1932.
'Hoard and grow poor', F.W. Pethick-Lawrence, *The New Clarion*, 19 November 1932.
'Break the strangle hold on trade', Francis Williams, *Daily Herald*, 6 December 1932.
'Conference chatter', *The New Clarion*, 28 January 1933.
'BU', *La Tribune*, Geneva, 15 March 1933.
'Employment and unemployment', *Industrial and Labour Information*, 24 April 1933.
'BU', *Tribune de Genève*, 27 April 1933.
'Before and after advent of Roosevelt', Brooklyn, *Daily Herald*, 8 August 1933.
'Roosevelt is a He-Man', (ext. from Bull. no. 27), *National Sphere*, September 1933.

The Economic Lessons of 1929–1931 (EL)

'Cost of world slump', *Evening Standard*, 1932.
(o. m.), *The Financial Times*, 9 July 1932.

(o. m.), *Evening Transcript*, 16 July 1932.
'Current economics', *Birmingham Gazette*, 21 July 1932.
(o. m.), *Manchester Guardian Commercial*, 30 July 1932.
'Diagnosis', G.D.H.C., *The New Clarion*, 30 July 1932.
(o. m.), *Statist*, 2 August 1932.
'Diagnosing the disease', *Aberdeen Press and Journal*, 5 August 1932.
'A moratorium for taxpayers', A. Emil Davies, *The Week-end Review*, 6 August 1932.
(o. m.), *The Nottingham Guardian*, 30 August 1932.
(o. m.), *Nottingham Evening Post*, 30 August 1932.
'Economic League. Meeting at Nuneaton', *Midland Daily Tribune*, 1 September 1932.
'To buy or not to buy', *Express & Star* and *Midland Counties Express*, 2/3 September 1932.
'EL', *The Star*, 3 September 1932.
'EL', *The Japan Chronicle*, 8 September 1932.
'EL', E.S., *International Cooperation*, October 1932.
'EL', A.L.F., *Daily Times* and *Otago Times*, 8 October 1932.
'EL', A.T.K. Grant, *International Affairs*, November 1932.
'EL', W.B., *Fabian News*, December 1932.
'EL', *International Labour Review*, December 1932.
'EL', D.H. Robertson, *The Economic Journal*, December 1932, XLII, 168: 612–14.
'EL', *Giornale degli Economisti*, December 1932: 5.
'El', G.R.W., *Journal of the Royal Statistical Society*, Part I, 1933.
'EL', A.F.W.P., *Canadian Forum*, Toronto, January 1933.
'EL', J.C. Coyajee, *The Mysore Economic Journal*, January 1933.
'EL', C.E. Ayres, *The American Economic Review*, March 1933, vol. 23, 1: 110–12.
'EL', *The American Economic Journal*, March 1933.
'EL', J. Baker White, *The Sphere*, 25 March 1933.
'Les richesses du monde', *Journal de Genève*, 31 March 1933.
'EL', mg, *Weltwirtschaftliches Archiv*, Band 37, Heft 2, April 1933.

The Search for Confidence in 1932 (SC)

'SC', *The Mysore Economic Journal*, 1933.
'World Buying', *The Financial Times*, 12 June 1933.
(o. m.), *Boston Evening Transcript*, 4 June 1933.
'SC', *Bankers' Magazine*, July 1933.
'SC', *The Banker*, July 1933.
'Righting the world', *Aberdeen Press and Journal*, 5 July 1933.
(o. m.), *Manchester Guardian Commercial*, 8 July 1933.
'SC', Francis Williams, *Daily Herald*, 14 July 1933.
'SC', *The Financial News*, 15 July 1933.
'SC', *The Economist*, 29 July 1933.
'Kindergarten for statesmen', A. Emil Davies, *The New Clarion*, 5 August 1933.
'SC', *Boston Evening Transcript*, 19 August 1933.
'SC', *The Times Literary Supplement*, 31 August 1933.
'SC', A.T. Grant, *International Affairs*, September 1933.
'SC', A. Campolongo, *Giornale degli Economisti*, November 1933.
'Money and goods', J.A. Hobson, *New Statesman and Nation*, 6 January 1934.
'Theory and practice. The year's business books', *Manchester Guardian Commercial*, 27 January 1934.

Economic Readjustment in 1933 (ER)

ER', *International Affairs*, 1934.
'Unclaimed wealth & how to claim it', *The Manchester Guardian*, 30 April 1934.
'Economic readjustment third phase. Will reflationary influences defeat the deflationist?',
   Francis Williams, *Daily Herald*, 2 May 1934.
'ER', *Annalist*, 11 May 1934.
'Unclaimed wealth', *The Times*, 15 May 1934.
'ER', *The Financial Times*, 22 May 1934.
'City man from Geneva', *Evening Standard*, 24 May 1934.
'ER', *The Times. Literary Supplement*, 24 May 1934.
'ER', *The Financial News*, 30 May 1934.
(o m.), *The Economic Journal*, June 1934.
'ER', *International Labour Review*, June 1934.
'ER', *Review of Reviews*, June 1934.
'ER', *Bankers' Magazine*, June 1934.
'ER', *The Banker*, June 1934.
'ER', *The Economist*, 9 June 1934.
'Purchasers and depression', *The Morning Post*, 15 June 1934.
(o. m.), *Manchester Guardian Commercial*, 30 June 1934.
'ER', *Review of Reviews*, July 1933.
'Unclaimed wealth', *The Japan Chronicle*, 1 July 1934.
'ER', *The Chicago American*, 20 July 1934.
'ER', *Labour Magazine*, August 1934.
'ER', *The Industan Review*, October 1934.
'ER', *Weltwirtschaftliches Archiv*, 3 November 1934.
'ER', Harold Barger, *The Economic Journal*, December 1934, XLIV, 176: 697.
(o. m.), *Manchester Guardian Commercial*, 1 February 1935.

Italy and the Abyssinian War (IA)

'IA', *Paisley Daily Express*, 16 May 1936.
'Un inglese di buon senso', *Gazzetta del Popolo della Sera*, 20 May 1936.
'Sidelights on Abyssinia', *Express & Star*, 21 May 1936.
'IA', 'Koko', *Harrogate Advertiser*, 23 May 1936.
(o. m.), *Statist*, 23 May 1936.
'Behind the fascist façade', A.F. Magri, *Labour*, June 1936.
'A limit to British quixotism', *The Daily Gazette*, 17 June 1936.

The Outlook for Interest Rates and for Stock Exchange Prices in England

'Cheap money must be continued', *Evening Standard*, 10 July 1936.
'Interest rates and security prices', *Investors' Review*, 8 August 1936.

Towards Full Employment (TF)

'TF', *The Times*, 12 January 1946.
'TF', *News & Book Trade Review*, 19 January 1946.

'TF', *Welsh Gazette*, 24 January 1946.
'TF', *Economic Reform Club*, February 1946.
'Who will buy?', *Truth*, 8 February 1946.
'When buyers become fewer again', *Eastbourne Courier*, 22 February 1946.
'TF', *The British Trade Journal and Export World*, March 1946.
'TF', *Rotary Service*, April 1946.
'TF', *Irish Banking Magazine*, April 1946.
'TF', W.J.R., *The Catholic Gazette*, April 1946.
'When buyers become fewer', (L), K.F. Williamson, *Eastbourne Courier*, 18 April 1946.
'A challenging economist', *The Times Literary Supplement*, 27 April 1946.
'TF', *International Labour Review*, May/June 1946.
(o. m.), *News & Book Trade Review*, 11 May 1946.
'Making everybody better off', (L), K.F. Williamson, *Eastbourne Courier*, 6 and 28 June 1946.

Lord Keynes' Central Thesis and the Concept of Unclaimed Wealth (LK)

'The missing money', W.D.L., *The New English Weekly*, 8 January 1948.
'LK', D.A., *Economic Reform Club Bulletin*, February 1948.
'LK', *The Economic Journal*, June 1948.

Other Writings

(World debt maze), *Review of Reviews*, September 1934.
(*id.*) 'Topics of the month', *The Nottingham Guardian*, 1 September 1934.
(*id.*) 'Review of Reviews', *Cork Examiner*, 5 September 1934.
(*id.*) 'Review of Reviews', *Canada*, 6 September 1934.
(*id.*) *Universe*, 7 September 1934.
(*id.*) 'Review of Reviews', *City & East London Observer*, 8 September 1934.
'Is labour missing the mark', *The Courier,* Tunbridge Wells; *Tunbridge Wells Advertiser; Tunbridge Free Press,* 31 January 1936.
(*id.*) (L), Fair Play, *Tunbridge Wells Advertiser*, February 1936.
'The farmers' freedom', (L), Hamil Westwood, *The Farmers Weekly*, 12 January 1945.
(*id.*), (L), John C. Hiatt, *The Farmers Weekly*, 19 January 1945.
'Farm training: a butcher's view', (L), *The Farmer Weekly*, 22 June 1945.
'The wartime butcher', (L), B. Mitchell, *The Farmer Weekly*, 13 July 1945.
'Butcher and farmer', (L), Onlooker, *The Farmer Weekly*, 3 August 1945.
(Abbati's conceptual priority), (L), H.A. Fountain, *Economic Reform Club Bulletin*, September 1946.
'The Argentine agreement', (L), C. Morgan-Webb, *Economic Reform Club*, April 1948.
'Levies on capital and income', (L), L.C. Jackson and O.L. Mathews, *Economic Reform Club Bulletin*, June 1948.
'Dollar and pound', (L), R.G. Hawtrey, *The Times*, 29 June 1948.
'Sterling and Marshall aid', (L), C. Morgan-Webb, *The New English Weekly*, 29 July 1948.
'Dismantling the sterling area', (L), C. Morgan-Webb, *The New English Weekly*, 21 October 1948.
'Reduction of National debt', (L), D.J. Mitchell, *The Economist*, 12 March 1949.

'Before Keynes and after', W.D. Law, *The New English Weekly*, 30 June 1949.

'The Whitehall handicap', *Rural Economy*, October 1952.

(Britain's Oversea Investments), Harold Wincott, *The Financial Times*, 5 and 12 May 1953.

'Tax relief on earned income', (L), J. Riddoch, *The Financial Times*, 7 July 1953.

'Replacing "invisible" ', *Rural Economy*, August/September 1953.

'Rising commodity prices', (L), *The Financial Times*, 4 June 1954.

(Post-war inflation), (L), H.P. Drewry, *The Financial Times*, 5 July 1955.

'Fiduciary issue', (L), J.F. Eggleston, *The Financial Times*, 6 June 1956.

Bibliography of Abbati's writings

L = Letter

1924a   *The Unclaimed Wealth. How Money Stops Production*, with an *Introduction* by J.A. Hobson, London: George Allen & Unwin.

1924b   'The Unclaimed Wealth', (L), *The Economist*, 22 November: 823.

1924c   'National debt and taxation', (L), *The Economic Review*, 5 December: 500–1.

1924d   'The Unclaimed Wealth', (L), *The Economic Review*, 12 December: 523.

1925a   'Gently, Mr Keynes', *The Economic Review*, 14 August: 145–7.

1925b   'A reply to Sir Josiah Stamp: the standard of living', *The Economic Review*, 11 December: 518–9.

1925c   'What is saved?', *The Economic Review*, 18 December: 540–1.

1925d   'What is trade depression?', *The Economic Review*, 25 December: 561–2.

1928   *The Final Buyer*, London: King & Son.

1929   'Causes of deflation', (L), *The Times*, 13 September.

1931a   'Attacking the trade depression', (Bull. no. 2), *The Star*, 7 June.

1931b   'La crise et l'Assemblée', *Journal des Nations*, September.

1931c   'Budgetary deficits', (L), *The Times*, 11 December.

1931d   'Taxation', (L), *The New Statesman and Nation*, 12 December.

1932a   *The Economic Lessons of 1929–1931*, (Bulletins of the *Unclaimed Wealth Utilization Committee* [UWUC] issued in 1931), with an *Introduction* by T.E. Gregory, London: King & Son, (reviewed by D. H. Robertson in *The Economic Journal*, December 1932).

1932b   'Debts between nations', *The Times*, 19 January.

1932c   ' "To buy or not to buy". Aspects of financial policy', (L), *Express & Star* and *Midland Daily Tribune*, 16 September.

1932–58 Correspondence between H.A. Abbati and D.H. Robertson, in *D.H. Robertson Papers*, Wren Library, Trinity College, Cambridge and private archive.

1933a   *The Search for Confidence in 1932*, (Bulletins of the UWUC issued in 1932), with an *Introduction* by B.P. Blacket, London: King & Son.

1933b   Letter to E. Cannan, February, in *E. Cannan Collection*, 1033, British Library of Political and Economic Science, London School of Economic, London.

1933c   'A Moratorium for taxpayers', *The New Clarion*, 18 March.

1933d   'The Search for confidence in 1932', (L), *The Japan Chronicle*, 9 September.

1934a   *Economic Readjustment in 1933*, (Bulletins of the UWUC issued in 1933), London: King & Son.

1934b   'Review' of Edwin Cannan, *Economic Scares, Fabian News*, September.

1934c   'The world debt maze and a way out', *Review of Reviews*, September.

1935   'Italy and Abyssinia. The weakened League', (L), *The Morning Post*, 3 September.

1936a   'Is the Labour Party missing the mark?', Lecture delivered to Tonbridge Division Liberal Association, Tunbridge, Wells, 27 January.

1936b   *The Outlook for Interest Rates and for Stock Exchange Prices in England*, London, 10 June (Marshall Library of Economics, University of Cambridge).

1936c   *Italy and the Abyssinian War*, London: London General Press.

1936d   'Italy and the Abyssinian war', *Labour*, October.

1937a   'An analysis of the gold scare', *The Financial Times*, 13 May.

1937b   'International capital movements', (L), *The Economist*, 15 May: 402.

1937c   'Value of gold', (L), *The Financial News, The Morning Post* and *The Times*, 22 June.

1937d   'League reform idea', *Daily Herald*, 28 October.

1937e   'Public works and slumps', *The Times*, 24 December.

1938   'The long term budget problem', (L), *The Economist*, 16 July: 121.

1939a   'Corsica and France', (L), *The Daily Telegraph*, 23 February.

1939b   'Savings and investment in the U.S.A.', (L), *The Economist*, 12 August: 319.

1943a   'Acquisition of land', (L), *The Farmers Weekly*, 22 October.

1943b   'Ploughing in Wales', (L), *The Farmers Weekly*, 5 November.

1944a   'Why not a farmers' party', (L), *The Farmers Weekly*, 14 January.

1944b   'Questions for Mr Hudson', (L), *The Farmers Weekly*, 4 February.

1944c   'Mr Hudson – "Deflationist": An economist's view', *The Farmers Weekly*, 31 March.

1944d   'Fees for forms', (L), *The Farmers Weekly*, 29 September.

1944e   'Giving up farming', (L), *Welsh Gazette*, 23 November.

1944f   'Output per worker', (L), *The Farmers Weekly*, 24 November.

1944g   'Milk output per worker', (L), *The Farmers Weekly*, 8 December.

1944h   '"Forced" losses', (L), *The Farmers Weekly*, 15 December.

1945a   *Towards Full Employment*, London: Baskerville Press.

1945b   'Farm women's gratuities', (L), *Welsh Gazette*, 22 March.

1945c   'What does the butcher get?', (L), *The Farmers Weekly*, 29 June.

1945d   'What does the butcher get?', (L), *The Farmers Weekly*, 20 July.

1946a   'When buyers become fewer', (L), *Eastbourne Courier*, 24 May.

1946b   'Making everybody better off', (L), *Eastbourne Courier*, 21 June.

1946c   (on his conceptual priority) (L), *Economic Reform Club Bulletin*, July.

1946d   (*id.*), (L), *Economic Reform Club Bulletin*, November.

1947a   *Lord Keynes' Central Thesis and the Concept of Unclaimed Wealth*, Cardiff: William Lewis (printers).

1947b   (on the inflation) (L), *Economic Reform Club Bulletin*, January.

1947c   'Money and prices', (L), *New English Weekly*, 13 February.

1948a   'The Argentine agreement', (L), *Economic Reform Club Bulletin*, February.

1948b   'Electricity in Geneva', (L), *The Times*, 3 March.

1948c   'Levies on capital and income', *Economic Reform Club Bulletin*, May.

1948d   'Dollar value of the pound', (L), *The Times*, 16 June.

1948e   'Dollar and pound', *Weekly Edition*, 23 June.

1948f   'Sterling and Marshall Aid', (L), *The New English Weekly*, 15 July.

1948g   (on Anglo-American film agreement), (L), *Economic Reform Club Bulletin*, July/August.

1948h   'Dismantling the sterling area', (L), *The New English Weekly*, 9 September.

1948i   'The special account', (L), *The New English Weekly*, 21 October.

1948j   'Hoarded deposits', (L), *Economic Reform Club Bulletin*, December.

1948–50 Correspondence between H.A. Abbati and Roy Harrod, in *The Sir Roy Harrod Papers*, Chiba University of Commerce, Ichikawa, Japan and private archive.

1949a   'Brakes that didn't hold', (L), *The New English Weekly*, 13 January.

1949b   'Planning and mis-planning', (L), *The Financial Times*, 14 January.

1949c   'Protecting exporters', (L), *The Financial Times*, 1 February.

1949d   'Reduction of National Debt', (L), *The Economist*, 5 March: 416.

1949e   'Higher salaries for civil servants', (L), *The New English Weekly*, 24 March.

1949f   'Argentine beef. Too high a price?', (L), *The Financial Times*, 31 March.

1949g   'Government spending. Upsetting the balance', (L), *The Financial Times*, 9 April.

1949h   'The price of gold', (L), *The New English Weekly*, 21 April.

1949i   'Stability of the currency unit', (L), *Economic Reform Club Bulletin*, March/April.

1949j   'Government buying. Whole nation may suffer', (L), *The Financial Times*, 9 May.

1949k   'The price of gold', (L), *The New English Weekly*, 19 May.

1949l   'The economic future of farming. (i) Why farmers are uneasy', *Rural Economy*, May.

1949m   'The mistiming of investment' (L), *The New English Weekly*, 16 June.

1949n   'Bulk-buying contracts. Short-term or long?', (L), *The Financial Times*, 17 June.

1949o   'The economic future of farming. (ii) The turn of the tide', *Rural Economy*, June.

1949p   'Argentine pact. Points in doubt', (L), *The Financial Times*, 4 July.

1949q   'The so-called labour shortage', (L), *The New English Weekly*, 28 July.

1949r   'Cheap oil for Argentina', by 'Drewynt', (L), *The Financial Times*, 15 September.

1949s   'The new position of agriculture. (i) Wartime methods and mistakes', *Rural Economy*, September.

1949t   'The new position of agriculture. (ii) The low cost fallacy', *Rural Economy*, October.

1949u   'Sterling & Dollar. Freedom or balance?', by 'Drewynt', (L), *The Financial Times*, 26 October.

1949v   'Exchequer Bond redemption', (L), *The Statist*, 10 December.

1949w   'Taxation of farm wages and cheap food. (i) The question of farm cost. (ii) How P.A.Y.E. raises production costs', *Rural Economy*, December.

1950a   'Investors' plight. Mexico-and elsewhere', (L), *The Financial Times*, 21 January.

1950b   'Interest rate', (L), *The Financial Times*, 26 January.

1950c   'U.K. overall payments in surplus?', (L), *The Statist*, 25 February.

1951a   'Causes of world inflation. Inflation of prices', (L), *The Financial Times*, 8 February.

1951b   'Farm wages and taxation', *Rural Economy*, March.

1951c   'Currency debasement', (L), *The Financial Times*, 2 April.

1951d   'Deflation before revaluation', (L), *The Financial Times*, 5 May.

1951e	'Fool's paradise', *Rural Economy*, June.
1951f	'Road to recovery?', (L), *The Financial Times*, 3 September.
1951g	'The dollar price of gold', (L), *The Financial Times*, 10 September.
1951h	'Unrequited exports', (L), *The Financial Times*, 10 October.
1951i	'Treasury bill rates', (L), *The Financial Times*, 19 November.
1951l	'Local borrowing', (L), *The Financial Times*, 20 December.
1951m	'Vicious spiral', (L), *The Financial Times*, 14 December.
1952a	'Credit restriction', (L), *The Economist*, 19 January: 136.
1952b	'Churchill right about the trapdoor', (L), *Western Mail*, 8 August.
1952c	'Whitehall and the farmer', (L), *Western Mail*, 23 August.
1953a	*Britain's Oversea Investments, National Income and Population*, unpublished, expounded and reviewed by Harold Wincott in *The Financial Times*, 5 and 12 May.
1953b	'Under-the-line', (L), *The Financial Times*, 21 February.
1953c	'Price stability', (L), *Western Mail*, 27 February.
1953d	'Income tax relief', (L), *The Financial Times*, 1 July.
1953e	'The Ceylon export duty', (L), *The Financial Times*, 20 November.
1953f	'What about cafe concerts at the Winter Gardens on Saturdays', (L), *Bournemouth Daily Echo*, 12 December.
1954a	'Rising prices of raw materials. Another round of currency debasement?', (L), *The Financial Times*, 3 June.
1954b	'Towards a new pattern', (L), *The Financial Times*, 7 July.
1954c	'World food', (L), *The Financial Times*, 24 August.
1954d	'Convertibility risk', (L), *The Financial Times*, 14 September.
1955a	*The New Economic Theories and the Great Depression of 1930–1933*, unpublished.
1955b	'University means test', (L), *The Times*, 28 January.
1955c	'Trustee stocks & inflation', (L), *The Financial Times*, 23 April.
1955d	'Trustee stocks & inflation', (L), *The Financial Times*, 4 July.
1955e	'A floating pound', (L), *The Financial Times*, 21 September.
1955f	(*id.*), (L), *The Financial Times*, 27 September.
1955g	'Fixed or floating pound', (L), *The Financial Times*, 3 October.
1955h	'Purchasing power parity', (L), *The Financial Times*, 12 October.
1956a	'Smoking in cinemas', *Bournemouth Daily Echo*, 19 April.
1956b	'Fiduciary issue', (L), *The Financial Times*, 2 June.
1956c	'The fiduciary issue', (L), *The Financial Times*, 11 June.
1956d	'Independent old lady?', (L), *The Financial Times*, 29 June.
1956e	'Independent old lady?', (L), *The Financial Times*, 11 July.
1956f	'Dear Money Plateau. Government's part', (L), *The Financial Times*, 3 August.
1956g	'Too old a Bradshaw', (L), *The Financial Times*, 1 September.
1956h	'Facing the truth', (L), *The Financial Times*, 17 December.
1957a	'Inflation', (L), *Eastbourne Gazette*, 5 June.
1957b	'Liquidity ratios', (L), *The Financial Times*, 17 July.
1957c	'Inflation and governmental and/or banking action', Evidence submitted by H.A. Abbati to the Committee on the Working of the Monetary System (Radcliffe Committee), December, The National Archives, Kew, U.K.
1958a	'Unrequited exports', (L), *The Financial Times*, 25 February.
1958b	'Freight rates. Reducing the supply of shipping', (L), *The Financial Times*, 25 March.

1958c   'Deflation and rising living costs. No mystery involved?', (L), *The Financial Times*, 11 April.

1958d   'The wrong door', (L), *The Financial Times*, 7 May.

1958e   'Pensioners trying to avoid queues', *Eastbourne Herald*, 12 July.

1958f   'The "strategy" of visiting motorists', *Eastbourne Herald*, 16 August.

1958g   'Saving and investment', (L), *The Economist*, 18 October: 223.

1959   'Burnt toast, new cars, illness and expansion', *Eastbourne Herald*, 10 October.

1960a   'The speculator', (L), *The Financial Times*, 30 June.

1960b   'Control of spending', (L), *The Financial Times*, 15 September.

1961a   'Onward and upward', (L), *The Financial Times*, 9 June.

1961b   'Repaying the fund', (L), *The Financial Times*, 30 October.

1961c   'A floating exchange rate', (L), *The Financial Times*, 7 December.

1961d   '. . . and purchasing power', (L), *The Financial Times*, 15 December.

1962a   'Hard bargaining', (L), *The Financial Times*, 12 March.

1962b   'Limit on savings', (L), *The Financial Times*, 14 April.

1962c   'Wall Street', (L), *The Financial Times*, 16 May.

Bibliography

Besomi, D. (ed.) (2003) *The Collected Interwar Papers and Correspondence of Roy Harrod*, Cheltenham: Edward Elgar.

Beveridge, W. (1944) *Full Employment in a Free Society. A Report*, London: George Allen and Unwin.

Brown, C.C. (1940) *Liquidity and Instability*, New York: Columbia University Press.

Cannan, E. (1921) 'The meaning of bank deposits', *Economica*, 1, January: 28–36.

— (1933) *Economic Scares*, London: P.S. King & Son.

Clark, J.M. (1925) 'Review' of H.A. Abbati, *The Unclaimed Wealth*, *The Journal of Political Economy*: 476–7.

— (1950) *Alternative to Serfdom*, New York: Alfred A. Knopf.

Coppock, D.J. (1954) 'The theory of effective Demand in the 1920s', *The Manchester School of Economic and Social Studies*, 22, 1: 62–89.

Curtis, M. and Townshend, H. (1937) *Modern Money*, London: G.Harrop, Ltd.

Di Gaspare, S. (2005) ' "To buy or not to buy". The problem of effective demand in Abbati's theory', *Studi Economici*, 60, 86: 69–100.

Douglas C.H. (1920) *Credit-Power and Democracy*, London: Palmer.

— (1930) Evidence Submitted to the MacMillan Committee of Finance and Industry. Reprinted from the Official Minutes of Evidence, 24th day, 1 May.

Ellis, H.S. (1934) *German Monetary Theory*, Cambridge, Mass.: Harward University Press.

Everyman's Encyclopaedia (1958), London: J.M.Dent & Sons Ltd.

Foster W., Catchings W. (1925) *Profits*, New York: Houghton Mifflin Co.

— (1927) *Business without a Buyer*, Boston: Houghton Mifflin Co.

— (1928) *The Road to Plenty*, New York: Houghton Mifflin Co.

Hahn L.A. (1920) *Volkswirtschaftliche Theorie des Bankkredits*, Tübingen: Verlag J.C.B. Mohr.

— (1945) 'Compensating reactions to compensatory spending', *The American Economic Review*, March: 28–39.

Haney, L.H. (1910) [2nd ed. 1920] *History of Economic Thought*, New York: MacMillan Company.

Harrod, R.F. (1951) [2nd ed. 1952] *The Life of John Maynard Keynes*, London: Macmillan & Co.

Hawtrey R. (1923), *Currency and Credit*, London: Longmans, Green & Co.

— (1927), *The Gold Standard in Theory and Practice*, London: Longmans, Green & Co.

Hayek F.A. (1932) 'Reflections on the pure theory of money of Mr J.M. Keynes (continued)', *Economica*, 35: 22–44; reprinted in *The Collected Works of F.A. Hayek* (1995), vol. 9, London: Routledge.

— (1933), *Monetary Theory and the Trade Cycle*, London: J. Cape.

Hessling, W. (1931) *The Distinction between Saving and Investment*, in Abbati (1932a).

Hobson, J.A. and Mummery, A.F. (1889) *The Physiology of Industry: An Exposure of Certain Fallacies in Existing Theories of Economics*, London: J. Murray.

Hobson J.A. (1922), *Economics of Unemployment*, London: George Allen & Unwin.

Johannsen, N. (1908) *A Neglected Point in Connection with Crises*, New York: The Bankers Publishing Co.

Keynes, J.M. (1919) *The Economic Consequences of the Peace*, London: Macmillan (reprinted in *The Collected Writings of J.M.Keynes* (CWK), vol. II).

— (1923) *A Tract on Monetary Reform*, London: Macmillan (reprinted in CWK, vol. IV).

— (1925) *The Economic Consequences of Mr Churchill*, London: Macmillan (reprinted in CWK, vol. IX).

— (1930a) *A Treatise on Money*, 2 vols. London: Macmillan (reprinted in CWK, vol. V).

— (1930b) Letter to Montagu Norman, 22 May, in CWK, vol. XX.

— (1931) 'A rejoinder', *The Economic Journal*, September, 163, XLI: 412–23.

— (1936) *The General Theory of Employment, Interest and Money*, London: Macmillan (reprinted in CWK, vol. VII).

Lavington, F. (1922) *The Trade Cycle: An Account of the Causes Producing Changes in the Activity of Business*, London: P.S. King and Staples.

Luxemburg, R. (1913) *Die Akkumulation des Kapitals. Ein Beitrag zur ökonomischen Erklärung des Imperialismus*, Berlin: Buchhandlung Vorwärts Paul Singer GmbH.

Martin, P.W. (1924) *The Flaw in the Price System*, London: P.S. King & Son.

Marx, K. (1895) *Das Kapital. Kritik der politischen Ökonomie*, Berlin: Dietz Verlag.

Mehta, G. (1977), *The Structure of the Keynesian Revolution*, London: Martin Robertson & Co. Ltd.

Mises, L. (1912) *Theorie des Geldes und der Umlaufsmittel*, Muenchen und Leipzig: Duncker & Humblot.

Mizen, P., Moggridge, D. and Presley, J. (1997) 'The Papers of Dennis Robertson: the discovery of unexpected riches', *History of Political Economy*, 29: 573–92.

Patinkin, D. (1982) *Anticipations of the General Theory? And Other Essays on Keynes*, Oxford: Basil Blackwell.

Pigou, A. (1929) *Industrial Fluctuations*, London: Macmillan.

Robertson, D.H. (1915), *A Study of Industrial Fluctuation. An Enquiry into the Character and Causes of the so-called Cyclical Movements of Trade*, London: P.S. King & Son. Reprinted with a new Introduction in *Reprints of Scarce Works on Political Economy*, The London School of Economics and Political Science, 1948.

— (1922) *Money*, Cambridge Economic Handbooks, London: Nisbet & Co. Revised editions 1924, 1928. New edition (with two new chapters) 1948.

— (1926) *Banking Policy and the Price Level. An Essay in the Theory of the Trade Cycle*, London: P.S. King & Son. Revised edition 1932.

— (1931) 'Mr. Keynes theory of money', *The Economic Journal*, September, 163, XLI: 395–411.

— (1932) 'Review' of H.A. Abbati, *The Economic Lessons of 1929–31, The Economic Journal*, XLII, 168: 612–14.

— (1933) 'Saving and hoarding', *The Economic Journal*, September, 171, XLIII: 399–413.

— (1950) Letter to R.F. Harrod, 14 (or 4) April, *The Sir Roy Harrod Papers*, Chiba University of Commerce, Ichikawa, Japan.

Robinson, J. (1938) 'The concept of hoarding', *The Economic Journal*, June, 190, XLVIII: 231–6.

Schumpeter J.A. (1912) *Theorie der wirtschaftlichen Entwicklung*, Leipzig: Duncker & Humblot.

Smith A. (1776), *An Inquiry into the Nature and Causes of the Wealth of Nations*, reprinted New York: The Modern Library Inc, 1937.

Tugan-Baranovskij M.J. (1905), *Theoretische Grundlagen des Marxismus*, Leipzig.

Wicksell, K. (1898), *Interest and Prices*, reprinted London: MacMillan, 1936.

Index

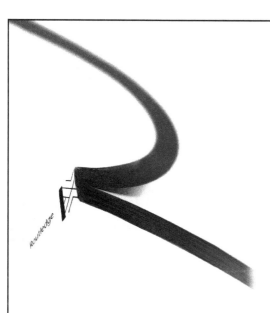

For Product Safety Concerns and Information please contact our EU
representative GPSR@taylorandfrancis.com
Taylor & Francis Verlag GmbH, Kaufingerstraße 24, 80331 München, Germany

www.ingramcontent.com/pod-product-compliance
Ingram Content Group UK Ltd.
Pitfield, Milton Keynes, MK11 3LW, UK
UKHW021834240425
457818UK00006B/198

* 9 7 8 0 4 1 5 5 7 3 4 5 0 *